The GUINNESS® *book of*
Sporting Facts

Stan Greenberg

St Michael®

COVER ILLUSTRATION

Daley Thompson, Britain's Olympic champion in the decathlon

Title page picture: the Opening Ceremony of the 1982 soccer World Cup at the Bernabeu Stadium in Madrid, Spain

ACKNOWLEDGEMENTS

The author wishes to acknowledge the following important sources: *The Guinness Book of Records, The Guinness Book of Winners and Champions, The Guinness Facts and Feats* series, national and international governing bodies of the various sports, and sporting experts too numerous to mention individually.

Editorial: Beatrice Frei, Peter Matthews, Beverley Waites and Karin Ilsen
Design and Layout: David Roberts

Illustrations: All-Sport Photographic Ltd, except for the following illustrations on pages 14 (Syndication International); 21, 39 (Mel Franks); 45 (Press Association); 50, 53 (Hulton Picture Library); 66 (*Darts World*); 73 (Richard Walker); 76 (Mansell Collection); 78 (Badminton Collection); 93 (Gerry Cranham's); 124 (Nigel Snowdon); 130–31 (Stan Greenberg); 141 (Hulton Picture Library); 144, 148 (Associated Sports); 149 (Novosti); 155 (David Muscroft); 158 (Impact Photos/GSL); 179. Cover illustration (Colorsport)

THE AUTHOR

Stan Greenberg was born (in 1931) and educated in the East End of London. Always a keen, and not unskilful, player of various sports, his enthusiasm for athletics particularly was kindled by a visit to the 1948 Olympic Games in London. Before long that enthusiasm had become an obsession, and Stan is now one of the acknowledged world experts on the sport. After a long career in information and library work with Unilever Limited, and then the Greater London Council, he was invited to become the Sports Editor of *The Guinness Book of Records*, a position he held for six years. During that period he greatly expanded his knowledge of all forms of sporting activity. He has attended five Olympic Games, five Commonwealth Games and numerous other meetings abroad, usually as statistician to the BBC Television athletics commentary team. Currently a freelance author and statistician, Stan indulges in his other interests, music, theatre, cinema and travel whenever possible. He is married, to Carole, and has two children, Karen and Keith.

This edition published exclusively
for Marks and Spencer plc
by Guinness Superlatives Ltd,
2 Cecil Court, London Road, Enfield, Middlesex, Great Britain

Set in 9/10 pt and 8/9 pt Plantin
Photoset and printed by Redwood Burn Limited,
Trowbridge, Wiltshire, Great Britain
Bound by Pegasus Bookbinding, Melksham, Wiltshire,
Great Britain

ISBN 0–85112–407–0

List of Country Abbreviations

Arg—Argentina
Aus—Australia
Aut—Austria
Bah—Bahamas
Bar—Barbados
Bel—Belgium
Ber—Bermuda
Bol—Bolivia
Bra—Brazil
Bul—Bulgaria
Can—Canada
Chi—Chile
Chn—China
Col—Colombia
Cub—Cuba
Cz—Czechoslovakia
Den—Denmark
Dom—Dominican Republic
Egy—Egypt
Eng—England
Eth—Ethiopia
Fin—Finland
Fra—France
FRG—Federal Republic of Germany
GB—Great Britain
GDR—German Democratic Republic
Ger—Germany
Gha—Ghana

Gre—Greece
Hol—Holland
Hun—Hungary
Ina—Indonesia
Ind—India
Ire—Ireland
Irn—Iran
Isr—Israel
Ita—Italy
Jam—Jamaica
Jap—Japan
Ken—Kenya
Kor—Korea
Lie—Liechtenstein
Lux—Luxembourg
Mal—Malaysia
Mex—Mexico
Mta—Malta
Ngr—Nigeria
Nic—Nicaragua
NI—Northern Ireland
NK—North Korea
Nor—Norway
NZ—New Zealand
Pak—Pakistan
Pan—Panama
Par—Paraguay
Phi—Philippines

PNG—Papua New Guinea
Pol—Poland
Por—Portugal
PR—Puerto Rico
Rho—Rhodesia
Rom—Romania
Saf—South Africa
Sco—Scotland
Sin—Singapore
SK—South Korea
Spa—Spain
Sri—Sri Lanka
Swe—Sweden
Swi—Switzerland
Tan—Tanzania
Tha—Thailand
Tri—Trinidad & Tobago
Tun—Tunisia
Tur—Turkey
Uga—Uganda
USSR—Union of Soviet Socialist Republics
Uru—Uruguay
USA—United States
Ven—Venezuela
VI—Virgin Islands
Wal—Wales
Yug—Yugoslavia
Zim—Zimbabwe

Conversion Table

DISTANCE

1 cm	¼ in
2 cm	¾ in
1 in	0·25 cm
5 cm	2 in
10 cm	4 in
20 cm	7¾ in
1 ft	30 cm
50 cm	1 ft 7¾ in
1 yd	0.91 m
1 m	3 ft 3¼ in
2 m	6 ft 6¾ in
5 m	16 ft 4¾ in
10 m	32 ft 9¾ in
100 ft	30·48 m
50 m	164 ft
100 yd	91·44 m
100 m	328 ft 1 in
500 m	546 yd 2 ft 5 in
1 km	1093 yd 1 ft 10 in
1 mile	1609 m
5 km	3 miles 188 yd
10 km	6 miles 376 yd
20 km	12 miles 752 yd
50 km	31 miles 120 yd
100 km	62 miles 241 yd 1 ft
100 miles	160·9 km
200 km	124 miles 482 yd 2 ft
500 km	310 miles 1206 yd 2 ft
1000 km	621 miles 653 yd 1 ft

WEIGHT

1 gram	0·03 oz
5 grams	0·17 oz
10 grams	0·35 oz
1 oz	28·34 grams
50 grams	1·76 oz
100 grams	3·52 oz
1 lb	453 grams
500 grams	1 lb 1·6 oz
1 kg	2.20 lb
5 kg	11·02 lb
10 kg	22·04 lb
100 lb	45·35 kg
50 kg	110·23 lb
100 kg	220·46 lb
500 lb	226·79 kg
1000 lb	453·59 kg
500 kg	1102·3 lb
1000 kg	2204·6 lb
1 ton	1016 kg

SPEED

1 km/h	0·62 mph
1 mph	1·609 km/h
10 km/h	6·21 mph
10 mph	16·09 km/h
50 km/h	31·06 mph
50 mph	80·46 km/h
100 km/h	62·13 mph
100 mph	160·9 km/h

Contents

Contents

American Football

A direct descendant of the English games of soccer and rugby, it evolved at the great American universities, such as Harvard, Yale and Princeton. Harvard played what was known as the 'Boston Game' from 1871, but changed from this largely soccer-based game to something more akin to rugby when they played McGill University of Montreal in 1874. Two years later the Intercollegiate Football Association was founded by five colleges, and from then the game has steadily evolved into its present form.

The professional game, which has a few differences in rules from college football, dates from August 1895 when Latrobe played Jeannette, at Latrobe, Pennsylvania. In 1919 the American Professional Football Association was formed. This became the National Football League in 1922, and it was divided into two divisions in 1933. The American Football League was formed in 1960. In 1970 the two leagues merged, and, under the aegis of the NFL the teams were reorganised into the National Football Conference (NFC) and the American Football Conference (AFC). The Canadian game developed independently and, while very similar, differs primarily in number of players, 12 to the American 11, and size of pitch.

SUPER BOWL: Instituted in 1967 as a competition between the champions of the NFL and AFL, since 1970 it has been between the champions of the National and American Conferences.

1967 Green Bay Packers (NFL)	1975 Pittsburgh Steelers (AFC)
1968 Green Bay Packers (NFL)	1976 Pittsburgh Steelers (AFC)
1969 New York Jets (AFL)	1977 Oakland Raiders (AFC)
1970 Kansas City Chiefs (AFL)	1978 Dallas Cowboys (NFC)
1971 Baltimore Colts (AFC)	1979 Pittsburgh Steelers (AFC)
1972 Dallas Cowboys (NFC)	1980 Pittsburgh Steelers (AFC)
1973 Miami Dolphins (AFC)	1981 Oakland Raiders (AFC)
1974 Miami Dolphins (AFC)	1982 San Francisco 49ers (NFC)
	1983 Washington Redskins (NFC)

The highest aggregate score in the Super Bowl was in 1979 when Pittsburgh beat Dallas by 35–31, with Pittsburgh equalling the record score of 35 by the Green Bay Packers in 1967.

PROFESSIONAL RECORDS

Most points—career 2002 George Blanda 1949–75.—*season* 176 Paul Hornung (Green Bay) 1960.—*game* 40 Ernie Nevers (Chicago Cardinals) *v* Chicago Bears 1929.

Most touchdowns—career 126 Jim Brown (Cleveland) 1957–65.—*season* 23 O. J. Simpson (Buffalo) 1975.—*game* 6 Ernie Nevers (Chicago Cardinals) *v* Chicago Bears 1929. 6 Dub Jones (Cleveland) *v* Chicago Bears 1951. 6 Gale Sayers (Chicago) *v* San Francisco 1965.

Most yards gained rushing—career 12 312 Jim Brown (Cleveland) 1957–65.—*season* 2003 O. J. Simpson (Buffalo) 1975.—*game* 275 Walter Payton (Chicago Bears) *v* Minnesota 1977.

Most passes completed—career 3686 Fran Tarkenton (Minnesota, NY Giants) 1961–78.—*season* 360 Dan Fouts (San Diego) 1981.

Most yards gained passing—season 4802 Dan Fouts (San Diego) 1981.

Most passes intercepted by—season 14 Richard Lane (Los Angeles) 1952.

COLLEGE FOOTBALL

The college season culminates in a number of Bowl games which are frequently contests between the winners of various conferences. The oldest is the Rose Bowl at Pasadena, California, played on New Year's Day, first in 1902, and then annually from 1916, between the champions of the Big Ten (Midwest) and Pacific Coast conferences. The most wins have been 17 by the University of Southern California (USC) between 1923 and 1980.

College records (Players have a maximum of four years in a college team).

Most points—career 356 Tony Dorsett (Pittsburgh) 1973–76.—*season* 174 Lydell Mitchell (Penn State) 1971.—*game* 43 Jim Brown (Syracuse) *v* Colgate 1956.

Most touchdowns—career 59 Glenn Davis (Army) 1943–46. 59

Tony Dorsett (Pittsburgh) 1973–76.—*season* 29 Lydell Mitchell (Penn State) 1971.—*game* 7 Arnold Boykin (Mississippi) *v* Mississippi State 1951.

Most yards gained rushing—career 6082 Tony Dorsett (Pittsburgh) 1973–76.—*season* 2342 Marcus Allen (USC) 1981.
Most yards gained passing—season 4571 Jim McMahon (Brigham Young) 1980.
Most passes completed—season 296 Bill Anderson (Tulsa) 1965.
Most passes intercepted by—season 14 Al Worley (Washington) 1968.

HIGHEST TEAM SCORES
The most points scored in a college football game is 222 by Georgia Tech against Cumberland University(0) in October 1916. The score included a record 32 touchdowns.

Football, American style, is the most popular sport in the United States. The amateur game, as typified here by a clash between the University of Southern California and California State University, also attracts big crowds.

9

Archery

Archery did not become an organised sport until the 3rd century AD although it had been a hunting skill *c* 8000 BC. In Britain the Royal Company of Archers, the Sovereign's bodyguard in Scotland, dates from 1676. The world governing body, the Fédération Internationale de Tir à l'Arc (FITA) was formed in 1931.

WORLD TARGET CHAMPIONSHIPS: They were first held in 1931 in Warsaw, Poland. Since 1957 the championships are held biennially with individual and team competitions consisting of a Double FITA round—a total of 144 arrows shot from four different distances. The most titles won is seven by Janina Spychajowa-Kurkowska (Pol) between 1931 and 1947, while the male record is four by Hans Deutgen (Swe) 1947–50. *Winners from 1971:*

Men	Individual	Points	Team (3 scoring)	Points
1971	John Williams (USA)	2445	USA	7050
1973	Viktor Sidoruk (USSR)	2185	USA	6400
1975	Darrell Pace (USA)	2548	USA	7444
1977	Richard McKinney (USA)	2501	USA	7444
1979	Darrell Pace (USA)	2474	USA	7409
1981	Kyosti Laasonen (Fin)	2541	USA	7547

Women	Individual	Points	Team (3 scoring)	Points
1971	Emma Gapchenko (USSR)	2380	Poland	6907
1973	Linda Myers (USA)	2204	USSR	6389
1975	Zebiniso Rustamova (USSR)	2465	USSR	7252
1977	Luann Ryon (USA)	2515	USA	7379
1979	Jin Ho-Kim (SK)	2507	South Korea	7314
1981	Natalia Butuzova (USSR)	2514	USSR	7455

FLIGHT SHOOTING: The greatest distance achieved with a handbow is 1231 yd 1 ft 10 in (1126·18 m) by Alan Webster (GB) at Ivanpah Dry Lake, California on 2 October 1982. At the same venue on 4 October 1980 April Moon (USA) set a women's record of 923 yd 1 ft 6 in (844·45 m). With a footbow, Harry Drake shot an arrow 1 mile 268 yd (1854·4 m) in 1971.

The greatest distance shot by a British woman is 456 yd (417·47 m) by Julie Ingleby, at Burton Constable, near Hull, in 1979.

Right: **Darrell Pace (USA) set a world record to win his Olympic title in 1976, finishing a record 69 points ahead of his nearest opponent.**

OLYMPIC GAMES: Archery was included in the Games in 1900–08 and 1920 and re-introduced in 1972. Hubert van Innis (Bel) won a record six gold and three silver medals in 1900 and 1920.

Men		Points	Women	Points
1972	John Williams (USA)	2528	Doreen Wilbur (USA)	2424
1976	Darrell Pace (USA)	2571	Luann Ryon (USA)	2499
1980	Tomi Poikolainen (Fin)	2455	Keto Losaberidze (USSR)	2491

Records

		Points	World		Points	British	
Double FITA Round	Men	2571	Darrell Pace (USA)	1976	2466	Dennis Savory	1980
	Women	2515	Luann Ryon (USA)	1977	2520	Rachel Fenwick	1980
Single FITA Round	Men	1341	Darrell Pace (USA)	1979	1294	Steve Hallard	1982
	Women	1324	Natalia Butuzova (USSR)	1982	1271	Rachel Fenwick	1979

WORLD RECORDS

Men

Event	Points	Name/Country	Year
90 m	322	Vladimir Esheyev (USSR)	1980
70 m	338	Sante Spigarelli (Ita)	1978
50 m	340	Sante Spigarelli (Ita)	1976
30 m	356	Darrell Pace (USA)	1978
Team	3887	USSR	1981

Women

Event	Points	Name/Country	Year
70 m	328	Natalia Butuzova (USSR)	1979
60 m	336	Kim Jin Ho (Kor)	1980
50 m	331	Paivi Meriluoto (Fin)	1982
30 m	353	Valentina Radionova (USSR)	1981
Team	3979	USSR	1979

Association Football (Soccer)

Ball kicking games were played very early in human history. One of the earliest of which there are details was Tsu-Chu in China around 400 BC. A more recognisable game, Calcio, existed in Italy in 1410. The earliest official reference to football in Britain was Edward II's Edict banning the game in London in 1314. Further proscribing of ball kicking games occurred under later sovereigns. In 1846 the first soccer rules were formulated at Cambridge University, and on 26 October 1863 the Football Association was founded in England. The oldest club still in existence is Sheffield FC, formed in 1857. The Fédération Internationale de Football Association (FIFA) was founded in Paris on 21 May 1904.

WORLD CUP: Instituted in 1930, and held every four years. The only country to win three times is Brazil, who have uniquely played in all 12 competitions, losing only nine of a total of 52 matches played to 1978. Antonio Carbajal (Mex) played in a record five competitions 1950–66. The greatest margin of victory in a World Cup match occurred when New Zealand beat Fiji by 13–0 in a qualifying round in Auckland, NZ, on 16 August 1981. England had beaten Northern Ireland 13–1 in 1956. The most goals scored in the final stages of the Cup are 13 by Just Fontaine (Fra) in 1958 and the most goals scored in a Final were three by Geoff Hurst (Eng) in 1966. The fastest goal in the competition was in 27 sec by England's Bryan Robson *v* France at Bilbao on 16 June 1982.

	Winner	Venue		Winner	Venue
1930	**Uruguay**	Uruguay	1962	**Brazil**	Chile
1934	**Italy**	Italy	1966	**England**	England
1938	**Italy**	France	1970	**Brazil**	Mexico
1950	**Uruguay**	Brazil	1974	**W.Germany**	W.Germany
1954	**W.Germany**	Switzerland	1978	**Argentina**	Argentina
1958	**Brazil**	Sweden	1982	**Italy**	Spain

EUROPEAN CHAMPIONSHIP: Instituted in 1958 as the Nations Cup. Held every four years and played over a two-year period.

1960 USSR
1964 Spain
1968 Italy
1972 W.Germany
1976 Czechoslovakia
1980 W.Germany

EUROPEAN CHAMPION CLUBS CUP: Instituted in 1955, as the European Cup, and contested annually by the League champions of the member countries of the Union of European Football Associations (UEFA).

1955–56	Real Madrid (Spa)	1969–70	Feyenoord (Hol)
1956–57	Real Madrid (Spa)	1970–71	Ajax (Hol)
1957–58	Real Madrid (Spa)	1971–72	Ajax (Hol)
1958–59	Real Madrid (Spa)	1972–73	Ajax (Hol)
1959–60	Real Madrid (Spa)	1973–74	Bayern Munich (FRG)
1960–61	Benfica (Por)	1974–75	Bayern Munich (FRG)
1961–62	Benfica (Por)	1975–76	Bayern Munich (FRG)
1962–63	A C Milan (Ita)	1976–77	Liverpool (Eng)
1963–64	Inter Milan (Ita)	1977–78	Liverpool (Eng)
1964–65	Inter Milan (Ita)	1978–79	Nottingham Forest (Eng)
1965–66	Real Madrid (Spa)	1979–80	Nottingham Forest (Eng)
1966–67	Celtic (Sco)	1980–81	Liverpool (Eng)
1967–68	Manchester United (Eng)	1981–82	Aston Villa (Eng)
1968–69	A C Milan (Ita)	1982–83	SV Hamburg (FRG)

EUROPEAN CUP-WINNERS CUP: Instituted in 1960 for National Cup winners (or the runners-up if the winners are in the European Cup).

1960–61 Fiorentina (Ita)
1961–62 Atletico Madrid (Spa)
1962–63 Tottenham Hotspur (Eng)
1963–64 Sporting Lisbon (Por)
1964–65 West Ham United (Eng)

1965–66 Borussia Dortmund (FRG)
1966–67 Bayern Munich (FRG)
1967–68 A C Milan (Ita)
1968–69 Slovan Bratislava (CZ)
1969–70 Manchester City (Eng)
1970–71 Chelsea (Eng)
1971–72 Rangers (Sco)
1972–73 A C Milan (Ita)
1973–74 Magdeburg (GDR)
1974–75 Dynamo Kiev (USSR)
1975–76 Anderlecht (Bel)
1976–77 SV Hamburg (FRG)
1977–78 Anderlecht (Bel)
1978–79 Barcelona (Spa)
1979–80 Valencia (Spa)
1980–81 Dinamo Tbilisi (USSR)
1981–82 Barcelona (Spa)
1982–83 Aberdeen (Sco)

UEFA CUP: Instituted in 1955 as the Inter-City Fairs Cup. Originally contested over three years, since 1960 it is held annually.

1955–58 Barcelona (Spa)
1958–60 Barcelona (Spa)
1960–61 A S Roma (Ita)
1961–62 Valencia (Spa)
1962–63 Valencia (Spa)
1963–64 Real Zaragossa (Spa)
1964–65 Ferencvaros (Hun)
1965–66 Barcelona (Spa)
1966–67 Dynamo Zagreb (Yug)
1967–68 Leeds United (Eng)
1968–69 Newcastle United (Eng)
1969–70 Arsenal (Eng)
1970–71 Leeds United (Eng)
1971–72 Tottenham Hotspur (Eng)
1972–73 Liverpool (Eng)
1973–74 Feyenoord (Hol)
1974–75 Borussia Mönchengladbach (FRG)
1975–76 Liverpool (Eng)
1976–77 Juventus (Ita)
1977–78 PSV Eindhoven (Hol)
1978–79 Borussia Mönchengladbach (FRG)
1979–80 Eintracht Frankfurt (FRG)
1980–81 Ipswich Town (Eng)
1981–82 IFK Gothenburg (Swe)
1982–83 Anderlecht (Bel)

EUROPEAN SUPER CUP: Instituted in 1972 for contest between the winners of the European Champion Clubs Cup and the European Cup-Winners Cup.

1972	Ajax (Hol)	1978	Anderlecht (Bel)
1973	Ajax (Hol)	1979	Nottingham Forest (Eng)
1974	not held	1980	Valencia (Spa)
1975	Dynamo Kiev (USSR)	1981	not held
1976	Anderlecht (Bel)	1982	Aston Villa (Eng)
1977	Liverpool (Eng)		

WORLD CLUB CHAMPIONSHIP: Instituted in 1960 for contest between the winners of the European Champion Clubs Cup and the Copa Libertadores (the South American championship).

1960	Real Madrid (Spa)	1974	Atletico Madrid (Spa)
1961	Penarol (Uru)	1975	not held
1962	Santos (Bra)	1976	Bayern Munich (FRG)
1963	Santos (Bra)	1977	Boca Juniors (Arg)
1964	Inter Milan (Ita)	1978	not held
1965	Inter Milan (Ita)	1979	Olimpia (Par)
1966	Penarol (Uru)	1980	Nacional (Uru)
1967	Racing Club (Arg)	1981	Flamengo (Bra)
1968	Estudiantes (Arg)	1982	Penarol (Uru)
1969	AC Milan (Ita)		
1970	Feyenoord (Hol)		
1971	Nacional (Uru)		
1972	Ajax (Hol)		
1973	Independiente (Arg)		

Twenty-one-year old Argentine goal scoring star Diego Maradona, the most highly valued footballer in the world, stands 1·63 m (5 ft 4 in) tall and could be worth £25 000 a centimetre. He was in his national team at the age of 17. Such success is the dream of all South American boys, like this Brazilian youngster in the back streets of Rio, whose ball juggling skills may well one day make him into another Pele.

Willie 'Fatty' Foulke, the largest man ever to play soccer for England.

In the early 1900s when Willie 'Fatty' Foulke played in goal for England he stood 1·90 m (6 ft 3 in) tall and weighed over 141 kg (22 stone). Later, playing for Bradford City, his weight reached a record 165 kg (26 stone).

The fastest authenticated time for a goal from kick-off is 6 sec by Albert Mundy in 1958, by Barrie Jones in 1962, by Keith Smith in 1964, and by Tommy Langley in 1980, although wind-aided goals in 3 sec have been widely reported.

The Coleridge FC of the Cambridgeshire FA, formed in 1954, have never had a player disciplined by a referee. In contrast, in February, 1975, Glencraig United of Faifley near Clydebank had all 11 players and two substitutes booked before they left the dressing room due to the referee taking exception to the chant which greeted his arrival.

Two teams from Callinafercy Soccer Club, Co. Derry, played a marathon game of 65 hr 1 min for charity in August 1980.

Terry McDermott of Liverpool and Bryan Robson of Manchester United playing for England against Romania in 1981. McDermott won both the Footballer of the Year award (from the Football Writers Association) and the Player of the Year trophy (from the Professional Footballers Association) in 1980. The following year Robson was transferred from West Bromwich Albion to Manchester for a British record fee of approximately £1 500 000.

FOOTBALL ASSOCIATION (FA) CHALLENGE CUP:

Instituted in 1871. Since 1923 the finals have been played at Wembley. Aston Villa and Tottenham Hotspur have won a record seven times (the latter in seven final appearances) but Newcastle United have appeared in the final 11 times, winning six. The highest score in an FA Cup match is 26–0 by Preston North End *v* Hyde in 1887. There was a record crowd, estimated at 160 000, at the first Wembley Final in 1923 between Bolton Wanderers and West Ham United. The 1980 final accrued record receipts of £729 000 (excluding radio and television fees), whereas the 1872 final had a gate of £100. The youngest player ever in the competition was Scott Endersby (Kettering Town), aged 15 yr 288 days in 1977. The youngest in a final was Paul Allen (West Ham), aged 17 yr 256 days in 1980, while the youngest to score in a final was Norman Whiteside (Manchester United) aged 18 yr 20 days in 1983.

1872 Wanderers	1946 Derby County
1873 Wanderers	1947 Charlton Athletic
1874 Oxford University	1948 Manchester United
1875 Royal Engineers	1949 Wolverhampton Wanderers
1876 Wanderers	1950 Arsenal
1877 Wanderers	1951 Newcastle United
1878 Wanderers	1952 Newcastle United
1879 Old Etonians	1953 Blackpool
1880 Clapham Rovers	1954 West Bromwich Albion
1881 Old Carthusians	1955 Newcastle United
1882 Old Etonians	1956 Manchester City
1883 Blackburn Olympic	1957 Aston Villa
1884 Blackburn Rovers	1958 Bolton Wanderers
1885 Blackburn Rovers	1959 Nottingham Forest
1886 Blackburn Rovers	1960 Wolverhampton Wanderers
1887 Aston Villa	1961 Tottenham Hotspur
1888 West Bromwich Albion	1962 Tottenham Hotspur
1889 Preston North End	1963 Manchester United
1890 Blackburn Rovers	1964 West Ham United
1891 Blackburn Rovers	1965 Liverpool
1892 West Bromwich Albion	1966 Everton
1893 Wolverhampton Wanderers	1967 Tottenham Hotspur
1894 Notts County	1968 West Bromwich Albion
1895 Aston Villa	1969 Manchester City
1896 Sheffield Wednesday	1970 Chelsea
1897 Aston Villa	1971 Arsenal
1898 Nottingham Forest	1972 Leeds United
1899 Sheffield United	1973 Sunderland
1900 Bury	1974 Liverpool
1901 Tottenham Hotspur	1975 West Ham United
1902 Sheffield United	1976 Southampton
1903 Bury	1977 Manchester United
1904 Manchester City	1978 Ipswich Town
1905 Aston Villa	1979 Arsenal
1906 Everton	1980 West Ham United
1907 Sheffield Wednesday	1981 Tottenham Hotspur
1908 Wolverhampton Wanderers	1982 Tottenham Hotspur
1909 Manchester United	1983 Manchester United
1910 Newcastle United	
1911 Bradford City	
1912 Barnsley	
1913 Aston Villa	
1914 Burnley	
1915 Sheffield United	
1920 Aston Villa	
1921 Tottenham Hotspur	
1922 Huddersfield Town	
1923 Bolton Wanderers	
1924 Newcastle United	
1925 Sheffield United	
1926 Bolton Wanderers	
1927 Cardiff City	
1928 Blackburn Rovers	
1929 Bolton Wanderers	
1930 Arsenal	
1931 West Bromwich Albion	
1932 Newcastle United	
1933 Everton	
1934 Manchester City	
1935 Sheffield Wednesday	
1936 Arsenal	
1937 Sunderland	
1938 Preston North End	
1939 Portsmouth	

FOOTBALL LEAGUE CUP:

Instituted in 1960 and from 1982 to 1983 known as the Milk Cup. It has been won a record three times by Aston Villa (from a record five final appearances) and by Liverpool.

1961 Aston Villa
1962 Norwich City
1963 Birmingham City
1964 Leicester City
1965 Chelsea
1966 West Bromwich Albion
1967 Queen's Park Rangers
1968 Leeds United
1969 Swindon Town
1970 Manchester City
1971 Tottenham Hotspur
1972 Stoke City
1973 Tottenham Hotspur
1974 Wolverhampton Wanderers
1975 Aston Villa
1976 Manchester City
1977 Aston Villa
1978 Nottingham Forest
1979 Nottingham Forest
1980 Wolverhampton Wanderers
1981 Liverpool
1982 Liverpool
1983 Liverpool

The pride of Scotland and Liverpool, Kenny Dalglish, was voted Footballer of the Year in 1978–79 and 1982–83. Prior to joining Liverpool he had played for Celtic in over 300 matches.

FOOTBALL LEAGUE: Formed in 1888 by 12 clubs. There are now four divisions, with 22 clubs in divisions one and two, and 24 in divisions three and four (92 in all).

In Division I the most championships won is 14 by Liverpool, who also scored the highest number of points, 68, in 1978–79. The narrowest winning margin was in 1924 when Huddersfield won from Cardiff by 0·02 of a goal.

The League Champions (Division I) have been:

1888–89 Preston North End	1970–71 Arsenal
1889–90 Preston North End	1971–72 Derby County
1890–91 Everton	1972–73 Liverpool
1891–92 Sunderland	1973–74 Leeds United
1892–93 Sunderland	1974–75 Derby County
1893–94 Aston Villa	1975–76 Liverpool
1894–95 Sunderland	1976–77 Liverpool
1895–96 Aston Villa	1977–78 Nottingham Forest
1896–97 Aston Villa	1978–79 Liverpool
1897–98 Sheffield United	1979–80 Liverpool
1898–99 Aston Villa	1980–81 Aston Villa
1899–1900 Aston Villa	1981–82 Liverpool
1900–01 Liverpool	1982–83 Liverpool
1901–02 Sunderland	
1902–03 Sheffield Wednesday	
1903–04 Sheffield Wednesday	
1904–05 Newcastle United	
1905–06 Liverpool	
1906–07 Newcastle United	
1907–08 Manchester United	
1908–09 Newcastle United	
1909–10 Aston Villa	
1910–11 Manchester United	
1911–12 Blackburn Rovers	
1912–13 Sunderland	
1913–14 Blackburn Rovers	
1914–15 Everton	
1919–20 West Bromwich Albion	
1920–21 Burnley	
1921–22 Liverpool	
1922–23 Liverpool	
1923–24 Huddersfield Town	
1924–25 Huddersfield Town	
1925–26 Huddersfield Town	
1926–27 Newcastle United	
1927–28 Everton	
1928–29 Sheffield Wednesday	
1929–30 Sheffield Wednesday	
1930–31 Arsenal	
1931–32 Everton	
1932–33 Arsenal	
1933–34 Arsenal	
1934–35 Arsenal	
1935–36 Sunderland	
1936–37 Manchester City	
1937–38 Arsenal	
1938–39 Everton	
1946–47 Liverpool	
1947–48 Arsenal	
1948–49 Portsmouth	
1949–50 Portsmouth	
1950–51 Tottenham Hotspur	
1951–52 Manchester United	
1952–53 Arsenal	
1953–54 Wolverhampton Wanderers	
1954–55 Chelsea	
1955–56 Manchester United	
1956–57 Manchester United	
1957–58 Wolverhampton Wanderers	
1958–59 Wolverhampton Wanderers	
1959–60 Burnley	
1960–61 Tottenham Hotspur	
1961–62 Ipswich Town	
1962–63 Everton	
1963–64 Liverpool	
1964–65 Manchester United	
1965–66 Liverpool	
1966–67 Manchester United	
1967–68 Manchester City	
1968–69 Leeds United	
1969–70 Everton	

Kevin Keegan (second from left), one of the mainstays of the England team, in the colours of Southampton against Birmingham City, soon after returning to the Football League from playing with SV Hamburg. Prior to his £500 000 transfer to the German team he had won League championship, FA Cup, UEFA Cup and European Cup medals with Liverpool. Also in the picture are Keith Bertschin (left), Mike Channon, and Archie Gemmell.

Brilliant goalkeeper Pat Jennings has gained the record number of caps by a Northern Ireland player. His skill has also graced the teams of Watford, Spurs and Arsenal.

SCOTTISH FA CUP: Instituted 1873 and won a record 26 times by Celtic between 1892 and 1980.

1874	Queen's Park	1891	Hearts
1875	Queen's Park	1892	Celtic
1876	Queen's Park	1893	Queen's Park
1877	Vale of Leven	1894	Rangers
1878	Vale of Leven	1895	St Bernard's
1879	Vale of Leven	1896	Hearts
1880	Queen's Park	1897	Rangers
1881	Queen's Park	1898	Rangers
1882	Queen's Park	1899	Celtic
1883	Dumbarton	1900	Celtic
1884	Queen's Park	1901	Hearts
1885	Renton	1902	Hibernian
1886	Queen's Park	1903	Rangers
1887	Hibernian	1904	Celtic
1888	Renton	1905	Third Lanark
1889	Third Lanark	1906	Hearts
1890	Queen's Park	1907	Celtic

Stanley Matthews was the first footballer to be knighted, in 1965, when he retired from the game aged 50, after 34 years and 701 League matches.

1908 Celtic	1932 Rangers	1958 Clyde	1971 Celtic
1909 Not decided	1933 Celtic	1959 St Mirren	1972 Celtic
1910 Dundee	1934 Rangers	1960 Rangers	1973 Rangers
1911 Celtic	1935 Rangers	1961 Dunfermline	1974 Celtic
1912 Celtic	1936 Rangers	1962 Rangers	1975 Celtic
1913 Falkirk	1937 Celtic	1963 Rangers	1976 Rangers
1914 Celtic	1938 East Fife	1964 Rangers	1977 Celtic
1915–19 Not held	1939 Clyde	1965 Celtic	1978 Rangers
1920 Kilmarnock	1940–46 Not held	1966 Rangers	1979 Rangers
1921 Partick Thistle	1947 Aberdeen	1967 Celtic	1980 Celtic
1922 Morton	1948 Rangers	1968 Dunfermline	1981 Rangers
1923 Celtic	1949 Rangers	1969 Celtic	1982 Aberdeen
1924 Airdrieonians	1950 Rangers	1970 Aberdeen	1983 Aberdeen
1925 Celtic	1951 Celtic		
1926 St Mirren	1952 Motherwell		
1927 Celtic	1953 Rangers		
1928 Rangers	1954 Celtic		
1929 Kilmarnock	1955 Clyde		
1930 Rangers	1956 Hearts		
1931 Celtic	1957 Falkirk		

The 'Tartan Army' of Scotland's fans seen here at Wembley are in the same mould as the record 149 547 crowd which saw Scotland beat England (3–1) at Hampden Park, Glasgow in 1937. Of the 101 games between the countries so far, Scotland have won 39 to England's 40, with 22 drawn.

SCOTTISH LEAGUE CUP: Instituted in 1946, it has been won a record 10 times by Rangers.

1947	Rangers	1965	Rangers
1948	East Fife	1966	Celtic
1949	Rangers	1967	Celtic
1950	East Fife	1968	Celtic
1951	Motherwell	1969	Celtic
1952	Dundee	1970	Celtic
1953	Dundee	1971	Rangers
1954	East Fife	1972	Partick Thistle
1955	Hearts	1973	Hibernian
1956	Aberdeen	1974	Dundee
1957	Celtic	1975	Celtic
1958	Celtic	1976	Rangers
1959	Hearts	1977	Aberdeen
1960	Hearts	1978	Rangers
1961	Rangers	1979	Rangers
1962	Rangers	1980	Dundee United
1963	Hearts	1981	Dundee United
1964	Rangers	1982	Celtic

SCOTTISH LEAGUE CHAMPIONS: The Scottish League was formed in 1890. Rangers won the title 34 times (and one shared) till 1975 when the League was reformed into a Premier Division of 10 clubs and first and second divisions of 14 clubs each.

First Division Champions:

		1935	Rangers
1891	Dumbarton	1936	Celtic
1892	Dumbarton	1937	Rangers
1893	Celtic	1938	Celtic
1894	Celtic	1939	Rangers
1895	Hearts	1940–46	Not held
1896	Celtic	1947	Rangers
1897	Hearts	1948	Hibernian
1898	Celtic	1949	Rangers
1899	Rangers	1950	Rangers
1900	Rangers	1951	Hibernian
1901	Rangers	1952	Hibernian
1902	Rangers	1953	Rangers
1903	Hibernian	1954	Celtic
1904	Third Lanark	1955	Aberdeen
1905	Celtic	1956	Rangers
1906	Celtic	1957	Rangers
1907	Celtic	1958	Hearts
1908	Celtic	1959	Rangers
1909	Celtic	1960	Hearts
1910	Celtic	1961	Rangers
1911	Rangers	1962	Dundee
1912	Rangers	1963	Rangers
1913	Rangers	1964	Rangers
1914	Celtic	1965	Kilmarnock
1915	Celtic	1966	Celtic
1916	Celtic	1967	Celtic
1917	Celtic	1968	Celtic
1918	Rangers	1969	Celtic
1919	Celtic	1970	Celtic
1920	Rangers	1971	Celtic
1921	Rangers	1972	Celtic
1922	Celtic	1973	Celtic
1923	Rangers	1974	Celtic
1924	Rangers	1975	Rangers
1925	Rangers		
1926	Celtic	*Premier Division Champions:*	
1927	Rangers	1976	Rangers
1928	Rangers	1977	Celtic
1929	Rangers	1978	Rangers
1930	Rangers	1979	Celtic
1931	Rangers	1980	Aberdeen
1932	Motherwell	1981	Celtic
1933	Rangers	1982	Celtic
1934	Rangers	1983	Dundee United

MOST GOALS

Career 1329 Artur Friedenreich (Brazil) 42 years
Season 126 Edson Arantes do Nascimento (Pele) (Brazil) 1959
Match 16 Stephan Stanis, Racing Club de Lens v Aubry-Asturies (France) 13 Dec 1942

MOST INTERNATIONAL APPEARANCES

England 108 Bobby Moore (West Ham and Fulham) 1962–73
Ireland 96 Pat Jennings (Watford, Tottenham Hotspur, Arsenal) 1964–83
Scotland 90 Kenny Dalglish (Celtic and Liverpool) 1971–83
Wales 68 Ivor Allchurch (Swansea, Newcastle, Cardiff, Worcester City) 1950–68

Youngest 17 yr 42 days Norman Whiteside (Manchester United) for Northern Ireland v Yugoslavia, 1982
Oldest 45 yr 229 days Billy Meredith (Manchester City and United) for Wales v England 1920

OLYMPIC GAMES: Soccer was included from 1908, after unofficial competitions in 1900, 1904 and 1906. The highest score has been 17 by Denmark v France (1) in 1908.

1908 Great Britain	1936 Italy	1968 Hungary
1912 Great Britain	1948 Sweden	1972 Poland
1920 Belgium	1952 Hungary	1976 GDR
1924 Uruguay	1956 USSR	1980 Czechoslovakia
1928 Uruguay	1960 Yugoslavia	
1932 not held	1964 Hungary	

The most famous soccer player of recent years, Pele, who scored 1283 goals in first class soccer. An international at 17, his 111 appearances for Brazil included playing on three winning World Cup teams, in 1958, 1962 and 1970.

A Peruvian player about to give a 'bravura' performance after being brought down by a Pole in the World Cup. The histrionics of many of the players in the 1982 tournament saddened supporters of the game.

BIGGEST CROWDS

World 205 000 (*199 854 paid*) Brazil *v* Uruguay, Maracana Stadium, Rio de Janeiro, 16 July 1950.
Britain 149 547 Scotland *v* England, Hampden Park, Glasgow, 17 April 1937

HIGH SCORING GAMES

The highest score achieved in a first class match was the 36–0 defeat of Bon Accord by Arbroath in the Scottish Cup competition on 5 September 1885. However, it is only just the record as in the same competition on the same day Dundee Harp beat Aberdeen Rovers by 35–0. The Bon Accord goalkeeper was reported to have had a bad leg, but no excuse was given for his colleague in the Aberdeen Rovers team.

The record score at international level was when England beat France in an amateur match at Ipswich in 1910 by 20–0. The record in the International Championship is England's 13–0 defeat of Ireland at Belfast in 1882.

In minor football even higher scores have been reached, as when an under-14 team in Kent, Midas FC ran out winners against Courage Colts in 1976, by a margin of 59–1, even though the Colts had scored first. In women's soccer Edinburgh Dynamos beat Lochend Thistle by 42–0 in 1975. But the score to end all scores came in a promotion match in Yugoslavia in 1979, when the Ilinden and Mladost teams connived, with the help of the referee, for Ilinden to win by 134–1. Their nearby rivals in the promotion race (which was dependent on goal average) won their match, also with the collusion of all concerned, by 88–0. Apparently local police used their walkie-talkie radios to inform the adversaries of the respective scores. Not surprisingly, all participants were suspended by the national football authorities.

Currently the record holder for heading a ball non-stop, Sweden's Mikael Palmqvist is also the former holder of the ball juggling record, having kept it going for ten hours and 80 357 repetitions without the ball ever touching his hands or the ground.

BALL JUGGLING

Alan Nyanjong Abuto (Ken) kept a ball off the ground for 11 hr 36 min 19 sec (85 295 repetitions) in February 1982, using only his feet, legs and head. Mikael Palmqvist (Sweden) headed a ball non-stop for 3 hr 26 min 12 sec in August 1982.

21

Athletics

There is evidence that running was involved in early Egyptian rituals at Memphis c 3800 BC, but organised athletics is usually dated from the ancient Olympic Games c 1370 BC. In the British Isles the earliest references are the legendary accounts of the Tailteann Games in Ireland being founded in 1829 BC. The first recorded Olympic champion was Coroibos of Elis who won the Stadium foot race, about 180–185 m (164–169 yd) in 776 BC. Initially that was the only event but later the *diaulos*, double course, was introduced, followed by the *dolichos*, long race.

WORLD RECORDS

The greatest number of official IAAF world records (in events on the current schedule) broken by one athlete is 14, by Paavo Nurmi (Fin) at various events between 1921 and 1931, and by Iolanda Balas (Rom) in the high jump from 1956 to 1961. Nurmi also set eight marks in events no longer recognised, giving him a grand total of 22. The most achieved by a British athlete is nine by Sebastian Coe from 1979 to 1982, while the record for a British woman is five by 400 m/800 m runner Pat Lowe-Cropper in relays from 1967 to 1970.

PROGRESSIVE WORLD 1 MILE RECORD

Min. sec.	Name and Nationality	Place	Date
4:55·0	J. Heaviside (Ire)	Dublin	1 Apr 1861
4:49·0	J. Heaviside (Ire)	Dublin	27 May 1861
4:46·0	N. Greene (Ire)	Dublin	27 May 1861
4:33·0	George Farran (Ire)	Dublin	23 May 1862
4:29·6	Walter Chinnery (GB)	Cambridge	10 Mar 1868
4:28·8	Walter Gibbs (GB)	London	3 Apr 1868
4:28·6	Charles Gunton (GB)	London	31 Mar 1873
4:26·0	Walter Slade (GB)	London	30 May 1874
4:24·5	Walter Slade (GB)	London	19 June 1875
4:23·2	Walter George (GB)	London	16 Aug 1880
4:19·4	Walter George (GB)	London	3 June 1882
4:18·4	Walter George (GB)	Birmingham	21 June 1884
4:17·8	Thomas Conneff (Ire/USA)	Cambridge, USA	26 Aug 1893
4:17·0	Fred Bacon (GB)	London	6 July 1895
4:15·6	Thomas Conneff (Ire/USA)	New York	30 Aug 1895
4:15·4	John Paul Jones (USA)	Cambridge, USA	27 May 1911
4:14·4	John Paul Jones (USA)	Cambridge, USA	31 May 1913
4:12·6	Norman Taber (US)	Cambridge, USA	16 July 1915
4:10·4	Paavo Nurmi (Fin)	Stockholm, Sweden	23 Aug 1923
4:09·2	Jules Ladoumegue (Fra)	Paris, France	4 Oct 1931
4:07·6	Jack Lovelock (NZ)	Princeton, USA	15 July 1933
4:06·7**	Glenn Cunningham (USA)	Princeton, USA	16 June 1934
4:06·4	Sydney Wooderson (GB)	Motspur Park	28 Aug 1937
4:06·1**	Gunder Hägg (Swe)	Gothenburg, Sweden	1 July 1942
4:06·2	Arne Andersson (Swe)	Stockholm, Sweden	10 July 1942
4:04·6	Gunder Hägg (Swe)	Stockholm, Sweden	4 Sept 1942
4:02·6	Arne Andersson (Swe)	Gothenburg, Sweden	1 July 1943
4:01·6	Arne Andersson (Swe)	Malmo, Sweden	18 July 1944
4:01·3**	Gunder Hägg (Swe)	Malmo, Sweden	17 July 1945
3:59·4	Roger Bannister (GB)	Oxford	6 May 1954
3:57·9**	John Landy (Aus)	Turku, Finland	21 June 1954
3:57·2	Derek Ibbotson (GB)	London	19 July 1957
3:54·5	Herb Elliott (Aus)	Dublin	6 Aug 1958
3:54·4	Peter Snell (NZ)	Wanganui, NZ	27 Jan 1962
3:54·1	Peter Snell (NZ)	Auckland, NZ	17 Nov 1964
3:53·6	Michel Jazy (Fra)	Rennes, France	9 June 1965
3:51·3	Jim Ryun (USA)	Berkeley, USA	17 July 1966
3:51·1	Jim Ryun (USA)	Bakersfield, USA	23 June 1967
3:51·0	Filbert Bayi (Tan)	Kingston, Jamaica	17 May 1975
3:49·4	John Walker (NZ)	Gothenburg, Sweden	12 Aug 1975
3:49·0	Sebastian Coe (GB)	Oslo, Norway	17 July 1979
3:48·8	Steve Ovett (GB)	Oslo, Norway	1 July 1980
3:48·53	Sebastian Coe (GB)	Zurich, Switzerland	19 Aug 1981
3:48·40	Steve Ovett (GB)	Coblenz, Germany	26 Aug 1981
3:47·33	Sebastian Coe (GB)	Brussels, Belgium	28 Aug 1981

**Ratified marks were 4:06:8, 4:06:2, 4:01:4 and 3:58:0 respectively.*

Note: The following professional times were superior to the then accepted amateur mark.

Min. sec.	Name and Nationality	Place	Date
4:23·0	Thomas Horspool (GB)	—	1858
4:22¼	Siah Albison (GB)	Manchester	27 Oct 1860
4:20·5	Edward Mills (GB)	—	23 Apr 1863
4:20·0	Edward Mills (GB)	Manchester	25 June 1864
4:17¼	William Lang (GB) & William Richards (GB)	Manchester	19 Aug 1865
4:16·2	William Cummings (GB)	Preston	14 May 1881
4:12¾	Walter George (GB)	London	23 Aug 1886

One of the greatest sprinter/long jumpers the world has seen, Jesse Owens. He dominated the 1936 Olympic Games, winning four gold medals. He set an unprecedented six world records in one afternoon in 1935, and his long jump mark that day lasted for over 25 years.

Jesse Owens (USA) set six world marks within one hour on 25 May 1935, at Ann Arbor, Michigan, with 100 yd in 9·4 sec, 220 yd (and 200 m) in 20·3 sec, 220 yd (and 200 m) hurdles in 22·6 sec, and the long jump 26 ft 8¼ in (8·13 m). Nurmi broke the 1500 m and 5000 m records within one hour on 19 June 1924 as part of his Olympic preparations.

BARRIERS

As a sport governed primarily by the stop watch and the tape measure, there have been various 'barriers' to be broken. The first important one of these was the 6 ft (1·83 m) high jump, which was cleared by the Hon Marshall Brooks of Oxford University in 1876. Brooks, a rugby international, reputedly did much of his jumping in a high hat. The first man over 7 ft (2·13 m) was Charlie Dumas (USA) who jumped 7 ft 0½ in (2·15 m) in June 1956. The time of 10 sec for 100 yd (91·44 m) was first beaten by John Owen (USA) when winning the American title in 9·8 sec in October 1890. The most famous barrier was the four-minute mile, which was also first achieved by an Oxford man, Roger Bannister, when he clocked 3 min 59·4 sec on 6 May 1954. Since then four minutes has been broken by another 388 athletes from 40 countries, to the end of 1982. That total includes 72 Britons and a record single country total of 123 from the USA. Former world record holder John Walker (NZ) has the most with 74. The youngest runner to achieve the distinction was Jim Ryun (USA) with 3 min 59·0 sec in 1964, when aged 17 yr 37 days, and the oldest was his countryman George Young, aged 34 yr 220 days when he clocked 3 min 59·6 sec in 1972.

The camera has caught Bob Beamon jumping into the 21st century. For the young American long jumper is about to clear the extraordinary distance of 8·90 m (29 ft 2½ in) to win the 1968 Olympic title in the rarified altitude of Mexico City. Experts have predicted that his record will not be beaten in this century. Fifteen years later only one man has jumped within 30 cm (12 in) of the mark.

RECORDS (As at 31 May 1983)

Men

Event	World			Olympic			British		
	min sec	Name/Country	Year	min sec	Name/Country	Year	min sec	Name	Year
100 m	9·95★	Jim Hines (USA)	1968	9·95★	Jim Hines (USA)	1968	10·11	Allan Wells	1980
200 m	19·72★	Pietro Mennea (Ita)	1979	19·83★	Tommie Smith (USA)	1968	20·21	Allan Wells	1980
400 m	43·86★	Lee Evans (USA)	1968	43·86★	Lee Evans (USA)	1968	44·93	David Jenkins	1975
800 m	1 41·73	Sebastian Coe (GB)	1981	1 43·50	Alberto Juantorena (Cub)	1976	1 41·73	Sebastian Coe	1981
1000 m	2 12·18	Sebastian Coe (GB)	1981	—	—	—	2 12·18	Sebastian Coe	1981

Every runner knows that behind the championship medals and record breaking achievements lie hours of hard training in all weather conditions. The shore near Steve Ovett's home is not always the hospitable place that the summer tourist knows, but even on grey, stormy days like this, he churns out the lonely miles which must be run to have the successes of the summer.

RECORDS *MEN continued*

	World				Olympic				British		
1500 m	3 31·36	Steve Ovett (GB)	1980	3 34·91	Kip Keino (Ken)	1968		3 31·36	Steve Ovett	1980
1 Mile	3 47·33	Sebastian Coe (GB)	1981	—	—			3 47·33	Sebastian Coe	1981
2000 m	4 51·4	John Walker (NZ)	1976	—	—			4 57·71	Steve Ovett	1982
3000 m	7 32·1	Henry Rono (Ken)	1981	—	—			7 32·79	David Moorcroft	1982
5000 m	13 00·41	David Moorcroft (GB)	1982	13 20·34	Brendan Foster (GB)	1976		13 00·41	David Moorcroft	1982
10 000 m	27 22·4	Henry Rono (Ken)	1978	27 38·35	Lasse Viren (Fin)	1972		27 30·3	Brendan Foster	1978
3000 m Steeplechase	8 05·37	Henry Rono (Ken)	1978	8 08·02	Anders Garderud (Swe)	1976		8 18·80	Colin Reitz	1982
110 m Hurdles	12·93	Renaldo Nehemiah (USA)	1981	13·24	Rod Milburn (USA)	1972		13·43	Mark Holtom	1982
400 m Hurdles	47·13	Ed Moses (USA)	1980	47·64	Ed Moses (USA)	1976		48·12	David Hemery	1968
4 × 100 m Relay	38·03	USA	1977	38·19*	USA	1968		38·62	National Team	1980
4 × 400 m Relay	2 56·16*	USA	1968	2 56·16*	USA	1968		3 00·46	National Team	1972
	metres			*metres*				*metres*		
High Jump	2·36	Gerd Wessig (GDR)	1980	2·36	Gerd Wessig (GDR)	1980		2·24	Mark Naylor	1980
Pole Vault	5·81	Vladimir Polyakov (SU)	1981	5·78	Wladyslaw Kozakiewicz (Pol)	1980		5·65	Keith Stock	1981
Long Jump	8·90*	Bob Beamon (USA)	1968	8·90*	Bob Beamon (USA)	1968		8·23	Lynn Davies	1968
Triple Jump	17·89*	Joao Carlos de Oliveira (Bra)	1975	17·39*	Viktor Saneyev (USSR)	1968		17·57	Keith Connor	1982
Shot	22·15	Udo Beyer (GDR)	1978	21·35	Vladimir Kiselyev (USSR)	1980		21·68	Geoff Capes	1980
Discus	71·88	Yuri Dumchev (USSR)	1983	68·28	Mac Wilkins (USA)	1976		64·32	Bill Tancred	1974
Hammer	83·98	Sergey Litvinov (USSR)	1982	81·80	Yuri Sedykh (USSR)	1980		75·08	Robert Weir	1982
Javelin	99·72	Tom Petranoff (USA)	1983	94·58	Miklos Nemeth (Hun)	1976		85·52	David Ottley	1980
Decathlon	8743 pts	Daley Thompson (GB)	1982	8617 pts	Bruce Jenner (USA)	1976		8743 pts	Daley Thompson	1982

★ Achieved at Mexico City at an altitude of 2240 m (7347 ft)

World record holder Renaldo Nehemiah (USA), the only man to run faster than 13·0 sec in the 110 metres hurdles. Favourite for the 1980 Olympic title until the American withdrawal, he is seen here winning the 1979 World Cup race from the man next to him, Thomas Munkelt (GDR), who went on to win in Moscow. Beyond both of them is Alejandro Casanas (Cub) who won the silver medal in 1980, as he had in 1976.

RECORDS
Women

Event	World min sec	World Name/Country	World Year	Olympic min sec	Olympic Name/Country	Olympic Year	British min sec	British Name	British Year
100 m	10·88	Marlies Oelsner (GDR)	1977	11·01	Annegret Richter (FRG)	1976	11·10	Kathy Smallwood	1981
200 m	21·71	Marita Koch (GDR)	1979	22·03	Barbel Wöckel (GDR)	1980	22·13	Kathy Smallwood	1982
400 m	48·16	Marita Koch (GDR)	1982	48·88	Marita Koch (GDR)	1980	50·46	Kathy Smallwood	1982
800 m	1 53·43	Nadezda Olizarenko (USSR)	1980	1 53·43	Nadezda Olizarenko (USSR)	1980	1 59·05	Christina Boxer	1979
1500 m	3 52·47	Tatyana Kazankina (USSR)	1980	3 56·56	Tatyana Kazankina (USSR)	1980	4 01·53	Christine Benning	1979
1 Mile	4 17·44	Maricica Puica (Rom)	1982	—	—	—	4 30·20	Christina Boxer	1979
3000 m	8 26·78	Svetlana Ulmasova (USSR)	1982	—	—	—	8 46·01	Wendy Smith	1982
5000 m	15 08·26	Mary Decker-Tabb (USA)	1982	—	—	—	15 14·51	Paula Fudge	1981
10 000 m	31 35·01	Ludmila Baranova (USSR)	1983	—	—	—	32 57·17	Kathy Binns	1980
100 m Hurdles	12·36	Grazyna Rabsztyn (Pol)	1980	12·56	Vera Komisova (USSR)	1980	13·06	Shirley Strong	1980
400 m Hurdles	54·28	Karin Rossley (GDR)	1980	—	—	—	56·06	Christine Warden	1979
4 × 100 m Relay	41·60	GDR	1980	41·60	GDR	1980	42·43	National Team	1980
4 × 400 m Relay	3 19·04	GDR	1982	3 19·23	GDR	1976	3 25·82	National Team	1982
	metres			metres			metres		
High Jump	2·02	Ulrike Meyfarth (FRG)	1982	1·97	Sara Simeoni (Ita)	1980	1·95	Diana Elliott	1982
Long Jump	7·21	Anisoara Cusmir (Rom)	1983	7·06	Tatyana Kolpakova (USSR)	1980	6·76	Mary Rand	1964
Shot	22·45	Ilona Slupianek (GDR)	1980	22·41	Ilona Slupianek (GDR)	1980	18·99	Margaret Ritchie	1983
Discus	73·26	Galina Savinkova (USSR)	1983	69·96	Evelin Jahl (GDR)	1980	67·48	Margaret Ritchie	1981
					Maria Colon (Cub)	1980	69·70	Tessa Sanderson	1980
Javelin	74·20	Sofia Sakorafa (Gre)	1982	68·40	Nadezda Tkachenko	1980	4408 pts	Susan Longden	1980
Pentathlon	5083 pts	Nadezda Tkachenko (USSR)	1980	5083 pts	(USSR)				
				—			6286 pts	Judy Livermore	1982
Heptathlon	6772 pts	Ramona Neubert (GDR)	1982	—					

Below: **Gerd Wessig (GDR)** achieved the ultimate in his sport when he won an Olympic gold medal with a world record breaking effort. He jumped 6 cm (2¼ in) higher than ever before and some 40 cm (15¾ in) over his own height to set a world best of 2·36 m (7 ft 8¾ in). *Left:* British and Commonwealth record holder Tessa Sanderson in the javelin.

OLYMPIC TITLES: The greatest number of gold medals ever won in track and field events is 10 by the American Ray Ewry in the three standing jumps between 1900 and 1908. The most by a woman is four, by Fanny Blankers-Koen (Hol) in 1948, by Betty Cuthbert (Aus) in 1956 and 1964, and by Barbel Wöckel (GDR) in 1972–76. The highest total by a runner is nine by the 'Flying Finn' Paavo Nurmi 1920–28. He also achieved a single Games record of five gold medals in 1924. The only athlete to win the same event in four editions of the Games is Al Oerter, the American discus thrower from 1956 to 1968. The only runner to win a gold medal in the same event three times consecutively is the sprinter Frank Wykoff (USA) who ran on America's winning relay team in 1928, 1932 and 1936.

Paavo Nurmi holds the all-time medals record total with twelve by winning three silver medals as well as the nine golds. The equivalent female record is seven by Shirley Strickland-de la Hunty (Aus) 1948–56, and by Irena Kirszenstein-Szewinska (Pol) 1964–76. Unofficially, the Australian's total is eight as a photo-finish picture—then only used to judge places if thought necessary—indicates that the judges were wrong and that she was actually third in a final in which she was officially placed fourth in 1948. The record number of medals won by an athlete representing Great Britain is four by runner Guy Butler in the 400 m and 4 × 400 m relay in 1920–24. The most by a British woman is three by sprinter Dorothy Hyman 1960–64, and by long jumper Mary Bignal-Rand in 1964.

Among many examples of multiple wins in the Games, perhaps the most remarkable are the 1500 m and 5000 m victories by Nurmi in July 1924 within an hour and a half on the same afternoon, and the unique triple by Emil Zatopek (Cz) when he won the 5000 m, 10 000 m and the marathon in 1952. His wife, Dana, who was born on exactly the same day as Emil, won the women's javelin title on the same day as his 5000 m victory.

MEN
100 metres
1896 Thomas Burke (USA) 12·0
1900 Francis Jarvis (USA) 11·0
1904 Archie Hahn (USA) 11·0
1906 Archie Hahn (USA) 11·2
1908 Reginald Walker (Saf) 10·8
1912 Ralph Craig (USA) 10·8
1920 Charles Paddock (USA) 10·8
1924 Harold Abrahams (GB) 10·6
1928 Percy Williams (Can) 10·8
1932 Eddie Tolan (USA) 10·3
1936 Jesse Owens (USA) 10·3
1948 Harrison Dillard (USA) 10·3
1952 Lindy Remigino (USA) 10·4
1956 Bobby-Joe Morrow (USA) 10·5
1960 Armin Hary (Ger) 10·2
1964 Robert Hayes (USA) 10·05
1968 James Hines (USA) 9·95
1972 Valeriy Borzov (USSR) 10·14
1976 Hasely Crawford (Tri) 10·06
1980 Allan Wells (GB) 10·25

200 metres
1896 Not held
1900 Walter Tewksbury (USA) 22·2
1904 Archie Hahn (USA) 21·6
1906 Not held
1908 Robert Kerr (Can) 22·6
1912 Ralph Craig (USA) 21.7
1920 Allen Woodring (USA) 22·0

The 1980 Olympic 1500 metres final, which was the scene of one of the great comebacks in sport. Sebastian Coe (254), who had been beaten into second place in the 800 metres by Steve Ovett (279) six days previously, returned 'from oblivion' to take the gold medal with Ovett in third place. Jurgen Straub (338) of the GDR split them to win the silver medal. Britain's third finalist was Steve Cram (257).

1924 Jackson Scholz (USA) 21·6
1928 Percy Williams (Can) 21·8
1932 Eddie Tolan (USA) 21·2
1936 Jesse Owens (USA) 20·7
1948 Melvin Patton (USA) 21·1
1952 Andrew Stanfield (USA) 20·7
1956 Bobby-Joe Morrow (USA) 20·6
1960 Livio Berrutti (Ita) 20·5
1964 Henry Carr (USA) 20·36
1968 Tommie Smith (USA) 19·83
1972 Valeriy Borzov (USSR) 20·00
1976 Donald Quarrie (Jam) 20·23
1980 Pietro Mennea (Ita) 20·19

400 metres
1896 Thomas Burke (USA) 54·2
1900 Maxie Long (USA) 49·4
1904 Harry Hillman (USA) 49·2
1906 Paul Pilgrim (USA) 53·2
1908 Wyndham Halswelle (GB) 50·0
1912 Charles Reidpath (USA) 48·2
1920 Bevil Rudd (Saf) 49·6
1924 Eric Liddell (GB) 47·6
1928 Ray Barbuti (USA) 47·8
1932 Bill Carr (USA) 46·2
1936 Archie Williams (USA) 46·5
1948 Arthur Wint (Jam) 46·2
1952 George Rhoden (Jam) 45·9
1956 Charles Jenkins (USA) 46·7
1960 Otis Davis (USA) 44·9
1964 Michael Larrabee (USA) 45·15
1968 Lee Evans (USA) 43·86
1972 Vincent Matthews (USA) 44·66
1976 Alberto Juantorena (Cub) 44·26
1980 Viktor Markin (USSR) 44·60

800 metres
1896 Edwin Flack (Aus) 2:11·0
1900 Alfred Tysoe (GB) 2:01·2
1904 James Lightbody (USA) 1:56·0
1906 Paul Pilgrim (USA) 2:01·5
1908 Mel Sheppard (USA) 1:52·8
1912 James Meredith (USA) 1:51·9
1920 Albert Hill (GB) 1:53·4
1924 Douglas Lowe (GB) 1:52·4
1928 Douglas Lowe (GB) 1:51·8
1932 Tom Hampson (GB) 1:49·7
1936 John Woodruff (USA) 1:52·9
1948 Malvin Whitfield (USA) 1:49·2
1952 Malvin Whitfield (USA) 1:49·2
1956 Thomas Courtney (USA) 1:47·7
1960 Peter Snell (NZ) 1:46·3
1964 Peter Snell (NZ) 1:45·1
1968 Ralph Doubell (Aus) 1:44·3
1972 David Wottle (USA) 1:44·9
1976 Alberto Juantorena (Cub) 1:43·5
1980 Steven Ovett (GB) 1:45·4

1500 metres
1896 Edwin Flack (Aus) 4:33·2
1900 Charles Bennett (GB) 4:06·2
1904 James Lightbody (USA) 4:05·4
1906 James Lightbody (USA) 4:12·0
1908 Mel Sheppard (USA) 4:03·4
1912 Arnold Jackson (GB) 3:56·8
1920 Albert Hill (GB) 4:01·8
1924 Paavo Nurmi (Fin) 3:53·6
1928 Harri Larva (Fin) 3:53·2
1932 Luigi Beccali (Ita) 3:51·2
1936 Jack Lovelock (NZ) 3:47·8
1948 Henry Eriksson (Swe) 3:49·8
1952 Josef Barthel (Lux) 3:45·1
1956 Ron Delany (Ire) 3:41·2
1960 Herbert Elliott (Aus) 3:35·6
1964 Peter Snell (NZ) 3:38·1
1968 Kipchoge Keino (Ken) 3:34·9
1972 Pekka Vasala (Fin) 3:36·3
1976 John Walker (NZ) 3:39·2
1980 Sebastian Coe (GB) 3:38·4

5000 metres
1896–1908 Not held
1912 Hannes Kolehmainen (Fin) 14:36·6
1920 Joseph Guillemot (Fra) 14:55·6
1924 Paavo Nurmi (Fin) 14:31·2
1928 Ville Ritola (Fin) 14:38·0
1932 Lauri Lehtinen (Fin) 14:30·0
1936 Gunnar Hockert (Fin) 14:22·2
1948 Gaston Reiff (Bel) 14:17·6
1952 Emil Zatopek (Cz) 14:06·6
1956 Vladimir Kuts (USSR) 13:39·6
1960 Murray Halberg (NZ) 13:43·4
1964 Robert Schul (USA) 13:48·8
1968 Mohamed Gammoudi (Tun) 14:05·0
1972 Lasse Viren (Fin) 13:26·4
1976 Lasse Viren (Fin) 13:24·8
1980 Miruts Yifter (Eth) 13:21·0

10 000 metres
1896–1908 Not held
1912 Hannes Kolehmainen (Fin) 31:20·8
1920 Paavo Nurmi (Fin) 31:45·8
1924 Ville Ritola (Fin) 30:23·2
1928 Paavo Nurmi (Fin) 30:18·8
1932 Janusz Kusocinski (Pol) 30:11·4
1936 Ilmari Salminen (Fin) 30:15·4
1948 Emil Zatopek (Cz) 29:59·6
1952 Emil Zatopek (Cz) 29:17·0
1956 Vladimir Kuts (USSR) 28:45·6
1960 Pyotr Bolotnikov (USSR) 28:32·2
1964 William Mills (USA) 28:24·4
1968 Naftali Temu (Ken) 29:27·4
1972 Lasse Viren (Fin) 27:38·4
1976 Lasse Viren (Fin) 27:40·4
1980 Miruts Yifter (Eth) 27:42·7

Marathon
1896 Spyridon Louis (Gre) 2:58:50·0
1900 Michel Theato (Fra) 2:59:45·0
1904 Thomas Hicks (USA) 3:28:35·0
1906 William Sherring (Can) 2:51:23·6
1908 John Hayes (USA) 2:55:18·4
1912 Kenneth McArthur (Saf) 2:36:54·8
1920 Hannes Kolehmainen (Fin) 2:32:35·8
1924 Albin Stenroos (Fin) 2:41:22·6
1928 Mohamed El Ouafi (Fra) 2:32:57·0
1932 Juan Zabala (Arg) 2:31:36·0
1936 Kitei Son (Jap) 2:29:19·2
1948 Delfo Cabrera (Arg) 2:34:51·6
1952 Emil Zatopek (Cz) 2:23:03·2
1956 Alain Mimoun (Fra) 2:25:00·0
1960 Abebe Bikila (Eth) 2:15:16·2
1964 Abebe Bikila (Eth) 2:12:11·2
1968 Mamo Wolde (Eth) 2:20:26·4
1972 Frank Shorter (USA) 2:12:19·8
1976 Waldemar Cierpinski (GDR) 2:09:55·0
1980 Waldemar Cierpinski (GDR) 2:11:03·0

4 × 100 metres relay		
1896–1908 Not held	1964 USA 39·06	1932 USA 3:08·2
1912 GB 42·4	1968 USA 38·23	1936 GB 3:09·0
1920 USA 42·2	1972 USA 38·19	1948 USA 3:10·4
1924 USA 41·0	1976 USA 38·33	1952 Jamaica 3:03·9
1928 USA 41·0	1980 USSR 38·26	1956 USA 3:04·8
		1960 USA 3:02·2
1932 USA 40·0	**4 × 400 metres relay**	1964 USA 3:00·7
1936 USA 39·8	1896–1908 Not held	1968 USA 2:56·1
1948 USA 40·6	1912 USA 3:16·6	1972 Kenya 2:59·8
1952 USA 40·1	1920 GB 3:22·2	1976 USA 2:58·7
1956 USA 39·5	1924 USA 3:16·0	1980 USSR 3:01·1
1960 Germany 39·5	1928 USA 3:14·2	

110 metres hurdles
1896 Thomas Curtis (USA) 17·6
1900 Alvin Kraenzlein (USA) 15·4
1904 Fred Schule (USA) 16·0
1906 R. Leavitt (USA) 16·2
1908 Forrest Smithson (USA) 15·0
1912 Fred Kelly (USA) 15·1
1920 Earl Thomson (Can) 14·8
1924 Daniel Kinsey (USA) 15·0
1928 Sydney Atkinson (Saf) 14·8
1932 George Saling (USA) 14·6
1936 Forrest Towns (USA) 14·2
1948 William Porter (USA) 13·9
1952 Harrison Dillard (USA) 13·7
1956 Lee Calhoun (USA) 13·5
1960 Lee Calhoun (USA) 13·8
1964 Hayes Jones (USA) 13·67

1968 Willie Davenport (USA) 13·33
1972 Rodney Milburn (USA) 13·24
1976 Guy Drut (Fra) 13·30
1980 Thomas Munkelt (GDR) 13·39

400 metres hurdles
1896 Not held
1900 Walter Tewksbury (USA) 57·6
1904 Harry Hillman (USA) 53·0
1906 Not held
1908 Charles Bacon (USA) 55·0
1912 Not held
1920 Frank Loomis (USA) 54·0
1924 Morgan Taylor (USA) 52·6
1928 Lord Burghley (GB) 53·4
1932 Robert Tisdall (Ire) 51·7
1936 Glen Hardin (USA) 52·4
1948 Roy Cochran (USA) 51·1
1952 Charles Moore (USA) 50·8
1956 Glenn Davis (USA) 50·1
1960 Glenn Davis (USA) 49·3
1964 Warren 'Rex' Cawley (USA) 49·69
1968 David Hemery (GB) 48·12
1972 John Akii-Bua (Uga) 47·82
1976 Edwin Moses (USA) 47·64
1980 Volker Beck (GDR) 48·70

3000 metres steeplechase
1896–1912 Not held
1920 Percy Hodge (GB) 10:00·4
1924 Ville Ritola (Fin) 9:33·6
1928 Toivo Loukola (Fin) 9:21·8
1932 Volmari Iso-Hollo (Fin) 10:33·4*
1936 Volmari Iso-Hollo (Fin) 9:03·8
1948 Tore Sjöstrand (Swe) 9:04·6
1952 Horace Ashenfelter (USA) 8:45·4
1956 Christopher Brasher (GB) 8:41·2
1960 Zdzislaw Krzyszkowiak (Pol) 8:34·2
1964 Gaston Roelants (Bel) 8:30·8
1968 Amos Biwott (Ken) 8:51·0
1972 Kipchoge Keino (Ken) 8:23·6
1976 Anders Garderud (Swe) 8:08·0
1980 Bronislaw Malinowski (Pol) 8:09·7
* Due to lap counting error distance was 3460 metres

20 000 metres walk
1896–1952 Not held
1956 Leonid Spirin (USSR) 1:31:27·4
1960 Vladimir Golubnichiy (USSR) 1:34:07·2
1964 Kenneth Matthews (GB) 1:29:34·0
1968 Vladimir Golubnichiy (USSR) 1:33:58·4
1972 Peter Frenkel (GDR) 1:26:42·4
1976 Daniel Bautista (Mex) 1:24:40·6
1980 Maurizio Damilano (Ita) 1:23:35·5

50 000 metres walk
1896–1928 Not held
1932 Thomas Green (GB) 4:50:10·0
1936 Harold Whitlock (GB) 4:30:41·1
1948 John Ljunggren (Swe) 4:41:52·0
1952 Giuseppe Dordoni (Ita) 4:28:07·8
1956 Norman Read (NZ) 4:30:42·8
1960 Don Thompson (GB) 4:25:30·0
1964 Abdon Pamich (Ita) 4:11:12·4
1968 Christophe Höhne (GDR) 4:20:13·6
1972 Bernd Kannenberg (GDR) 3:56:11·6
1976 Not held
1980 Hartwig Gauder (GDR) 3:49:24·0

High jump
1896 Ellery Clark (USA) 1·81
1900 Irving Baxter (USA) 1·90
1904 Samuel Jones (USA) 1·80
1906 Con Leahy (GB) 1·77
1908 Harry Porter (USA) 1·90
1912 Alma Richards (USA) 1·93
1920 Richard Landon (USA) 1·94
1924 Harold Osborn (USA) 1·98
1928 Robert King (USA) 1·94
1932 Duncan McNaughton (Can) 1·97
1936 Cornelius Johnson (USA) 2·03
1948 John Winter (Aus) 1·98
1952 Walter Davis (USA) 2·04

1956 Charles Dumas (USA) 2·12
1960 Robert Shavlakadze (USSR) 2·16
1964 Valeriy Brumel (USSR) 2·18
1968 Richard Fosbury (USA) 2·24
1972 Yuriy Tarmak (USSR) 2·23
1976 Jacek Wszola (Pol) 2·25
1980 Gerd Wessig (GDR) 2·36

Pole vault
1896 William Hoyt (USA) 3·30
1900 Irving Baxter (USA) 3·30
1904 Charles Dvorak (USA) 3·50
1906 Fernand Gonder (Fra) 3·40
1908 Edward Cooke (USA) 3·70
1912 Harry Babcock (USA) 3·95
1920 Frank Foss (USA) 4·09
1924 Lee Barnes (USA) 3·95
1928 Sabin Carr (USA) 4·20
1932 Bill Miller (USA) 4·31
1936 Earle Meadows (USA) 4·35
1948 Guinn Smith (USA) 4·30
1952 Robert Richards (USA) 4·55
1956 Robert Richards (USA) 4·56
1960 Donald Bragg (USA) 4·70
1964 Frederick Hansen (USA) 5·10
1968 Robert Seagren (USA) 5·40
1972 Wolfgang Nordwig (GDR) 5·50
1976 Tadeusz Slusarski (Pol) 5·50
1980 Wladyslaw Kozakiewicz (Pol) 5·78

Long jump
1896 Ellery Clark (USA) 6·35
1900 Alvin Kraenzlein (USA) 7·18
1904 Myer Prinstein (USA) 7·34
1906 Myer Prinstein (USA) 7·20
1908 Francis Irons (USA) 7·48
1912 Albert Gutterson (USA) 7·60
1920 William Pettersson (Swe) 7·15
1924 William De Hart Hubbard (USA) 7·44
1928 Edward Hamm (USA) 7·73
1932 Edward Gordon (USA) 7·63
1936 Jesse Owens (USA) 8·06
1948 William Steele (USA) 7·82
1952 Jerome Biffle (USA) 7·57
1956 Gregory Bell (USA) 7·83
1960 Ralph Boston (USA) 8·12
1964 Lynn Davies (GB) 8·07
1968 Robert Beamon (USA) 8·90
1972 Randy Williams (USA) 8·24
1976 Arnie Robinson (USA) 8·35
1980 Lutz Dombrowski (GDR) 8·54

Triple jump
1896 James Connolly (USA) 13·71
1900 Myer Prinstein (USA) 14·47
1904 Myer Prinstein (USA) 14·35
1906 Peter O'Connor (GB) 14·07
1908 Tim Ahearne (GB) 14·91
1912 Gustaf Lindblom (Swe) 14·76
1920 Vilho Tuulos (Fin) 14·50
1924 Anthony Winter (Aus) 15·52
1928 Mikio Oda (Jap) 15·21
1932 Chuhei Nambu (Jap) 15·72
1936 Naoto Tajima (Jap) 16·00
1948 Arne Ahman (Swe) 15·40
1952 Adhemar Ferreira da Silva (Bra) 16·22
1956 Adhemar Ferreira da Silva (Bra) 16·35
1960 Jozef Schmidt (Pol) 16·81
1964 Jozef Schmidt (Pol) 16·85
1968 Viktor Saneyev (USSR) 17·39
1972 Viktor Saneyev (USSR) 17·35
1976 Viktor Saneyev (USSR) 17·29
1980 Jaak Uudmae (USSR) 17·35

Shot
1896 Robert Garrett (USA) 11·22
1900 Richard Sheldon (USA) 14·10
1904 Ralph Rose (USA) 14·80
1906 Martin Sheridan (USA) 12·32
1908 Ralph Rose (USA) 14·21
1912 Patrick McDonald (USA) 15·34
1920 Ville Porhola (Fin) 14·81
1924 Clarence Houser (USA) 14·99

The 5000 metres final at the 1980 Olympics, illustrating the current dominance of African runners in the distance races. Leading is Mohamed Kedir (Eth-178) who had won a bronze in the 10 km. In second place is the eventual winner Miruts Yifter, the 36-year-old Ethiopian, who added this gold medal to that won at double the distance, and lying third is eventual silver medallist Suleiman Nyambui of Tanzania. Karlo Maaninka (Fin-208) was the bronze medallist, while Ireland's Eamonn Coghlan (403) finished fourth.

1928 John Kuck (USA) 15·87
1932 Leo Sexton (USA) 16·00
1936 Hans Wöllke (Ger) 16·20
1948 Wilbur Thompson (USA) 17·12
1952 Parry O'Brien (USA) 17·41
1956 Parry O'Brien (USA) 18·57
1960 William Nieder (USA) 19·68
1964 Dallas Long (USA) 20·33
1968 Randel Matson (USA) 20·54
1972 Wladyslaw Komar (Pol) 21·18
1976 Udo Beyer (GDR) 21·05
1980 Vladimir Kiselyov (USSR) 21·35

Discus
1896 Robert Garrett (USA) 29·15
1900 Rudolf Bauer (Hun) 36·04
1904 Martin Sheridan (USA) 39·28
1906 Martin Sheridan (USA) 41·46
1908 Martin Sheridan (USA) 40·89
1912 Armas Taipale (Fin) 45·21
1920 Elmer Niklander (Fin) 44·68
1924 Clarence Houser (USA) 46·15
1928 Clarence Houser (USA) 47·32
1932 John Anderson (USA) 49·49
1936 Ken Carpenter (USA) 50·48
1948 Adolfo Consolini (Ita) 52·78
1952 Sim Iness (USA) 55·03
1956 Alfred Oerter (USA) 56·36
1960 Alfred Oerter (USA) 59·18
1964 Alfred Oerter (USA) 61·00
1968 Alfred Oerter (USA) 64·78
1972 Ludvik Danek (Cz) 64·40
1976 Mac Wilkins (USA) 67·50
1980 Viktor Rasschupkin (USSR) 66·64

Hammer
1896 Not held
1900 John Flanagan (USA) 49·73
1904 John Flanagan (USA) 51·23
1906 Not held
1908 John Flanagan (USA) 51·92
1912 Matt McGrath (USA) 54·74
1920 Patrick Ryan (USA) 52·87
1924 Fred Tootell (USA) 53·29
1928 Pat O'Callaghan (Ire) 51·39
1932 Pat O'Callaghan (Ire) 53·92
1936 Karl Hein (Ger) 56·49

1948 Imre Nemeth (Hun) 56·07
1952 Jozsef Csermak (Hun) 60·34
1956 Harold Connolly (USA) 63·19
1960 Vasiliy Rudenkov (USSR) 67·10
1964 Romuald Klim (USSR) 69·74
1968 Gyula Zsivotzky (Hun) 73·36
1972 Anatoliy Bondarchuk (USSR) 75·50
1976 Yuriy Syedikh (USSR) 77·52
1980 Yuriy Syedikh (USSR) 81·80

Javelin
1896–1904 Not held
1906 Erik Lemming (Swe) 53·90
1908 Erik Lemming (Swe) 54·82
1912 Erik Lemming (Swe) 60·64
1920 Jonni Myyra (Fin) 65·78
1924 Jonni Myyra (Fin) 62·96
1928 Erik Lundkvist (Swe) 66·60
1932 Matti Järvinen (Fin) 72·71
1936 Gerhard Stöck (Ger) 71·84
1948 Tapio Rautavaara (Fin) 69·77
1952 Cyrus Young (USA) 73·78
1956 Egil Danielsen (Nor) 85·71
1960 Viktor Tsibulenko (USSR) 84·64
1964 Pauli Nevala (Fin) 82·66
1968 Janis Lusis (USSR) 90·10
1972 Klaus Wolfermann (Ger) 90·48
1976 Miklos Nemeth (Hun) 94·58
1980 Dainis Kula (USSR) 91·20

Decathlon
1896–1908 Not held
1912 Hugo Weislander (Swe) 6162
1920 Helge Lovland (Nor) 5970
1924 Harold Osborn (USA) 6668
1928 Paavo Yrjola (Fin) 6774
1932 James Bausch (USA) 6986
1936 Glenn Morris (USA) 7421
1948 Robert Mathias (USA) 6825
1952 Robert Mathias (USA) 7731
1956 Milton Campbell (USA) 7708
1960 Rafer Johnson (USA) 8001
1964 Willi Holdorf (Ger) 7887
1968 William Toomey (USA) 8193
1972 Nikolai Avilov (USSR) 8454
1976 Bruce Jenner (USA) 8618
1980 Daley Thompson (GB) 8495

WOMEN

100 metres
1928 Elizabeth Robinson (USA) 12·2
1932 Stanislawa Walasiewicz (Pol) 11·9
1936 Helen Stephens (USA) 11·5
1948 Fanny Blankers-Koen (Hol) 11·9
1952 Marjorie Jackson (Aus) 11·5
1956 Betty Cuthbert (Aus) 11·5
1960 Wilma Rudolph (USA) 11·0
1964 Wyomia Tyus (USA) 11·49
1968 Wyomia Tyus (USA) 11·07
1972 Renate Stecher (GDR) 11·07
1976 Annegret Richter (Ger) 11·08
1980 Lyudmila Kondratyeva (USSR) 11·06

200 metres
1928–1936 Not held
1948 Fanny Blankers-Koen (Hol) 24·4
1952 Marjorie Jackson (Aus) 23·7
1956 Betty Cuthbert (Aus) 23·4
1960 Wilma Rudolph (USA) 24·0
1964 Edith Maguire (USA) 23·05
1968 Irena Szewinska (Pol) 22·58
1972 Renate Stecher (GDR) 22·40
1976 Barbel Eckert (GDR) 22·37
1980 Barbel Wöckel (née Eckert) (GDR) 22·03

400 metres
1928–1960 Not held
1964 Betty Cuthbert (Aus) 52·01
1968 Colette Besson (Fra) 52·03
1972 Monika Zehrt (GDR) 51·08
1976 Irena Szewinska (Pol) 49·29
1980 Marita Koch (GDR) 48·88

800 metres
1928 Lina Radke (Ger) 2:16·8
1932–56 Not held
1960 Lyudmila Shevtsova (USSR) 2:04·3
1964 Ann Packer (GB) 2:01·1
1968 Madeline Manning (USA) 2:00·9
1972 Hildegard Falck (Ger) 1:58·6
1976 Tatyana Kazankina (USSR) 1:54·9
1980 Nadyezhda Olizarenko (USSR) 1:53·5

1500 metres
1928–68 Not held
1972 Lyudmila Bragina (USSR) 4:01·4
1976 Tatyana Kazankina (USSR) 4:05·5
1980 Tatyana Kazankina (USSR) 3:56·6

80 metres hurdles
1928 Not held
1932 Mildred Didrikson (USA) 11·7
1936 Trebisonda Valla (Ita) 11·7
1948 Fanny Blankers-Koen (Hol) 11·2
1952 Shirley Strickland (Aus) 10·9
1956 Shirley Strickland (Aus) 10·7
1960 Irina Press (USSR) 10·8
1964 Karin Balzer (GDR) 10·5
1968 Maureen Caird (Aus) 10·3

100 metres hurdles
1972 Annelie Ehrhardt (GDR) 12·59
1976 Johanna Schaller (GDR) 12·77
1980 Vera Komisova (USSR) 12·56

High jump
1928 Ethel Catherwood (Can) 1·59
1932 Jean Shiley (USA) 1·65
1936 Ibolya Csak (Hun) 1·60
1948 Alice Coachman (USA) 1·68
1952 Esther Brand (Saf) 1·67
1956 Mildred McDaniel (USA) 1·76
1960 Iolanda Balas (Rom) 1·85
1964 Iolanda Balas (Rom) 1·90
1968 Miloslava Rezkova (Cz) 1·82
1972 Ulrike Meyfarth (Ger) 1·92
1976 Rosi Ackermann (GDR) 1·93
1980 Sara Simeoni (Ita) 1·97

Long jump
1928–36 Not held
1948 Olga Gyarmati (Hun) 5·69
1952 Yvette Williams (NZ) 6·24
1956 Elzbieta Krzesinska (Pol) 6·35
1960 Vyera Krepkina (USSR) 6·37
1964 Mary Rand (GB) 6·76
1968 Viorica Viscopoleanu (Rom) 6·82
1972 Heide Rosendahl (Ger) 6·78
1976 Angela Voigt (GDR) 6·72
1980 Tatyana Kolpakova (USSR) 7·06

Shot
1928–36 Not held
1948 Micheline Ostermeyer (Fra) 13·75
1952 Galina Zybina (USSR) 15·28
1956 Tamara Tishkyevich (USSR) 16·59

1960 Tamara Press (USSR) 17·32
1964 Tamara Press (USSR) 18·14
1968 Margitta Gummel (GDR) 19·61
1972 Nadyezhda Chizhova (USSR) 21·03
1976 Ivanka Khristova (Bul) 21·16
1980 Ilona Slupianek (GDR) 22·41

Discus
1928 Helena Konopacka (Pol) 39·62
1932 Lillian Copeland (USA) 40·58
1936 Gisela Mauermayer (Ger) 47·63
1948 Micheline Ostermeyer (Fra) 41·92
1952 Nina Ponomaryeva (USSR) 51·42
1956 Olga Fikotova (Cz) 53·69
1960 Nina Ponomaryeva (USSR) 55·10
1964 Tamara Press (USSR) 57·27
1968 Lia Manoliu (Rom) 58·28
1972 Faina Melnik (USSR) 66·62
1976 Evelin Schlaak (GDR) 69·00
1980 Evelin Jahl (née Schlaak) (GDR) 69·96

Javelin
1928 Not held
1932 Mildred Didrikson (USA) 43·68
1936 Tilly Fleischer (Ger) 45·18
1948 Herma Bauma (Aut) 45·57
1952 Dana Zatopkova (Cz) 50·47
1956 Inese Jaunzeme (USSR) 53·86
1960 Elvira Ozolina (USSR) 55·98
1964 Mihaela Penes (Rom) 60·54
1968 Angela Nemeth (Hun) 60·36
1972 Ruth Fuchs (GDR) 63·88
1976 Ruth Fuchs (GDR) 65·94
1980 Maria Colon (Cub) 68·40

4 × 100 metres relay

		4 × 400 metres relay
1928 Canada 48·4	1960 USA 44·5	1928–68 Not held
1932 USA 47·0	1964 Poland 43·69	1972 GDR 3:23·0
1936 USA 46·9	1968 USA 42·87	1976 GDR 3:19·2
1948 Netherlands 47·5	1972 W. Ger 42·81	1980 USSR 3:20·2
1952 USA 45·9	1976 GDR 42·55	
1956 Australia 44·5	1980 GDR 41·60	

Pentathlon
80 m hurdles, Shot, High jump, Long jump, 200 m 1964–68: 100 m hurdles replaced 80 mh from 1972 and 800 m replaced 200 m from 1976.

1928–60 Not held
1964 Irina Press (USSR) 4702
1968 Ingrid Becker (Ger) 4559
1972 Mary Peters (GB) 4801
1976 Sigrun Siegl (GDR) 4745
1980 Nadyezhda Tkachenko (USSR) 5083
(1964 and 1968 scores re-totalled on current scoring tables)

MISCELLANEOUS—*Jumping*
The greatest height cleared above an athlete's own head is 59 cm (23¼ in) by Franklin Jacobs (USA), who, 1·73 m (5 ft 8 in) tall, jumped over a bar at 2·32 m (7 ft 7¼ in) in January 1978. The equivalent record for a woman is 30·5 cm (12 in) by Cindy Holmes (USA), 1·525 m (5 ft) tall, who jumped 1·83 m (6 ft) in June 1982.

The standing high, long and triple jumps were once very popular events, achieving Olympic status, but are now rarely contested. The best amateur performances recorded are 1·90 m (6 ft 2¾ in) in the high jump by Rune Almen (Swe) in 1980, and 3·71 m (12 ft 2¼ in) in the long jump by Arne Tverrvaag (Nor) in 1968. A professional jumper, Joe Darby (GB), had long jumped a reported 3·69 m (12 ft 1½ in) back in 1890. The women's records are a 1·50 m (4 ft 11 in) high jump by Grete Bjordalsbakke (Nor) in 1979, and a long jump of 2·92 m (9 ft 7 in) by Annelin Mannes (Nor) in 1981.

In April 1981 the one-legged Canadian Arnie Boldt cleared a high jump bar at 2·04 m (6 ft 8¼ in) in Rome.

MISCELLANEOUS—*Running*
Two former American Olympic medallists, Harry Hillman and Lawson Robertson, recorded 11·0 sec for 100 yards in a three-legged race in 1909, a time which has never been bettered. Paul Wilson of New Zealand ran 100 yards backwards in 13·1 sec in 1979.

The oldest continually held race has been at Carnwath Scotland since 1508 for a prize of hand-knitted knee length red hose.

When Johnny Salo won the 1929 Trans-America race from New York to Los Angeles his total elapsed time of 525 hr 57 min 20 sec gave him a margin of only 2 min 47 sec over second placed Peter Gavuzzi—after 5898 km (3665 miles).

OLDEST AND YOUNGEST
The oldest person to break a world record was Gerhard Weidner of Germany who set a 20 mile walk record on 25 May 1974, aged 41 yr 71 days. The oldest woman was Dana Zatopkova (Cz), aged 35 yr 255 days when she broke the javelin record in June 1958. The youngest to break a record was Carolina Gisolf (Hol) only 15 yr 5 days when she set the high jump mark of 1·61 m (5 ft 3¼ in) at Maasricht on 18 July 1928. The youngest male was Tom Ray (GB) who set a record in the pole vault with 3·42 m (11 ft 2¾ in) in 1879 when aged 17 yr 198 days.

The oldest Olympic champion was Irish-born Patrick 'Babe' McDonald (USA), a New York policeman, when he took the 56 lb weight throw title in 1920 at Antwerp, aged 42 yr 26 days. The oldest woman was Romania's Lia Manoliu who won the 1968 discus at the age of 36 yr 176 days. The youngest gold medallist was Barbara Jones (USA), aged 15 yr 123 days, when a member of the USA 4 × 100 m team in 1952, while the youngest male champion was Bob Mathias (USA) who won the decathlon in 1948, at 17 yr 263 days.

The oldest British Olympic champion was Tommy Green, aged 39 yr 126 days when he took the 1932 50 km Walk at Los Angeles. However, the oldest Briton to win an international championship was Jack Holden who won the 1950 European marathon title aged 43 yr 163 days. The youngest to win an Olympic gold medal in the colours of Great Britain was Irish-born Harold Macintosh in the 1912 sprint relay aged 20 yr 29 days. The youngest individual event winner was Arnold Strode-Jackson, winner of the 1912 1500 m when 21 yr 96 days. Of the only two British Olympic women champions, Mary Peters was 33 yr 59 days old when she won the 1972 Pentathlon event, and Mary Bignal-Rand, the 1964 long jump champion, was 24 yr 247 days old.

LARGE FIELDS
The largest gathering of runners competing in one race was the 80 000 estimated to have run in the 10·5 km (6½ mile) Round the Bays race in Auckland, New Zealand in March 1982. Another enormous entry competes annually in the 22 km Stramilano event in Milan, Italy, which has had 50 000 runners in recent years. The biggest field in an actual marathon race, 26 miles 385 yd (42 195 m) is the 16 350 in the 1982 London marathon when 15 758 finished.

The largest race in Britain has been the 1982 Great North Run at South Shields with 20 400 runners of which about 17 500 completed the course.

MARATHONS
The inaugural marathon races were staged in Greece in 1896. They were two trial races before the first Olympic marathon at Athens. The race commemorated the legendary run of an unknown Greek courier, possibly Pheidippides, who in 490 BC

ran some 24 miles (38·6 km) from the Plain of Marathon to Athens with the news of a Greek victory over the numerically superior Persian army. Delivering his message—'Rejoice! We have won.'—he collapsed and died. The Olympic races were run over varying distances until 1924 when the distance was standardised at 26 miles 385 yd (42 195 m) the distance first instituted in the 1908 Games in London.

There are no official records for the distance due to the variety of courses used and their varying severity, but the following are generally accepted to be the progressive best known times on record:

MARATHON PROGRESSIVE BEST PERFORMANCES

Men

2:55:18·4	John Hayes (USA)	1908
2:52:45·4	Robert Fowler (USA)	1909
2:46:52·6	James Clark (USA)	1909
2:46:04·6	Albert Raines (USA)	1909
2:42:31·0	Fred Barrett (GB)	1909
2:38:16·2	Harry Green (GB)	1913
2:36:06·6	Johannes Kolehmainen (Fin)	1913
2:29:01·8	Albert Michelsen (USA)	1925
2:27:49·0	Fusashige Suzuki (Jap)	1925
2:26:44·0	Yasao Ikenaka (Jap)	1935
2:26:42·0	Kitei Son (Jap)	1935
2:25:39·0	Yun Bok Suh (SK)	1947
2:20:42·2	Jim Peters (GB)	1952
2:18:40·2	Jim Peters (GB)	1953
2:18:34·8	Jim Peters (GB)	1953
2:17:39·4	Jim Peters (GB)	1954
2:15:17·0	Sergey Popov (USSR)	1958
2:15:16·2	Abebe Bikila (Eth)	1960
2:15:15·8	Toru Terasawa (Jap)	1963
2:14:28·0*	Buddy Edelen (USA)	1963
2:13:55·0	Basil Heatley (GB)	1964
2:12:11·2	Abebe Bikila (Eth)	1964
2:12:00·0	Morio Shigematsu (Jap)	1965
2:09:36·4	Derek Clayton (Aus)	1967
2:08:33·6	Derek Clayton (Aus)	1969
2:08:13·0	Alberto Salazar (USA)	1981

*36 yd (about 6 sec) under standard distance.

Women

3:40:22·0	Violet Piercy (GB)	1926
3:37:07·0	Merry Lepper (USA)	1963
3:27:45·0	Dale Greig (GB)	1966
3:19:33·0	Mildred Sampson (NZ)	1964
3:15:22·0	Maureen Wilton (Can)	1967
3:07:26·0	Anni Pede-Erdkamp (Ger)	1967
3:02:53·0	Caroline Walker (USA)	1970
3:01:42·0	Elizabeth Bonner (USA)	1971
3:00:35·0	Sara Mae Berman (USA)	1971
2:46:30·0	Adrienne Beames (Aus)	1971
2:46:24·0	Chantal Langlace (Fra)	1974
2:43:54·5	Jackie Hansen (USA)	1974
2:42:24·0	Liane Winter (FRG)	1975
2:40:15·8	Christa Vahlensieck (FRG)	1975
2:38:19·0	Jackie Hansen (USA)	1975
2:35:10·4	Chantal Langlace (Fra)	1977
2:34:47·5	Christa Vahlensieck (FRG)	1977
2:32:30·0	Grete Waitz (Nor)	1978
2:27:33·0	Grete Waitz (Nor)	1979
2:25:42·0	Grete Waitz (Nor)	1980
2:25:29·0	Allison Roe (NZ)	1981
2:25:29·0	Grete Waitz (Nor)	1983
2:22:43·0	Joan Benoit (USA)	1983

An American, Jay Helgerson, ran a certified marathon or longer for 52 consecutive weeks in 1979–80. Donald Davis (USA) ran the Honolulu marathon backwards in 4 hr 20 min 36 sec in 1982. The oldest man known to have completed a marathon is 98-year-old Dimitrion Yordanidis who clocked 7 hr 33 min at Athens in October 1976. A Californian restaurant owner, Roger

The Italian Dorando Pietri in the 1908 Olympic marathon race. He entered the White City stadium in the lead, but fell five times before being helped over the line by anxious officials. He was disqualified, but Queen Alexandra presented him with a special gold cup.

Bourbon, ran the full marathon distance wearing waiter's uniform and carrying a bottle on a tray in 2 hr 47 min 21 sec in London on 9 May 1982.

WORLD CUP

Held biennially from 1977 and contested by male and female teams representing the five continents—Europe, Asia, Africa, Oceania, the Americas—and individual teams from the United States, and the two strongest teams from Europe (the first two in the European Cup Finals). Each team enters one athlete per event. In 1981 the host country, Italy, also fielded a team, having specially constructed an extra, ninth, lane at the Rome Olympic stadium for that purpose. The most events won by one athlete in the World Cup have been four by Miruts Yifter (Africa/Ethiopia) with both the 5 km and 10 km in 1977 and 1979, and by Evelyn Ashford (USA) with the 100 m and 200 m in 1979 and 1981. The same event has been won on all three occasions by Ed Moses (USA)—400 m hurdles, Joao Carlos de Oliveira (Americas/Brazil)—Triple Jump, Udo Beyer (GDR)—Shot, and the GDR women's 4 × 400 m Relay teams.

Year	Venue	Men	Points	Women	Points
1977	Dusseldorf	GDR	127	Europe	107
1979	Montreal	USA	119	GDR	105
1981	Rome	Europe	147	GDR	120½

EUROPEAN CUP

Instituted in 1965 as a contest between the best European countries for the Bruno Zauli trophy, named after the man whose idea the competition was. Each team, male and female, is represented by one athlete per event. The greatest number of individual victories is five by Renate Stecher (GDR) with two 100 m and three 200 m wins, 1970–75. She was also in two winning relay teams. The most by a man is three individual wins by eight athletes.

Year	Venue	Men	Points	Women	Points
1965	Stuttgart (men)	USSR	86		
	Kassel (women)			USSR	56
1967	Kiev	USSR	81	USSR	51
1970	Stockholm (men)	GDR	102		
	Budapest (women)			GDR	70
1973	Edinburgh	USSR	82½	GDR	72
1975	Nice	GDR	112	GDR	97
1977	Helsinki	GDR	125	GDR	106
1979	Turin	GDR	125	GDR	102
1981	Zagreb	GDR	128	GDR	108½

The last decade has seen a tremendous growth in long distance running. Regularly thousands of people compete in road races from 10 km up to the full marathon distance, and enormous fields have become commonplace. An example is seen here in the annual Bay to Breakers race in San Francisco in which thousands of men and women of all ages and abilities compete. The ultimate so far has been about 80 000 entries for a similar race in Auckland, New Zealand.

Badminton

The modern game is traditionally thought to have evolved in about 1870 at Badminton Hall, Avon. There is strong evidence that it came direct from a game played in India at about the same period, and where the first modern rules were formulated in 1876. However, a similar game had been played in China over two thousand years previously.

WORLD CHAMPIONSHIPS: Instituted in 1977 and held triennially.

	Men	Women	Mixed Doubles
1977	Flemming Delfs (Den)	Lene Koppen (Den)	Steen Stovgaard & Lene Koppen (Den)
1980	Rudy Hartono (Ina)	Wiharjo Verawaty (Ina)	Hadinata Christian & Imelda Wigoeno (Ina)
1983	Icuk Sugiarto (Ina)	Li Lingwei (Chn)	Thomas Kihlstrom (Swe) & Nora Perry (GB)

	Men's Doubles	Women's Doubles
1977	Johan Wahjudi & Tjun Tjun (Ina)	Etsuko Tuganoo & Emiko Vero (Jap)
1980	Ade Chandra & Hadinata Christian (Ina)	Nora Perry & Jane Webster (GB)
1983	Steen Fladberg & Jesper Helledie (Den)	Liu Ying & Wu Dixi (Chn)

ALL ENGLAND CHAMPIONSHIPS: Inaugurated in 1899, and, until the institution of the World Championships, considered to be the premier tournament in the world.

G. A. (later Sir George) Thomas won a record 21 championships comprising four singles, nine men's doubles and eight mixed doubles from 1903 to 1928. The most by a woman is 17 by Muriel Lucas (England) with six singles, ten women's doubles and one mixed, 1899–1910, and by Judy Devlin-Hashman (USA), a record ten singles and seven women's doubles, 1954–67. Rudy Hartono (Indonesia) has won a record eight men's singles.

Men's singles

1899	Not held
1900	S. Smith (Eng)
1901	H. Davies (Eng)
1902	Ralph Watling (Eng)
1903	Ralph Watling (Eng)
1904	H. Marrett (Eng)
1905	H. Marrett (Eng)
1906	Norman Wood (Eng)
1907	Norman Wood (Eng)
1908	H. Marrett (Eng)
1909	Frank Chesterton (Eng)
1910	Frank Chesterton (Eng)
1911	George Sautter (Eng)
1912	Frank Chesterton (Eng)
1913	George Sautter (Eng)
1914	George Sautter (Eng)
1915–19	Not held
1920	George Thomas (Eng)
1921	George Thomas (Eng)
1922	George Thomas (Eng)
1923	George Thomas (Eng)
1924	G. Mack (Ire)
1925	Frank Devlin (Ire)
1926	Frank Devlin (Ire)
1927	Frank Devlin (Ire)
1928	Frank Devlin (Ire)
1929	Frank Devlin (Ire)
1930	Donald Hume (Eng)
1931	Frank Devlin (Ire)
1932	Ralph Nichols (Eng)
1933	Raymond White (Eng)
1934	Ralph Nichols (Eng)
1935	Raymond White (Eng)
1936	Ralph Nichols (Eng)
1937	Ralph Nichols (Eng)
1938	Ralph Nichols (Eng)
1939	Tage Madsen (Den)
1940–46	Not held
1947	Conny Jepsen (Swe)
1948	Jorn Skaarup (Den)
1949	Dave Freeman (USA)
1950	Wong Peng Soon (Mal)
1951	Wong Peng Soon (Mal)
1952	Wong Peng Soon (Mal)
1953	Eddie Choong (Mal)
1954	Eddie Choong (Mal)
1955	Wong Peng Soon (Mal)
1956	Eddie Choong (Mal)
1957	Eddie Choong (Mal)
1958	Erland Kops (Den)
1959	Tan Joe Hok (Ina)
1960	Erland Kops (Den)
1961	Erland Kops (Den)
1962	Erland Kops (Den)
1963	Erland Kops (Den)
1964	Knud Nielsen (Den)
1965	Erland Kops (Den)
1966	Tan Aik Huang (Mal)
1967	Erland Kops (Den)
1968	Rudy Hartono (Ina)
1969	Rudy Hartono (Ina)
1970	Rudy Hartono (Ina)
1971	Rudy Hartono (Ina)
1972	Rudy Hartono (Ina)
1973	Rudy Hartono (Ina)
1974	Rudy Hartono (Ina)
1975	Svend Pri (Den)
1976	Rudy Hartono (Ina)
1977	Flemming Delfs (Den)
1978	Liem Swie King (Ina)
1979	Liem Swie King (Ina)
1980	Prakash Padukone (Ina)
1981	Liem Swie King (Ina)
1982	Morten Frost (Den)
1983	Luan Jin (Chn)

Women's singles

1899	Not held
1900	Ethel Thomson (Eng)
1901	Ethel Thomson (Eng)
1902	Muriel Lucas (Eng)
1903	Ethel Thomson (Eng)
1904	Ethel Thomson (Eng)
1905	Muriel Lucas (Eng)
1906	Ethel Thomson (Eng)
1907	Muriel Lucas (Eng)
1908	Muriel Lucas (Eng)
1909	Muriel Lucas (Eng)
1910	Muriel Lucas (Eng)
1911	Margaret Larminie (Eng)
1912	Margaret Larminie-Tragett (Eng)
1913	Lavinia Radeglia (Eng)
1914	Lavinia Radeglia (Eng)
1915–19	Not held
1920	Kitty McKane (Eng)
1921	Kitty McKane (Eng)
1922	Kitty McKane (Eng)
1923	Lavinia Radeglia (Eng)
1924	Kitty McKane (Eng)
1925	Margaret Stocks (Eng)
1926	Marjorie Barrett (Eng)
1927	Marjorie Barrett (Eng)
1928	Margaret Larminie-Tragett (Eng)
1929	Marjorie Barrett (Eng)
1930	Marjorie Barrett (Eng)
1931	Marjorie Barrett (Eng)
1932	Leonie Kingsbury (Eng)
1933	Alice Woodroffe (Eng)
1934	Leonie Kingsbury (Eng)
1935	Betty Uber (Eng)
1936	Thelma Kingsbury (Eng)
1937	Thelma Kingsbury (Eng)
1938	Daphne Young (Eng)
1939	Dorothy Walton (Can)
1940–46	Not held
1947	Marie Ussing (Den)
1948	Kirsten Thorndahl (Den)
1949	Aase Jacobsen (Den)
1950	Tonny Olsen-Ahm (Den)
1951	Aase Jacobsen (Den)
1952	Tonny Olsen-Ahm (Den)
1953	Marie Ussing (Den)
1954	Judy Devlin (USA)
1955	Margaret Varner (USA)
1956	Margaret Varner (USA)
1957	Judy Devlin (USA)
1958	Judy Devlin (USA)
1959	Heather Ward (Eng)
1960	Judy Devlin (USA)
1961	Judy Devlin-Hashman (USA)
1962	Judy Devlin-Hashman (USA)
1963	Judy Devlin-Hashman (USA)
1964	Judy Devlin-Hashman (USA)
1965	Ursula Smith (Eng)
1966	Judy Devlin-Hashman (USA)
1967	Judy Devlin-Hashman (USA)
1968	Eva Twedberg (Swe)
1969	Hiroe Yuki (Jap)
1970	Etsuko Takenaka (Jap)
1971	Eva Twedberg (Swe)
1972	Noriko Nakayama (Jap)
1973	Margaret Beck (Eng)
1974	Hiroe Yuki (Jap)
1975	Hiroe Yuki (Jap)
1976	Gillian Gilks (Eng)
1977	Hiroe Yuki (Jap)
1978	Gillian Gilks (Eng)
1979	Lene Köppen (Den)
1980	Lene Köppen (Den)
1981	Sun Ai Hwang (SK)
1982	Zang Ailing (Chn)
1983	Zang Ailing (Chn)

Men's doubles

1899	D. Oakes & S. Massey (Eng)
1900	H. Mellersh & F. Collier (Eng)
1901	H. Mellersh & F. Collier (Eng)
1902	H. Mellersh & F. Collier (Eng)
1903	S. Massey & E. Huson (Eng)
1904	A. Prebble & H. Marrett (Eng)
1905	S. Massey & C. Barnes (Eng)
1906	George Thomas & H. Marrett (Eng)
1907	A. Prebble & Norman Wood (Eng)
1908	George Thomas & H. Marrett (Eng)
1909	A. Prebble & Frank Chesterton (Eng)
1910	George Thomas & H. Marrett (Eng)
1911	P. Fitton & Edward Hawthorn (Eng)
1912	George Thomas & H. Marrett (Eng)
1913	George Thomas & Frank Chesterton (Eng)
1914	George Thomas & Frank Chesterton (Eng)
1915–19	Not held
1920	Alfred Engelbach & Robert du Roveray (Eng)
1921	George Thomas & Francis Hodge (Eng)
1922	Frank Devlin (Ire) & George Sautter (Eng)
1923	Frank Devlin & G. Mack (Ire)
1924	George Thomas & Francis Hodge (Eng)
1925	Herbert Huber & A. Jones (Eng)
1926	Frank Devlin & G. Mack (Ire)
1927	Frank Devlin & G. Mack (Ire)
1928	George Thomas & Francis Hodge (Eng)
1929	Frank Devlin & G. Mack (Ire)

1930 Frank Devlin & G. Mack (Ire)
1931 Frank Devlin & G. Mack (Ire)
1932 Donald Hume & Raymond White (Eng)
1933 Donald Hume & Raymond White (Eng)
1934 Donald Hume & Raymond White (Eng)
1935 Donald Hume & Raymond Whote (Eng)
1936 Ralph Nichols & Leslie Nichols (Eng)
1937 Ralph Nichols & Leslie Nichols (Eng)
1938 Ralph Nichols & Leslie Nichols (Eng)
1939 Tom Boyle & James Rankin (Ire)
1940–46 Not held
1947 Tage Madsen & Poul Holm (Den)
1948 Preben Dabelsteen & Borge Frederiksen (Den)
1949 Ooi Teik Hock & Teoh Seng Khoon (Mal)
1950 Preben Dabelsteen & Jorn Skaarup (Den)
1951 Eddie Choong & David Choong (Mal)
1952 Eddie Choong & David Choong (Mal)
1953 Eddie Choong & David Choong (Mal)
1954 Ooi Teik Hock & Ong Poh Lim (Mal)
1955 Finn Kobbero & Jurgen Hammergaard Hansen (Den)
1956 Finn Kobbero & Jurgen Hammergaard Hansen (Den)
1957 Joseph Alston (USA) & Hock Aun Heah (Mal)
1958 Erland Kops & Per Nielsen (Den)
1959 Lim Say Hup & Teh Kew San (Mal)
1960 Finn Kobbero & Per Nielsen (Den)
1961 Finn Kobbero & Jurgen Hammergaard Hansen (Den)
1962 Finn Kobbero & Jurgen Hammergaard Hansen (Den)
1963 Finn Kobbero & Jurgen Hammergaard Hansen (Den)
1964 Finn Kobbero & Jurgen Hammergaard Hansen (Den)
1965 Ng Boon Bee & Tan Yee Khan (Mal)
1966 Ng Boon Bee & Tan Yee Khan (Mal)
1967 Erland Kops & Henning Borch (Den)
1968 Erland Kops & Henning Borch (Den)
1969 Erland Kops & Henning Borch (Den)
1970 Tom Backer & Paul Petersen (Den)
1971 Ng Boon Bee & Punch Gunalan (Mal)
1972 Hadinata Christian & Ade Chandra (Ina)
1973 Hadinata Christian & Ade Chandra (Ina)
1974 Tjun Tjun & Johan Wahjudi (Ina)
1975 Tjun Tjun & Johan Wahjudi (Ina)
1976 Bengt Froman & Thomas Kihlstrom (Swe)
1977 Tjun Tjun & Johan Wahjudi (Ina)
1978 Tjun Tjun & Johan Wahjudi (Ina)
1979 Tjun Tjun & Johan Wahjudi (Ina)
1980 Tjun Tjun & Johan Wahjudi (Ina)
1981 Rudy Hartono & Rudy Heryanto (Ina)
1982 Razif Sidek & Jalaini Sidek (Mal)
1983 Stefan Karlsson & Thomas Kihlstrom (Swe)

Women's doubles

1889 Muriel Lucas & Miss Graeme (Eng)
1900 Muriel Lucas & Miss Graeme (Eng)
1901 Miss St John & E Moseley (Eng)
1902 Muriel Lucas & Ethel Thomson (Eng)
1903 M Hardy & Dorothea Douglass (Eng)
1904 Muriel Lucas & Ethel Thomson (Eng)
1905 Muriel Lucas & Ethel Thomson (Eng)
1906 Muriel Lucas & Ethel Thomson (Eng)
1907 Muriel Lucas & G Murray (Eng)
1908 Muriel Lucas & G Murray (Eng)
1909 Muriel Lucas & G Murray (Eng)
1910 Mary Bateman & Muriel Lucas (Eng)
1911 A. Gowenlock & Dorothy Cundall (Eng)
1912 A. Gowenlock & Dorothy Cundall (Eng)
1913 Hazel Hogarth & Mary Bateman (Eng)
1914 Margaret Larminie-Tragett & Eveline Peterson (Eng)
1915–19 Not held
1920 Lavinia Radeglia & Violet Elton (Eng)
1921 Kitty McKane & Margaret McKane (Eng)
1922 Margaret Larminie-Tragett & Hazel Hogarth (Eng)
1923 Margaret Larminie-Tragett & Hazel Hogarth (Eng)
1924 Margaret McKane-Stocks & Kitty McKane (Eng)
1925 Margaret Larminie-Tragett & Hazel Hogarth (Eng)
1926 A. Head & Violet Elton (Eng)
1927 Margaret Larminie-Tragett & Hazel Hogarth (Eng)
1928 Marjorie Barrett & Violet Elton (Eng)
1929 Marjorie Barrett & Violet Elton (Eng)
1930 Marjorie Barrett & Violet Elton (Eng)
1931 Betty Uber & Marianne Horsley (Eng)
1932 Marjorie Barrett & Leonie Kingsbury (Eng)
1933 Thelma Kingsbury & Marjorie Bell-Henderson (Eng)
1934 Thelma Kingsbury & Marjorie Bell-Henderson (Eng)
1935 Thelma Kingsbury & Marjorie Bell-Henderson (Eng)

1936 Thelma Kingsbury & Marjorie Bell-Henderson (Eng)
1937 Betty Uber & Diana Doveton (Eng)
1938 Betty Uber & Diana Doveton (Eng)
1939 Ruth Dalsgard & Tonny Olsen (Den)
1940–46 Not held
1947 Tonny Olsen-Ahm & Kirsten Thorndahl (Den)
1948 Tonny Olsen-Ahm & Kirsten Thorndahl (Den)
1949 Betty Uber & Queenie Allen (Eng)
1950 Tonny Olsen-Ahm & Kirsten Thorndahl (Den)
1951 Toony Olsen-Ahm & Kirsten Thorndahl (Den)
1952 Tonny Olsen-Ahm & Aase Jacobsen (Den)
1953 Iris Cooley & June White (Eng)
1954 Judy Devlin & Susan Devlin (USA)
1955 Iris Cooley & June White (Eng)
1956 Judy Devlin & Susan Devlin (USA)
1957 Kirsten Thorndahl-Granlund & Ami Hammergaard Hansen (Den)
1958 Margaret Varner & Heather Ward (Eng)
1959 Iris Cooley-Rogers & June White-Timperley (Eng)
1960 Judy Devlin & Susan Devlin (USA)
1961 Judy Devlin-Hashman (USA) & Susan Devlin-Peard (Ire)
1962 Judy Devlin-Hashman (USA) & T. Holst-Christensen (Den)
1963 Judy Devlin-Hashman (USA) & Susan Devlin-Peard (Ire)
1964 Karen Jorgensen & Ulla Rasmussen (Den)
1965 Karen Jorgensen & Ulla Rasmussen (Den)
1966 Judy Devlin-Hashman (USA) & Susan Devlin-Peard (Ire)
1967 Irme Rietveld (Hol) & Ulla Rasmussen-Strand (Den)
1968 Retno Koestijah & Miss Minarni (Ina)
1969 Margaret Boxall & Sue Whetnall (Eng)
1970 Margaret Boxall & Sue Whetnall (Eng)
1971 Noriko Takagi & Hiroe Yuki (Jap)
1972 Machiko Aizawa & Etsuko Takenaka (Jap)
1973 Machiko Aizawa & Etsuko Takenaka (Jap)
1974 Margaret Beck & Gillian Gilks (Eng)
1975 Machiko Aizawa & Etsuko Takenaka (Jap)
1976 Gillian Gilks & Sue Whetnall (Eng)
1977 Etsuko Tuganoo (née Takenaka) & Emiko Ueno (Jap)
1978 Atsuko Tokuda & Mikiko Takada (Jap)
1979 Wiharjo Verawaty & Imelda Wigoeno (Ina)
1980 Gillian Gilks & Nora Perry (Eng)
1981 Nora Perry & Jane Webster (Eng)
1982 Liu Ying & Wu Dixi (Chn)
1983 Xu Rong & Wu Jianqiu (Chn)

Mixed doubles

1899 D. Oakes & Miss St John (Eng)
1900 D. Oakes & Miss St John (Eng)
1901 F. Collier & Miss E. Stawell-Brown (Eng)
1902 L. Ransford & Miss E. Moseley (Eng)
1903 George Thomas & Ethel Thomson (Eng)
1904 H. Marrett & Dorothea Douglass (Eng)
1905 H. Marrett & Hazel Hogarth (Eng)
1906 George Thomas & Ethel Thomson (Eng)
1907 George Thomas & Miss G. Murray (Eng)
1908 Normand Wood & Muriel Lucas (Eng)
1909 A. Prebble & Miss D. Boothby (Eng)
1910 George Sautter & Dorothy Cundall (Eng)
1911 George Thomas & Margaret Larminie (Eng)
1912 Edward Hawthorn & Hazel Hogarth (Eng)
1913 George Sautter & Miss M. Mayston (Eng)
1914 George Thomas & Hazel Hogarth (Eng)
1915–19 Not held
1920 George Thomas & Hazel Hogarth (Eng)
1921 George Thomas & Hazel Hogarth (Eng)
1922 George Thomas & Hazel Hogarth (Eng)
1923 G. Mack (Ire) & Margaret Larminie-Tragett (Eng)
1924 Frank Devlin (Ire) & Kitty McKane (Eng)
1925 Frank Devlin (Ire) & Kitty McKane (Eng)
1926 Frank Devlin (Ire) & Eveline Peterson (Eng)
1927 Frank Devlin (Ire) & Eveline Peterson (Eng)
1928 A. Harbot & Margaret Larminie-Tragett (Eng)
1929 Frank Devlin (Ire) & Marianne Horseley (Eng)
1930 Herbert Uber & Betty Uber (Eng)
1931 Herbert Uber & Betty Uber (Eng)
1932 Herbert Uber & Betty Uber (Eng)
1933 Donald Hume & Betty Uber (Eng)
1934 Donald Hume & Betty Uber (Eng)
1935 Donald Hume & Betty Uber (Eng)
1936 Donald Hume & Betty Uber (Eng)
1937 Ian Maconachie (Ire) & Thelma Kingsbury (Eng)
1938 Raymond White & Betty Uber (Eng)
1939 Ralph Nichols & Bessie Staples (Eng)
1940–46 Not held

1947 Poul Holm & Tonny Olsen-Ahm (Den)	1954 John Best & Iris Cooley (Eng)
1948 Jorn Skaarup & Kirsten Thorndahl (Den)	1955 Finn Kobbero & Kirsten Thorndahl (Den)
1949 Cliton Stephens & Mrs Stephens (USA)	1956 Tony Jordan & June White-Timperley (Eng)
1950 Poul Holm & Tonny Olsen-Ahm (Den)	1957 Finn Kobbero & Kirsten Thorndahl-Granlund (Den)
1951 Poul Holm & Tonny Olsen-Ahm (Den)	1958 Tony Jordan & June White-Timperley (Eng)
1952 Poul Holm & Tonny Olsen-Ahm (Den)	1959 Per Nielsen & Mrs I Hansen (Den)
1953 Eddie Choong (Mal) & June White (Eng)	1960 Finn Kobbero & Kirsten Thorndahl (Den)

Liem Swie King of Indonesia, three times winner of the All-England badminton title, winds up for a smash. He and his countrymen have monopolised the singles championship, winning 12 times in the last 16 years.

1961 Finn Kobbero & Kirsten Thorndahl (Den)
1962 Finn Kobbero & Ulla Rasmussen (Den)
1963 Finn Kobbero & Ulla Rasmussen (Den)
1964 Tony Jordan & Miss H Pritchard (Eng)
1965 Finn Kobbero & Ulla Rasmussen-Strand (Den)
1966 Finn Kobbero & Ulla Rasmussen-Strand (Den)
1967 S. Andersen & Ulla Rasmussen-Strand (Den)
1968 Tony Jordan & Sue Pound (Eng)
1969 Roger Mills & Gillian Perrin (Eng)
1970 Per Walsöe & Pernille Mölgaard Hansen (Den)
1971 Svend Pri & Ulla Strand (Den)
1972 Svend Pri & Ulla Strand (Den)
1973 Derek Talbot & Gillian Gilks (Eng)
1974 David Eddy & Sue Whetnall (Eng)
1975 Elliott Stuart & Nora Gardner (Eng)
1976 Derek Talbot & Gillian Gilks (Eng)
1977 Derek Talbot & Gillian Gilks (Eng)
1978 Mike Tredgett & Nora Perry (née Gardner) (Eng)
1979 Hadinata Christian & Imelda Wigoeno (Ina)
1980 Mike Tredgett & Nora Perry (Eng)
1981 Mike Tredgett & Nora Perry (Eng)
1982 Martin Dew & Gillian Gilks (Eng)
1983 Thomas Kihlstrom (Swe) & Nora Perry (Eng)

THOMAS CUP: The Cup was donated by Sir George Thomas in 1939 for an international men's team championship. Due to the War the first competition was delayed until the 1948–49 season. Teams of six players compete triennially on a knockout basis in four geographic zones.

1949 Malaya	1967 Malaysia
1952 Malaya	1970 Indonesia
1955 Malaya	1973 Indonesia
1958 Indonesia	1976 Indonesia
1961 Indonesia	1979 Indonesia
1964 Indonesia	1982 China

UBER CUP: Donated by Betty Uber for an international women's team championship, first held in 1956–57. Teams of up to six players compete triennially on a knockout basis in four geographic zones.

1957 USA	1972 Japan
1960 USA	1975 Indonesia
1963 USA	1978 Japan
1966 Japan	1981 Japan
1969 Japan	

Keep it in the family

The Devlin family have achieved a unique record in the All-England championships winning a total of 35 titles between them. Frank won six singles, seven men's doubles and five mixed doubles representing Ireland from 1922 to 1931, while daughters Sue (later Peard) and Judy (later Hashman) representing the United States won six ladies doubles, and Judy won another doubles plus her record 10 singles. Judy, perhaps the greatest woman player the game has yet seen, also won 29 US titles.

Baseball

The first game under the Cartwright rules, which form the basis of the modern game in the United States, was at Hoboken, New Jersey on 19 June 1846. However, a game of the same name was played in England prior to 1700.

MAJOR LEAGUES
There are two major leagues, the National (NL) founded in 1876, and the American (AL) founded in 1901.

Batting Records

Batting average—season	0·438	Hugh Duffy (NL)	1894
	0·422	Napoleon Lajoie (AL)	1901
—career	0·367	Ty Cobb (AL)	1905–28
Runs batted in—career	2297	'Hank' Aaron	1954–76
Runs batted in—season	190	'Hack' Wilson	1930
Runs batted in—game	12	James Bottomley	16 Sept 1924
Runs batted in—innings	7	Edward Cartwright	23 Sept 1890
Home runs—career	755	'Hank' Aaron	1954–76
Home runs—season	61	Roger Maris	1961
Base hits—season	257	George Sisler	1920
—career	4191	Ty Cobb (AL)	1905–28
Consecutive games batted safely	56	Joe DiMaggio	15 May–16 July 1941
Stolen bases—career	938	Lou Brock	1961–79
Stolen bases—season	130	Rickey Henderson	1982
Consecutive games played	2130	Lou Gehrig	1 Jun 1925–30 Apr 1939

Pitching Records

Games won—career	511	'Cy' Young	1890–1911
Games won—season	60	Charles Gardner Radbourne	1884
Consecutive games won	24	Carl Hubbell	1936–37
Shutouts—career	113	Walter Johnson	1907–27
Shutouts—season	16	George Bradley	1876
	16	Grover Cleveland Alexander	1916
Strikeouts—career	3509	Nolan Ryan	1966–83
Strikeouts—season	383	Nolan Ryan	1973
No-hit games—career	5	Nolan Ryan	1966–81
Earned run av.—season	0·90	Ferdinand Schupp (140 inn)	1916
	1·01	Hubert Leonard (222 inn)	1914
	1·12	Robert Gibson (305 inn)	1968
Complete games—career	751	'Cy' Young	1890–1911

MISCELLANEOUS
A record pitching speed of 100·9 mph (162·3 km/h) has been attributed to Nolan Ryan, measured in 1974 when playing for the California Angels.

The longest hit home run was 618 ft (188·4 m) by Dizzy Carlyle in a minor league game in 1929. The major league record is held by the legendary Babe Ruth who hit a 587 ft (178·9 m) home run for the Boston Red Sox *v* New York Giants in 1919. A Canadian, Glen Gorbous, threw a baseball weighing 5–5¼ oz (141–148 g) 445 ft 10 in (135·88 m) in August 1957. The female record is 296 ft (90·22 m) by Olympic athlete Babe Didrikson-Zaharias in July 1931.

WORLD SERIES
The winners of each League meet annually in a best of seven series of games. The first such end-of-season duel was in 1882, but the competition was not permanently established until 1905. The most wins have been by the New York Yankees with 22 between 1922 and 1978 including a record five consecutively 1949–53. The single game attendance record is 92 706 at Los Angeles on 6 October 1959. In that series of six games in which

the Los Angeles Dodgers (formerly Brooklyn) beat the Chicago White Sox, there was a record total attendance of 420 784. *Winners from 1970:*

1970 Baltimore Orioles (AL)
1971 Pittsburgh Pirates (NL)
1972 Oakland Athletics (AL)
1973 Oakland Athletics (AL)
1974 Oakland Athletics (AL)
1975 Cincinnati Reds (NL)
1976 Cincinnati Reds (NL)
1977 New York Yankees (AL)
1978 New York Yankees (AL)
1979 Pittsburgh Pirates (NL)
1980 Philadelphia Phillies (NL)
1981 Los Angeles Dodgers (NL)
1982 St Louis Cardinals (NL)

Right: **The record pitching speed of Nolan Ryan has made him one of the outstanding baseball pitchers of recent years, earning $1 million a year. Playing for the California Angels and the Houston Astros, his records include five no-hit games, 19 strikeouts in one game, and 383 strikeouts in a season.**

Basketball

The modern game was devised by Canadian-born Dr James Naismith at the International YMCA College, Springfield, Massachusetts in December 1891. A game of similar concept was played in Mexico in the 10th century.

WORLD CHAMPIONSHIPS: A championship for amateur teams was instituted in 1950 for men, and in 1953 for women, and both are now contested every four years.

MEN		WOMEN	
1950 Argentina	1970 Yugoslavia	1953 USA	1971 USSR
1954 USA	1974 USSR	1957 USA	1975 USSR
1959 Brazil	1978 Yugoslavia	1959 USSR	1979 USA
1963 Brazil	1982 USSR	1964 USSR	
1967 USSR		1967 USSR	

Sunderland Maestros on the way to beating Crystal Palace (winners of the National League title for the seventh time) in the 1983 Just Juice National Championships.

OLYMPIC GAMES: A men's event has been held at each Games from 1936. The United States has won a record eight finals and they also had a record run of 63 consecutive Olympic match victories from 1936 to the 1972 final. A women's event has been held since 1976 and won by the USSR on both occasions.

1936 USA	1964 USA
1948 USA	1968 USA
1952 USA	1972 USSR
1956 USA	1976 USA
1960 USA	1980 Yugoslavia

AMERICAN PROFESSIONAL LEAGUE: One of the most popular games in the United States, the major competition is for the National Basketball Association (NBA) championship (instituted 1947). The Boston Celtics won a record 14 titles between 1957 and 1981. *Winners from 1970:*

1970 New York Knicks	1977 Portland Trailblazers
1971 Milwaukee Bucks	1978 Washington Bullets
1972 Los Angeles Lakers	1979 Seattle Supersonics
1973 New York Knicks	1980 Los Angeles Lakers
1974 Boston Celtics	1981 Boston Celtics
1975 Golden State Warriors	1982 Los Angeles Lakers
1976 Boston Celtics	

HIGHEST SCORES
The highest aggregate score in the NBA is 337 points, when the San Antonio Spurs beat the Milwaukee Bucks 171–166 in 1982. The most points scored by a single team is 173 by Boston against Minneapolis in 1959. In 1962 Wilt 'The Stilt' Chamberlain scored a record 100 individual points for the Philadelphia Warriors when they beat the New York Knickerbockers 169–147. He also holds the career scoring mark of 31 419 points from 1960 to 1973.

BASKETBALL IN ENGLAND
The most men's National Championships (instituted 1936 for the George Williams cup) is eight by the London Central YMCA between 1957 and 1969. The English National League title (instituted 1972) has been won seven times by Crystal Palace. The National Cup (held separately from the National Championships from 1979) has been won twice by Crystal Palace in 1980 and 1981.

The women's National Cup (instituted 1965) has been won on a record eight occasions by the Tigers between 1972 and 1982. They have also won the National League (instituted 1975) a record three times.

TALLEST PLAYERS
The tallest ever has been Sulieman Ali Nashnush, who stood 2·45 m (8 ft) when he played for Libya in 1962. The tallest currently playing is 23 yr old Aleksandr Sisorenko, at 2·37 m (7 ft 9¼ in), who is in the Soviet national team. The tallest woman player was 2·18 m (7 ft 2 in) Iuliana Semenova who played in the 1976 Olympics for the USSR. The tallest British player has been Chris Greener 2·29 m (7 ft 6¼ in) who played for England in 1969.

Billiards

The earliest recorded reference to the game was in France in 1429, when it was probably played on grass. Louis XI of France (1461–83) is believed to be the first to have played the game on a table. The first known public billiards room in England was the Piazza at Covent Garden, London, in the early part of the 19th century.

WORLD CHAMPIONSHIPS: The most professional titles (instituted 1870) won is eight by John Roberts Jr (Eng) from 1870 to 1885. The greatest number of amateur titles (instituted 1926) is four by Bob Marshall (Aus) from 1936 to 1962. *Winners from 1971:*

Professional	*Amateur*
1971 Rex Williams (Eng)	1971 Norman Dagley (Eng)
1973 Rex Williams (Eng)	1973 Mohammed Lafir (Sri)
1974 Rex Williams (Eng)	1975 Norman Dagley (Eng)
1976 Rex Williams (Eng)	1977 Michael Ferreira (Ind)
1980 Fred Davis (Eng)	1979 Paul Mifsud (Mta)
1982 Rex Williams (Eng)	1981 Michael Ferreira (Ind)
1983 Rex Williams (Eng)	

UK PROFESSIONAL CHAMPIONSHIPS: Instituted 1934, these championships lasted until 1951, and were revived in 1979. Joe Davis won a record seven titles from 1934 to 1947. More recently Rex Williams won in 1979 and 1981, Jack Karnehm 1980, and Mark Wildman in 1982.

ENGLISH AMATEUR CHAMPIONSHIPS: Instituted 1888, the most titles won is 13 by Norman Dagley between 1965 and 1982. The women's championship (instituted 1931) has been won a record eight times by Vera Selby.

HIGHEST BREAKS
Because of the great many changes in rules over the years, the various records at different times are listed.

Professional records
Unofficial break of 499 135 (including 249 152 anchor cannons—with the two object balls caught in a pocket opening) by Tom Reece (Eng) in London from 3 June–6 July 1907.

Official break of 42 746 (using the anchor cannon) by William Cook (Eng) from 29 May – 7 June 1907.

Official break (before the baulk line rule—which stipulated that the cue-ball must cross the line in every 100 points during large breaks) of 4137 by Walter Lindrum (Aus) in January 1932.

Official break (under the then baulk line rule) of 1784 by Joe Davis in May 1936.

Amateur records
Break of 1149 (under the 5 pot rule—which only allows the red to be sunk five times consecutively) by Michael Ferreira (Ind) in December 1978.

Break of 630 (under the 3 pot rule) by Michael Ferreira (Ind) in the World Championships at New Delhi, India in November 1981.

Fastest 100 points
Walter Lindrum's official record is 46·0 sec, in Sydney in 1941, but unofficially he was timed in 27·5 sec in October 1952.

Board Sailing

One of the fastest-growing sports of recent years, board sailing has received the ultimate accolade with its inclusion in the 1984 Olympic Games at Los Angeles.

'Windsurfing' is the common name for this sport, although strictly speaking a 'windsurfer' is a particular brand of sail board, first designed by Hoyle Schweitzer in 1968. However, sail boards were first made in California in 1964 by Newman Darby. His idea enabled surfers to continue practising their sport even when there were no waves. The sport has been included in the Olympic Games for 1984, but continuing argument about standardisation of boards may preclude it at the last moment.

WORLD CHAMPIONSHIPS: The world title has been won a record three times by Robby Naish (USA) who was only 13 years old when he first won it in 1976.

SPEED
The official record for board sailing is held by a Frenchman, Pascal Maka, with 27·82 knots, 51·55 km/h (32·03 mph) at Weymouth, England on 13 October 1982. The fastest by a Briton is the previous world record of 22·95 knots, 42·53 km/h (26·42 mph) set up by Clive Colenso on *Olympic Gold* at Portland Harbour, Dorset in October 1979.

DISTANCE
The first man to cross the English Channel on a board was Frédéric Beauchêne (Fra), in 1978. The record for the crossing is 1 hr 4 min 33 sec by Baron Arnaud de Rosnay (Fra) in July 1982 at an average speed of 31·3 km/h (19·5 mph). He then made the return trip in 1 hr 4 min 37 sec. The longest verified distance covered in 24 hours (actually 23 hr 25 min) was a sail of 330 km (205 miles) in the West Indies by Thomas Staltmaier (FRG) on 2–3 February 1981.

Christian Marty (Fra) made the first trans-Atlantic crossing from Dakar, Senegal to Kourou, Guyana, a distance of 4800 km (2982 miles) in 37 days from 12 December 1981 to 18 January 1982.

Bobsleigh

The first known sledge came from Heinola, Finland and is dated c 6500 BC. The first bobsleigh race took place at Davos, Switzerland in 1899. Bobs have two pairs of runners and streamlined cowls and steering is by means of cables attached to the front runners, which are flexible.

WORLD CHAMPIONSHIPS: The 4-man bob title has been won 14 times by Switzerland since it was inaugurated in 1924, and the 2-man (instituted 1931) record is 14 by Italy. Eugenio Monti (Ita) was a member of 11 world championship winning crews. In Olympic years the Olympic champion is also world champion.

OLYMPICS: The 4-man title has been won four times by Switzerland, while four countries, United States, Switzerland, Italy and West Germany, have won the 2-man (boblet) on two occasions. The most gold medals won by an individual is three by the East Germans, Meinhard Nehmer and Bernard Germeshausen. The greatest number of medals won is six by Eugenio Monti (Ita) with two gold, two silver and two bronze. *Winners of world and Olympic titles from 1970:*

4-Man (*Olympic championship)

1970	Italy	1977	GDR
1971	Switzerland	1978	GDR
1972*	Switzerland	1979	W. Germany
1973	Switzerland	1980*	GDR
1974	W. Germany	1981	GDR
1975	Switzerland	1982	Switzerland
1976*	GDR	1983	Switzerland

2-Man (*Olympic championship)

1970	W. Germany	1977	Switzerland
1971	Italy	1978	Switzerland
1972*	W. Germany	1979	Switzerland
1973	W. Germany	1980*	Switzerland
1974	W. Germany	1981	GDR
1975	Italy	1982	Switzerland
1976*	GDR	1983	Switzerland

TOBOGGANING

The name of the sport comes from a Micmac American Indian word *Tobaakan*. The oldest tobogganing club is the St Moritz in Switzerland, founded in 1887, but the Cresta Run dates from 1884. The course is 1212·25 m (3977 ft) long and the record for the full run is 53·24 sec by Poldi Berchtold (Swi) in 1975. Speeds of 145 km/h (90 mph) are sometimes reached.

LUGEING

In lugeing the rider sits, or lies back, as opposed to lying prone face down as in tobogganing. The first official international competition was in 1881 at Klosters, Switzerland. World titles were first contested in 1955 with Olympic champions automatically taking the world crown.

The Swiss number II bob team of Erich Schärer and Josef Benz winning the 1980 Olympic title at Lake Placid, a week after they won silver medals in the Swiss 4-man bob team. In 1976 they had placed third in the 2-man event. Schärer has also been on world championship teams on a further four occasions.

Tobogganing on the Cresta Run at St Moritz, Switzerland, where speeds of 90 mph are achieved by the experts. Olympic titles have been held in this sport on two occasions, in 1928 and 1948.

Bowls

A game similar to modern bowls is believed to have been common in ancient Egypt. The Southampton Bowling Club was formed in 1299, and a green dating to 1294 is claimed by the Chesterfield club. Modern rules were formulated in Scotland in 1848–9.

WORLD CHAMPIONSHIPS *(men)*: Instituted in 1966, and currently held every four years. In 1976 the South African team won an unprecedented clean sweep of the titles. David Bryant (Eng) has won a record three titles with two singles and one triples.

	Singles	Pairs	Triples	Fours
1966	David Bryant (Eng)	Australia	Australia	New Zealand
1972	Malwyn Evans (Wal)	Hong Kong	USA	England
1976	Doug Watson (Saf)	South Africa	South Africa	South Africa
1980	David Bryant (Eng)	Australia	England	Hong Kong

LEONARD TROPHY *(Team title)*: 1966 Australia 1972 Scotland 1976 South Africa 1980 England

WORLD CHAMPIONSHIPS *(women)*: First held in 1969 and currently every four years.

	Singles	Pairs	Triples	Fours
1969	Gladys Doyle (PNG)	South Africa	South Africa	South Africa
1973–74	Elsie Wilke (NZ)	Australia	New Zealand	New Zealand
1977	Elsie Wilke (NZ)	Hong Kong	Wales	Australia
1981	Norma Shaw (Eng)	Ireland	Hong Kong	England

TEAM TROPHY: 1969 South Africa 1973–74 New Zealand 1977 Australia 1981 England.

INTERNATIONAL CHAMPIONSHIPS: The Home Countries international championships (instituted 1903) have been won a record 34 times by Scotland including a record 11 consecutively 1965–75.

ENGLISH (EBA) CHAMPIONSHIPS: First held in 1903. David Bryant has won a record 15 titles including six singles crowns.

1970	Harry Kershaw	1977	Chris Ward
1971	David Bryant	1978	Charles Burch
1972	David Bryant	1979	David Cutler
1973	David Bryant	1980	Tom Buller
1974	Bill Irish	1981	Andy Thomson
1975	David Bryant	1982	Chris Ward
1976	Anthony O'Connell		

INDOOR BOWLS: The World Championship (instituted 1979) has been won on three occasions by David Bryant (Eng). He has also won a record eight National Singles titles (instituted 1961).

1979	David Bryant (Eng)
1980	David Bryant (Eng)
1981	David Bryant (Eng)
1982	John Watson (Sco)
1983	Bob Sutherland (Sco)

HIGHEST SCORES
The highest score ever achieved in an outdoor international match was 63–1 by Swaziland *v* Japan in the 1980 World Championships. The record score in an indoor match was Scotland's 52–3 victory over Wales in 1972.

COMMONWEALTH GAMES: Bowls was introduced in 1930, omitted in 1966, but is currently held every four years. A women's event was included in 1982. David Bryant (Eng) won a record five gold medals between 1962 and 1978, comprising four consecutive singles titles and a fours medal in 1962.

Twice world singles champion, David Bryant has won virtually every honour open to him in bowls, including a CBE from the Queen for services to the game. He held the Commonwealth Games title for 20 years, first winning it in 1962.

MEN

	Singles	Pairs	Fours
1930	Robert Colquhoun (Eng)	England	England
1934	Robert Sprot (Sco)	England	England
1938	Horace Harvey (Saf)	New Zealand	New Zealand
1950	James Pirret (NZ)	New Zealand	South Africa
1954	Ralph Hodges (S Rho)	N. Ireland	South Africa
1958	Pinkie Danilowitz (Saf)	New Zealand	England
1962	David Bryant (Eng)	New Zealand	England
1970	David Bryant (Eng)	England	Hong Kong
1974	David Bryant (Eng)	Scotland	New Zealand
1978	David Bryant (Eng)	Hong Kong	Hong Kong
1982	William Wood (Sco)	Scotland	Australia

WOMEN

	Triples
1982	Zimbabwe

Boxing

As a competitive sport boxing originated in Ancient Greece—a fresco of boxing with gloves on the Isle of Thera dates from 1520 BC—and it was one of the first Olympic sports. The first prizering rules were formulated in England in 1743 by the famous pugilist Jack Broughton. They were followed in 1867 by the Queensberry Rules, formulated by the 9th Marquess of Queensberry, which were the foundation of modern boxing. The first permanent arena was opened near Oxford Street, London by James Figg in 1719, but from 1750 to 1901 boxing was not a legal sport in Britain. There are two governing bodies, the World Boxing Association (formed as the National Boxing Association in the USA in 1920) and the World Boxing Council (formed in 1963). At most weights separate champions are recognised by these two organisations.

WORLD HEAVYWEIGHT CHAMPIONSHIP: The first generally accepted title fight took place in 1810 when Tom Cribb beat Tom Molineaux, but the first under modern rules, with gloves and three-minute rounds, was in 1892 when 'Gentleman Jim' Corbett beat John L. Sullivan at New Orleans, USA.

	Titleholder
Oldest	Jersey Joe Walcott (USA) 38 yr 236 days in 1952
Youngest	Floyd Patterson (USA) 21 yr 331 days in 1956
Tallest	Primo Carnera (Ita) 6 ft 5¾ in (1·96 m) in 1933
Shortest	Tommy Burns (Can) 5 ft 7 in (1·70 m) in 1906
Heaviest	Primo Carnera (Ita) 270 lb (122 kg) in 1934
Lightest	Bob Fitzsimmons (Eng) 167 lb (75 kg) in 1897
Most defences	25 by Joe Louis (USA) 1937–49
Most times gained title	3 by Muhammad Ali (Cassius Clay) 1964, 1974, 1978
Biggest Chest	Primo Carnera (Ita) 53 in (134 cm) in 1933
Longest Reach	Primo Carnera (Ita) 85½ in (217 cm) in 1933
Largest Fists	Sonny Liston (USA) 15 in (38 cm) in 1962
Greatest Weight Difference	86 lb (39 kg) Primo Carnera v Tommy Loughran (USA) 1934

Larry Holmes has had little need to cool down since taking the world heavyweight (WBC) championship in 1978, although he has made 13 successful defences of the title to the end of 1982.

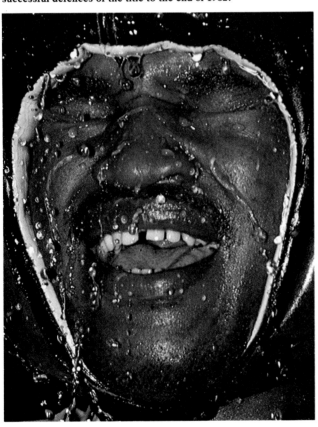

WORLD CHAMPIONS (As at 31 May 1983)
Below are listed all heavyweight champions since 1882, and the champions in other weights since 1965, or from the time when the category was established.

Heavyweight
1882 John L. Sullivan (USA)
1892 James J. Corbett (USA)
1897 Bob Fitzsimmons (GB)
1899 James J. Jeffries (USA)
1905 Marvin Hart (USA)
1906 Tommy Burns (Can)
1908 Jack Johnson (USA)
1915 Jess Willard (USA)
1919 Jack Dempsey (USA)
1926 Gene Tunney (USA)
1930 Max Schmeling (Ger)
1932 Jack Sharkey (USA)
1933 Primo Carnera (Ita)
1934 Max Baer (USA)
1935 James J. Braddock (USA)
1937 Joe Louis (USA)
1949 Ezzard Charles (USA)
1951 Jersey Joe Walcott (USA)
1952 Rocky Marciano (USA)
1956 Floyd Patterson (USA)
1959 Ingemar Johansson (Swe)
1960 Floyd Patterson (USA)
1962 Sonny Liston (USA)
1964 Cassius Clay/Muhammad Ali (USA)
1965 Ernie Terrell (USA)—WBA only till 1967
1968 Joe Frazier (USA)—NY State
1968 Jimmy Ellis (USA)—WBA
1970 Joe Frazier (USA)—undisputed
1973 George Foreman (USA)
1974 Muhammad Ali (USA)
1978 Leon Spinks (USA)
1978 Ken Norton (USA)—WBC
1978 Muhammad Ali (USA)—WBA
1978 Larry Holmes (USA)—WBC
1979 John Tate (USA)—WBA
1980 Mike Weaver (USA)—WBA
1982 Mike Dokes (USA)—WBA

Cruiserweight limit—190 lb
1980 Marvin Camel (USA)—WBC
1980 Carlos DeLeon (PR)—WBC
1982 Ossie Ocasio (PR)—WBA
1982 S.T. Gordon (PR)—WBC

Light heavyweight limit—175 lb
1965 Jose Torres (USA)
1966 Dick Tiger (Ngr)
1968 Bob Foster (USA)
1971 Vincente Rondon (Ven)—WBA
1974 John Conteh (GB)—WBC
1974 Victor Galindez (Arg)—WBA
1977 Miguel Cuello (Arg)—WBC
1978 Mate Parlov (Yug)—WBC
1978 Mike Rossman (USA)—WBA
1978 Marvin Johnson (USA)—WBC
1979 Matthew Saad Muhammad (USA)—WBC
1979 Victor Galindez (Arg)—WBA
1979 Marvin Johnson (USA)—WBA
1980 Eddie Mustafa Muhammad (USA)—WBA
1981 Michael Spinks (USA)—WBA
1981 Dwight Muhammad Qawi (USA)—WBC
1983 Michael Spinks (USA)—both

Middleweight limit—160 lb
1965 Dick Tiger (Ngr)
1966 Emile Griffith (VI)
1967 Nino Benvenuti (Ita)
1967 Emile Griffith (VI)
1968 Nino Benvenuti (Ita)
1970 Carlos Monzon (Arg)
1974 Carlos Monzon (Arg)—WBA
1974 Rodrigo Valdes (Col)—WBC

1976 Carlos Monzon (Arg)—both
1977 Rodrigo Valdes (Col)
1978 Hugo Corro (Arg)
1979 Vito Antuofermo (Ita)
1980 Alan Minter (GB)
1980 Marvin Hagler (USA)

Light middleweight limit—153½ lb
1965 Nino Benvenuti (Ita)
1966 Kim Ki-Soo (SK)
1968 Sandro Massinghi (Ita)
1969 Freddie Little (USA)
1970 Carmelo Bossi (Ita)
1971 Koichi Wajima (Jap)
1974 Oscar Albarado (USA)
1975 Koichi Wajima (Jap)
1975 Miguel de Oliveira (Bra)—WBC
1975 Jae Do Yuh (SK)—WBA
1975 Elisha Obed (Bah)—WBC
1976 Eckhard Dagge (FRG)—WBC
1976 Koichi Wajima (Jap)—WBA
1976 Jose Duran (Spa)—WBA
1976 Miguel Castellini (Arg)—WBA
1977 Rocky Mattioli (Ita)—WBC
1977 Eddie Gazo (Nic)—WBA
1978 Masashi Kudo (Jap)—WBA
1979 Maurice Hope (GB)—WBC
1980 Ayub Kalule (Uga)—WBA
1981 Wilfred Benitez (PR)—WBC
1981 Sugar Ray Leonard (USA)—WBA
1981 Tadashi Mihara (Jap)—WBA
1982 Davey Moore (USA)—WBA
1982 Thomas Hearns (USA)—WBC

Welterweight limit—147 lb
1966 Curtis Cokes (USA)
1969 Jose Napoles (Cub)
1970 Billy Backus (USA)
1971 Jose Napoles (Cub)
1975 John H. Stracey (GB)—WBC
1975 Angel Espada (PR)—WBA
1976 Carlos Palomino (Mex)—WBC
1976 Jose Cuevas (Mex)—WBA
1979 Wilfredo Benitez (PR)—WBC
1979 Sugar Ray Leonard (USA)—WBC
1980 Roberto Duran (Pan)—WBC
1980 Thomas Hearns (USA)—WBA
1980 Sugar Ray Leonard (USA)—WBC
1981 Sugar Ray Leonard—both
1983 Donald Curry (USA)—WBA

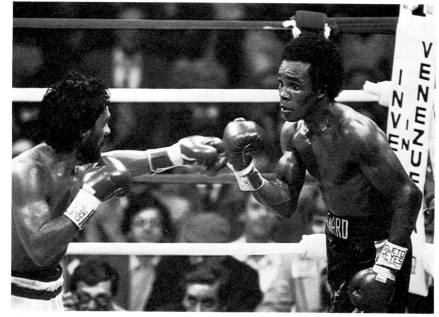

Sugar Ray Leonard taunting Panama's Roberto Duran in their second fight for the world welterweight (WBC) crown in 1980, in which he regained the title. His boxing career was put in jeopardy in May 1982 with the diagnosis of a detached retina, leading the boxing authorities to bring pressure on Leonard to retire from the ring.

LARGEST PURSE, EARNINGS
Sugar Ray Leonard (USA) won a reported $11 million when he beat Thomas Hearns (USA) for the undisputed welterweight title at Las Vegas, Nevada in September 1981. He had previously received a then record sum of $8½ million when he lost to Roberto Duran (Pan) in June 1980. Muhammad Ali (formerly Cassius Clay) earned a total estimated at $68 million from some 60 fights, comprising 539 rounds, from October 1960 to October 1980.

Charlie Magri beat Eleoncio Mercedes of the Dominican Republic in March 1983 to win the WBC Flyweight title, so regaining it for Britain after a gap of 17 years.

The car park of Caesar's Palace in Las Vegas, on the occasion of the world title fight between Larry Holmes and Muhammad Ali in 1981. Later in the year it was also the venue of the last Grand Prix of the motor racing season. The course, reported to be among the most difficult ever raced on, consisted of 75 laps, each comprising 14 sharp corners of which seven were hairpin bends.

Light welterweight limit—140 lb
1965 Carlos Hernandez (Ven)
1966 Sandro Lopopolo (Ita)
1967 Paul Fuji (USA)
1968 Pedro Adigue (Phi)—WBC
1968 Nicolino Loche (Arg)—WBA
1970 Bruno Arcari (Ita)—WBC
1972 Alfonso Frazer (Pan)—WBA
1972 Antonio Cervantes (Col)—WBA
1974 Perico Fernandez (Spa)—WBC
1975 Saensak Muangsurin (Tha)—WBC
1976 Miguel Velasquez (Spa)—WBC
1976 Wilfredo Benitez (PR)—WBA
1976 Antonio Cervantes (Col)—WBA
1978 Kim Sang-Hyun (SK)—WBC
1980 Saul Mamby (USA)—WBC
1980 Aaron Pryor (USA)—WBA
1982 Leroy Haley (USA)—WBC
1983 Bruce Curry (USA)—WBC

Lightweight limit—135 lb
1965 Carlos Ortiz (PR)
1968 Carlos Teo Cruz (Dom)
1969 Mando Ramos (USA)
1970 Ismael Laguna (Pan)
1970 Ken Buchanan (GB)
1971 Pedro Carrasco (Spa)—WBC
1971 Ken Buchanan (GB)—WBA
1972 Mando Ramos (USA)—WBC
1972 Roberto Duran (Pan)—WBA
1972 Chango Carmona (Mex)—WBC
1972 Rodolfo Gonzales (Mex)—WBC
1974 Guts Ishimatsu (Jap)—WBA
1974 Roberto Duran (Pan)—WBA
1976 Esteban de Jesus (PR)—WBC
1978 Roberto Duran (Pan)—both
1979 Jim Watts (GB)—WBC
1979 Ernesto Espana (Ven)—WBA
1980 Hilmer Kenty (USA)—WBA
1981 Sean O'Grady (USA)—WBA

1981 Alexis Arguello (Nic)—WBC
1981 Claude Noel (Tri)—WBA
1981 Arturo Frias (USA)—WBA
1982 Ray Mancini (USA)—WBA
1983 Edwin Rosario (PR)—WBC

Junior lightweight limit—130 lb
1967 Yoshiaki Numata (Jap)
1967 Hiroshi Kobayashi (Jap)
1969 Rene Barrientos (Phi)—WBC
1969 Hiroshi Kobayashi (Jap)—WBA
1970 Yoshiaki Numata (Jap)—WBC
1971 Ricardo Arredondo (Mex)—WBC
1971 Alfredo Marcano (Ven)—WBA
1972 Ben Villaflor (Phi)—WBA
1973 Kuniaki Shibata (Jap)—WBA
1973 Ben Villaflor (Phi)—WBA
1974 Kuniaki Shibata (Jap)—WBC
1975 Alfredo Escalera (PR)—WBC
1976 Sam Serrano (PR)—WBA
1978 Alexis Arguello (Nic)—WBC
1980 Yasatsune Uehara (Jap)—WBA
1980 Rafael Limon (Mex)—WBC
1981 Cornelius Boza-Edwards (GB)—WBC
1981 Sam Serrano (PR)—WBA
1981 Rolando Navarrete (Phi)—WBC
1982 Rafael Limon (Mex)—WBC
1982 Bobby Chacon (USA)—WBC
1983 Roger Mayweather (USA)—WBA

Featherweight limit—126 lb
1964 Vicente Saldivar (Mex)
1968 Howard Winstone (GB)—WBC
1968 Raul Rojas (USA)—WBA
1968 Jose Legra (Cub)—WBC
1968 Shozo Saijyo (Jap)—WBA
1969 Johnny Famechon (Fra)—WBC
1970 Vicente Saldivar (Mex)—WBC
1970 Kuniaki Shibata (Jap)—WBC
1971 Antonio Gomez (Ven)—WBA

1972 Clemente Sanchez (Mex)—WBC
1972 Ernesto Marcel (Pan)—WBA
1972 Jose Legra (Cub)—WBC
1973 Eder Jofre (Bra)—WBC
1974 Bobby Chacon (USA)—WBC
1974 Ruben Olivares (Mex)—WBA
1974 Alexis Arguello (Nic)—WBA
1975 Ruben Olivares (Mex)—WBC
1975 David Kotey (Gha)—WBC
1976 Danny Lopez (USA)—WBC
1977 Rafael Ortega (Pan)—WBA
1977 Cecilio Lastra (Spa)—WBA
1978 Eusebio Pedroza (Pan)—WBA
1980 Salvador Sanchez (Mex)—WBC
1982 Juan Laporte (USA)—WBC

Light featherweight limit—122 lb
1976 Rigoberto Riasco (Pan)—WBC
1976 Royal Kobayashi (Jap)—WBC
1976 Dong Kyun Yum (SK)—WBC
1977 Wilfredo Gomez (PR)—WBC
1977 Soo Hwan Hong (SK)—WBA
1978 Ricardo Cardona (Col)—WBA
1980 Sergio Palma (Arg)—WBA
1982 Leo Cruz (Dom)—WBA

Bantamweight limit—118 lb
1965 Masahiko Harada (Jap)
1968 Lionel Rose (Aus)
1969 Ruben Olivares (Mex)
1970 Jesus Castillo (Mex)
1971 Ruben Olivares (Mex)
1972 Rafael Herrera (Mex)
1972 Enrique Pinder (Pan)
1973 Rafael Herrera (Mex)—WBC
1973 Romero Anaya (Mex)—WBA
1973 Arnold Taylor (Saf)—WBA
1974 Rodolfo Martinez (Mex)—WBC
1974 Soo Hwan Hong (SK)—WBA
1975 Alfonso Zamora (Mex)—WBA

WORLD CHAMPIONSHIPS (Any weight)

	Titleholder
Oldest	Archie Moore (USA) *c* 45–48 yr Light heavyweight 1962
Youngest	Wilfredo Benitez (PR) 17 yr 180 days Light welter 1976
Smallest	Pascual Perez (Arg) 4 ft 11½ in (1·51 m) Flyweight 1954
Lightest	Pascual Perez (Arg) 107 lb (48½ kg) Flyweight 1954
Most times title won	Sugar Ray Robinson (USA) 5 Middleweight 1951 (2), 55, 57, 58
Most titles held simultaneously	Henry Armstrong (USA) 3 Feather, light, welter 1938
Most title bouts	George Dixon (Can) 33–34 Bantam & featherweight 1890–1901
Biggest crowd	135 132 Tony Zale *v* Billy Pryor at Milwaukee, USA 18 Aug 1941
Smallest crowd	2434 Cassius Clay *v* Sonny Liston at Lewiston, USA 25 May 1965

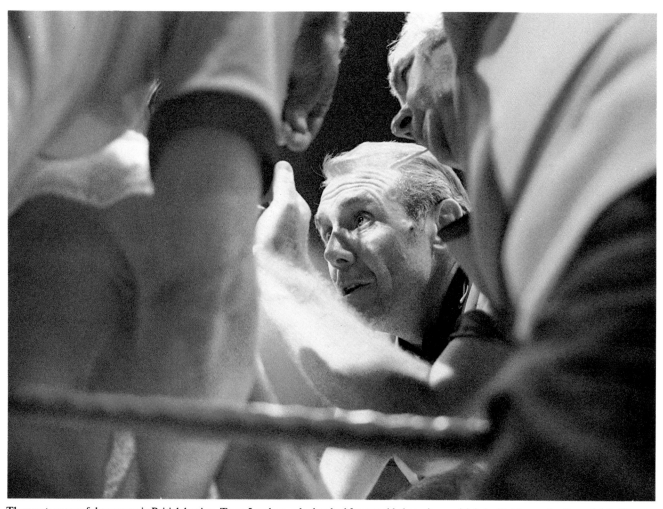

The most successful manager in British boxing, Terry Lawless, who has had four world champions, with John H. Stracey (welterweight), Maurice Hope (light middleweight), Jim Watt (lightweight) and Charlie Magri (flyweight). He has also managed numerous British champions including John L. Gardner.

1976 Carlos Zarate (Mex)—WBC
1977 Jorge Lujan (Pan)—WBA
1979 Lupe Pintor (Mex)—WBC
1980 Julian Solis (PR)—WBA
1980 Jeff Chandler (USA)—WBA

Super flyweight limit—115 lb
1980 Rafael Orono (Ven)—WBC
1981 Chul Ho Kim (SK)—WBC
1981 Gustavo Ballas (Arg)—WBA
1981 Rafael Pedroza (Pan)—WBA
1982 Jiro Watanabe (Jap)—WBA
1982 Rafael Orono (Ven)—WBC

Flyweight limit—112 lb
1965 Salvatore Burruni (Ita)
1966 Walter McGowan (GB)—WBC
1966 Horacio Accavallo (Arg)—WBA
1966 Chartchai Chionoi (Tha)—WBC
1969 Efren Torres (Mex)—WBC
1969 Hiroyuki Ebihara (Jap)—WBA
1970 Chartchai Chionoi (Tha)—WBC
1970 Bernabe Villacampo (Phi)—WBA
1970 Erbito Salavarria (Phi)—WBC

1970 Berkrerk Chartvanchai (Tha)—WBA
1970 Masao Ohba (Jap)—WBA
1971 Betulio Gonzalez (Ven)—WBC
1972 Venice Borkorsor (Tha)—WBC
1973 Betulio Gonzalez (Ven)—WBC
1973 Chartchai Chionoi (Tha)—WBA
1974 Shoji Oguma (Jap)—WBC
1974 Susumu Hanagata (Jap)—WBA
1975 Miguel Canto (Mex)—WBC
1975 Erbito Salavarria (Phi)—WBA
1976 Alfonso Lopez (Pan)—WBA
1976 Gustavo Espadas (Mex)—WBA
1978 Betulio Gonzalez (Ven)—WBA
1979 Chan-Hee Park (SK)—WBC
1979 Luis Ibarra (Pan)—WBA
1980 Kim Tae Shik (SK)—WBA
1980 Shoji Oguma (Jap)—WBC
1980 Peter Mathebula (Saf)—WBA
1981 Santos Laciar (Arg)—WBA
1981 Antonio Avelar (Mex)—WBC
1981 Luis Ibarra (Pan)—WBA
1981 Juan Herrera (Mex)—WBA
1982 Prudencio Cardona (Col)—WBC

1982 Santos Laciar (Arg)—WBA
1982 Freddie Castillo (Mex)—WBC
1982 Eleoncio Mercedes (Dom)—WBC
1983 Charlie Magri (GB)—WBC

Light flyweight limit—108 lb
1975 Franco Udella (Ita)—WBC
1975 Jaime Rios (Pan)—WBC
1975 Luis Estaba (Ven)—WBC
1976 Juan Guzman (Dom)—WBA
1976 Yoko Gushiken (Jap)—WBA
1978 Freddy Castillo (Mex)—WBC
1978 Netranoi Vorasingh (Tha)—WBC
1979 Kim Sung Jun (SK)—WBC
1980 Shigeo Nakejima (Jap)—WBC
1980 Hilario Zapata (Pan)—WBC
1981 Pedro Flores (Mex)—WBA
1981 Kim Hwan-Jin (SK)—WBA
1981 Katsuo Tokashiki (Jap)—WBA
1982 Amado Ursua (Mex)—WBC
1982 Tadeshi Tomori (Jap)—WBC
1982 Hilario Zapata (Pan)—WBC
1983 Chang Jung-Koo (SK)—WBC

Super heavy:	—		—		1982 Tyrell Biggs (USA)
Heavy:	1974 Teofilo Stevenson (Cub)		1978 Teofilo Stevenson (Cub)		1982 Aleksandr Iagubkin (USSR)
Light heavy:	1974 Mate Parlov (Yug)		1978 Sixto Soria (Cub)		1982 Pablo Romero (Cub)
Middle:	1974 Rufat Riskiev (USSR)		1978 Jose Gomez (Cub)		1982 Bernardo Comas (Cub)
Light middle:	1974 Rolando Garbey (Cub)		1978 Viktor Savchenko (USSR)		1982 Aleksandr Koshkin (USSR)
Welter:	1974 Emilio Correa (Cub)		1978 Valeriy Rachkov (USSR)		1982 Mark Breland (USA)
Light welter:	1974 Ayub Kalule (Uga)		1978 Valeriy Lvov (USSR)		1982 Carlos Garcia (Cub)
Light:	1974 Vasiliy Solomin (USSR)		1978 Andeh Davison (Nig)		1982 Angel Herrera (Cub)
Feather:	1974 Howard Davis (US)		1978 Angel Herrera (Cub)		1982 Adolfo Horta (Cub)
Bantam:	1974 Wilfredo Gomez (PR)		1978 Adolfo Horta (Cub)		1982 Floyd Favors (USA)
Fly:	1974 Douglas Rodriguez (Cub)		1978 Henryk Srednicki (Pol)		1982 Yuri Aleksandrov (USSR)
Light fly:	1974 Jorge Hernandez (Cub)		1978 Stephen Muchoki (Ken)		1982 Ismail Mustafov (Bul)

BRITISH CHAMPIONSHIPS

Since 1909 the winners of British title fights have been awarded a Lonsdale Belt—named after the 5th Earl of Lonsdale—to hold as long as the title is retained. The winner of three title fights keeps the Belt. The only man to win three outright is Henry Cooper between 1959 and 1971. The only men to have held British titles at three weights have been Ted 'Kid' Lewis, featherweight, welterweight and middleweight in the 1920s, and Len Harvey, middleweight, light heavyweight, and heavyweight in the 1930s. The greatest number of British heavyweight title defences were the 14 by 'Bombardier' Billy Wells between 1911 and 1919. The shortest ever British title fight was when Dave Charnley beat 'Darkie' Hughes for the lightweight crown in 40 sec in 1961.

Harry Mallin won two of Britain's four Olympic gold medals in the middleweight category.

UNDEFEATED

A professional record of 183 fights without defeat was set by an English lightweight, Hal Bagwell, from 1938 to 1948. Of these only five were drawn. Three world titleholders were unbeaten in their professional careers. They were James Barry (USA) bantamweight at the end of the 19th century, Jack McAuliffe (Ire) lightweight, 1886–96, and heavyweight champion Rocky Marciano (USA), 1947–56. The British amateur, double Olympic champion Harry Mallin, was undefeated in 300 bouts.

OLYMPIC GAMES: Two men have won three gold medals, Laszlo Papp (Hun) at middleweight 1948, and light middleweight 1952 and 1956, and Teofilo Stevenson (Cub) at heavyweight 1972–80. The only man to win two titles at the same Games is Oliver Kirk (USA) with the bantam and feather titles in 1904. The oldest boxer to win was Richard Gunn (GB) who was aged 38 yr when he won the featherweight gold medal in 1908. Britain's Harry Mallin was the first to retain an Olympic title when he won the middleweight title in 1920 and 1924.

AMATEUR BOXING ASSOCIATION (ABA)

The ABA was founded in 1880 and instituted British championships in 1881. The most titles won is six by Joseph Steers, three middleweight and three heavyweight from 1890 to 1893. Pat Floyd set a record when he won his first ABA heavyweight title in 1929 and his fourth and last 17 years later in 1946. The greatest number of titles won consecutively is five by Harry Mallin, middleweight 1919–23, his brother Fred, middleweight 1928–32, and flyweight Tom Pardoe 1929–33.

LONGEST AND SHORTEST FIGHTS

The longest fight on record, 7 hr 19 min, was between Andy Bowen and Jack Burke in New Orleans in 1893, when the contestants, wearing gloves, fought to a standstill after 110 rounds—the decision of 'no contest' was later changed to 'a draw'. The longest bare knuckle fight lasted 6 hr 15 min between James Kelly and Jack Smith in Australia in 1855. The greatest number of rounds has been 276, lasting 4 hr 30 min, between Jack Jones and Patsy Tunney in England in 1825. The record for a championship was 3 hr 16 min when Jim 'Deaf' Burke became the champion of England by beating Simon Byrne at St Albans in 1833—the latter dying three days later. The longest fight in Britain, with bare knuckles, was 6 hr 3 min between Bill Hayes and Mike Madden at Edenbridge, Kent in 1849. The record for a world title fight under the Queensberry Rules was in 1906 when Joe Gans (USA) beat Battling Nelson (Den) for the lightweight title after Nelson was disqualified in the 42nd round of a scheduled 45 round contest. The shortest fight was an amateur Golden Gloves contest at Minneapolis, USA in 1947 when Mike Collins knocked down Pat Brownson with the first punch of the fight and it was stopped only 4 sec from the start. The 10½ sec knockout (including a 10 sec count) attributed to Al Couture in America in 1947 is suspect as he was halfway across the ring when the bell sounded and hit Ralph Walton while he was still adjusting his gum shield. The shortest world title fight was 45 sec when Al McCoy beat George Chip for the middleweight crown in 1914. The record for the heavyweight title was a 1 min 28 sec win by Tommy Burns (Can) over Jem Roche (Ire) at Dublin in 1908.

The fastest knockout in British boxing was the 11 sec (including count) it took for Jack Cain to floor Harry Deamer in a lightweight fight at the National Sporting Club in 1922.

Canoeing

Representations of craft similar to canoes have been traced back to the Sumerian civilisation c 4000 BC, but modern canoes and kayaks originated among the Indians and Eskimos of North America. There are references to French trappers competing in canoe races in 1790, but canoeing as a sport is attributed to an English barrister, James Macgregor who founded the Royal Canoe Club in 1866.

Wild, or white, water canoeing is a real test of strength and skill, carried out on stretches of water on which a number of natural and artificial hazards are encountered. These include a torrential flow of water, strong currents, rapids, rocks and slalom gates. This shot of a Norwegian C–2 crewed by Eivind Schauffenberg and Sverre Gulbandsen indicates both the dangers and the exhilaration of the sport.

LONG JOURNEYS

The longest known journey by canoe is 14 290 km (8880 miles) by Jerry Pushcar (USA) from New Orleans to the Bering Sea and Alaska, via the Mississippi, Lake Superior and across Canada from January 1975 to November 1977. Some parts of the journey included portaging the canoes, ie carrying them around rapids and other unpassable stretches of water. The longest open sea trip was 3491 km (2170 miles) from Venezuela to Florida, USA by four Americans in 1977–78. The Texas Water Safari (instituted 1963) is the longest annual race, and the record for the 674 km (419 miles) on the San Marcos and Guadelupe rivers is 37 hr 18 min by Butch Hodges and Robert Chatham in 1976.

HIGHEST ALTITUDE

Dr Mike Jones and Mike Hopkinson of the British Everest expedition canoed down the lower slopes of Mt Everest on the Dudh Khosi from its source, a small ice-laden lake at the foot of the Khombu Glacier, 5334 m (17 500 ft) above sea level, in September 1976.

OLYMPIC GAMES: Canoeing was first included in the 1936 Games for men, and 1948 for women. The record number of gold medals is six by Gert Fredriksson (Swe) from 1948 to 1960, while the most by a woman is three by Ludmila Khvedosyuk-Pinayeva (USSR) 1964–72. Vladimir Parfenovich (USSR) won a record three golds in one Games, at Moscow in 1980.

WORLD CHAMPIONSHIPS: Instituted in 1938 under the auspices of the Internationale Repräsentationsschaft des Kanusports (founded 1924), they were later supervised by the International Canoe Federation (founded 1945). Yuri Lobanov (USSR) has won a record 11 titles between 1972 and 1979, while Ludmila Pinayeva (USSR) holds the female record with six from 1966 to 1973.

SPEED

The highest speed recorded for a canoe is 21·15 km/h (13·14 mph) by the USSR 4-man kayak (K4) in the 1980 Olympic Games.

Chess

The name chess is derived from the Persian word *Shah*, meaning a king or ruler, but it originated in India under the name *Chaturanga*—a military game. The earliest known chessmen have been dated *c* 200 AD. The game reached Britain about 1255.

WORLD CHAMPIONSHIPS: The first official champion dates from 1886 but unofficial champions were recognised before then. The youngest ever was Mikhail Tal (USSR) who won the title in 1960 at the age of 23 yr 180 days. The oldest was Wilhelm Steinitz (Ger), who was aged 58 yr when he lost his title in 1894 to Emanuel Lasker (Ger), who then held it for a record 27 years. The women's championship (instituted 1927) was held for 17 years by Vera Menchik-Stevenson (USSR/GB).

Men
1851–58 Adolph Anderssen (Ger)
1858–62 Paul Morphy (USA)
1862–66 Adolph Anderssen (Ger)
1866–94 Wilhelm Steinitz (Aut)
1894–1921 Emanuel Lasker (Ger)
1921–27 José Capablanca (Cub)
1927–35 Alexandre Alekhine (Fra)
1935–37 Max Euwe (Hol)
1937–47 Alexandre Alekhine (Fra)
1948–57 Mikhail Botvinnik (USSR)
1957–58 Vassiliy Smyslov (USSR)
1958–60 Mikhail Botvinnik (USSR)
1960–61 Mikhail Tal (USSR)
1961–63 Mikhail Botvinnik (USSR)
1963–69 Tigran Petrosian (USSR)
1969–72 Boris Spassky (USSR)
1972–75 Robert Fischer (USA)
1975–   Anatoliy Karpov (USSR)

Women
1927–44 Vera Menchik (GB)
1950–53 Lyudmila Rudenko (USSR)
1953–56 Elizaveta Bykova (USSR)
1956–58 Olga Rubtsova (USSR)
1958–62 Elizaveta Bykova (USSR)
1962–78 Nona Gaprindashvili (USSR)
1978–   Maya Chiburdanidze (USSR)

Men's Team
1927 Hungary
1928 Hungary
1930 Poland
1931 USA
1933 USA
1935 USA
1937 USA
1939 Germany
1950 Yugoslavia

1952 USSR
1954 USSR
1956 USSR
1958 USSR
1960 USSR
1962 USSR
1964 USSR
1966 USSR
1968 USSR
1970 USSR
1972 USSR
1974 USSR
1976 USA
1978 Hungary
1980 USSR
1982 USSR

Women's Team
1957 USSR
1963 USSR
1966 USSR
1969 USSR
1972 USSR
1974 USSR
1976 Israel
1978 USSR
1980 USSR
1982 USSR

GREATEST PLAYER

Such a description is always a contentious issue, but Bobby Fischer (USA) achieved the highest ever rating of 2785 on the official ELO System scoring. He also won 20 Grand Master games in succession in 1970–71. Anatoliy Karpov (USSR) has only lost 53 (6·16%) of his 859 games, winning 386 and tieing 420, from 1966 to the end of the 1981 World Championships.

LONG GAMES

When Yedael Stepak (Isr) beat Yaakov Mashian (Irn/Isr) in Tel Aviv in 1980, the event set Master game records of 24½ hr and 193 moves. Among minor chess players, two Americans, Stan Zygmunt and Ilya Schwartzman played for 168 hr from December 1979 to January 1980.

BRITISH CHAMPIONSHIPS

Rowena Dew-Bruce won a record 11 women's titles from 1937 to 1969. The men's record is 10 by Dr Jonathan Penrose between 1958 and 1969. *Winners since 1970:*

Men		Women	
1970	Robert Wade	1970–74	Jana Hartston
1971	Raymond Keene	1975	Sheila Jackson
1972	Brian Eley	1976–77	Jana Hartston
1973	William Hartston	1978	Sheila Jackson
1974	George Botterill	1979	Jana Hartston-Miles
1975	William Hartston	1980	Sheila Jackson
1976	Jonathan Mestel	1981	Sheila Jackson
1977	George Botterill	1982	Jan Garwell
1978	Jonathan Speelman		
1979	Robert Bellin		
1980	John Nunn		
1981	Paul Littlewood		
1982	Tony Miles		

Cricket

The earliest representation of a bat and ball game, resembling cricket, is a drawing dated *c* 1250. The game was played in Guildford, Surrey in 1550. In Australia, it was first played in 1803, and the first Australian touring team was an Aboriginal XI to England in 1868. However, the first English touring side had gone to North America in 1859. The first Test match between England and Australia was at Melbourne, Victoria in March 1877—Australia won. Coincidentally, the Centenary Test, in March 1977, again in Melbourne, was also won by Australia by exactly the same margin of 45 runs.

DEVELOPMENT
In the late 18th century the game was controlled by the Hambledon Club, but the formation of the MCC (Marylebone Cricket Club), which merged with the White Conduit Club in 1787, brought revision and codification of the rules in 1835. Among them was the acceptance of round-arm bowling, said to have been 'invented' in 1807 by a girl, Christina Willes, whose brother played for Kent.

LONGEST NAME
Unchallenged holder of the longest name in representative cricket is IlikeNa Bula, who toured New Zealand with the Fijian team in 1948. His surname, which he had shortened to Bula as a charitable act towards scorers and pressmen, contained 59 letters. It was—Talebulamaineiilikenamainavaleniveivakabulaimainakulalakeba.

BATTING FEAT EXTRAORDINARY
Possibly the greatest batting feat of all time occurred at Swansea on 31 August 1968, when Sir Garfield Sobers, the West Indian Test cricketer, playing for Nottinghamshire *v* Glamorgan, hit six consecutive sixes in one over for a first-class cricket record. The unfortunate bowler was Malcolm Nash, in whose favour it should be said that Sobers was nearly caught out by Roger Davis off the fifth ball. However, Sobers hit the last ball clean out of the ground with a hit that was suggested should have been credited with 'a 12'.

MOST RUNS OFF A BALL
The first-class record for runs off a single hit is 10 by Albert Hornby for Lancashire *v* Surrey at the Oval in July 1873, and by Samuel Hill Wood (later Sir Samuel Hill Hill-Wood) for Derbyshire *v* MCC at Lord's in May 1900. The minor cricket record is 11, all run, with no overthrows, by Lt Philip Mitford for the 2nd Battalion Queens Own Cameron Highlanders *v* 1st Battalion Kings Royal Rifles, in Malta in May 1903. There are reports, however, of matches such as the one in Lancashire in 1898 when the batsman hit the ball over a cliff. As it was still visible it was not ruled a 'lost ball' and by the time it was recovered the batsman had made 264 runs. In another similar case in Australia the ball lodged high in a tree and the batsmen ran 286 before it was shot down with a rifle.

HIGHEST INNINGS SCORE
The first-class record is the 499 hit by Hanif Mohammad of Pakistan, for Karachi *v* Bahawalpur at Karachi on 8–11 January 1959. The innings took 10 hr 35 min to play. The highest score in England is 424 runs in 7 hr 50 min by Archie MacLaren for Lancashire *v* Somerset at Taunton, 15–16 July 1895. The record for a Test match is 365 not out by Sir Garfield Sobers for West Indies *v* Pakistan at Kingston, Jamaica, taking 10 hr 14 min on 27 February–1 March 1958. In minor cricket 13-year-old Arthur Collins scored an outstanding 628 runs not out in a Junior House match at Clifton College, Bristol in June 1889. He took 6 hr 50 min spread over five afternoons of play, carrying his bat through his team's innings of 836. Collins, who also collected 11 wickets as a bowler in the match, was Mentioned in Despatches as a Captain in the Royal Engineers on the Western Front early in the First World War and was killed in action.

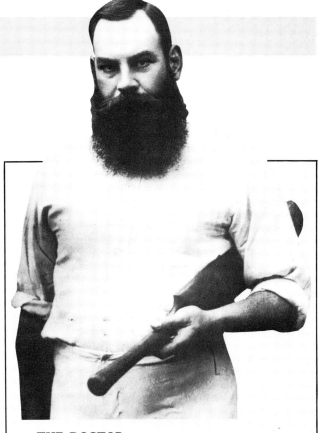

THE DOCTOR
Doctor William Gilbert 'W.G.' Grace dominated English cricket from the 1860s to the end of the century. The most famous and recognisable figure in the game's history, he held virtually all the major records in his day. These included a career total of 54 211 runs, of which 1098 were in Tests, 124 hundreds, 2809 wickets as a bowler, and 872 catches as a fielder. He set a season's record of 2739 runs in 1871, was the first man to score 1000 runs in May (actually in 22 days), and achieved his highest innings score of 344 for the MCC *v* Kent in 1876. Grace had other sporting interests which included lawn bowls—he was President of the English Bowling Association in 1903—and athletics, in his younger days.

FASTEST SCORING
In August 1920 Percy Fender scored the fastest ever hundred in first class cricket, in 35 min, when making 113 not out for Surrey *v* Northamptonshire at Northampton. The fastest hundred achieved in a Test match was one of 70 min duration by Jack Gregory for Australia *v* South Africa at Johannesburg in November 1921. Gloucestershire and England batsman Gilbert Jessop scored a hundred in an hour or less a record eleven times between 1897 and 1913. He also holds the record for a double hundred, in 120 min, achieved during his 286 for Gloucestershire *v* Sussex at Hove in June 1903. Clive Lloyd equalled the mark for the West Indians *v* Glamorgan at Swansea in August 1976. Three hundred in 181 min was scored by Denis Compton for the MCC *v* North-Eastern Transvaal at Benoni, South Africa in December 1948. The fastest 50 was scored in 8 min by Clive Inman playing for Leicestershire *v* Nottinghamshire at Trent Bridge in August 1965. One of the most outstanding fast scoring feats was when Edwin Alletson made 189 runs in 90 min for Nottinghamshire *v* Sussex at Hove in May 1911. In a minor cricket match in Australia in January 1979, Greg Beacroft scored 268 in 92 min playing for Yass Wallaroos *v* Williamsdale.

BATTING RECORDS (As at 20 February 1983)

Highest innings

Team—first-class	1107	Victoria v New South Wales at Melbourne	1926
—Test	903	England v Australia at The Oval	1938
—John Player	307	Worcestershire v Derbyshire at Worcester	1975
—Benson & Hedges	350	Essex v Combined Universities at Chelmsford	1979
—Nat West/Gillette Cup	371	Hampshire v Glamorgan at Southampton	1975
Individual—first-class	499	Hanif Mohammad, for Karachi v Bahawalpur, at Karachi	1959
—Test	365	Gary Sobers for West Indies v Pakistan, at Kingston	1958
—John Player	163	Gordon Greenidge for Hampshire v Warwickshire, at Edgbaston	1979
—Benson & Hedges	198	Graham Gooch for Essex v Sussex, at Hove	1982
—Nat West/Gillette Cup	177	Gordon Greenidge for Hampshire v Glamorgan, at Southampton	1975
Individual—first-class runs	61 237	Jack Hobbs (Surrey and England)	1905–34
—Test runs	8114	Geoffrey Boycott (Yorkshire and England)	1964–82
—season's runs	3816	Denis Compton (Middlesex and England)	1947
Career centuries	197	Jack Hobbs (Surrey and England)	1905–34
Test centuries	29	Don Bradman (Australia)	1928–48
Season's centuries	18	Denis Compton (Middlesex and England)	1947

Fastest scoring, first-class

50 runs	8 min	Clive Inman for Leicestershire v Nottinghamshire, at Trent Bridge	1965
100 runs	35 min	Percy Fender for Surrey v Northamptonshire, at Northampton	1920
200 runs	120 min	Gilbert Jessop for Gloucestershire v Sussex, at Hove	1903
	120 min	Clive Lloyd for West Indians v Glamorgan, at Swansea	1976
300 runs	181 min	Denis Compton for MCC v North-Eastern Transvaal, at Benoni	1948

BOWLING (As at 20 February 1983)

Most wickets—career	4187	Wilfred Rhodes (Yorkshire and England)	1898–1930
—Tests	332	Dennis Lillee (Australia)	1971–83
—season	304	'Tich' Freeman (Kent)	1928
—match	19	Jim Laker for England v Australia, at Old Trafford	1956
—day	17	Colin Blythe for Kent v Northamptonshire at Northampton	1907
	17	Hedley Verity for Yorkshire v Essex, at Leyton	1933
	17	Tom Goddard for Gloucestershire v Kent, at Bristol	1939
—innings	10	*	

Achieved many times, but only one man, 'Tich' Freeman (Kent) did it on three occasions

FIELDING (As at 20 February 1983)

Most catches—career	1018	Frank Woolley (Kent and England)	1906–38
—Tests	120	Colin Cowdrey (Kent and England)	1954–75
—season	78	Walter Hammond (Gloucestershire and England)	1928
—match	10	Walter Hammond for Gloucestershire v Surrey, at Cheltenham	1928
—innings	7	Mike Stewart for Surrey v Northamptonshire, at Northampton	1957
	7	Tony Brown for Gloucestershire v Nottinghamshire, at Trent Bridge	1966
—Test innings	7	Greg Chappell for Australia v England, at Perth	1974
		Yajurvindra Singh for India v England, at Bangalore	1977

WICKETKEEPING (As at 20 February 1983)

Most dismissals—career	1543	Bob Taylor (Derbyshire and England)	1960–83
—Tests	334	Rodney Marsh (Australia)	1970–83
—season	127	Leslie Ames (Kent)	1929
—match	12	Edward Pooley for Surrey v Sussex, at The Oval	1868
	12	Don Tallon for Queensland v New South Wales, at Sydney	1939
	12	Brian Taber for New South Wales v South Australia, at Adelaide	1968
—innings	8	Wally Grout for Queensland v Western Australia, at Brisbane	1960
—Test innings	7	Wasim Bari for Pakistan v New Zealand, at Auckland	1979
	7	Bob Taylor for England v India, at Bombay	1980
Most catches—career	1375	Bob Taylor (Derbyshire and England)	1960–83

FASTEST BOWLER

In December 1975 the University of Western Australia's Department of Physical Education and Recreation set out to decide who was the world's fastest bowler. In experiments conducted during the Second Test match between Australia and the West Indies they found that Australia's Jeff Thomson was the fastest with a delivery speed of 99·7 mph (160·45 km/h). But that had not really ended the speculation as the second fastest man that day, Andy Roberts of the West Indies, at 93·62 mph (150·66 km/h), was said to have bowled faster on occasions when he was not being tested. Of all the bowlers for whom claims have been made, the longest lasting seem to be those for C. J. Kortwright of Essex in the 1890s.

LONGEST OVER

The longest over consisting of legal deliveries, with no no-balls or wides, was one of 14 by David Hill playing for British Guiana (now Guyana) v Barbados at Georgetown in September–October 1946. Apparently, the umpire, A. C. De Barros, miscounted the 8-ball over to a remarkable degree much to the physical distress of the bowler, who nevertheless was able to dismiss Everton Weekes, lbw, with the last, and 14th ball.

Sir John Berry 'Jack' Hobbs of Surrey was perhaps England's greatest batsman. His innings of 316 not out against Middlesex in 1926 is still the highest score ever made at Lord's. The previous year he had scored a total of 16 centuries, and in his career on six occasions he scored two centuries in a match.

WOMEN'S CRICKET

The first known women's match took place at Gosden Common, Surrey on 26 June 1745, when Hambleton beat Bramley by 127–119. The first Test match between Australia and England was played at Brisbane on 28–31 December 1934—England won the match and the series 2–0, with one drawn.

The highest score by a woman is 224 not out by Mabel Bryant playing for the Visitors v Residents at Eastbourne, Sussex in August 1901. The highest in a Test match is 189 by Betty Snowball for England v New Zealand at Christchurch, NZ in February 1935. Rachel Heyhoe-Flint scored a record 1594 runs in Test matches between 1960 and 1979, averaging 63·76 per innings.

LONGEST THROW

Robert Percival of Shildon, Durham threw a cricket ball (weighing $5\frac{1}{4}$ oz (155 g) 422 ft (128·6 m) on the Durham Sands Racecourse on an Easter Monday in the early 1880s. There have been doubts expressed about this feat, due to the failure of modern throwers to get even close to that mark, but there is also a reported, but highly suspect, throw of 441 ft (134·4 m) by an Australian Aboriginal named King Billy in Queensland in 1872.

Alan Knott making a spectacular diving catch against Australia. Knott is one of a long line of fine wicketkeepers produced by his county, Kent. His total of 1143 dismissals includes an English record of 269 in Test matches. An excellent batsman as well, he has scored 4389 runs for England in his 95 Test match appearances.

ATTENDANCES

The greatest number of people to watch a single cricket match was the 394 000 who attended the Fourth Test between India and England at Calcutta on 1–6 January 1982. The biggest crowd to watch a match on a single day was 90 800 on the second day of the Fifth Test between Australia and the West Indies at Melbourne on 11 February 1961. The greatest attendances in England have been 159 000 for the Fourth Test between England and Australia at Headingley, Leeds on 22–27 July 1948, and the one day record of an estimated 45 000 at the Lancashire *v* Yorkshire match at Old Trafford, Manchester on 2 August 1926. The English series record is 549 650 for that won by England 1–0, with 4 drawn, against Australia in 1953.

Right: West Indian cricket supporters epitomised by the famous King Dyal, whose yellow suit, seen here at the Third Test in Barbados in 1981, is only one of a series of brightly coloured outfits with which he graces the grounds. *Below:* Mike Brearley returned to captain England to victory in the 1981 series against Australia, after the situation had looked grim at the end of the first two Tests. Here he is batting in the Fourth Test which put England in the lead.

ENGLISH COUNTY CHAMPIONSHIP: Although officially constituted in 1890, cricket experts have been able to extend the title back to 1864. Since 1890 the title has been won most often by Yorkshire with 29 outright wins and one shared. The record for consecutive wins is seven by Surrey 1952–58. Northamptonshire holds the unenviable record of being last on 11 occasions.

1864	Surrey	1878	Undecided
1865	Nottinghamshire	1879	Nottinghamshire / Lancashire
1866	Middlesex		
1867	Yorkshire	1880	Nottinghamshire
1868	Nottinghamshire	1881	Lancashire
1869	Nottinghamshire / Yorkshire	1882	Nottinghamshire / Lancashire
1870	Yorkshire	1883	Nottinghamshire
1871	Nottinghamshire	1884	Nottinghamshire
1872	Nottinghamshire	1885	Nottinghamshire
1873	Gloucestershire / Nottinghamshire	1886	Nottinghamshire
1874	Gloucestershire	1887	Surrey
1875	Nottinghamshire	1888	Surrey
1876	Gloucestershire	1889	Surrey / Lancashire / Nottinghamshire
1877	Gloucestershire		

1890 Surrey	1914 Surrey	1948 Glamorgan	1970 Kent
1891 Surrey	1919 Yorkshire	1949 Middlesex / Yorkshire	1971 Surrey
1892 Surrey	1920 Middlesex	1950 Lancashire / Surrey	1972 Warwickshire
1893 Yorkshire	1921 Middlesex	1951 Warwickshire	1973 Hampshire
1894 Surrey	1922 Yorkshire	1952 Surrey	1974 Worcestershire
1895 Surrey	1923 Yorkshire	1953 Surrey	1975 Leicestershire
1896 Yorkshire	1924 Yorkshire	1954 Surrey	1976 Middlesex
1897 Lancashire	1925 Yorkshire	1955 Surrey	1977 Middlesex / Kent
1898 Yorkshire	1926 Lancashire	1956 Surrey	1978 Kent
1899 Surrey	1927 Lancashire	1957 Surrey	1979 Essex
1900 Yorkshire	1928 Lancashire	1958 Surrey	1980 Middlesex
1901 Yorkshire	1929 Nottinghamshire	1959 Yorkshire	1981 Nottinghamshire
1902 Yorkshire	1930 Lancashire	1960 Yorkshire	1982 Middlesex
1903 Middlesex	1931 Yorkshire	1961 Hampshire	
1904 Lancashire	1932 Yorkshire	1962 Yorkshire	
1905 Yorkshire	1933 Yorkshire	1963 Yorkshire	
1906 Kent	1934 Lancashire	1964 Worcestershire	
1907 Nottinghamshire	1935 Yorkshire	1965 Worcestershire	
1908 Yorkshire	1936 Derbyshire	1966 Yorkshire	
1909 Kent	1937 Yorkshire	1967 Yorkshire	
1910 Kent	1938 Yorkshire	1968 Yorkshire	
1911 Warwickshire	1939 Yorkshire	1969 Glamorgan	
1912 Yorkshire	1946 Yorkshire		
1913 Kent	1947 Middlesex		

GILLETTE/NAT WEST TROPHY: The Gillette Cup was the first inter-county one-day competition, featuring all 17 first-class counties, first held in 1963. The National Westminster Bank took over as sponsors in 1981 and the competition is now for the NatWest Bank Trophy. It is contested on a knock-out basis and the 1983 competition will include 13 minor counties, Ireland and Scotland. Sixty overs per side are played.

1963 Sussex	1982 Surrey
1964 Sussex	
1965 Yorkshire	
1966 Warwickshire	
1967 Kent	
1968 Warwickshire	
1969 Yorkshire	
1970 Lancashire	
1971 Lancashire	
1972 Lancashire	
1973 Gloucestershire	
1974 Kent	
1975 Lancashire	
1976 Northamptonshire	
1977 Middlesex	
1978 Sussex	
1979 Somerset	
1980 Middlesex	
1981 Derbyshire	

JOHN PLAYER LEAGUE: This one-day competition was first held in 1969, and contested by the 17 first-class counties on a league basis of 40-over matches.

1969 Lancashire	1982 Sussex
1970 Lancashire	
1971 Worcestershire	
1972 Kent	
1973 Kent	
1974 Leicestershire	
1975 Hampshire	
1976 Kent	
1977 Leicestershire	
1978 Hampshire	
1979 Somerset	
1980 Warwickshire	
1981 Essex	

BENSON & HEDGES CUP: A one-day competition instituted in 1972 and contested by the 17 first-class counties, and extra teams which have included Scotland, Ireland, representative Minor Counties Cricket Association teams, and Oxford and Cambridge Universities, either singularly or combined. Matches of 55 overs are played.

1972 Leicestershire	1982 Somerset
1973 Kent	
1974 Surrey	
1975 Leicestershire	
1976 Kent	
1977 Gloucestershire	
1978 Kent	
1979 Essex	
1980 Northamptonshire	
1981 Somerset	

SHEFFIELD SHIELD: The trophy donated by Lord Sheffield in 1892 is for the State championship of Australia. It has been won on a record 37 occasions by New South Wales between 1896 and 1983. In 1978 Western Australia won with a record total of 147 points. *Winners since 1970:*

1970 Victoria	1983 New South Wales
1971 South Australia	
1972 Western Australia	
1973 Western Australia	
1974 Victoria	
1975 Western Australia	
1976 South Australia	
1977 Western Australia	
1978 Western Australia	
1979 Victoria	
1980 Victoria	
1981 Western Australia	
1982 South Australia	

PLUNKET SHIELD / SHELL TROPHY: The Plunket Shield was presented in 1906 by Lord Plunket, then Governor-General, and is for the Inter-Provincial championship of New Zealand. Originally contested on a challenge basis, a league competition was introduced in 1922, which lasted until 1975. It was then replaced by the Shell Trophy in 1976. Wellington have won a record 16 times between 1924 and 1983. *Winners since 1976:*

1976 Canterbury	1983 Wellington
1977 Otago	
1978 Auckland	
1979 Otago	
1980 Northern Districts	
1981 Auckland	
1982 Wellington	

CURRIE CUP: Donated by Sir Donald Currie in 1889, originally for the South African team which performed best against the English touring team that year (which incidentally was captained by C. Aubrey Smith who, in the 1930s, became a famous film actor in Hollywood). The following year it became the trophy for the Inter-Provincial championship of South Africa. The record number of wins is 20 (plus four tied) by Transvaal between 1890 and 1983. *Winners since 1974:*

1974 Natal	1983 Transvaal
1975 Western Province	
1976 Natal	
1977 Natal	
1978 Western Province	
1979 Transvaal	
1980 Transvaal	
1981 Natal	
1982 Western Province	

RANJI TROPHY: Established in 1934 in memory of Kumar Shri Ranjitsinhji, who played for England, and captained Sussex from 1899 to 1903. The trophy, donated by H.H. the Maharaja Bhupendra Singh of Patiala, is awarded to India's champion State or Province. Bombay has won it most often with 28 wins between 1935 and 1981, including 15 consecutively, 1959–73. *Winners since 1974:*

1974 Karnataka	1983 Karnataka
1975 Bombay	
1976 Bombay	
1977 Bombay	
1978 Karnataka	
1979 Delhi	
1980 Delhi	
1981 Bombay	
1982 Delhi	

SHELL SHIELD: The principal domestic competition in the West Indies has been held since 1966, with the exception of 1968. Barbados has won a record nine times plus once shared. *Winners since 1974:*

1974 Barbados	1983 Guyana
1975 Guyana	
1976 { Barbados / Trinidad & Tobago	
1977 Barbados	
1978 Barbados	
1979 Barbados	
1980 Barbados	
1981 Combined Islands	
1982 Barbados	

Right: **Ian Botham putting on his pads before going out to face Australia in the First Test at Trent Bridge in 1981. His performances, both as batsman (399 runs) and bowler (34 wickets), were a prime factor in England taking the series. Born in Cheshire, he lives in Lincolnshire, but plays for Somerset. Botham set a number of records when he achieved the double of scoring 2000 runs and taking 200 wickets in Test cricket. He was the youngest ever, at 26 years 7 days, to perform the feat, in fewest Tests, 42, and he did it in the shortest period of time, 4 years 126 days. He also captained England in 12 of those Test matches. In the winter he sometimes plays League soccer for Scunthorpe United.**

SUMMARY OF ALL TEST MATCHES
(As at 1 June 1983)

The first figure shows the number of wins gained by the team shown in the left-hand column, the second figure is for the team shown above, and draws are shown within brackets.

	England	Australia	South Africa	West Indies	New Zealand	India	Pakistan	Sri Lanka	Totals
England	—	83–95(73)	46–18(38)	21–25(34)	27–1(25)	28–8(31)	13–2(21)	1–0(0)	219–149(222)
Australia	95–83(73)	—	29–11(13)	26–13(12)★	8–2(5)	20–8(11)	9–8(6)	1–0(0)	188–125(120)
South Africa	18–46(38)	11–29(13)	—	—	9–2(6)	—	—	—	38–77(57)
West Indies	25–21(34)	13–26(12)★	—	—	5–3(9)	17–5(21)	7–4(8)	—	67–59(84)
New Zealand	1–27(25)	2–8(5)	2–9(6)	3–5(9)	—	4–10(11)	1–8(12)	2–0	13–67(68)
India	8–28(31)	8–20(11)	—	5–17(21)	10–4(11)	—	4–6(20)	0–0(1)	35–75(95)
Pakistan	2–13(21)	8–9(6)	—	4–7(8)	8–1(12)	6–4(20)	—	2–0(1)	30–34(68)
Sri Lanka	0–1(0)	0–1(0)		—	0–2	0–0(1)	0–2(1)	—	0–6(2)

★Plus one tied

Cross-Country

One of the earliest references to modern cross-country running was in the 1820s when Shrewsbury School, England held a hunt in which boys ran after the hounds. In 1834 Rugby School held a 4 miles (6·4 km) steeplechase. The Thames Rowing Club, at Putney, London held cross-country runs—the first was on 7 December 1867—as a means for oarsmen to keep fit during the winter, and the famous Thames Hare and Hounds club was formed in 1868. The earliest international race took place just outside Paris between England and France in March 1898—England won, with the minimum possible points.

WORLD (formerly International) CHAMPIONSHIPS: The first championship between England, Scotland, Ireland and Wales, was held at Hamilton Park racecourse, Scotland on 28 March 1903. France was invited in 1905, and other countries were added from time to time. In 1973 the race came under the auspices of the International Amateur Athletic Federation (IAAF). A women's race was held unofficially in 1931 in France, but the series proper began in 1967.

The greatest number of wins by an individual in the men's race is four by Jack Holden (Eng) in 1933–5, 1939, by Alain Mimoun (Fra) in 1949, 1952, 1954, 1956, and by Gaston Roelants (Bel) in 1962, 1967, 1969, 1972. The women's race has been won five times by Doris Brown-Heritage (USA) consecutively 1967–71, and by Grete Waitz (Nor) 1978–81 and 1983. The most team races have been won by England, with a record 45 victories (men) and 6 (women). England has been the only team to score a minimum of 21 points (the first six finishers), in 1924 and 1932. The greatest margin of victory in the individual race was 56 sec by Jack Holden (Eng) in 1934. The narrowest win was in 1983 when the timekeepers could not separate the first three finishers, with the fourth man one second behind. A Belgian, Marcel Van de Wattyne, ran in the race on a record 20 occasions between 1946 and 1965. The women's record is 15 appearances by Jean Lochhead (Wal) 1967–79, 1981 and 1983.

WINNERS OF THE INTERNATIONAL CHAMPIONSHIP RACES (MEN)

	Individual	Team
1903	Alfred Shrubb (Eng)	England
1904	Alfred Shrubb (Eng)	England
1905	Albert Aldridge (Eng)	England
1906	Charles Straw (Eng)	England
1907	A. Underwood (Eng)	England
1908	Archie Robertson (Eng)	England
1909	Edward Wood (Eng)	England
1910	Edward Wood (Eng)	England
1911	Jean Bouin (Fra)	England
1912	Jean Bouin (Fra)	England
1913	Jean Bouin (Fra)	England
1914	Arthur Nicholls (Eng)	England
1920	James Wilson (Sco)	England
1921	Walter Freeman (Eng)	England
1922	Joseph Guillemot (Fra)	France
1923	Charles Blewitt (Eng)	France
1924	William Cotterell (Eng)	England
1925	Jack Webster (Eng)	England
1926	Ernest Harper (Eng)	France
1927	Lewis Payne (Eng)	France
1928	Harry Eckersley (Eng)	France
1929	William Cotterell (Eng)	France
1930	Thomas Evenson (Eng)	England
1931	Tim Smythe (Ire)	England
1932	Thomas Evenson (Eng)	England
1933	Jack Holden (Eng)	England
1934	Jack Holden (Eng)	England
1935	Jack Holden (Eng)	England
1936	William Eaton (Eng)	England
1937	James Flockhart (Sco)	England
1938	John Emery (Eng)	England
1939	Jack Holden (Eng)	France
1946	Raphael Pujazon (Fra)	France
1947	Raphael Pujazon (Fra)	France
1948	John Doms (Bel)	Belgium
1949	Alain Mimoun (Fra)	France
1950	Lucien Theys (Bel)	France
1951	Geoffrey Saunders (Eng)	England
1952	Alain Mimoun (Fra)	France
1953	Franjo Mihalic (Yug)	England
1954	Alain Mimoun (Fra)	England
1955	Frank Sando (Eng)	England
1956	Alain Mimoun (Fra)	France
1957	Frank Sando (Eng)	Belgium
1958	Stanley Eldon (Eng)	England
1959	Fred Norris (Eng)	England
1960	Abdesselem Rhadi (Fra)	England
1961	Basil Heatley (Eng)	Belgium
1962	Gaston Roelants (Bel)	England
1963	Roy Fowler (Eng)	Belgium
1964	Francesco Arizmendi (Spa)	England
1965	Jean Fayolle (Fra)	England
1966	Ben Assou El Ghazi (Mor)	England
1967	Gaston Roelants (Bel)	England
1968	Mohamed Gammoudi (Tun)	England
1969	Gaston Roelants (Bel)	England
1970	Michael Tagg (Eng)	England
1971	David Bedford (Eng)	England
1972	Gaston Roelants (Bel)	England
1973	Pekka Paivarinta (Fin)	Belgium
1974	Eric De Beck (Bel)	Belgium
1975	Ian Stewart (Sco)	NZ
1976	Carlos Lopes (Por)	England
1977	Leon Schots (Bel)	Belgium
1978	John Treacy (Ire)	France
1979	John Treacy (Ire)	England
1980	Craig Virgin (USA)	England
1981	Craig Virgin (USA)	Ethiopia
1982	Mohamed Kedir (Eth)	Ethiopia
1983	Bekele Debele (Eth)	Ethiopia

BIGGEST FIELDS
The largest field in any cross-country race was 10 055 starters, of whom 9650 finished, in the 30 km (18·6 miles) Lidingöloppet, held near Stockholm, Sweden on 4 October 1981. The largest British field was in the National championship with 1782 starters, 1610 finishers, at Luton in 1983. A record 1627 finished from 1710 starters in 1980.

WOMEN			JUNIORS		
	Individual	Team		Individual	Team
			1961	Colin Robinson (Eng)	England
1967	Doris Brown (USA)	England	1962	Abdeslam Bouchta (Mor)	England
1968	Doris Brown (USA)	USA	1963	Not held	
1969	Doris Brown (USA)	USA	1964	Ian McCafferty (Sco)	England
1970	Doris Brown (USA)	England	1965	Johnny Dumon (Bel)	Belgium
1971	Doris Brown (USA)	England	1966	Mike Tagg (Eng)	England
1972	Joyce Smith (Eng)	England	1967	Edward Knox (Sco)	England
1973	Paola Cacchi (Ita)	England	1968	John Bednarski (Eng)	England
1974	Paola Cacchi (Ita)	England	1969	David Bedford (Eng)	England
1975	Julie Brown (USA)	USA	1970	John Hartnett (Ire)	England
1976	Carmen Valero (Spa)	USSR	1971	Nick Rose (Eng)	England
1977	Carmen Valero (Spa)	USSR	1972	Aldo Tomasini (Ita)	Italy
1978	Grete Waitz (Nor)	Romania	1973	Jim Brown (Sco)	Spain
1979	Grete Waitz (Nor)	USA	1974	Richard Kimball (USA)	USA
1980	Grete Waitz (Nor)	USSR	1975	Robert Thomas (USA)	USA
1981	Grete Waitz (Nor)	USSR	1976	Eddie Hulst (USA)	USA
1982	Maricica Puica (Rom)	USSR	1977	Thom Hunt (USA)	USA
1983	Grete Waitz (Nor)	USA	1978	Mick Morton (Eng)	England
			1979	Eddy de Paauw (Bel)	Spain
			1980	Jordi Garcia (Spa)	USSR
			1981	Mohammed Chouri (Tun)	USA
			1982	Zurubachev Gelaw (Eth)	Ethiopia
			1983	Fesseha Abebe (Eth)	Ethiopia

ENGLISH CHAMPIONSHIPS: After an inauspicious start in 1876, when all 32 runners went off course and the race had to be declared void, the championship proper began in 1877. The most successful team has been Birchfield Harriers with 28 victories, including one tie, between 1880 and 1953. The most senior individual titles have been four by Percy Stenning 1877–80, and Alfred Shrubb 1901–04. Only two athletes have won titles at all three age groups. Walter Hesketh won the Youth

Typical cold, wet and muddy conditions for the 1981 National championships. Former British steeplechase record holder Andy Holden came tenth and his club Tipton Harriers won its fifth title.

race in 1948, the Junior in 1950 and 1951, and the Senior in 1952, while David Black won the three titles in 1971, 1972 and 1974 respectively. The biggest margin of victory in the Senior race was 1 min 55 sec by Julian Goater in 1981, and the narrowest was when Ron Hill beat Mike Turner in 1966 by inches.

ENGLISH CHAMPIONSHIP WINNERS:

	Individual	*Team*
1946	Jack Holden	Belgrave H
1947	Archie Robertson	Sutton H
1948	Sydney Wooderson	Belgrave H
1949	Frank Aaron	Sutton H
1950	Frank Aaron	Sutton H
1951	Frank Aaron	Sutton H
1952	Walter Hesketh	Victoria Park AAC
1953	Gordon Pirie	Birchfield H
1954	Gordon Pirie	Bolton United H
1955	Gordon Pirie	South London H
1956	Ken Norris	Sheffield United H
1957	Frank Sando	South London H
1958	Alan Perkins	South London H
1959	Fred Norris	Sheffield United H
1960	Basil Heatley	Derby & Co
1961	Basil Heatley	Derby & Co
1962	Gerry North	Derby & Co
1963	Basil Heatley	Coventry Godiva H
1964	Mel Batty	Portsmouth AC

1965	Mel Batty	Portsmouth AC
1966	Ron Hill	North Staffs & Stone H
1967	Dick Taylor	Portsmouth AC
1968	Ron Hill	Coventry Godiva H
1969	Mike Tagg	Tipton H
1970	Mike Tagg	City of Stoke AC
1971	David Bedford	Shettleston H
1972	Mal Thomas	Tipton H
1973	David Bedford*	Gateshead H
1974	David Black	Derby & Co
1975	Tony Simmons	Gateshead H
1976	Bernie Ford	Gateshead H
1977	Brendan Foster	Gateshead H
1978	Bernie Ford	Tipton H
1979	Mike McLeod	Gateshead H
1980	Nick Rose	Tipton H
1981	Julian Goater	Tipton H
1982	David Clarke	Tipton H
1983	Tim Hutchings	Aldershot, Farnham & District AC

Actually won by a guest, Rod Dixon (NZ).

Cycling

The first known race was won by Dr James Moore (GB) over 2 km (1·2 miles) in Paris on 31 May 1868. In the early 1870s the main centres in Britain were at the Star Grounds, Fulham, and Aston Cross, Birmingham. The Road Records Association in Britain was formed in 1888, and in 1891 the first cement racing track was built at Putney, London. The time-trial was devised in 1889–90 by F. T. Bidlake as a means of avoiding the traffic congestion caused by ordinary mass road racing.

TOUR DE FRANCE: This race is the longest lasting non-mechanical sporting event in the world, taking 23 days to stage annually. The longest ever was in 1926 when it lasted for 29 days. It is estimated that as many as 10 million people watch some part of it, and the cost to the French economy has been estimated to be in excess of £1000 million.

The longest distance over which it has been run is 5745 km (3569 miles) in 1926. The greatest number of riders to take part was 162 in 1928, but only 41 finished.

The most wins have been five by Jacques Anquetil (Fra) 1957, 1961–64, and Eddy Merckx (Bel) 1969–72, 1974. The fastest average speed was by Bernard Hinault (Fra) in 1981 when he averaged 37·84 km/h (23·51 mph). The closest race ever was in 1968 when Jan Janssen (Hol) beat Herman van Springel (Bel) by 38 sec after 25 days and 4665 km (2898·7 miles).

Winners from 1970:

1970 Eddy Merckx (Bel)
1971 Eddy Merckx (Bel)
1972 Eddy Merckx (Bel)
1973 Luis Ocana (Spa)
1974 Eddy Merckx (Bel)
1975 Bernard Thevenet (Fra)
1976 Lucien van Impe (Bel)
1977 Bernard Thevenet (Fra)
1978 Bernard Hinault (Fra)
1979 Bernard Hinault (Fra)
1980 Joop Zoetemelk (Hol)
1981 Bernard Hinault (Fra)
1982 Bernard Hinault (Fra)

Right: **The Belgian cyclist Eddy Merckx in the position he held so often, the lead, in the greatest free show in sport, the Tour de France. Seen wearing the traditional yellow jersey of the race leader, his record in the 23-day event, watched by some ten million spectators annually, is unsurpassed, with five victories and one second placing.**

CYCLING—WORLD RECORDS (As at 31 May 1983)

Professionals

Event	min	sec	Open Air Tracks Name/Country	Venue	Year	min	sec	Indoor Tracks Name/Country	Venue	Year
Flying start										
200 m		10·8	Antonio Maspes (Ita)	Rome	1960		10·99	Oskar Plattner (Swi)	Zurich	1961
500 m		28·75	Robert Dill-Bundi (Swi)	Zurich	1982		28·60	Oskar Plattner (Swi)	Zurich	1956
1 km	1	02·46	Patrick Sercu (Fra)	Milan	1973	1	01·23	Patrick Sercu (Fra)	Antwerp	1967
Standing start										
1 km	1	06·79	Urs Freuler (Swi)	Zurich	1981	1	06·603	Urs Freuler (Swi)	Zurich	1981
5 km	5	50·71	Hans-Henrik Oersted (Den)	Mexico City	1980	5	59·099	Hans-Henrik Oersted (Den)	Copenhagen	1980
10 km	11	53·2	Eddy Merckx (Bel)	Mexico City	1972	12	26·8	Roger Rivière (Fra)	Paris	1958
20 km	24	06·8	Eddy Merckx (Bel)	Mexico City	1972	25	18·0	Siegfried Adler (FRG)	Zurich	1968
1 Hour	49	431 m	Eddy Merckx (Bel)	Mexico City	1972	46	847 m	Siegfried Adler (FRG)	Zurich	1968

Amateurs

Event	min	sec	Open Air Tracks Name/Country	Venue	Year	min	sec	Indoor Tracks Name/Country	Venue	Year
Flying start										
200 m		10·58	Gordon Singleton (Can)	Mexico City	1980		10·369	Sergei Kopylov (USSR)	Moscow	1981
500 m		27·31	Gordon Singleton (Can)	Mexico City	1980		28·040	Sergei Kopylov (USSR)	Moscow	1982
1 km		59·682	Anthony Cuff (NZ)	Mexico City	1980	1	00·279	Sergei Kopylov (USSR)	Moscow	1982
Standing start										
1 km	1	02·547	Marc Malchow (GDR)	Mexico City	1980	1	02·955	Lothar Thoms (GDR)	Moscow	1980
4 km	4	40·23	Hans-Henrik Oersted (Den)	Mexico City	1979	4	39·96	Harald Wolf (GDR)	Moscow	1980
5 km	5	50·68	Hans-Henrik Oersted (Den)	Mexico City	1979	5	50·21	Aleksandr Krasnov (USSR)	Moscow	1983
10 km	11	54·906	Hans-Henrik Oersted (Den)	Mexico City	1979	12	06·29	Hans-Henrik Oersted (Den)	Copenhagen	1978
20 km	24	35·63	Hans-Henrik Oersted (Den)	Mexico City	1979	24	52·83	Mikhail Svechnikov (USSR)	Moscow	1983
1 Hour	48	200 m	Hans-Henrik Oersted (Den)	Mexico City	1979	46	745 m	Daniel Gisiger (Swi)	Zurich	1977

Women

Event	min	sec	Open Air Tracks Name/Country	Venue	Year	min	sec	Indoor Tracks Name/Country	Venue	Year
Flying start										
200 m		11·547	Natalia Krouchelnitskaya (USSR)	Moscow	1982		11·914	Galina Tsareva (USSR)	Moscow	1980
500 m		31·112	Natalia Krouchelnitskaya (USSR)	Moscow	1982		32·302	Galina Tsareva (USSR)	Moscow	1980
						1	09·077	Galina Tsareva (USSR)	Moscow	1980
1 km	1	12·36	Erika Saloumian (USSR)	Erevan	1982					
Standing start										
1 km	1	14·97	Sylvia Burka (Can)	Montreal	1982	1	15·66	Rosella Galbiatti (Ita)	Milan	1981
3 km	3	52·50	Tatyana Garkouchkina (USSR)	Montreal	1974		—			
5 km	6	41·75	Mandy Jones (GB)	Leicester	1982	6	42·273	Galina Tsareva (USSR)	Moscow	1982
10 km	13	34·39	Cornelia Hage (Hol)	Munich	1978		—			
20 km	27	26·66	Cornelia Hage (Hol)	Munich	1978		—			
1 Hour	43	082 m	Cornelia Hage (Hol)	Munich	1978		—			

TOUR OF BRITAIN: First held in 1951 and known as the 'Milk Race', it is for amateurs only. It has been won twice by Bill Bradley (GB) 1959 and 1960, Les West (GB) 1965 and 1967, and Fedor den Hertog (Hol) 1969 and 1971. The fastest speed was in 1971 when Fedor den Hertog averaged 40·55 km/h (25·20 mph) over 1763·8 km (1096 miles). The longest race was in 1953 over a distance of 2624·8 km (1631 miles). The closest finish was in 1976 when Bill Nickson (GB) beat Joe Waugh (GB) by 5 sec after 14 days and 1665·6 km (1035 miles).

Individual winners from 1970:

1970 Jiri Mainus (Cz)
1971 Fedor den Hertog (Hol)
1972 Hennie Kuiper (Hol)
1973 Piet van Katwijk (Hol)
1974 Roy Schuiten (Hol)
1975 Bernt Johansson (Swe)
1976 Bill Nickson (GB)
1977 Said Gusseinov (USSR)
1978 Jan Brzezny (Pol)
1979 Yuri Kachinine (USSR)
1980 Ivan Mitchtenko (USSR)
1981 Sergei Krivocheyev (USSR)
1982 Yuri Kashurin (USSR)
1983 Matt Eaton (USA)

WORLD CHAMPIONSHIPS: Amateur titles were instituted in 1893 and followed two years later by professional championships. The most titles won by an amateur is eight (including an Olympic gold medal) sprint titles by Daniel Morelon (Fra) 1966–67, 1969–73, and 1975. The most by a professional is seven, also sprint titles, by Jef Scherens (Bel) 1932–37 and 1947, and by Antonio Maspes (Ita) 1955–56, 1959–62 and 1964. The most titles by a woman is seven on track and road by Beryl Burton (GB) between 1959 and 1967, and Yvonne Reynders (Bel) between 1959 and 1966.

OLYMPIC GAMES: Cycling has been in the Games since 1896. The most wins have been three by Paul Masson (Fra) in 1896, Francisco Verri (Ita) in 1906 and Robert Charpentier (Fra) in 1936, although in the highly unofficial events of the 1904 Games, the American Marcus Hurley won four.

BRITISH CHAMPIONSHIPS: Among the men, Albert White won 12 track championships at varying distances. He was also one of the pair who won three tandem titles from 1920 to 1925. However, all men are overshadowed by the number of titles acquired by Beryl Burton in a 22-year career. Her current total includes 23 times British all-round champion, 14 track pursuit titles, 12 British Cycling Federation road race championships, and 68 Road Time Trials Council titles.

The tactics of sprint cycling on the track. Timing is taken for the last 200 m only and the rest of the distance consists of manoeuvring for position. During this phase of the competition riders will sometimes remain virtually stationary in the effort to make opponents take the lead.

SPEED: The highest speed ever attained on a bicycle is 226·1 km/h (140·5 mph) by Allan Abbott (USA) on the Bonneville Salt Flats, USA in August 1973, on his home-built machine behind a wind shield mounted on a car. In June 1899 Charles 'Mile-a-Minute' Murphy (USA) achieved the then seemingly impossible speed of 100·23 km/h (62·28 mph) behind a train on the Long Island Railroad, New York. A special wooden surface was laid over the sleepers on the line.

The greatest distance covered in one hour is 122·7 km (76 miles 504 yd) on the Montlhery Motor Circuit, France, by Leon Vanderstuft (Bel) in 1928. He was paced by a motorcycle. The record distance covered in 24 hours is 1384·3 km (860 miles 367 yd) by Hubert Opperman (Aus) in Melbourne in 1932, also paced.

SIX-DAY RACING: Introduced around the turn of the century, the Six-Day race reached the height of popularity in the 1920s and 1930s, but is still very popular on the Continent. The former Belgian sprint star Patrick Sercu has gained a record 88 victories at this form of racing, over a period of 19 years, to 31 May 1983.

BRITISH ROAD RECORDS (As at 31 May 1983)

Distance	hr	min	sec	Name	Date
25 miles		46	23	Alan Richards	1 Sept 1977
50 miles	1	35	45	David Lloyd	26 Oct 1974
100 miles	3	28	40	Ray Booty	28 Sept 1956
1000 miles	2 days 10	40	00	Reg Randel	19–21 Aug 1960

PLACE-TO-PLACE

	hr	min	sec	Name	Date
London–York (197 miles)	7	41	13	Bob Addy	6 Aug 1972
Land's End–London (287 miles)	12	34	00	Robert Maitland	17 Sept 1954
London–Edinburgh (380 miles)	18	49	42	Cliff Smith	2 Nov 1965
Land's End–John O'Groats (847 miles)	1 day 21	03	16	John Woodburn	13–15 Aug 1982
Land's End–John O'Groats (Women)	2 days 11	07	00	Eileen Sheridan	9–11 June 1954

LONG DISTANCE

A German-born lecturer, Walter Stolle, who now lives in Romford, Essex, spent 18 years, from January 1959 to December 1976, touring the world. Visiting 159 countries he covered over 643 700 km (402 000 miles) on his bicycle—suffering more than 1000 punctures.

Starting in 1922 Englishman Tommy Chambers kept a note of his mileage, and by the end of 1973 he had ridden 1 286 517 km (799 405 miles). After 51 years of riding he had a bad fall on Christmas Day 1973 and had to stop his cycling exploits. In June 1980, John Marino (USA) cycled across the United States, from Santa Monica, California to New York in 12 days 3 hr 41 min breaking his own record for the 4604 km (2861 miles) by 22 hours.

Competitors in the gruelling sport of Cyclo-Cross carrying their machines over a ridge. The sport involves racing over rough country, which often necessitates the rider having to manhandle or carry his bicycle. Championships were held unofficially on the Continent in the 1920s and 1930s, and officially from 1950. In 1967 amateurs and professionals were separated into their own races.

Darts

Darts developed from the heavily weighted throwing arrows used in Roman and Greek warfare. It is said that the Pilgrim Fathers played darts on the *Mayflower* on their way to the New World in 1620. The modern game had its beginnings in 1896 when a Lancashire carpenter, Brian Gamlin, devised the present numbering system on the board. The first known score of 180—three treble 20s—was by John Reader at the Highbury Tavern in Sussex in 1902.

Maureen Flowers, one of the few women in the game of darts who can match all but the very best of the men. Here she is holding the British Ladies Pony Individual trophy after her second win in 1980.

WORLD PROFESSIONAL CHAMPIONSHIP
(instituted in 1978)
1978 Leighton Rees (Wal) beat John Lowe (Eng)
1979 John Lowe (Eng) beat Leighton Rees (Wal)
1980 Eric Bristow (Eng) beat Bobby George (Eng)
1981 Eric Bristow (Eng) beat John Lowe (Eng)
1982 Jocky Wilson (Sco) beat John Lowe (Eng)
1983 Keith Deller (Eng) beat Eric Bristow (Eng)

WORLD MASTERS (instituted in 1974)
1974 Cliff Inglis (Devon) beat Harry Heenan (Glasgow)
1975 Alan Evans (Stockport) beat David Jones (Rhymney)
1976 John Lowe (Derbyshire) beat Phil Obbard (Pencoed)
1977 Eric Bristow (London) beat Paul Reynolds (Wakefield)
1978 Ron Davis (Newcastle) beat Tony Brown (Dover)
1979 Eric Bristow (London) beat Allan Hogg (Ontario, Can)
1980 John Lowe (Derbyshire) beat Rab Smith (Dumfries)
1981 Eric Bristow (London) beat John Lowe (Derbyshire)
1982 Dave Whitcombe (Kent) beat Jocky Wilson (Fife)

WORLD CUP: First held in 1977, for teams of four and an individual title.

	Individual	Team
1977	Leighton Rees (Wal)	Wales
1979	Nicky Virachkul (USA)	England
1981	John Lowe (Eng)	England

BRITISH OPEN CHAMPIONSHIP (instituted in 1975)
1975	Alan Evans (Wal)	1980	Cliff Lazarenko (Eng)
1976	Jack North (Eng)	1981	Eric Bristow (Eng)
1977	John Lowe (Eng)	1982	Jocky Wilson (Sco)
1978	Eric Bristow (Eng)	1983	Eric Bristow (Eng)
1979	Tony Brown (Eng)		

NEWS OF THE WORLD CHAMPIONSHIPS: Started in 1927 as a London area competition, it then encompassed other areas until the war stopped it in 1939. Restarted in 1947–48 as a national tournament. The format is best of three legs of 501, from a distance of 2·45 m (8 ft). Four men have won the title twice. *Winners from 1970:*

1970	Henry Barney	1977	Mick Norris
1971	Dennis Filkins	1978	Stefan Lord (Swe)
1972	Brian Netherton	1979	Bobby George
1973	Ivor Hodgkinson	1980	Stefan Lord (Swe)
1974	Peter Chapman	1981	John Lowe
1975	Derek White	1982	Roy Morgan
1976	Bill Lennard	1983	Eric Bristow

LEAST DARTS
Scores of 201, 301, 401, and 501, have been made with the minimum possible four, six, seven and nine darts respectively on numerous occasions. The best for 1001 is 19 (minimum possible 17) by Cliff Inglis in November 1975, scoring 160, 180, 140, 180, 121, 180, and 40. Alan Evans made 2001 in 52 darts (minimum 34) in 1976. A score of 3001 in 79 darts (minimum 51) was achieved by Charlie Ellix at the Victoria Hotel, Tottenham in April 1977, watched by British Open champion, John Lowe.

DOUBLE SPEED
Bill Duddy went round the board in doubles, including the bull, from a distance of 2·74 m (9 ft), retrieving his own darts, in 2 min 13 sec, at The Plough, Harringey in October 1972. He claims to have beaten that time in an unverified attempt.

ENDURANCE AND SKILL
In a 24-hour-period, 26–27 May 1981, eight players from the Royal Hotel, Newsome, Huddersfield, using only one board, scored a total of 1 358 731.

Another eight players, from the Sir John Barleycorn, Bitterne, Hampshire, scored 1 000 001 with 39 566 darts in April 1980—averaging over 25 per dart.

Two Australians, Bruce Campbell and Peter Dawson, scored 487 588 in a 10-hour period in October 1978, while Englishman Nick Korn scored 2814 doubles, also in 10 hours, at Newquay, Cornwall in March 1978.

Equestrianism

Men have ridden horses for 5000 years. The Athenian General and historian Xenophon wrote a treatise on horsemanship 2300 years ago but it was not until the 16th century that schools of horsemanship, or equitation, became established, primarily in Italy and then in France. In Britain the first official competitions were held in 1865 under the auspices of the Royal Dublin Society, while the first jumping contest was at the Agricultural Hall, Islington, London in 1869. The dressage event was a direct outcome of the exercises taught in the early Italian and French academies. The three-day event developed from cavalry endurance rides, one of the earliest being from Vienna to Berlin in 1892.

OLYMPIC GAMES: There was a jumping event in the Games of 1900, but a full equestrian programme was not instituted until 1912.

Hans-Günter Winkler (FRG) won a record five gold medals in jumping (team and individual events) from 1956 to 1972, although Pierre Jonquières d'Oriola (Fra) is the only man to win the individual title twice, in 1952 and 1964.

In dressage, Henri St Cyr (Swe) has won four golds, including a unique two in the individual competition 1952–56. St Cyr was also a member of the winning Swedish team in 1948, but subsequently they were disqualified because one of them was not a military officer as the rules at that time decreed. Emphasising the increasingly successful role of women in this sport, the most medals ever won is five by Liselott Linsenhoff (FRG) between 1956 and 1972.

In the three-day event, Charles Pahud de Mortanges (Hol) won a record four gold medals, including two individual titles, from 1924 to 1932, as well as a team silver. Britain's only triple equestrian gold medallist is Richard Meade with an individual gold in 1972 and team titles in 1968 and 1972.

OLDEST
The oldest British competitor in the Olympic equestrian events was Lorna Johnstone (GB) who was placed 12th in the 1972 dressage competition five days after celebrating her 70th birthday, at her third Games. As a youngster of 54 she had been placed 21st at Stockholm in 1956. Her appearance at Munich gave her the additional distinction of being Britain's oldest ever international representative, at any sport at such a high level.

The foremost lady three-day event rider in the world, Lucinda Prior-Palmer (now Mrs David Green). She has won two European championships as well as five titles at Badminton.

WORLD CHAMPIONSHIPS: In show jumping (instituted in 1953 and now held quadrennially) both Hans-Günter Winkler (FRG) in 1954 and 1955, and Raimondo d'Inzeo (Ita) in 1956 and 1960, have won two titles. The women's title (instituted 1965) which was held separately until 1974, was also won twice by Janou Lefebvre-Tissot (Fra) in 1970 and 1974.

Men		Women	
1953	Francisco Goyoago (Spa)	1965	Marion Coakes (GB)
1954	Hans-Günter Winkler (FRG)	1970	Janou Lefebvre (Fra)
1955	Hans-Günter Winkler (FRG)	1974	Janou Tissot (Fra)
1956	Raimondo d'Inzeo (Ita)		
1960	Raimondo d'Inzeo (Ita)		
1966	Pierre d'Oriola (Fra)		
1970	David Broome (GB)		
1974	Hartwig Steenken (FRG)	*Team*	
1978	Gerd Wiltfang (FRG)	1978	Great Britain
1982	Norbert Koof (FRG)	1982	France

Championships for dressage were first held in 1966.

	Individual	*Team*
1966	Josef Neckarmann (FRG)	West Germany
1970	Elena Petouchkova (USSR)	USSR
1974	Reiner Klimke (FRG)	West Germany
1978	Christine Stückelberger (Swi)	West Germany
1982	Reiner Klimke (FRG)	West Germany

The three-day event title has been won twice by Bruce Davidson (USA) since it was introduced in 1966.

	Individual	*Team*
1966	Carlos Moratorio (Arg)	Ireland
1970	Mary Gordon-Watson (GB)	Great Britain
1974	Bruce Davidson (USA)	USA
1978	Bruce Davidson (USA)	Canada
1982	Lucinda Green (GB)	Great Britain

PRESIDENT'S CUP: Awarded to the country with the best results in the series of Nations Cup competitions each season. Great Britain has won it a record nine times, since its institution in 1965.

1965	Great Britain	1974	Great Britain
1966	USA	1975	West Germany
1967	Great Britain	1976	West Germany
1968	USA	1977	Great Britain
1969	West Germany	1978	Great Britain
1970	Great Britain	1979	Great Britain
1971	West Germany	1980	France
1972	Great Britain	1981	West Germany
1973	Great Britain	1982	West Germany

BADMINTON THREE-DAY EVENT: Instituted in 1949, it has been won on five occasions by Lucinda Green (née Prior-Palmer) in 1973, 1976–77, 1979 and 1983. Capt Mark Phillips was successful in 1971–72, 1974 and 1981.

ROYAL INTERNATIONAL HORSE SHOW: First held at Olympia in 1907 it is now staged at Wembley every year. The two most important events are the King George V Gold Cup (first held 1911) and the Queen Elizabeth II Cup, for women, (first held 1949). The KGV Gold Cup has been won five times by David Broome between 1960 and 1981. The QEII Cup has been won four times by Liz Edgar between 1977 and 1982. Only one horse, *Sunsalve*, has won both cups, ridden by Elisabeth Anderson in 1957 and by David Broome in 1960.

BRITISH SHOW JUMPING ASSOCIATION CHAMPIONSHIPS: The most men's BSJA titles won is five by Alan Oliver between 1951 and 1970, but Pat Smythe won eight women's championships between 1952 and 1962. Her three victories on *Flanagan* in 1955, 1958 and 1962 make it the only horse to win three times.

JUMPING RECORDS
The official FEI (Fédération Equestre Internationale) high jump record is 2·47 m (8 ft 1¼ in) by Capt Alberto Morales

When 22-year-old Welshman Rowland Fernyhough was part of the British show jumping team at Montreal in 1976 it was his first competition in a major championship. He is seen here on his most successful horse, *Autumatic*, negotiating the infamous Bank at Hickstead.

(Chile) on *Huasó* at Santiago in 1949, but there are several reports of much higher jumps. The most extreme is a 2·89 m (9 ft 6 in) clearance by *Ben Bolt* at the 1938 Royal Horse Show in Sydney, Australia. Jack Martin rode *Golden Meade* over 2·59 m (8 ft 6 in) at Cairns, Queensland in July 1946, but the official Australian record stands at 2·54 m (8 ft 4 in) by *Flyaway*, ridden by Colin Russell in 1939, and *Golden Meade* in 1946, this time ridden by A. L. Payne. The greatest height reached by a woman is 2·34 m (7 ft 8 in) by Katrina Towns-Musgrove (Aus) on *Big John* at Cairns in 1978.

The official long jump record is 8·40 m (27 ft 6¾ in) by *Something* ridden by André Ferreira at Johannesburg, South Africa on 26 April 1975, but there have been many longer jumps recorded. These gain rather more credence when one considers that the official record is 60 cm (1 ft 11¾ in) less than the world record by a man. The Australian record is 10·00 m (32 ft 10 in) by *Monarch* at Brisbane in 1951, but *Solid Gold* jumped 11·05 m (36 ft 3 in) at the Wagga Show, New South Wales in 1936. In the United States *Heatherbloom*, ridden by Dick Donnelly, is reputed to have cleared 11·28 m (37 ft) when high jumping 2·51 m (8 ft 3 in) at Richmond, Virginia in 1903. The most extreme claim made is for *Jerry M*, the 1912 Grand National Steeplechase winner at Aintree who is alleged to have jumped 12·19 m (40 ft) over water there.

BRITISH RECORDS

The highest jump achieved in Britain is 2·32 m (7 ft 7¼ in) by *Lastic*, ridden by Nick Skelton, at Olympia in December 1978. At the same venue, in June 1937, the Lady Wright (formerly Margery Bullows) set a record for a woman rider of 2·23 m (7 ft 4 in) on *Jimmy Brown*, a liver chestnut horse.

Fencing

Swords have been in use as combat weapons since ancient times. The first indication of fencing as a sport or pastime is on a relief in the temple of Medinet Habu, Luxor, Egypt built by Ramses III about 1190 BC, although it seems likely that it was used in religious ceremonies some two centuries before. The modern sport developed directly from the duelling, often to the death, of the Middle Ages. In the early 14th century the Marxbrüder Fencing Guild was flourishing in Frankfurt, Germany. In Britain, Edward I had specifically banned fencing tournaments in the City of London in 1285. Henry VIII, some 250 years later, founded the Corporation of Masters of Defence which was probably the first governing body of any sport in the country. The mask was introduced by a Frenchman, La Boessière in about 1780.

There are three swords used today. With the foil, introduced in the 17th century, only the trunk of the body is acceptable as a target. The épée, established in the mid-19th century, is rather heavier and more rigid than the foil and has the whole body as a valid target. The sabre, introduced in the late-19th century, has cutting edges on the front and back of the blade, and can only score on the whole body from the waist upwards. In foil and épée hits are scored with the point of the weapon, but with the sabre scoring is allowed using all of the front edge and part of the back edge of the blade.

WORLD CHAMPIONSHIPS: Other than at the Olympic Games, genuine world championships were not introduced until 1937, although the European titles, inaugurated in 1921 for men, were styled 'world championships'. The most world titles won is four by Christian d'Oriola (Fra) in 1947, 1949, 1953–54, which, with his two Olympic gold medals, gives him a total of six individual titles. Aleksandr Romankov (USSR) also won four foil titles between 1974 and 1982. The women's title,

only with foil, established in 1929, has been won twice by Hélène Mayer (Ger), Ilona Elek (Hun) and Ellen Muller-Preis (Aut), but only Elek also won two Olympic titles. The team titles have been dominated by the USSR with 13 foil victories, Italy with 10 at épée, and Hungary with 17 sabre wins. The USSR have won the women's foil team title 14 times.

OLYMPIC GAMES: Fencing was included in the 1896 Games. The most individual gold medals won is three by Ramón Fonst (Cub) in 1900 and 1904, and Nedo Nadi (Ita) 1912 and 1920.

In 1920 Nadi also won three team golds making a record total of five in one Games. His countryman, Edoardo Mangiarotti, won a record 13 medals between 1936 and 1960, comprising six gold, five silver and two bronze. The most gold medals won by a woman is four by Elena Novikova-Belova (USSR), comprising one individual and three team from 1968 to 1976. Ildikó Sagi-Retjö (Hun) won a total of seven medals, two gold, three silver and two bronze, from 1960 to 1976.

BRITAIN AT THE OLYMPICS: The only Briton to win an Olympic fencing gold medal is Gillian Sheen who won the women's foil in 1956. The most medals won by a British fencer is three, all silver, by Edgar Seligman in the épée team from 1906 to 1912. Bill Hoskyns competed for Britain in the Olympic Games épée competitions from 1956 to 1976, six celebrations, which is a record for any British sportsman. He won a team silver in 1960 and an individual silver in 1964.

A Hungarian fencer, Laszlo Petho, in unusual guise—in the épée event. His country's strongest event has traditionally been the sabre, at which they have won 11 individual and nine team gold medals in Olympic competition. However, they have also managed to take the épée team gold medal on three occasions.

Fishing (Angling)

From time immemorial men have fished the seas and rivers of the world for food, but fishing for pleasure and leisure seems to have been practised in Egypt, according to wall paintings, from the 5th Dynasty, 2470–2320 BC. On Tomb inscriptions, Amenemhat, a prince of Beni Hasan, is described as 'overseer of the swamps of enjoyment', a reference interpreted as fishing grounds.

WORLD CHAMPIONSHIPS: Initially held as European championships in 1953, the World Championships were instituted in 1957, under the auspices of the Confédération Internationale de la Pêche Sportive. The individual title has been won, uniquely, three times by Robert Tesse (Fra) in 1959–60 and 1969. The French team has won on a record 12 occasions between 1956 and 1981. The greatest weight of fish totalled by a team is 34·715 kg (76 lb 8 oz 8 dr) by West Germany on the Neckar at Mannheim in September 1980. The record by a single angler is 16·990 kg (37 lb 7 oz 3 dr) by Wolf-Rüdiger Kremkus of that same German team on the previous day to the team title. The greatest number of fish caught in a world championship is 652 by Jacques Isenbaert (Bel) when winning at Dunajvaros, Yugoslavia in 1967.

BRITISH CHAMPIONSHIPS: It is estimated that there are 3¾ million anglers in Britain. The National Angling Championships first held in 1906, have been won seven times by the Leeds club, between 1909 and 1952. One of their members, James Bazley, is the only man to win the individual title twice, in 1909 and 1927. The greatest weight caught by a team is 62·120 kg (136 lb 15¼ oz) by Sheffield Amalgamated in the Huntspill, Somerset in 1955. David Burr of Rugby caught the record individual weight of 34·720 kg (76 lb 9 oz) also in the Huntspill in 1965. The largest single fish caught was a carp weighing 6·406 kg (14 lb 2 oz) by John Essex in the Nene at Peterborough in 1975.

LARGEST CATCH, FRESHWATER
The biggest single catch ever ratified was on the Snake River, Idaho, USA in 1956 when Willard Cravens caught a white sturgeon weighing 163·29 kg (360 lb). However, that may not be the last word as two years previously, in the same river, Glenn Howard claims to have caught one which weighed 178 kg (394 lb). At the other end of the scale is a smelt caught by Peter Christian in Norfolk, in 1977, which weighed all of one dram (1/16th oz), but which won him a competition, as none of the other 107 competitors caught anything.

The biggest catch made under non-competition conditions was in 1978 when a 188·6 kg (416 lb) Nile perch was netted in Lake Victoria, Kenya.

LARGEST CATCH, SALTWATER
For a fish to be officially ratified by the International Game Fish Association, very stringent rules, relating to equipment used and method caught, have to be complied with. The largest fish so recognised is a white shark of 1208 kg (2664 lb) caught by Alf Dean on a 58 kg (130 lb) line at Denial Bay, South Australia on 21 April 1959. However, a white shark of 1537 kg (3388 lb) was caught by Clive Green off the coast of Western Australia in 1976, but he used whale meat bait which is unacceptable for record purposes.

Even larger sharks have been harpooned, such as that 9·00 m (29 ft 6 in) long, weighing over 4536 kg (10 000 lb) which was landed after a lengthy fight by fishermen at San Miguel harbour in the Azores in June 1978.

But the ultimate in fishing stories must be the blue whale killed with a hand harpoon by Archer Davidson in Twofold Bay, New South Wales, in 1910. It measured 29·56 m (97 ft) in length with tail flukes 6·09 m (20 ft) across.

LARGEST BRITISH CATCHES
When Edward Crutch caught a 571·5 kg (1260 lb) black marlin in October 1973 off Cairns, Queensland, Australia it was the heaviest fish ever caught on a rod by a British fisherman. The largest freshwater fish caught in a British river was a sturgeon weighing 230 kg (507½ lb) which was accidentally netted in the Severn at Lydney, Gloucestershire in June 1937. Four years earlier a legendary fish in the Towy, South Wales, was caught by Alec Allen. It turned out to be a 175·99 kg (388 lb) sturgeon which measured 2·79 m (9 ft 2 in) in length, and Allen had to enlist the help of a friend to land it. It is reported that a third man who was watching them ran off in terror when he saw the size of the fish.

SELECTED WORLD RECORDS

Freshwater

Species	kg	lb	oz	Name of Angler	Location	Year
Bass, largemouth	10·09	22	4	George W. Perry	Montgomery Lake, Georgia, USA	1932
Carp	25·08	55	5	Frank J. Ledwein	Clearwater Lake, Minnesota, USA	1952
Catfish, blue	43·99	97	0	Edward B. Elliott	Missouri River, South Dakota, USA	1959
Char, Arctic	13·46	29	11	Jeanne P. Branson	Arctic River, N.W. Territories, Canada	1968
Gar, alligator	126·55	279	0	Bill Valverde	Rio Grande, Texas, USA	1951
Grayling, Arctic	2·69	5	15	Jeanne P. Branson	Katseyedie River, N.W. Territories, Canada	1967
Perch, white	2·15	4	12	Mrs Earl Small	Mesalonskee Lake, Maine, USA	1949
Perch, yellow	1·91	4	3	C. C. Abbot	Bordentown, New Jersey, USA	1865
Pike, northern	28·35	62	8	Jurg Notzli	Reuss-Weiher, Rickenbach, Switzerland	1979
Salmon, Atlantic	35·89	79	2	Henrik Henriksen	Tana River, Norway	1928
Salmon, chinook	42·18	93	0	Howard C. Rider	Kelp Bay, Alaska, USA	1977
Salmon, chum	12·33	27	3	Robert A. Jahnke	Raymond Cove, Alaska, USA	1977
Salmon, coho	14·06	31	0	Mrs Lee Hallberg	Cowichan Bay, British Colombia, Canada	1947
Shad, American	4·19	9	4	J. Edward Whitman	Delaware River, Pennsylvania, USA	1979
Trout, brook	6·57	14	8	W. J. Cook	Nipigon River, Ontario, Canada	1916
Trout, brown	16·30	35	15	Eugenio Cavaglia	Nahuel Huapi, Argentina	1952
Trout, cutthroat	18·59	41	0	John Skimmerhorn	Pyramid Lake, Nevada, USA	1925
Trout, golden	4·98	11	0	Charles S. Reed	Cook's Lake, Wyoming, USA	1948
Trout, lake	29·48	65	0	Larry Daunis	Great Bear Lake, N.W. Territories, Canada	1970
Trout, rainbow	19·10	42	2	David R. White	Bell Island, Alaska, USA	1970
Walleye	11·34	25	0	Mabry Harper	Old Hickory Lake, Tennessee, USA	1960
Whitefish, lake	6·32	13	15	Wayne Caswell	Meaford, Ontario, Canada	1981
Whitefish, mountain	2·26	5	0	Orville Welch	Athabasca River, Alberta, Canada	1963

Thar she blows! Sea fishing from the shore is a
popular pastime around the coasts of Britain.

SELECTED WORLD RECORDS

Saltwater

Species	kg	lb	oz	Name of Angler	Location	Year
Albacore	40·00	88	2	Siegfried Dickemann	Mogan Port, Gran Canaria, Canary Is.	1977
Amberjack, greater	70·59	155	10	Joseph Dawson	Bermuda	1981
Bass, giant sea	255·60	563	8	James D. McAdam Jr	Anacapa Island, California, USA	1968
Bonito, Atlantic	7·60	16	12	Rolf Fedderies	Puerto Rio, Gran Canaria, Canary Is.	1980
Bonito, Pacific	10·65	23	8	Anne Cochain	Victoria, Mahe, Seychelles	1975
Cobia	50·03	110	5	Eric Tinworth	Mombasa, Kenya	1964
Cod	44·79	98	12	Alphonse J. Bielevich	Isle of Shoals, New Hampshire, USA	1969
Mackerel, king	40·82	90	0	Norton I. Thornton	Key West, Florida, USA	1976
Marlin, black	707·61	1560	0	Alfred C. Glassell Jr	Cabo Blanco, Peru	1953
Marlin, Atlantic blue	581·51	1282	0	Larry Martin	St Thomas, Virgin Is.	1977
Marlin, Pacific blue	624·14	1376	0	Jay de Beaubie	Kona Court, Hawaii	1982
Marlin, striped	206·50	455	4	Bruce Jenkinson	Major Island, New Zealand	1982
Marlin, white	82·49	181	14	Evando Luiz Coser	Vitoria, Brazil	1979
Sailfish, Atlantic	58·10	128	1	Harm Steyn	Luanda, Angola	1974
Sailfish, Pacific	100·24	221	0	C. W. Stewart	Santa Cruz Island, Ecuador	1947
Shark, blue	198·22	437	0	Peter Hyde	Catherine Bay, New South Wales, Australia	1976
Shark, hammerhead	449.50	991	0	Allen Ogle	Sarusota, Florida, WA	1982
Shark, porbeagle	210·92	465	0	Jorge Potier	Padstow, Cornwall, England	1976
Shark, shortfin mako	489·88	1080	0	James L. Melanson	Montauk, New York, USA	1979
Shark, thresher	335·20	739	0	Brian Galvin	Tutukaka, New Zealand	1975
Shark, tiger	807·40	1780	0	Walter Maxwell	Cherry Grove, S. Carolina, USA	1964
Shark, white	1208·38	2664	0	Alfred Dean	Denial Bay, South Australia	1959
Snook	24·32	53	10	Gilbert Ponzi	Rio de Parasmina, Costa Rica	1978
Swordfish	536·15	1182	0	L. Marron	Iquique, Chile	1953
Tarpon	128·36	283	0	M. Salazar	Lake Maracaibo, Venezuela	1956
Tuna, Atlantic bigeye	170·32	375	8	Cecil Browne	Ocean City, Maryland, USA	1977
Tuna, Pacific bigeye	197·31	435	0	Russell V. Lee	Cabo Blanco, Peru	1957
Tuna, blackfin	19·05	42	0	Alan J. Card	Bermuda	1978
Tuna, bluefin	679·00	1496	0	Ken Fraser	Aulds Cove, Nova Scotia, Canada	1979
Tuna, dogtooth	88·00	194	0	Kim Chul I	Kwan-Tall Es, Che Ju-Do, Korea	1980
Tuna, longtail	35·90	79	2	Tim Simpson	Montague Island, New South Wales, Australia	1982
Tuna, skipjack	18·94	41	12	Bruno de Ravel	Black River, Mauritius	1982
Tuna, southern bluefin	158·00	348	5	Rex Wood	Whakatane, New Zealand	1981
Tuna, yellowfin	176·35	388	12	Curt Wiesenhutter	San Benedicto Island, Mexico	1977
Wahoo	67·58	149	0	John Pirovano	Cat Cay, Bahamas	1962
Yellowtail, California	32·65	71	15	Michael Carpenter	Alijos Rocks, Mexico	1979
Yellowtail, southern	50·34	111	0	A. F. Plim	Bay of Islands, New Zealand	1961

SELECTED BRITISH RECORDS

Freshwater

Species	kg	lb	oz	Name of Angler	Location	Year
Bream, common bronze	6·12	13	8	A. R. Heslop	Private water, Staffs	1977
Carp	19·95	44	0	R. Walker	Redmire Pool	1952
Catfish, Weis	19·73	43	8	R. J. Bray	Wilstone Reservoir, Tring, Herts	1970

Pete Thomas holds Richard Walker's record carp, which weighed in at 44 lb and is the largest coarse fish on the British record list.

Species	kg	lb	oz	Name of Angler	Location	Year
Char	0·80	1	12	C. Imperiale	Loch Insh, Inverness	1974
Chub	3·34	7	6	W. L. Warren	Royalty Fishery, Hants	1957
Dace	0·57	1	4	J. L. Gasson	Little Ouse, Thetford, Norfolk	1960
Eel	5·04	11	2	S. Terry	Kingfisher Lake, Hants	1978
Grayling	1·27	2	13	P. B. Goldsmith	River Test, Romsey, Hants	1981
Gudgeon	0·12	4	4	M. J. Brown	Fish Pond, Ebbw Vale, Gwent	1977
Perch	2·15	4	12	S. F. Baker	Oulton Broad, Suffolk	1962
Pike	18·14	40	0	P. D. Hancock	Horsey Mere, Norfolk	1967
Roach	1·84	4	1	R. G. Jones	Gravel Pit, Notts	1975
Salmon	29·03	64	0	Miss G. W. Ballantyne	River Tay, Scotland	1922
Tench	4·57	10	1¼	A. J. Chester	Wilstone Reservoir, Tring, Herts	1981
Trout, brown	8·88	19	9	J. A. Jackson	Loch Quoich, Inverness	1978
Trout, rainbow	8·84	19	8	A. Pearson	Avington Fishery, Hants	1977

Saltwater

Species	kg	lb	oz	Name of Angler	Location	Year
Bass	8·33	18	6	R. G. Slater	off Eddystone Reef	1975
Brill	7·25	16	0	A. H. Fisher	Isle of Man	1950
Coalfish	15·16	33	7	L. M. Saunders	Start Point, off Dartmouth, Devon	1980
Cod	24·04	53	0	G. Martin	Start Point, Devon	1972
Common Skate	102·73	226	8	R. S. Macpherson	Duny Voe, Shetland Is.	1970
Conger	49·61	109	6	R. W. Potter	SE of Eddystone Light	1976
Dab	1·25	2	12	R. Islip	Gairloch, Wester Ross, Scotland	1975
Flounder	2·59	5	11	A. G. Cobbledick	Fowey, Cornwall	1956
Haddock	6·21	13	11	G. Bones	off Falmouth, Cornwall	1978
Hake	11·49	25	5	H. W. Steele	Belfast Lough, N. Ireland	1962
Halibut	106·13	234	0	C. Booth	Dunnet Head, Highland	1979
Herring	0·48	1	1	Brett Barden	off Bexhill-on-Sea, East Sussex	1973
Ling	25·92	57	2	H. Solomons	off Megavissey, Cornwall	1975
Mackerel	2·45	5	6	S. Beasley	north of Eddystone Light	1969
Opah	58·05	128	0	A. R. Blewitt	Mounts Bay, Cornwall	1973
Plaice	4·63	10	3	H. Gardiner	Longa Sound, Scotland	1974
Pollack	11·36	25	0	R. J. Vines	Lyme Bay, Devon	1980
Ray, bottle-nosed	34·47	76	0	R. Bulpitt	off The Needles, Isle of Wight	1970
Ray, electric	43·57	96	1	N. J. Cowley	off Dadman Point, Cornwall	1975
Ray, sting	27·89	61	8	V. W. Roberts	Cardigan Bay, Gwynedd	1979
Shark, blue	98·87	218	0	N. Sutcliffe	Looe, Cornwall	1959
Shark, mako	226·78	500	0	Mrs Y. M. Yallop	off Eddystone Light	1971
Shark, porbeagle	210·91	465	0	Jorge Potier	off Padstow, Cornwall	1976
Shark, thresher	133·80	295	0	H. J. Aris	Dunose Head, Isle of Wight	1978
Sole	2·46	5	7	L. Dixon	Alderney, Channel Is.	1980
Sole, lemon	1·12	2	7	W. N. Callister	Douglas, Isle of Man	1980
Sunfish	48·98	108	0	T. F. Sisson	off Saundersfoot, Dyfed	1976
Tope	33·87	74	11	A. B. Harries	Caldy Island, Dyfed	1964
Tunny	385·99	851	0	L. Mitchell-Henry	Whitby, N. Yorkshire	1933
Turbot	15·30	33	12	R. Simcox	Salcombe, Devon	1980
Whiting	3·06	6	12	N. R. Croft	Falmouth, Cornwall	1981

Gliding

Man has sought to emulate the birds from early times, and the first successful 'glider pilot' may well have been the mythical Daedalus, of Athens, who made wings for himself and his son Icarus to escape captivity. Icarus soared too near the sun and melted the wax with which the wings were fastened, but according to legend his father flew from Crete to Sicily. In Italy, about AD 1500 Leonardo da Vinci defined the difference between gliding and powered flight in some drawings, and at the same period Danti of Perugia, an Italian mathematician, is said to have actually flown. However, the first authenticated man-carrying glider was designed by Sir George Cayley and bore his coachman across a valley in north Yorkshire in 1853.

WORLD CHAMPIONSHIPS: First held in 1937 and then biennially from 1948. The most world titles won is three by Helmut Reichman (FRG) in the Standard class 1970 and 1974, and 15 metre class in 1978, and by George Lee (GB) who won the Open class three times consecutively. *Winners from 1968:*

	Open Class	Standard Class	15 Metres Class
1968	Harro Wodl (Aut)	A. J. Smith (USA)	Not held
1970	George Moffat (USA)	Helmut Reichmann (FRG)	Not held
1972	Göran Ax (Swe)	Jan Wroblewski (Pol)	Not held
1974	George Moffat (USA)	Helmut Reichmann (FRG)	Not held
1976	George Lee (GB)	Ingo Renner (Aus)	Not held
1978	George Lee (GB)	Baer Selen (Hol)	Helmut Reichmann (FRG)
1981	George Lee (GB)	Marc Schroeder (Fra)	Göran Ax (Swe)

Soaring with the wind over 'a green and pleasant land'.

INTERNATIONAL GLIDING RECORDS (As at 31 March 1983)

Single-seaters

Discipline	Performance	Name/Nationality	Glider	Date
Height gain	12 894 m (42 303 ft)	P. F. Bikle (USA)	SGS 1–23E	25 Feb 1961
Absolute Altitude	14 102 m (46 266 ft)	P. F. Bikle (USA)	SGS 1–23E	25 Feb 1961
Straight Distance	1460·8 km (905·7 miles)	H. W. Grosse (FRG)	ASW–12	25 Apr 1972
Goal Flight	1254·26 km (777·6 miles)	B. L. Drake, D. N. Speight, S. H. Georgeson (NZ)	Nimbus 2	14 Jan 1978
Goal and Return	1634·7 km (1013·5 miles)	K. H. Striedieck (USA)	ASW–17	9 May 1977
Triangular Distance	1306·85 km (812·03 miles)	H. W. Grosse (FRG)	ASW–17	4 June 1981
100 km Triangle	195·18 km/h (121·28 mph)	I. Renner (Aus)	Nimbus 3	14 Dec 1982
300 km Triangle	158·67 km/h (98·59 mph)	H. W. Grosse (FRG)	ASW–17.	24 Dec 1980
500 km Triangle	151·28 km/h (94·00 mph)	G. Eckle (FRG)	ASW–17	10 Dec 1979
750 km Triangle	143·63 km/h (89·25 mph)	H. W. Grosse (FRG)	ASW–17	6 Jan 1982
1000 km Triangle	145·33 km/h (90·10 mph)	H. W. Grosse (FRG)	ASW–17	3 Jan 1979
1250 km Triangle	133·24 km/h (82·79 mph)	H. W. Grosse (FRG)	ASW–17	9 Dec 1980

Single-seaters (Women)

Discipline	Performance	Name/Nationality	Glider	Date
Height Gain	9119 m (29 918 ft)	Anne Burns (GB)	Skylark 3B	13 Jan 1961
Absolute Altitude	12 637 m (41 460 ft)	Sabrina Jackintell (USA)	Astir CS	14 Feb 1979
Straight Distance	949·7 km (590·11 miles)	Karla Karel (GB)	LS–3	20 Jan 1980
Goal Flight	731·6 km (453·6 miles)	Tamara Zaiganova (USSR)	A–15	29 July 1966
Goal and Return	1127·68 km (700·7 miles)	Doris Grove (USA)	Nimbus 2c	28 Sept 1981
Triangular Distance	814·01 km (505·8 miles)	Karla Karel (GB)	LS–3	9 Jan 1980
100 km Triangle	139·45 km/h (86·5 mph)	Susan Martin (Aus)	LS–3	2 Feb 1979
300 km Triangle	129·52 km/h (80·48 mph)	Susan Martin (Aus)	Ventus	5 Feb 1981
500 km Triangle	133·14 km/h (82·5 mph)	Susan Martin (Aus)	LS–3	29 Jan 1979
750 km Triangle	95·42 km/h (59·2 mph)	Karla Karel (GB)	LS–3	24 Jan 1979

Golf

As with so many games the origins of golf are not clear. The Chinese had *Ch'ui Wan*, a ball hitting game, which dates from the 2nd century BC, and the Romans played *paganica* with a bent stick and a leather covered ball stuffed with feathers. Other possible sources were the French *paille maille*, which came to Britain with the Normans in the 11th century AD, or the Dutch *Kolven*. This latter is referred to in a Brussels City Magistrates Ordinance of 1360 which prohibited the playing of the game. An earlier Belgian source refers to it being played on Boxing Day 1297 on a four-hole course in and around the village of Loenen aan de Vecht. It has also been suggested that golf originated with Scottish shepherds using their crooks to knock pebbles into rabbit holes. Somewhat firmer evidence exists in the stained glass window in Gloucester Cathedral, which dates from AD 1350 and portrays a golfer-like figure. In March 1457 'goff' was prohibited by an Act of Parliament in Scotland, and further bans were introduced by James III and James IV, although the latter is known to have played the game in 1504. There is a painting of Mary, Queen of Scots, playing at St Andrews in 1563, and at her trial in 1567, in connection with the murder of her husband Lord Henry Darnley, she was criticised for playing the game only a few days after his death. The first golf club of which there is written evidence is the Honourable Company of Edinburgh Golfers founded in March 1744, although the Royal Burgess Golfing Society of Edinburgh claims to date from 1735. The earliest golf balls were made of wood, and later of feathers inside a leather cover. In 1848 these were replaced by the 'guttie' or gutta percha ball, and then in 1902 by the rubber-cored ball invented by Coburn Haskell, an American dentist. Tournaments are conducted under match play or medal play conditions. In match play the game is decided by the number of holes won, whereas in medal or stroke play the result is decided by the total number of strokes taken in the round.

GOLF COURSES

The term 'links', which has become synonymous with golf course in recent years, originally referred to undulating sandy ground near seashore, and such sites in Scotland appear to have been the first golf courses. Undoubtedly the most famous course is that of the Royal and Ancient at St Andrews, where, although the club itself was not founded until 1754, golf had been played for the previous two centuries.

The longest course is the International GC, Bolton, Massachusetts. It was remodelled in 1969 by Robert Trent Jones to make it 7612 m (8325 yd) long from the 'Tiger' tees (par-77).

The young Mary, Queen of Scots, playing golf at St Andrews in 1563, following in the footsteps of her grandfather, James IV, who was the first golfer in history that we know by name.

76

The idyllic setting of the La Quinta Country Club at Palm Springs, California, whose 6904 yard, par-72, course is considered to be one of the more challenging on the American circuit.

The fifth (par-6) hole, 635 m (695 yd) long, has the largest green in the world, measuring over 2600 square metres (28 000 square feet). The largest bunker, or trap, known as 'Hell's Half Acre', is on the 535 m (585 yd) seventh hole at the Pine Valley GC, Clementon, New Jersey.

Golf was first played on the Moon in February 1971 by Capt Alan Shepard, Commander of the Apollo 14 spacecraft.

LONG HOLES
The longest hole in the world is the par-7 seventh on the Sano course, Satsuki GC, Japan which is 831 m (909 yd) long. The record for a British championship course is the 528 m (577 yd) sixth hole at Troon, Strathclyde.

WINNING
The most wins in the US Professional Golfers Association (PGA) tournaments in one season is 18, plus one tournament which did not have PGA Tour status, by Byron Nelson (USA) between March and August 1945. Included was a record 11 consecutive victories. The most official PGA Tour events won in a career is 84 by Sam Snead (USA) from 1936 to 1965. Snead has been credited with a total of 135 wins in all tournaments to the end of 1980.

The women's professional record is 84 victories by Kathy Whitworth (USA) between 1969 and 1983. Mickey Wright (USA) set a season record of 13 wins in 1963.

Jack Nicklaus (USA) is the only golfer to win five different major titles (The Open, US Open, Masters, PGA and US Amateur) on at least two occasions each, with a record 19 in total between 1959 and 1980. His unique record in the US Open consists of four first, seven second and two third places. The only man to achieve a Grand Slam of the US Open and Amateur and the British Open and Amateur was Bobby Jones (USA) in 1930.

The greatest number of club championship titles is 33 by Bernard Cusack (Aus) of Narembeen GC, Western Australia since 1943. The best by a British player is 27 by Eileen Ashton-Nairn at the Worsley GC, Manchester from 1925 to 1969.

The greatest margin of victory in a major tournament is 21 strokes by the 1976 US Open champion Jerry Pate when winning the Colombian Open in December 1981 with 262 (64, 67, 66, 65). Luis Arevalo (Col) was placed second with 283.

MOST SHOTS, ONE HOLE
The highest number of strokes taken at a single hole in a major tournament was achieved in the inaugural Open Championship at Prestwick in 1860, when an un-named player took 21. In the 1938 US Open, Ray Ainsley achieved instant fame when he took 19 strokes at the par-4 16th hole. Most of them were in an attempt to hit the ball out of a fast-moving brook. At Biarritz, France in 1888 it was reported that Chevalier von Cittern took 316 for 18 holes, thus averaging 17·55 strokes per hole. The story to top them all concerns a lady player in the qualifying round of a tournament in Shawnee-on-Delaware, Pennsylvania in the early part of the century. Her card showed she took 166 strokes for the short 118 m (130 yd) 16th hole. Her tee shot landed and floated in a nearby river, and with her meticulous husband she put out in a boat and eventually beached the ball about 2·4 km (1½ miles) downstream. From there she had to play through a wood until finally she holed the ball. It is reported that A. J. Lewis, playing at Peacehaven, Sussex in 1890 had 156 putts on one green without holing the ball.

HOLES IN ONE
The first recorded hole in one in a major tournament was in the 1868 Open at Prestwick when 'Young' Tom Morris did it at the eighth hole, 132·5 m (145 yd), on the way to the title. The American magazine *Golf Digest* recorded 35 757 such aces in 1981, which averages out to over 90 per day in the USA alone.

The longest straight hole, as opposed to a dog-leg or one with a curved fairway, aced was the 408 m (447 yd) tenth at Miracle Hills GC, Omaha, Nebraska achieved by Robert Mitera (USA) in October 1965. Mitera, a 21-year-old standing 1·68 m (5 ft 6 in) tall and weighing 75 kg (165 lb), was aided by generally downhill ground and a strong wind. The longest by a woman was 359 m (393 yd) by Marie Robie (USA) at the first hole of the Furnace Brook GC, Wollaston, Massachusetts in September 1949. The British male record is also 359 m (393 yd) by Peter Parkinson on the par-4 seventh hole at West Lancashire GC in June 1972.

The greatest reward for a hole in one was carried off when Isao Aoki (Jap) aced the 142 m (155 yd) second hole in the World Matchplay Championship at Wentworth, Surrey on 12 October 1979. He won a flat and furnishings valued at over £50 000 which had been put up as a prize for such a feat in that competition.

THE OPEN: It was first held on 17 October 1860, when it was organised by the Prestwick Club, Ayrshire. Originally played over 36 holes, since 1892 it has been contested annually over 72 holes of stroke play. The most victories have been six by Harry Vardon between 1896 and 1914. The greatest margin of victory was by 'Old' Tom Morris in 1862, 13 strokes ahead of Willie Park, who had won the first Open in 1860. Five years later, when he won his fourth title, Morris became the oldest ever

Four times winner of The Open, Tom Morris was only 47 when he received the accolade of 'Old' to differentiate him from his 17-year-old son 'Young' Tom who had taken his title from him in 1868.

Bernhard Langer, getting himself out of the rough and trouble in the 1981 Open. He became the first German golfer to head the European prize money list with a record £81 000 in 1981, in which year he also became the first home-bred golfer to win the German Open title. In the Benson and Hedges tournament at Fulford he received wide publicity for his televised wedge shot from up a tree.

Open champion at 46 yr 99 days. The following year, 1868, his son 'Young' Tom Morris became the youngest ever winner aged 17 yr 249 days. The lowest winning total is 268 (comprising rounds of 68, 70, 65, 65) by Tom Watson (USA) at Turnberry in 1977. The lowest round is 63 by Mark Hayes (USA) at Turnberry in 1977, and by Isao Aoki (Jap) at Muirfield in 1980. The record for the first 36 holes is 132 (67, 65) by Henry Cotton at Sandwich in 1934, while the best for 54 holes is 202 (68, 70, 64) by Tom Watson (USA) at Muirfield in 1980.

The first nine holes have been played in 29 strokes by Peter Thomson (Aus) and Tom Haliburton at Royal Lytham St Anne's in 1958, by Tony Jacklin at St Andrews in 1970, and by Bill Longmuir at Royal Lytham St Anne's in 1963. In the 64 tournaments between 1907 (when the title was first won by an overseas player—Arnaud Massy of France) and 1981, it has been won by foreign players on 45 occasions, including 28 by Americans, seven by South Africans, six by Australians and one each to French, Argentine, New Zealand and Spanish golfers.

		Score			Score
1860	Willie Park, Sr	174	1924	Walter Hagen (USA)	301
1861	Tom Morris, Sr	163	1925	James Barnes (USA)	300
1862	Tom Morris, Sr	163	1926	Robert T. Jones, Jr	
1863	Willie Park, Sr	168		(USA)	291
1864	Tom Morris, Sr	167	1927	Robert T. Jones, Jr	
1865	Andrew Strath	162		(USA)	285
1866	Willie Park, Sr	169	1928	Walter Hagen (USA)	292
1867	Tom Morris, Sr	170	1929	Walter Hagen (USA)	292
1868	Tom Morris, Jr	170	1930	Robert T. Jones, Jr	
1869	Tom Morris, Jr	154		(USA)	291
1870	Tom Morris, Jr	149	1931	Tommy Armour	
1871	Not held			(USA)	296
1872	Tom Morris, Jr	166	1932	Gene Sarazen (USA)	283
1873	Tom Kidd	179	1933	Denny Shute (USA)	292
1874	Mungo Park	159	1934	Henry Cotton	283
1875	Willie Park, Sr	166	1935	Alfred Perry	283
1876	Robert Martin	176	1936	Alfred Padgham	287
1877	Jamie Anderson	160	1937	Henry Cotton	283
1878	Jamie Anderson	157	1938	Reg Whitcombe	295
1879	Jamie Anderson	170	1939	Richard Burton	290
1880	Robert Ferguson	162	1946	Sam Snead (USA)	290
1881	Robert Ferguson	170	1947	Fred Daly	293
1882	Robert Ferguson	171	1948	Henry Cotton	284
1883	Willie Fernie	159	1949	Bobby Locke (Saf)	283
1884	Jack Simpson	160	1950	Bobby Locke (Saf)	279
1885	Bob Martin	171	1951	Max Faulkner	285
1886	David Brown	157	1952	Bobby Locke (Saf)	287
1887	Willie Park, Jr	161	1953	Ben Hogan (USA)	282
1888	Jack Burns	171	1954	Peter Thomson (Aus)	283
1889	Willie Park, Jr	155	1955	Peter Thomson (Aus)	281
1890	John Ball	164	1956	Peter Thomson (Aus)	286
1891	Hugh Kirkaldy	169	1957	Bobby Locke (Saf)	279
1892	Harold Hilton	305	1958	Peter Thomson (Aus)	278
1893	William Auchterlonie	322	1959	Gary Player (Saf)	284
1894	John Taylor	326	1960	Kel Nagle (Aus)	278
1895	John Taylor	322	1961	Arnold Palmer (USA)	284
1896	Harry Vardon	316	1962	Arnold Palmer (USA)	276
1897	Harry Hilton	314	1963	Bob Charles (NZ)	277
1898	Harry Vardon	307	1964	Tony Lema (USA)	279
1899	Harry Vardon	310	1965	Peter Thomson (Aus)	285
1900	John Taylor	309	1966	Jack Nicklaus (USA)	282
1901	James Braid	309	1967	Roberto de Vincenzo	
1902	Alexander Herd	307		(Arg)	278
1903	Harry Vardon	300	1968	Gary Player (Saf)	299
1904	Jack White	296	1969	Tony Jacklin	280
1905	James Braid	318	1970	Jack Nicklaus (USA)	283
1906	James Braid	300	1971	Lee Trevino (USA)	278
1907	Arnaud Massy (Fra)	312	1972	Lee Trevino (USA)	278
1908	James Braid	291	1973	Tom Weiskopf (USA)	276
1909	John Taylor	295	1974	Gary Player (Saf)	282
1910	James Braid	299	1975	Tom Watson (USA)	279
1911	Harry Vardon	303	1976	Johnny Miller (USA)	279
1912	Edward (Ted) Ray	295	1977	Tom Watson (USA)	268
1913	John Taylor	304	1978	Jack Nicklaus (USA)	281
1914	Harry Vardon	306	1979	Severiano Ballesteros	
1920	George Duncan	303		(Spa)	283
1921	Jock Hutchinson		1980	Tom Watson (USA)	271
	(USA)	296	1981	Bill Rogers (USA)	276
1922	Walter Hagen (USA)	300	1982	Tom Watson (USA)	284
1923	Arthur Havers	295			

US OPEN: First held on a nine-hole course at Newport, Rhode Island, in October 1895, after having been postponed for some weeks because it conflicted with the America's Cup yacht races. The first champion was Horace Rawlins, an Englishman, assistant professional at the Newport Club. The format is currently four 18-hole rounds, making a total of 72 holes of stroke play. There was a record entry of 4897 players for the qualifying rounds in 1978. The oldest champion was Ted Ray (GB) in 1920 aged 43 yr 4 months 16 days, and the youngest was John McDermott at 19 yr 10 months 14 days in 1911. The most wins is four by Willie Anderson from 1901 to 1905, Bobby Jones from 1923 to 1930, Ben Hogan from 1948 to 1953, and Jack Nicklaus from 1962 to 1980. The biggest margin of victory was 11 strokes by Willie Smith over George Low in 1899. The lowest score has been 272 by Jack Nicklaus in 1980, while the lowest round has been one of 63 by Johnny Miller in 1973, and by both Tom Weiskopf and Jack Nicklaus in 1980. The 36-hole record is 134 (63, 71) by Jack Nicklaus in 1980, while he (63, 71, 70) and Isao Aoki (Jap) (68, 68, 68) both set the 54-hole standard of 204, in 1980.

		Score			Score
1895	Horace Rawlins	173	1938	Ralph Guldahl	284
1896	James Foulis	152	1939	Byron Nelson	284
1897	Joe Lloyd	162	1940	Lawson Little	287
1898	Fred Herd	328	1941	Craig Wood	284
1899	Willie Smith	315	1946	Lloyd Mangrum	284
1900	Harry Vardon (GB)	313	1947	Lew Worsham	282
1901	Willie Anderson	331	1948	Ben Hogan	276
1902	Laurie Auchterlonie	307	1949	Gary Middlecoff	286
1903	Willie Anderson	307	1950	Ben Hogan	287
1904	Willie Anderson	303	1951	Ben Hogan	287
1905	Willie Anderson	314	1952	Julius Boros	281
1906	Alex Smith	295	1953	Ben Hogan	283
1907	Alex Ross	302	1954	Ed Furgol	284
1908	Fred McLeod	322	1955	Jack Fleck	287
1909	George Sargent	290	1956	Gary Middlecoff	281
1910	Alex Smith	298	1957	Dick Mayer	282
1911	John McDermott	307	1958	Tommy Bolt	283
1912	John McDermott	294	1959	Billy Casper	282
1913	Francis Ouimet	304	1960	Arnold Palmer	280
1914	Walter Hagen	290	1961	Gene Littler	281
1915	Jerome Travers	297	1962	Jack Nicklaus	283
1916	Charles Evans, Jr	286	1963	Julius Boros	293
1919	Walter Hagen	301	1964	Ken Venturi	278
1920	Edward Ray (GB)	295	1965	Gary Player (Saf)	282
1921	Jim Barnes	289	1966	Billy Casper	278
1922	Gene Sarazen	288	1967	Jack Nicklaus	275
1923	Robert T. Jones, Jr	296	1968	Lee Trevino	275
1924	Cyril Walker	297	1969	Orville Moody	281
1925	Willie Macfarlane	291	1970	Tony Jacklin (GB)	281
1926	Robert T. Jones, Jr	293	1971	Lee Trevino	280
1927	Tommy Armour	301	1972	Jack Nicklaus	290
1928	Johnny Farrell	294	1973	Johnny Miller	279
1929	Robert T. Jones, Jr	294	1974	Hale Irwin	287
1930	Robert T. Jones, Jr	287	1975	Lou Graham	287
1931	Billy Burke	292	1976	Jerry Pate	277
1932	Gene Sarazen	286	1977	Hubert Green	278
1933	John Goodman	287	1978	Andy North	285
1934	Olin Dutra	293	1979	Hale Irwin	284
1935	Sam Parks, Jr	299	1980	Jack Nicklaus	272
1936	Tony Manero	282	1981	David Graham (Aus)	273
1937	Ralph Guldahl	281	1982	Tom Watson (USA)	282

US MASTERS

First held in 1934 and always played over 72 holes of stroke play at the Augusta National Golf Course, Georgia. It has been won most often by Jack Nicklaus with five victories between 1963 and 1975. The oldest champion was Gary Player (Saf) at 42 yr 5 months 9 days in 1978, and the youngest was Severiano Ballesteros (Spa) aged 23 yr 4 days in 1980. The biggest margin of victory was nine strokes by Jack Nicklaus over Arnold Palmer and Gary Player in 1965. The lowest aggregate is 271 (67, 71, 64, 69) by Nicklaus in 1965, and Raymond Floyd (65, 66, 70, 70) in 1976. The lowest single round is 64, by Lloyd Mangrum in 1940, Jack Nicklaus in 1965, Maurice Bembridge (GB) in 1974, Hale Irwin in 1975, Gary Player (Saf) in 1978, and by

Of Mexican descent, but Texas-born, Lee Trevino is as renowned for his sunny disposition and constant banter on the course as for the quality of his play. He is only the fourth player to win The Open and the US Open in the same year.

Miller Barber in 1979. The 36-hole record is 131 (65, 66) by Raymond Floyd in 1976, when he also set the 54-hole standard with 201 by adding a round of 70.

18 days in 1968 and the youngest was Gene Sarazen aged 20 yr 5 months 20 days in 1922. Since 1958 the greatest margin of victory has been the seven-stroke lead by Nicklaus in 1980. The lowest aggregate was 271 by Bobby Nichols at Columbus, Ohio in 1964, and the lowest round was 63 by Bruce Crampton in 1975 and Ray Floyd in 1982. The lowest score for 36 holes has been 134 by Jerry Barber (69, 65) in 1959, Bruce Crampton (71, 63) in 1975 and Gil Morgan (66, 68) in 1976. The 54-hole mark is 202 (69, 66, 67) by Raymond Floyd in 1969.

		Score				Score
1934	Horton Smith	284	1962	Arnold Palmer		280
1935	Gene Sarazen	282	1963	Jack Nicklaus		286
1936	Horton Smith	285	1964	Arnold Palmer		276
1937	Byron Nelson	283	1965	Jack Nicklaus		271
1938	Henry Picard	285	1966	Jack Nicklaus		288
1939	Ralph Gudahl	279	1967	Gay Brewer		280
1940	Jimmy Demaret	280	1968	Bob Goalby		277
1941	Craig Wood	280	1969	George Archer		281
1942	Byron Nelson	280	1970	Billy Casper		279
1946	Herman Keiser	282	1971	Charles Coody		279
1947	Jimmy Demaret	281	1972	Jack Nicklaus		286
1948	Claude Harmon	279	1973	Tommy Aaron		283
1949	Sam Snead	282	1974	Gary Player (Saf)		278
1950	Jimmy Demaret	283	1975	Jack Nicklaus		276
1951	Ben Hogan	280	1976	Ray Floyd		271
1952	Sam Snead	286	1977	Tom Watson		276
1953	Ben Hogan	274	1978	Gary Player (Saf)		277
1954	Sam Snead	289	1979	Fuzzy Zoeller		280
1955	Cary Middlecoff	279	1980	Severiano Ballesteros		
1956	Jack Burke	289		(Spa)		275
1957	Doug Ford	283	1981	Tom Watson		280
1958	Arnold Palmer	284	1982	Craig Stadler		284
1959	Art Wall	284	1983	Severiano Ballesteros		
1960	Arnold Palmer	282		(Spa)		280
1961	Gary Player (Saf)	280				

US PROFESSIONAL GOLFERS' ASSOCIATION (PGA):

The PGA championship was first held in 1916 as a match play tournament but since 1958 it has been contested over 72 holes of stroke play. It has been won a record five times by Walter Hagan between 1921 and 1927, and Jack Nicklaus between 1963 and 1980. The oldest champion was Julian Boros at 48 yr

				Score
1916	James Barnes	1952	Jim Turnesa	
1919	James Barnes	1953	Walter Burkemo	
1920	Jock Hutchison	1954	Chick Harbert	
1921	Walter Hagen	1955	Doug Ford	
1922	Gene Sarazen	1956	Jack Burke	
1923	Gene Sarazen	1957	Lionel Hebert	Score
1924	Walter Hagen	1958	Dow Finsterwald	276
1925	Walter Hagen	1959	Bob Rosburg	277
1926	Walter Hagen	1960	Jay Hebert	281
1927	Walter Hagen	1961	Jerry Barber	277
1928	Leo Diegel	1962	Gary Player (Saf)	278
1929	Leo Diegel	1963	Jack Nicklaus	279
1930	Tommy Armour	1964	Bob Nichols	271
1931	Tom Creavy	1965	Dave Marr	280
1932	Olin Dutra	1966	Al Geiberger	280
1933	Gene Sarazen	1967	Don January	281
1934	Paul Runyan	1968	Julius Boros	281
1935	Johnny Revolta	1969	Ray Floyd	276
1936	Denny Shute	1970	Dave Stockton	279
1937	Denny Shute	1971	Jack Nicklaus	281
1938	Paul Runyan	1972	Gary Player (Saf)	281
1939	Henry Picard	1973	Jack Nicklaus	277
1940	Byron Nelson	1974	Lee Trevino	276
1941	Vic Ghezzi	1975	Jack Nicklaus	276
1942	Sam Snead	1976	Dave Stockton	281
1943	Not held	1977	Lanny Wadkins	282
1944	Bob Hamilton	1978	John Mahaffey	276
1945	Byron Nelson	1979	David Graham (Aus)	272
1946	Ben Hogan	1980	Jack Nicklaus	274
1947	Jim Ferrier	1981	Larry Nelson	273
1948	Ben Hogan	1982	Ray Floyd (USA)	272
1949	Sam Snead			
1950	Chandler Harper			
1951	Sam Snead			

Left: **The American comedian Bob Hope, illustrating the keen interest taken in the game by the entertainment profession. A number of major tournaments in the United States bear witness to this fact, such as the Bob Hope Desert Classic, the Bing Crosby National Pro-Am, the Glen Campbell/Los Angeles Open, and the Sammy Davis Jr/Greater Hartford Open.** *Below:* **In 1982 Tom Watson (USA) won the US Open and The Open, the latter for the fourth time. He seems the golfer most likely to challenge Jack Nicklaus for most major wins.**

THE AMATEUR: Instituted by the Royal Liverpool Club in April 1885, it is contested as a match play tournament open to all amateur players. John Ball won a record eight times between 1888 and 1912. The oldest winner has been the Hon Michael Scott who was 54 yr 297 days in 1933, while the youngest were John Beharrell in 1956, and Bobby Cole (USA) in 1966, both of whom were aged 18 yr 1 month.

1885 Allan MacFie (GB)	1934 Lawson Little (USA)
1886 Horace Hutchinson (GB)	1935 Lawson Little (USA)
1887 Horace Hutchinson (GB)	1936 Hector Thomas (GB)
1888 John Ball (GB)	1937 Robert Sweeny (USA)
1889 John Laidlay (GB)	1938 Charles Yates (USA)
1890 John Ball (GB)	1939 Alec Kyle (GB)
1891 John Laidlay (GB)	1940–45 Not held
1892 John Ball (GB)	1946 James Bruen (GB)
1893 Peter Anderson (GB)	1947 Willie Turnesa (USA)
1894 John Ball (GB)	1948 Frank Stranahan (USA)
1895 Leslie Balfour-Melville (GB)	1949 Sam McCready (GB)
1896 Fred Tait (GB)	1950 Frank Stranahan (USA)
1897 Jack Allan (GB)	1951 Richard Chapman (USA)
1898 Fred Tait (GB)	1952 Harvie Ward (USA)
1899 John Ball (GB)	1953 Joseph Carr (GB)
1900 Harold Hilton (GB)	1954 Doug Bachli (Aus)
1901 Harold Hilton (GB)	1955 Joseph Conrad (USA)
1902 Charles Hutchings (GB)	1956 John Beharrell (GB)
1903 Robert Maxwell (GB)	1957 Reid Jack (GB)
1904 Walter Travis (USA)	1958 Joseph Carr (GB)
1905 Gordon Barry (GB)	1959 Deane Beman (USA)
1906 James Robb (GB)	1960 Joseph Carr (GB)
1907 John Ball (GB)	1961 Michael Bonallack (GB)
1908 E. Lassen (GB)	1962 Richard Davies (USA)
1909 Robert Maxwell (GB)	1963 Michael Lunt (GB)
1910 John Ball (GB)	1964 Gordon Clark (GB)
1911 Harold Hilton (GB)	1965 Michael Lunt (GB)
1912 John Ball (GB)	1966 Robert Cole (Saf)
1913 Harold Hilton (GB)	1967 Robert Dickson (USA)
1914 J. Jenkins (GB)	1968 Michael Bonallack (GB)
1915–19 Not held	1969 Michael Bonallack (GB)
1920 Cyril Tolley (GB)	1970 Michael Bonallack (GB)
1921 Willie Hunter (GB)	1971 Steve Melnyk (USA)
1922 Ernest Holderness (GB)	1972 Trevor Homer (GB)
1923 Roger Wethered (GB)	1973 Dick Siderowf (USA)
1924 Ernest Holderness (GB)	1974 Trevor Homer (GB)
1925 Robert Harris (GB)	1975 Marvin Giles (USA)
1926 Jesse Sweetser (USA)	1976 Dick Siderowf (USA)
1927 William Tweddell (GB)	1977 Peter McAvoy (GB)
1928 Phil Perkins (GB)	1978 Peter McAvoy (GB)
1929 Cyril Tolley (GB)	1979 Jay Sigel (USA)
1930 Robert T. Jones Jr. (USA)	1980 Duncan Evans (GB)
1931 Eric Martin Smith (GB)	1981 Philippe Ploujoux (Fra)
1932 John de Forest (GB)	1982 Martin Thompson (GB)
1933 Hon Michael Scott (GB)	1983 Philip Parkin (GB)

US AMATEUR: Initially held in the same week and at the same venue as the first US Open in 1895. Bobby Jones won a record five times between 1924 and 1930, having first qualified for the tournament in 1916, aged 14 yr 5½ months, the youngest ever to do so. The oldest player to win the title was Jack Westland, aged 47 yr 8 months 9 days in 1952, while the youngest was Robert Gardner at 19 yr 5 months in 1909. (Three years later, in 1912, Gardner broke the world pole vault record becoming the first man to clear 13 ft.)

1895 Charles Macdonald	1902 Louis James
1896 H. J. Whigham	1903 Walter Travis
1897 H. J. Whigham	1904 Chandler Egan
1898 Findlay Douglas	1905 Chandler Egan
1899 H. M. Harriman	1906 Eben Byers
1900 Walter Travis	1907 Jerome Travers
1901 Walter Travis	1908 Jerome Travers

1909	Robert Gardner	1949	Charles Coe
1910	William Fownes, Jr	1950	Sam Urzetta
1911	Harold Hilton (GB)	1951	Billy Maxwell
1912	Jerome Travers	1952	Jack Westland
1913	Jerome Travers	1953	Gene Littler
1914	Francis Ouimet	1954	Arnold Palmer
1915	Robert Gardner	1955	Harvie Ward
1916	Charles Evans, Jr	1956	Harvie Ward
1919	Davidson Herron	1957	Hillman Robbins
1920	Charles Evans, Jr	1958	Charles Coe
1921	Jesse Gullford	1959	Jack Nicklaus
1922	Jesse Sweetser	1960	Deane Beman
1923	Max Marston	1961	Jack Nicklaus
1924	Robert T. Jones, Jr	1962	Labron Harris
1925	Robert T. Jones, Jr	1963	Deane Beman
1926	George Von Elm	1964	Bill Campbell
1927	Robert T. Jones, Jr	1965	Bob Murphy
1928	Robert T. Jones, Jr	1966	Gary Cowan (Can)
1929	Harrison Johnston	1967	Bob Dickson
1930	Robert T. Jones, Jr	1968	Bruce Fleisher
1931	Francis Ouimet	1969	Steve Melnyk
1932	Ross Somerville (Can)	1970	Lanny Wadkins
1933	George Dunlap, Jr	1971	Gary Cowan (Can)
1934	Lawson Little	1972	Marvin Giles
1935	Lawson Little	1973	Craig Stadler
1936	John Fisher	1974	Jerry Pate
1937	John Goodman	1975	Fred Ridley
1938	William Turnesa	1976	Bill Sander
1939	Marvin Ward	1977	John Fought
1940	Richard Chapman	1978	John Cook
1941	Marvin Ward	1979	Mark O'Meara
1946	Stanley Bishop	1980	Hal Sutton
1947	Robert Riegel	1981	Nathaniel Crosby
1948	William Turnesa	1982	Jay Sigel

US WOMEN'S OPEN:

US WOMEN'S OPEN: First held in 1946, and currently played over 72 holes of stroke play. Betsy Rawls won a record four times between 1951 and 1960, and this was equalled by Mickey Wright between 1958 and 1964. The oldest champion was Fay Crocker (Uru) at 40 yr 11 months in 1955, while the youngest was Catherine Lacoste (Fra) at 22 yr 5 days in 1967, when she became the only amateur player to win the title. The greatest margin of victory was by Babe Didrikson-Zaharias who beat Betty Hicks by 12 strokes in 1954. The lowest aggregate has been 280 (70, 70, 68, 72) by Amy Alcott in 1980, and the lowest round was 65 by Sally Little in 1978. The record for 36 holes is 139 by Carol Mann and Donna Caponi in 1970, the latter going on to a 54-hole score of 210.

		Score			_Score_
1946	Patty Berg beat		1965	Carol Mann	290
	Betty Jameson 5 and 4		1966	Sandra Spuzich	297
1947	Betty Jameson	295	1967	Catherine Lacoste	
1948	Mildred Zaharias	300		(Fra)	294
1949	Louise Suggs	291	1968	Sue Berning	289
1950	Mildred Zaharias	291	1969	Donna Caponi	294
1951	Betsy Rawls	293	1970	Donna Caponi	287
1952	Louise Suggs	284	1971	JoAnne Carner	288
1953	Betsy Rawls	302	1972	Sue Maxwell Berning	290
1954	Mildred Zaharias	291	1973	Sue Maxwell Berning	290
1955	Fay Crocker (Uru)	299	1974	Sandra Haynie	295
1956	Kathy Cornelius	302	1975	Sandra Palmer	295
1957	Betsy Rawls	299	1976	JoAnne Carner	292
1958	Mickey Wright	290	1977	Hollis Stacy	298
1959	Mickey Wright	287	1978	Hollis Stacy	289
1960	Betsy Rawls	292	1979	Jerilyn Britz	284
1961	Mickey Wright	293	1980	Amy Alcott	280
1962	Murle Lindstrom	301	1981	Pat Bradley	279
1963	Mary Mills	289	1982	Janet Alex	283
1964	Mickey Wright	290			

BRITISH LADIES' OPEN CHAMPIONSHIP:

BRITISH LADIES' OPEN CHAMPIONSHIP: First held in 1976 and contested over 72 holes of stroke play.

1976	Jennifer Lee Smith	299	1981	Debbie Massey	
1977	Vivien Saunders	306		(USA)	295
1978	Janet Melville	310	1982	Marta Figueras-	
1979	Alison Sheard (Saf)	301		Dotti (Spa)	296
1980	Debbie Massey				
	(USA)	294			

US WOMEN'S AMATEUR:

US WOMEN'S AMATEUR: Instituted in November 1895, and currently 36 final holes of match play after 36 qualifying holes of stroke play. Glenna Collett-Vare won a record six titles between 1922 and 1935. The oldest champion was Dorothy Campbell-Hurd (GB) aged 41 yr 4 months when winning her third title in 1924, and the youngest was Laura Baugh at 16 yr 2 months 21 days in 1971. Margaret Curtis beat her sister, Harriot, in the 1907 final—they later presented the Curtis Cup for competition between the United States and Great Britain.

1895	C. S. Brown	1939	Betty Jameson
1896	Beatrix Hoyt	1940	Betty Jameson
1897	Beatrix Hoyt	1941	Elizabeth Hicks Newell
1898	Beatrix Hoyt	1942–45	No Championships.
1899	Ruth Underhill	1946	Mildred Zaharias
1900	Frances Griscom	1947	Louise Suggs
1901	Genevieve Hecker	1948	Grace Lenczyk
1902	Genevieve Hecker	1949	Dorothy Germain Porter
1903	Bessie Anthony	1950	Beverly Hanson
1904	Georgianna Bishop	1951	Dorothy Kirby
1905	Pauline Mackay	1952	Jacqueline Pung
1906	Harriot Curtis	1953	Mary Lena Faulk
1907	Margaret Curtis	1954	Barbara Romack
1908	Catherine Harley	1955	Patricia Lesser
1909	Dorothy Campbell (GB)	1956	Marlene Stewart (Can)
1910	Dorothy Campbell (GB)	1957	JoAnne Gunderson
1911	Margaret Curtis	1958	Anne Quast
1912	Margaret Curtis	1959	Barbara McIntire
1913	Gladys Ravenscroft (GB)	1960	JoAnne Gunderson
1914	Catherine Harley-Jackson	1961	Anne Quast-Decker
1915	C. H. Vanderbeck	1962	JoAnne Gunderson
1916	Alexa Stirling	1963	Anne Quast-Welts
1919	Alexa Stirling	1964	Barbara McIntire
1920	Alexa Stirling	1965	Jean Ashley
1921	Marion Hollins	1966	JoAnne Gunderson-Carner
1922	Glenna Collett	1967	Mary Lou Dill
1923	Edith Cummings	1968	JoAnne Gunderson-Carner
1924	Dorothy Campbell Hurd	1969	Catherine Lacoste (Fra)
1925	Glenna Collett	1970	Martha Wilkinson
1926	Helen Stetson	1971	Laura Baugh
1927	Miriam Burns Horn	1972	Mary Ann Budke
1928	Glenna Collett	1973	Carol Semple
1929	Glenna Collett	1974	Cynthia Hill
1930	Glenna Collett	1975	Beth Daniel
1931	Helen Hicks	1976	Donna Horton
1932	Virginia van Wie	1977	Beth Daniel
1933	Virginia van Wie	1978	Cathy Sherk (Can)
1934	Virginia van Wie	1979	Carolyn Hill
1935	Glenna Collett-Vare	1980	Juli Inkster
1936	Pamela Barton (GB)	1981	Juli Inkster
1937	Estelle Page	1982	Juli Inkster
1938	Patty Berg		

BRITISH LADIES' AMATEUR:

BRITISH LADIES' AMATEUR: First held in 1893, and currently a match play contest. It has been won on four occasions by Cecilia Leitch between 1914 and 1926, and Joyce Wethered (later Lady Heathcoat-Amory) between 1922 and 1929. The oldest champion was Jessie Valentine aged 42 yr 3 months in 1958, and the youngest was May Hezlet at 17 yr 7 days in 1899.

1893	Lady Margaret Scott	1914	Cecilia Leitch
1894	Lady Margaret Scott	1919	Abandoned
1895	Lady Margaret Scott	1920	Cecilia Leitch
1896	Amy Pascoe	1921	Cecilia Leitch
1897	Edith C. Orr	1922	Joyce Wethered
1898	L. Thomson	1923	Doris Chambers
1899	May Hezlet	1924	Joyce Wethered
1900	Rhona Adair	1925	Joyce Wethered
1901	Miss Graham	1926	Cecilia Leitch
1902	May Hezlet	1927	Miss Thion de la Chaume (Fra)
1903	Rhona Adair	1928	Nanette Le Blan (Fra)
1904	Lottie Dod	1929	Joyce Wethered
1905	B. Thompson	1930	Diana Fishwick
1906	Mrs Kennion	1931	Enid Wilson
1907	May Hezlet	1932	Enid Wilson
1908	M. Titterton	1933	Enid Wilson
1909	Dorothy Campbell	1934	Helen Holm
1910	Miss Grant Suttie	1935	Wanda Morgan
1911	Dorothy Campbell	1936	Pam Barton
1912	Gladys Ravenscroft	1937	Jessie Anderson
1913	Muriel Dodd	1938	Helen Holm

Seven years after winning the 1973 American Girls Junior title, Amy Alcott won the US Women's Open with a record low score for the tournament.

1939	Pam Barton	1964	Carol Sorenson (USA)
1946	Jean Hetherington	1965	Brigitte Varangot (Fra)
1947	Mildred Zaharias (USA)	1966	Elizabeth Chadwick
1948	Louise Suggs (USA)	1967	Elizabeth Chadwick
1949	Frances Stephens	1968	Brigitte Varangot (Fra)
1950	Vicomtesse de Saint Sauveur	1969	Catherine Lacoste (Fra)
	(Fra)	1970	Dinah Oxley
1951	P. G. MacCann	1971	Michelle Walker
1952	Moira Paterson	1972	Michelle Walker
1953	Marlene Stewart (Can)	1973	Ann Irvin
1954	Frances Stephens	1974	Carol Semple (USA)
1955	Jessie Valentine	1975	Nancy Syms (USA)
1956	Margaret Smith	1976	Catherine Panton
1957	Philomena Garvey	1977	Angela Uzielli
1958	Jessie Valentine	1978	Edwina Kennedy (Aus)
1959	Elizabeth Price	1979	Maureen Madill (Ire)
1960	Barbara McIntire (USA)	1980	Ann Sander
1961	Marley Spearman	1981	Belle Robertson
1962	Marley Spearman	1982	Katrina Douglas
1963	Brigitte Varangot (Fra)		

RYDER CUP: First held in 1927 as a contest between professional teams from Great Britain and Ireland and the United States. Since 1977 the British team has been extended to include Europeans. Played biennially the Cup has been won most often by the United States with 20 outright victories to three by Britain and one match halved. Billy Casper (USA) played in 37 matches and won a record 20 of them, between 1961 and 1975. Neil Coles (GB&I) played in a record 40 matches between 1961 and 1977. Christy O'Connor Sr (GB&I) made 10 appearances between 1955 and 1973. The oldest competitor was Ted Ray (GB&I) at 50 yr 2 months 5 days in 1927, and the youngest was Nick Faldo (GB&I) who was 20 yr 59 days in 1977.

WALKER CUP: Instituted in 1922, and now held biennially, it is contested by teams of amateurs from the USA and the British Isles. Over two days eight 18-hole foursomes and sixteen 18-hole singles are played. The USA has won on 26 occasions, Britain twice, with the 1965 match halved. William Campbell (USA) has won seven singles and halved one and been in foursomes which won six, halved one and lost three from 1951 to 1975. Joseph Carr (GB) played in a record nine consecutive matches from 1947 to 1963, and again in 1967. The oldest player was the Hon Michael Scott (GB) aged 55 yr 273 days in 1934, and the youngest was James Bruen (Ire) at 18 yr 25 days in 1938.

CURTIS CUP: Instituted in 1932 for teams of women amateurs representing the USA and the British Isles. The teams play six 18-hole foursomes and twelve 18-hole singles, over two

days. The USA has won 19 times, Britain twice, and two matches have been halved. The youngest player to be in the competition has been Jane Connachan (GB) aged 16 yr 102 days in 1980.

WORLD AMATEUR TEAM TROPHY: Instituted in 1958 and held biennially for the Eisenhower Trophy—named after the then US President who was a keen golfer. It is contested over 72 holes of stroke play by teams of four with the best three scores aggregated. In 1980 at Pinehurst, North Carolina a record 39 countries competed. The USA has won most times with eight victories. The lowest team total was 834 by the USA in 1960, while the lowest individual score is 269 (66, 67, 68, 68) by Jack Nicklaus (USA) also in 1960. The lowest for a round has been 66 by Nicklaus in 1960, Ronald Shade (GB), Deane Beman (USA) and Juan Estrada (Mex) all in 1962, and Michael Bonallack (GB) in 1968. The oldest player was W. J. Gibb (Mal) in 1958, the only year in which there has been a play-off, when Australia beat the USA. *Winners from 1970:*

Year	Team	Venue
1970	USA	Madrid, Spain
1972	USA	Buenos Aires, Argentine
1974	USA	La Romana, Dominican Republic
1976	GB	Penina, Portugal
1978	USA	Pacific Harbour, Fiji
1980	USA	Pinehurst, N. Carolina, USA
1982	USA	Lausanne, Switzerland

WOMEN'S WORLD AMATEUR TEAM CHAMPIONSHIP: Instituted by the French Golf Federation in 1964 for the Espirito Santo Trophy. Held biennially over 72 holes of stroke play by teams of three with the best two scores aggregated. There were a record 28 teams in 1980. The lowest aggregate has been 580 by the USA in 1966, with the lowest individual score being 289 (74, 71, 70, 74) by Marlene Stewart-Streit (Can) also in 1966 at Mexico City. The lowest round was 68 by Jane Bastenchury-Booth (USA), Marlene Stewart-Streit (Can) and Claudine Cros-Rubin (Fra), all in 1972. The youngest competitors were 14-year-old Maria de la Guardia and Silvia Corrie, both from the Dominican Republic in 1974. *Winners from 1970:*

Year	Team	Venue
1970	USA	Madrid, Spain
1972	USA	Buenos Aires, Argentine
1974	USA	La Romana, Dominican Republic
1976	USA	Vilamoura, Portugal
1978	Australia	Pacific Harbour, Fiji
1980	USA	Pinehurst, N. Carolina, USA
1982	USA	Geneva, Switzerland

WORLD CUP: Instituted in 1953 by an American, John Jay Hopkins, and originally known as the Canada Cup after the first venue. Contested over 72 holes of stroke play by teams of two players with the scores aggregated. The United States have won on 15 occasions. Arnold Palmer (USA) and Jack Nicklaus (USA) have each been on six winning teams, and Nicklaus has

been the best individual on three occasions. The Australian winners in 1970, Bruce Devlin and David Graham, totalled the lowest aggregate of 545 for the 144 holes. The lowest individual score has been 269 (64, 67, 68, 70) by Roberto de Vicenzo (Arg) also in 1970. *Winners from 1970:*

Year	Team	Best individual	Venue
1970	Australia	Roberto de Vicenzo (Arg)	Buenos Aires, Argentine
1971	USA	Jack Nicklaus (USA)	Palm Beach, Florida, USA
1972	Taiwan	Hsieh Min Nam (Tai)	Melbourne, Australia
1973	USA	Johnny Miller (USA)	Marbella, Spain
1974	South Africa	Bobby Cole (Saf)	Caracas, Venezuela
1975	USA	Johnny Miller (USA)	Bangkok, Thailand
1976	Spain	Ernesto Perez Acosta (Mex)	Palm Springs, California, USA
1977	USA	Gary Player (Saf)	Manila, Philippines
1978	USA	John Mahaffey (USA)	Hanalei, Hawaii, USA
1979	USA	Hale Irwin (USA)	Glyfada, Greece
1980	Canada	Sandy Lyle (Sco)	Bogota, Colombia
1981	Not held	—	—
1982	Spain	Manuel Pinero (Spa)	Acapulco, Mexico

Greyhound Racing

Greyhounds as a breed developed in England probably from the Celtic hound interbred with Greek hounds. This view is supported by etymologists who note that the word 'grey' derives from the old Latin word for Greek. They were first used in sport at coursing—the chasing of hares by pairs of dogs—which was brought to England by the Normans in 1067. The first attempt to introduce an artificial quarry was at Hendon, North London in 1876, when there was a short-lived experiment using a dummy hare fixed to a rail and pulled by a windlass over a straight course. The perfecting of a mechanical hare operating around a circular course was the necessary spur to the introduction of modern greyhound racing. After tentative experiments in America such as the one at Salt Lake City, Utah in 1906, when the hare was pulled by a motorcycle, the first regular track was opened at Emeryville, California in 1919 by Owen Smith. In the United Kingdom the Belle Vue track, Manchester was built in 1926 and the first race in Britain was won by a dog named *Mistley* on 24 July 1926.

Greyhounds skilfully negotiating one of the bends of the track at Hackney, London. The sport has experienced fluctuating fortunes in Britain with the post-War boom culminating in a record-breaking crowd of 58 000 at the 1946 Derby at White City. This was followed by a gradual decline into the 1970s, but currently the crowds are beginning to return.

HIGHEST SPEEDS

The greatest speed achieved by a greyhound in a timed race is 67·14 km/h (41·72 mph) by an Australian dog *The Shoe* at Richmond, New South Wales on 25 April 1968, on a straight track. It has been estimated that he reached a top speed of 73·14 km/h (45·45 mph) during the race. The record speed achieved in Britain is 62·97 km/h (39·13 mph) by *Beef Cutlet*, over a straight course at Blackpool, on 13 May 1933. The fastest timing over the now standard circular track is 29·62 sec for 515 m by *Glen Miner* at Brighton in 1982. This represents an average speed of 62·59 km/h (38·89 mph). Over 500 m hurdles the record is 29·71 sec by *Wotchit Buster* at Brighton in 1978, averaging 60·58 km/h (37·64 mph).

GREYHOUND DERBY: The major race in Britain is the Derby, instituted in 1927, and held at London's White City Stadium, currently over a distance of 500 m (546 yd). Only two dogs have won the title twice, *Mick the Miller*, in 1929 and 1930, and *Patricia's Hope* in 1972 and 1973. 'Mick' was probably the most famous greyhound who ever lived, and, after his death in 1939, was preserved in the Natural History Museum, London. *Winners from 1970:*

1970 John Silver
1971 Dolores Rocket
1972 Patricia's Hope
1973 Patricia's Hope
1974 Jimsun
1975 Tartar Khan
1976 Mutts Silver
1977 Ballinska Band
1978 Lacca Champion
1979 Sarah's Bunny
1980 Indian Joe
1981 Parkdown Jet
1982 Laurie's Panther

GRAND NATIONAL: Also instituted in 1927, and currently held over a distance of 500 m, incorporating five flights of hurdles. The only three-time winner is *Sherry's Prince* between 1970 and 1972. *Winners from 1973:*

1973 Killone Flash
1974 Shanney's Darkie
1975 Pier Hero
1976 Weston Pete
1977 Salerno
1978 Top O' The Tide
1979 Top O' The Tide
1980 Gilt Edge Flyer
1981 Bobcol
1982 Face The Mutt
1983 Sir Winston

CATS AND DOGS

An interesting experiment was carried out at Harringey, London in September 1937 when cheetahs were matched against greyhounds in a series of races after a mechanical hare. The cheetahs, considered to be the swiftest animals on earth, were somewhat bemused by the unfamiliar conditions, but won quite easily. The fastest, named Helen, recorded an average speed of 69·8 km/h (43·4 mph).

MOST SUCCESSFUL GREYHOUND

The longest series of consecutive wins in greyhound racing is 31 by the American dog *Joe Dump* in the United States between November 1978 and June 1979. The British record streak is 20 by *Westpark Mustard* between January and October 1974.

Gymnastics

Tumbling and similar exercises were performed *c* 2600 BC as religious rituals in China, but it was the Greeks who coined the word gymnastics. A primitive form was practised in the ancient Olympic Games, but it was not until Johann Friedrich Simon began to teach at Basedow's Gymnasium in Dessau, Germany in 1776 that the foundations of the modern sport were laid. He was followed by Per Ling (Swe), Ludwig Jahn (Ger) and Johann Guts Muth (Ger) in perfecting the techniques of modern gymnastics. The first national federation was formed in Germany in 1860 and the International Gymnastics Federation was founded in Liège, Belgium in 1881. The sport was included at the first modern Olympic Games at Athens in 1896.

Current events for men are: floor exercises, horse vault, rings, pommel horse, parallel bars and horizontal bar, while for women they are: floor exercises, horse vault, asymmetrical bars, and balance beam.

Aleksandr Ditiatin from Leningrad is the only competitor to win medals in all sections of the men's competition at one Games. Unusually tall for a top class gymnast, at 1·77 m (5 ft 9¾ in) he improved on his 1976 silver placing in the rings, probably his best event, to take the gold medal as well as the overall title in Moscow.

Maria Filatova, one of the world's top gymnasts, was a member of the Soviet gold medal winning teams in the 1976 and 1980 Olympic Games. A silver medallist in the overall title in the 1981 world championships, she was involved in a highly unusual three-way tie for the bronze medal in the Moscow Games asymmetric bars event.

WORLD AND OLYMPIC CHAMPIONSHIPS:

The Olympic title is also the world championship title, and since 1950 a separate world meeting has been held biennially between Games. The greatest number of individual titles won by a man is 10 by Boris Shakhlin (USSR), who also was in three winning teams, between 1954 and 1964. Of these a record six were in the Olympics, a total he shares with fellow countryman Nikolai Andrianov, between 1972 and 1980. The latter also holds the aggregate record of 28 medals of all colours, of which 15 were Olympic. Japan have won the team title on 11 occasions, including five of them in the Games.

The female record for gold medals is 12, plus five with the winning team, by Larissa Latynina (USSR), who also holds the record for all medals with 31. Of these, 18 were won in the Olympics, which is the greatest total of medals ever won by either sex in any sport. The most Olympic gold medals won by a woman gymnast is seven by Vera Caslavska (Cz) in 1964 and 1968. Teams from the USSR have won the women's title on 14 occasions, including eight Olympic victories.

The only man to win a medal in all eight categories open to him at one Olympic Games is Aleksandr Ditiatin (USSR) with three golds, four silvers and a bronze at Moscow in 1980.

OVERALL CHAMPIONS (since 1948)

	Men	Women
1948*	Veikko Huhtanen (Fin)	Not held
1950	Walter Lehmann (Swi)	Helena Rokoczy (Pol)
1952*	Viktor Chukarin (USSR)	Maria Gorokhovskaya (USSR)
1954	Valentin Muratov (USSR) / Viktor Chukarin (USSR)	Galina Roudiko (USSR)
1956*	Viktor Chukarin (USSR)	Larissa Latynina (USSR)
1958	Boris Shakhlin (USSR)	Larissa Latynina (USSR)
1960*	Boris Shakhlin (USSR)	Larissa Latynina (USSR)
1962	Yuri Titov (USSR)	Larissa Latynina (USSR)
1964*	Yukio Endo (Jap)	Vera Caslavska (Cz)
1966	Mikhail Voronin (USSR)	Vera Caslavska (Cz)

	Men	Women
1968*	Sawao Kato (Jap)	Vera Caslavska (Cz)
1970	Eizo Kenmotsu (Jap)	Ludmila Tourischeva (USSR)
1972*	Sawao Kato (Jap)	Ludmila Tourischeva (USSR)
1974	Shigeru Kasamatsu (Jap)	Ludmila Tourischeva (USSR)
1976*	Nikolai Andrianov (USSR)	Nadia Comaneci (Rom)
1978	Nikolai Andrianov (USSR)	Elena Mukhina (USSR)
1980*	Aleksandr Ditiatin (USSR)	Elena Davidova (USSR)
1981	Yuriy Korolyev (USSR)	Olga Bicherova (USSR)

* *Olympics*

The delightful Nelli Kim (USSR) won the 1976 Olympic gold medal for the floor exercises in gymnastics with a maximum possible score of 10·00 points. In 1980 she retained her floor title and repeated her team gold medal of four years before.

BRITISH CHAMPIONSHIPS: Arthur Whitford won a record 10 individual titles from 1928 to 1939. He also was on four winning teams. The female record is eight by Pat Hirst between 1947 and 1956. *Overall champions from 1970:*

	Men	Women
1970	Stan Wild (Leeds AI)	Margaret Bell (Ladywell GC)
1971	Stan Wild (Leeds AI)	Pamela Hopkins (Penarth GC)
1972	Bill Norgrave (Army GU)	Barbara Alred (Leeds)
1973	Stan Wild (Leeds AI)	Ann Parkinson (Saltaire GC)
1974	Stan Wild (Leeds AI)	Avril Lennox (Charles Keene Coll)
1975	Tommy Wilson (Hendon GC)	Avril Lennox (Charles Keene Coll)
1976	Ian Neale (Coventry OGC)	Avril Lennox (Charles Keene Coll)
1977	Edward Arnold (Leeds AI)	Avril Lennox (Charles Keene Coll)
1978	Ian Neale (Coventry OGC)	Susan Cheeseborough (Tameside GC)
1979	Jeff Davis (Bush Harlow OGC)	Susan Cheeseborough (Tameside GC)
1980	Jeff Davis (Bush Harlow OGC)	Suzanne Dando (Ladywell GC)
1981	Keith Langley (Coventry OGC)	Mandy Gornall (Fylde Coast GC)
1982	Barry Winch (Bush Harlow OGC)	Cheryl Weatherstone (Darien, Connecticut)

MODERN RHYTHMIC GYMNASTICS

This recent addition to the female side of the sport incorporates exercises with different hand-held apparatus, including ribbons, balls, ropes, hoops and Indian clubs. The most overall titles won in world championships is three by Maria Guigova (Bul) while the most individual apparatus titles is nine by Guigova and Galina Shugurova (USSR). The latter has also won a record total of 14 medals. This category of the sport will be included in the Olympic Games for the first time in 1984.

Erica Schiller (USSR) in the ribbon discipline of the new sport of Rhythmic Gymnastics. Aesthetically more pleasing than the traditional gymnastic exercises, the sport will be included in the Olympics for the first time at Los Angeles in 1984.

HIGHEST SCORE

Nadia Comaneci (Rom) became the first gymnast in the Olympic Games to score a maximum of 10·00 points, at Montreal in 1976. She then proceeded to notch up another six such perfect scores. At the same Games, Nelli Kim (USSR) also scored two, and since then a number of other gymnasts, male and female, have achieved that standard of excellence.

LARGEST DISPLAY

The greatest number of gymnasts to give a display at the same time are the 30 000–40 000 from the Sokol movement who perform annually in the Strahov Stadium in Prague, Czechoslovakia before some 240 000 spectators.

SARGENT JUMP

Devised by, and named after, an eminent American professor of physical education in the 1920s, this exercise measures the differential between the height reached by a person's finger tips with their feet flat on the ground, and that reached by jumping. The record is 1·22 m (48 in) by Darrell Griffith of the University of Louisville, USA, in 1976.

SOMERSAULTS

Lance Corporal Wayne Wright of the Royal Engineers did a dive and tucked somersault over 37 men, lined up behind each other at Dover, Kent on 30 July 1980. In Japan, Shigeru Iwasaki somersaulted backwards over a 50 metres course in 10·8 sec in March 1980. An American, Ashrita Furman, did 6773 forward rolls to cover 16·09 km (10 miles) in Central Park, New York in November 1980.

Hang Gliding

Having much of the same basic history as ordinary gliding, differences can be noted from quite early times. In the 11th century a monk named Elmer is said to have flown by means of an elementary form of hang glider, from the tower of Malmesbury Abbey, Wiltshire. However, the earliest pioneer of the modern sport was Otto Lilienthal (Ger) who made numerous flights from 1893 until his death in a crash in 1896. The sport received a tremendous fillip through the development of a 'wing' in the early 1960s by Professor Francis Rogallo, as a spin-off of his researches into reusable space shuttles for the National Aeronautics and Space Agency (NASA) in America.

WORLD CHAMPIONSHIPS: An unofficial championship meeting was held in 1975, at Kossen, Austria, with the only individual title going to David Cronk (USA). The following year saw the first official championships. The highest placed Briton in individual events has been Johnny Carr with his second in Class I in 1979. In 1981 18 countries were represented.

1976 (Kossen, Austria) *Team*—Austria
Class I—Standard, Christian Steinbach (Aut)
Class II—High Aspect Ratio, Terry Delore (NZ)
Class III—Open, Ken Battle (Aus)
1979 (Grenoble, France) *Team*—France
Class I—Weight Shift, Josef Guggenmos (FRG)
Class II—Movable Surfaces, Rex Miller (USA)
1981 (Beppu, Japan) *Team*—Great Britain
Class I—Weight Shift, Pepe Lopes (Bra)
Class II—Movable Surfaces, Graeme Bird (NZ)

CHANNEL FLIGHT
The English Channel was first crossed by 37-year-old Ken Messenger (GB) in July 1971. Released from under a hot air balloon at 5486 m (18 000 ft) over Dover, he landed among cattle in a field at Sangatte, near Calais 35·4 km (22 miles) and 45 min later. His friend Brian Milton was less fortunate and came down in the Channel, but was rescued by a Russian freighter. The traditional maritime rules, of power giving way to sail, were observed with air traffic controllers diverting flights between London, Paris and Brussels to give Messenger safe passage.

WORLD RECORDS (As at 31 Dec 1982)
(As recognised by the Fédération Aéronautique Internationale-FAI)

Distance

Rigid Wing: 228 km (142 miles) by Robert Thompson (USA) in a Comet 165 over Arizona, USA on 29 June 1982
Flexible Wing: 178·07 km (110·65 miles) by George Worthington (USA) with a Moyes Maxi II from Cerro Gordo, California to Boundary Peak, Nevada on 25 July 1980

Distance to declared goal

Rigid Wing: 53·15 km (33 miles) by George Worthington (USA) with a Mitchell Wing on 3 August 1978
Flexible Wing: 153·61 km (95·4 miles) by George Worthington (USA) with a ASG-21 over California on 21 July 1977

Out and return distance to a goal

Rigid Wing: 76·38 km (47·46 miles) by George Worthington (USA) with a Mitchell Wing over California on 23 July 1977
Flexible Wing: 70·06 km (44·23 miles) by George Worthington (USA) with a Seagull 10-metre over California on 17 July 1979

Gain of height

Rigid Wing: 2701 m (8861 ft) by George Worthington (USA) with a Mitchell Wing over California on 22 July 1980
Flexible Wing: 4175 m (13 700 ft) by Ian Kibblewhite (NZ) in a Lightning 195 over California on 22 July 1981

Hang glider enthusiast taking off down a sloping runway prior to achieving the nearest that man has come to emulating the birds.

Hockey

An Egyptian tomb painting, which shows two players with curved sticks and a round object in a 'bully' position, has been found at Beni Hasan, on the Nile, and dated to c 2050 BC. Early Greek wall carvings c 500 BC indicate that hockey-like games were played then. There is a reference to a similar game played in Lincolnshire in 1277 but the word 'hockey' was first used in the 19th century. The first hockey club was Blackheath founded in 1861 or earlier in London. However, the Teddington HC, formed in 1871, has the oldest continuous history, and is credited with introducing standardised rules, curbs on dangerous stick use, umpires, and the circle, first used in a match against Surbiton at Bushey Park in December 1876. The first club for women was at East Molesey, Surrey in 1887.

A first attempt at organisation came with the foundation of a Hockey Association in April 1875. It was short-lived and it was only in January 1886 that the present English Hockey Association was formed. The first international match was when Ireland beat Wales 3–0 at Rhyl, Wales on 20 January 1895. The Fédération Internationale de Hockey (FIH) was set up in January 1924.

OLYMPIC GAMES: First included in 1908 and 1920, when England were the winners on both occasions. Hockey was re-introduced on a permanent basis in 1928. Since then the title has been won eight times by India 1928–56, 1964 and 1980. They have also had one silver and two bronze medal teams, but in 1976 India finished seventh, one of the greatest upsets in international sport. A women's competition was held for the first time in 1980 and was won by Zimbabwe. Three gold medals have been won by seven Indian players but of these, Leslie Claudius and Udham Singh also won a silver medal.

Olympic champions from 1960:

1960	Pakistan	1972	Germany
1964	India	1976	New Zealand
1968	Pakistan	1980	India

While not quite up to the standard of their countrymen, the Indian women's hockey team gave a good account of themselves when the distaff side of the game was represented in the Games for the first time in 1980. They narrowly lost to the Soviet team in the match to decide the bronze medallists.

SCORING FEATS

The biggest score in an international game was the 24–1 defeat of the United States by India in the 1932 Olympic Games. In that match Roop Singh scored 12 goals which remains an individual record. In the three Olympic tournaments of 1928, 1932 and 1936, the Indian teams scored a total of 102 goals and only had three scored against them, much to the disgust of their goalkeeper, Richard Allen. The highest score in women's international hockey is the 23–0 win by England over France at Merton, Surrey in 1923. The record for an England male team is 16–0 also against France at Beckenham in 1922.

The highest male individual score in one game is 19 by M. C. Marckx playing for Bowdon 2nd XI against Brooklands 2nd XI on the last day of 1910.

The highest known score in a club match is the 40–0 victory by Ross Ladies over Wyeside Ladies in January 1929, when Edna Blakelock scored a record 21 individual goals.

The record number of goals scored in an international hockey career is 150 by Paul Litjens in 112 games for Holland. In a lower level of hockey Fred Wagner scored 1832 goals between 1923 and 1958 playing for club teams and the County in Nottinghamshire.

WORLD CUP: First held for men in 1971. A women's cup was instituted in 1974 by the FIH as a world championship.

Men		Women	
1971	Pakistan	1974	Holland
1973	Holland	1976	Germany
1975	India	1978	Holland
1978	Pakistan	1981	Germany
1982	Pakistan	1983	Netherlands

The International Federation of Women's Hockey Associations (IFWHA) organised their own world championships in 1975. Held quadrennially, the first title was won by England, and the second, in 1979, by Holland.

ENGLISH COUNTY CHAMPIONSHIPS: Instituted in 1957 for men and 1968 for women. The men's title has been won four times by Middlesex in 1959, 1961, 1977 and 1981, and by Kent in 1964–65, 1975 and 1979. Lancashire have won the women's title on six occasions outright and twice shared. *Winners from 1975:*

	Men	Women
1975	Kent	Surrey, Leicestershire
1976	Hertfordshire	Lancashire
1977	Middlesex	Lancashire
1978	Lancashire	Hertfordshire
1979	Kent	Lancashire
1980	Buckinghamshire	Leicestershire, Suffolk
1981	Middlesex	Staffordshire
1982	Buckinghamshire	Suffolk
1983	Lancashire	Leicestershire

BIGGEST CROWD

The greatest number of spectators to attend a hockey match was 65 165, mainly schoolgirls, at the Empire Stadium, Wembley for the England v United States women's match on 11 March 1978.

Horse Racing

There is evidence that men were riding horses, as distinct from riding in chariots pulled by horses, in Assyria and Egypt *c* 1400 BC. However, early organised racing appears to have been confined to chariots, for which the Roman method used riders with a foot on each of two horses. The first racing on horseback was by the Greeks in the 33rd Olympic Games in 648 BC. The earliest recorded race in Britain was at Netherby, Cumbria in AD 210 between Arabian horses brought to the country by the Roman Emperor, Lucius Septimius Severus. The first recognisable regular race meeting was that held at Smithfield, London at the weekly horse fairs on Fridays in 1174. The first known prize money was a purse of gold presented by Richard I (the Lionheart) in 1195 for a race between knights over a distance of three miles.

THE THOROUGHBRED

All thoroughbred horses in the world today are descended from at least one of three great stallions, which were imported into Britain in the 17th and 18th centuries. The *Darley Arabian* was brought from Aleppo, Syria by the British Consul Richard Darley of Yorkshire *c* 1704; the *Byerley Turk* was brought to England from Turkey *c* 1685 and used by Captain Byerley as a charger in Ireland; and the *Godolphin Barb*—the latter word derived from the Barbary Coast of North Africa—was originally brought from France by Edward Coke in about 1735 and then acquired by the Earl of Godolphin.

SPEED

The fastest recorded speed by a racehorse is 69·62 km/h (43·36 mph) by a Mexican horse, *Big Racket*, when it ran 440 yd in 20·8 sec at Mexico City on 5 February 1945. The fastest time for a mile is 1 min 31·8 sec by *Soueida* in 1963, and by *Loose Cover* in 1966, both at Brighton, Sussex. As the course there includes a rather sharp descent for about a quarter of the distance, a more acceptable mark is 1 min 32·2 sec by *Dr Fager* at Arlington, Illinois on 24 August 1968. The greatest combination of endurance and speed was shown by *Champion Crabbet* who covered 482 km (300 miles) in 52 hr 33 min in 1920 carrying 111 kg (17½ stone). In 1831 Squire George Osbaldeston, Member of Parliament for East Retford, rode 321 km (200 miles) at Newmarket in 8 hr 42 min using 50 different horses, so averaging 36·99 km/h (22·99 mph).

The colour and excitement of the sport of kings illustrated here by an autumn handicap race at Newmarket.

In 1977 Steve Cauthen, then only 17 years of age, became a real-life six-million-dollar man when he led the US jockey table with winnings of $6 151 750.

HORSES FOR COURSES

The most prize money won by a horse is $3 371 610 by *John Henry* in the USA, to June 1982. The record winnings in a year is $1 798 030 also by *John Henry* in 1981. The most won by a mare in its career is $1 535 443 by *Dahlia* from 1972 to 1976. The greatest amount of prize money won by an English-trained horse is £450 428 by *Troy* in 1978–79. The highest first prize of $600 000 was won by *John Henry* in the Arlington Million, at Chicago on 30 August 1981. The richest prize in British racing was £166 820 won by *Henbit* in the Derby at Epsom on 4 June 1980.

The horse with the best win–loss record was *Kincsem*, a mare foaled in Hungary in 1874, unbeaten in 54 races including the 1878 Goodwood Cup. *Camarero* died in 1956 after his 73rd win in 77 races, which included a 56 consecutive win streak. The most expensive horse is *Conquistador Cielo*, which was syndicated in the USA in August 1982 for $36 400 000. In Britain only a filly can win all five Classic races, comprising the 1000 Guineas, 2000 Guineas, Derby, Oaks and the St Leger. The 1000 Guineas and the Oaks are open to fillies only, while the other three are for colts or fillies. In practice, fillies rarely contest either the 2000 Guineas or the Derby nowadays. In 1902 *Sceptre* won all but the Derby. The same four races had been won by *Formosa* in 1868, but she had deadheated in the 2000 Guineas.

In 1856 *Fisherman* won a record 23 races in one season. A unique performance was set by *Dr Syntax* when it won the Preston Gold Cup for seven successive years 1815–21. The oldest known horse to win a flat race was *Marksman* who won at Ashford, Kent in 1826 when 18 years old. On 28 February 1980 *Sonny Somers* was the oldest horse this century to win over jumps, when he won at Lingfield Park, Surrey, also at 18 years of age.

COURSES FOR HORSES

The largest turfed training area in the world is Newmarket Heath, Suffolk, about 2500 acres in size, in the middle of which is the Newmarket racecourse, founded in 1636. It comprises the July Course and the Rowley Mile Course, whose grandstands are about a mile apart. The Rowley course is named after Charles II, a racing enthusiast, whose nickname of 'Old Rowley' derived from a horse he owned. The largest grandstand at a racecourse is at Belmont Park, Long Island, New York. It is 402 m (440 yd) long and seats 30 000 people. In Britain in 1981 there were 59 racecourses in use, comprising 16 solely for flat racing, 25 for steeplechasing and hurdling, and 18 which were dual purpose.

JOCKEYS

Willie Shoemaker (USA) is the most successful jockey ever, having ridden over 8100 winners and won over $87 million in 33 years of riding. Weighing only 1·13 kg (2½ lb) at birth, he is 43 kg (94 lb) now and stands 1·50 m (4 ft 11 in). His wife is nearly 30 cm (1 ft) taller than he is. Britain's greatest jockey was Sir Gordon Richards, knighted in 1953 having won his first Derby after 28 attempts. Elsewhere he was far more successful, winning 4870 races between 1920 and 1954. He was champion jockey a record 26 times, and in October 1933 had a winning streak of 12 races over three days.

BRITISH CHAMPION JOCKEYS FROM 1946

	Flat Racing	Wins	National Hunt	Wins
1946	Gordon Richards	212	Fred Rimell	54
1947	Gordon Richards	269	Jack Dowdeswell	58
1948	Gordon Richards	224	Bryan Marshall	66
1949	Gordon Richards	261	Tim Molony	60
1950	Gordon Richards	201	Tim Molony	95
1951	Gordon Richards	227	Tim Molony	83
1952	Gordon Richards	231	Tim Molony	99
1953	Gordon Richards	191	Fred Winter	121
1954	Doug Smith	129	Dick Francis	76
1955	Doug Smith	168	Tim Molony	67
1956	Doug Smith	155	Fred Winter	74
1957	Scobie Breasley	173	Fred Winter	80
1958	Doug Smith	165	Fred Winter	82
1959	Doug Smith	157	Tim Brookshaw	83
1960	Lester Piggott	170	Stan Mellor	68
1961	Scobie Breasley	171	Stan Mellor	118
1962	Scobie Breasley	179	Stan Mellor	80
1963	Scobie Breasley	176	Josh Gifford	70
1964	Lester Piggott	140	Josh Gifford	94
1965	Lester Piggott	166	Terry Biddlecombe	114
1966	Lester Piggott	191	Terry Biddlecombe	102
1967	Lester Piggott	117	Josh Gifford	122
1968	Lester Piggott	139	Josh Gifford	82
1969	Lester Piggott	163	Bob Davies	77
			Terry Biddlecombe	77
1970	Lester Piggott	162	Bob Davies	91
1971	Lester Piggott	162	Graham Thorner	74
1972	Willie Carson	132	Bob Davies	89
1973	Willie Carson	163	Ron Barry	125
1974	Pat Eddery	148	Ron Barry	94
1975	Pat Eddery	164	Tommy Stack	82
1976	Pat Eddery	162	Johnny Francome	96
1977	Pat Eddery	176	Tommy Stack	97
1978	Willie Carson	182	JonJo O'Neill	149
1979	Joe Mercer	164	Johnny Francome	95
1980	Willie Carson	165	JonJo O'Neill	117
1981	Lester Piggott	179	Johnny Francome	105
1982	Lester Piggott	188	Johnny Francome / Peter Scudamore	120

The most races won within one year in the USA is 546 by Chris McCarron (USA) in 1974 from a record 2199 mounts, an average of six races a day.

The youngest known winning jockey was Frank Wootton, later English champion jockey for four years, who rode his first winner, in South Africa, when aged 9 yr 10 months, in 1903. Frank Buckle won a record 27 Classic races between 1792 and 1827, comprising five Derbys, nine Oaks, six 1000 Guineas, five 2000 Guineas, and two St Legers. Weighing in than 29 kg (64 lb) he was known as 'The Pocket Hercules'.

The National Hunt jockey with most wins is Stan Mellor with 1049 (plus three wins on the flat) between 1952 and 1972. The most NH wins in one season is 149 by JonJo O'Neill in 1977–78, while the most NH championships won is seven by Gerald Wilson between 1933 and 1941.

OWNERS

Dan Lasater (USA) had a record 494 winners in 1974, for a money record of $3 022 960. The most successful in Britain was

Lester Piggott and *The Minstrel*, receiving admiring glances from the Queen and the Duchess of Kent. The horse gave Lester his eighth victory in the Derby in 1977. He has won every English and Irish Classic at least once, and his total of English Classic wins (26) is only one short of the record.

HH Aga Khan III who headed the leading owner table on a record 13 occasions between 1924 and 1952. The greatest number of winners in a season was 115 owned by David Robinson in 1973, while the most first-prize money won is £441 654 by HH Aga Khan IV in 1981. Horses belonging to the 4th Duke of Grafton won 20 Classic races from 1813 to 1831.

TRAINERS

Jack Van Berg (USA) trained a record 494 winners in 1976, while the most prize money won in a year is $3 953 906 by Charles Whittingham (USA) in 1981. The record prize money won by a British trainer is £872 704 by Henry Cecil in 1982. The most races won in a year is 146 by John Day in 1867. The British trainers' list was headed 12 times by Alec Taylor between 1907 and 1925, and John Scott trained a record 41 Classic winners between 1827 and 1862. The National Hunt prize money record is £351 133 by Michael Dickinson in 1982–83, and the most wins in a season is 115, also by Michael Dickinson in 1982–83.

THE DERBY: First run on 4 May 1780 and named after the 12th Earl of Derby, it was originally run over 1 mile (1609 m) but in 1784 the distance was increased to 1½ miles (2414 m). It has always been run at Epsom Downs, Surrey, except during the two War periods when it was held at Newmarket. It is for three-year-old colts and fillies. The fastest time ever recorded was 2 min 33·8 sec by *Mahmoud* in 1936, at an average speed of 56·42 km (35·06 mph), when ridden by Charlie Smirke. The most successful jockey has been Lester Piggott with nine wins between 1954 and 1983. Three trainers have had seven winners: Robert Robson between 1793 and 1823, John Porter from 1868 to 1899, and Fred Darling from 1922 to 1941. Two owners, the 3rd Earl of Egremont and HH Aga Khan III have had five winners, but only the former owned all five outright.

Only six fillies have ever won the race, in 1801, 1857, 1882,

1908, 1912 and 1916. The highest odds on a winner were 100–1 in 1898, 1908 and 1913. The most runners were 34 in 1862 and the smallest field was four in 1794. The greatest winning margin was 10 lengths by *Shergar* over *Glint of Gold* in 1981. The oldest winning jockey was John Forth, over 60 when he rode *Frederick* to victory in 1829, and the youngest was John Parsons, only 16 when he won on *Caractacus* in 1862. There have been two dead heats, in 1828 when *Cadland* beat *The Colonel* in a run-off, and in 1884 when the prize was shared between *Harvester* and *St Gatien*. Starting stalls were first used in the 1967 race.

Winners from 1870:

1870	Kingcraft	T. French
1871	Favonius	T. French
1872	Cremorne	C. Maidment
1873	Doncaster	F. Webb
1874	George Frederick	H. Custance
1875	Galopin	J. Morris
1876	Kisber	C. Maidment
1877	Silvio	F. Archer
1878	Sefton	H. Constable
1879	Sir Bevys	G. Fordham
1880	Bend Or	F. Archer
1881	Iroquois	F. Archer
1882	Shotover	T. Cannon
1883	St Blaise	C. Wood
1884	St Gatien	C. Wood
	Harvester	S. Loates
1885	Melton	F. Archer
1886	Ormonde	F. Archer
1887	Merry Hampton	J. Watts
1888	Ayrshire	F. Barrett
1889	Donovan	T. Loates
1890	Sainfoin	J. Watts
1891	Common	G. Barrett
1892	Sir Hugo	F. Allsopp
1893	Isinglass	T. Loates
1894	Ladas	J. Watts

1895	Sir Visto	S. Loates	
1896	Persimmon	J. Watts	
1897	Galtee More	C. Wood	
1898	Jeddah	O. Madden	
1899	Flying Fox	M. Cannon	
1900	Diamond Jubilee	H. Jones	
1901	Volodyovski	L. Reiff	
1902	Ard Patrick	J. H. Martin	
1903	Rock Sand	D. Maher	
1904	St Amant	K. Cannon	
1905	Cicero	D. Maher	
1906	Spearmint	D. Maher	
1907	Orby	J. Reiff	
1908	Signorinetta	W. Bullock	
1909	Minoru	H. Jones	
1910	Lemberg	B. Dillon	
1911	Sunstar	G. Stern	
1912	Tagalie	J. Reiff	
1913	Aboyeur	E. Piper	
1914	Durbar II	M. MacGee	
1915	Pommern	S. Donoghue	
1916	Fifinella	J. Childs	
1917	Gay Crusader	S. Donoghue	
1918	Gainsborough	J. Childs	
1919	Grand Parade	F. Templeman	
1920	Spion Kop	F. O'Neill	
1921	Humorist	S. Donoghue	
1922	Captain Cuttle	S. Donoghue	
1923	Papyrus	S. Donoghue	
1924	Sansovino	T. Weston	
1925	Manna	S. Donoghue	
1926	Coronach	J. Childs	
1927	Call Boy	E. C. Elliott	
1928	Felstead	H. Wragg	
1929	Trigo	J. Marshall	
1930	Blenheim	H. Wragg	
1931	Cameronian	F. Fox	
1932	April the Fifth	F. Lane	
1933	Hyperion	T. Weston	
1934	Windsor Lad	C. Smirke	
1935	Bahram	F. Fox	
1936	Mahmoud	C. Smirke	
1937	Mid-day Sun	M. Beary	
1938	Bois Roussel	E. C. Elliott	
1939	Blue Peter	E. Smith	
1940	Pont l'Eveque	S. Wragg	
1941	Owen Tudor	Willie Nevett	
1942	Watling Street	Harry Wragg	
1943	Straight Deal	Tom Carey	
1944	Ocean Swell	Willie Nevett	
1945	Dante	Willie Nevett	
1946	Airborne	Tom Lowrey	
1947	Pearl Diver	George Bridgland	
1948	My Love	Rae Johnstone	
1949	Nimbus	Charlie Elliott	
1950	Galcador	Rae Johnstone	
1951	Arctic Prince	Charles Spares	
1952	Tulyar	Charlie Smirke	
1953	Pinza	Gordon Richards	
1954	Never Say Die	Lester Piggott	
1955	Phil Drake	Fred Palmer	
1956	Lavandin	Rae Johnstone	
1957	Crepello	Lester Piggott	
1958	Hard Ridden	Charlie Smirke	
1959	Parthia	Harry Carr	
1960	St Paddy	Lester Piggott	
1961	Psidium	Roger Poincelet	
1962	Larkspur	Neville Sellwood	
1963	Relko	Yves Saint-Martin	
1964	Santa Claus	Scobie Breasley	
1965	Sea Bird II	Pat Glennon	
1966	Charlottown	Scobie Breasley	
1967	Royal Palace	George Moore	
1968	Sir Ivor	Lester Piggott	
1969	Blakeney	Ernie Johnson	
1970	Nijinsky	Lester Piggott	
1971	Mill Reef	Geoff Lewis	
1972	Roberto	Lester Piggott	
1973	Morston	Edward Hide	
1974	Snow Knight	Brian Taylor	
1975	Grundy	Pat Eddery	
1976	Emprey	Lester Piggott	

1977	The Minstrel	Lester Piggott
1978	Shirley Heights	Greville Starkey
1979	Troy	Willie Carson
1980	Henbit	Willie Carson
1981	Shergar	Walter Swinburn
1982	Golden Fleece	Pat Eddery
1983	Teenoso	Lester Piggott

1000 GUINEAS: First run in 1814, the race is restricted to three-year-old fillies, and is over 1 mile (1609 m) at Newmarket. The fastest time is 1 min 37 sec by *Camaree*, ridden by Rae Johnstone in 1950. The most successful jockey has been George Fordham who rode seven winners between 1859 and 1883. The most wins by a trainer have been eight by Robert Robson, who also gave the owner's record to the 4th Duke of Grafton, between 1819 and 1827. The largest field was 29 in 1926. In 1825 *Tontine* became the only horse to win a British Classic race by a walkover.

1814	Charlotte	W. Clift
1815	Selim filly	W. Clift
1816	Rhoda	S. Barnard
1817	Nava	W. Arnull
1818	Corinne	F. Buckle
1819	Catgut	Unknown
1820	Rowena	F. Buckle
1821	Zeal	F. Buckle
1822	Whizgig	F. Buckle
1823	Zinc	F. Buckle
1824	Cobweb	J. Robinson
1825	Tontine	Unknown
1826	Problem	J. Day
1827	Arab	F. Buckle
1828	Zoe	J. Robinson
1829	Young Mouse	W. Arnull
1830	Charlotte West	J. Robinson
1831	Galantine	P. Conolly
1832	Galata	W. Arnull
1833	Tarantella	E. Wright
1834	May-Day	J. Day
1835	Preserve	E. Flatman
1836	Destiny	J. Day
1837	Chapeau d'Espagne	J. Day
1838	Barcarolle	E. Edwards
1839	Cara	G. Edwards
1840	Crucifix	J. Day
1841	Potentia	J. Robinson
1842	Firebrand	S. Rogers
1843	Extempore	S. Chifney
1844	Sorella	J. Robinson
1845	Pic-nic	W. Abdale
1846	Mendicant	S. Day
1847	Clementina	E. Flatman
1848	Canezou	F. Butler
1849	Flea	A. Day
1850	Lady Orford	F. Butler
1851	Aphrodite	J. Marson
1852	Kate	A. Day
1853	Mentmore Lass	J. Charlton
1854	Virago	J. Wells
1855	Habena	S. Rogers
1856	Manganese	J. Osborne
1857	Imperieuse	E. Flatman
1858	Governess	T. Ashmall
1859	Mayonaise	G. Fordham
1860	Sagitta	T. Aldcroft
1861	Nemesis	G. Fordham
1862	Hurricane	T. Ashmall
1863	Lady Augusta	A. Edwards
1864	Tomato	J. Wells
1865	Siberia	G. Fordham
1866	Repulse	T. Cannon
1867	Achievement	H. Custance
1868	Formosa	G. Fordham
1869	Scottish Queen	G. Fordham

1870	Hester	J. Grimshaw
1871	Hannah	C. Maidment
1872	Reine	H. Parry
1873	Cecilia	J. Morris
1874	Apology	J. Osborne
1875	Spinaway	F. Archer
1876	Camelia	T. Glover
1877	Belphoebe	H. Jeffery
1878	Pilgrimage	T. Cannon
1879	Wheel of Fortune	F. Archer
1880	Elizabeth	C. Wood
1881	Thebias	G. Fordham
1882	St Marguerite	C. Wood
1883	Hauteur	G. Fordham
1884	Busybody	T. Cannon
1885	Farewell	G. Barrett
1886	Miss Jummy	J. Watts
1887	Reve d'Or	C. Wood
1888	Briar-root	W. Warne
1889	Minthe	J. Woodburn
1890	Semolina	J. Watts
1891	Mimi	F. Rickaby
1892	La Fleche	G. Barrett
1893	Siffleuse	T. Loates
1894	Amiable	W. Bradford
1895	Galeottia	F. Pratt
1896	Thais	J. Watts
1897	Chelandry	J. Watts
1898	Nun Nicer	S. Loates
1899	Sibola	J. Sloan
1900	Winifreda	S. Loates
1901	Aida	D. Maher
1902	Sceptre	H. Randall
1903	Quintessence	H. Randall
1904	Pretty Polly	W. Lane
1905	Cherry Lass	G. McCall
1906	Flair	B. Dillon
1907	Witch Elm	B. Lynham
1908	Rhodora	L. Lyne
1909	Electra	B. Dillon
1910	Winkipop	B. Lynham
1911	Atmah	F. Fox
1912	Tagalie	L. Hewitt
1913	Jest	F. Rickaby, Jr
1914	Princess Dorrie	W. Huxley
1915	Vaucluse	F. Rickaby, Jr
1916	Canyon	F. Rickaby, Jr
1917	Diadem	F. Rickaby, Jr
1918	Ferry	B. Carslake
1919	Roseway	A. Whalley
1920	Cinna	W. Griggs
1921	Bettina	G. Bellhouse
1922	Silver Urn	B. Carslake
1923	Tranquil	E. Gardner
1924	Plack	E. C. Elliott
1925	Saucy Sue	F. Bullock
1926	Pillion	R. Perryman
1927	Cresta Run	A. Balding
1928	Scuttle	J. Childs
1929	Taj Mah	W. Sibbritt
1930	Fair Isle	T. Weston
1931	Four Course	E. C. Elliott
1932	Kandy	E. C. Elliott
1933	Brown Betty	J. Childs
1934	Campanula	H. Wragg
1935	Mesa	W. Johnstone
1936	Tide-Way	R. Perryman
1937	Exhibitionist	S. Donoghue
1938	Rockfel	S. Wragg
1939	Galatea II	R. A. Jones
1940	Godiva	D. Marks
1941	Dancing Time	R. Perryman
1942	Sun Chariot	G. Richards
1943	Herringbone	H. Wragg
1944	Picture Play	E. C. Elliott
1945	Sun Stream	H. Wragg
1946	Hypericum	Douglas Smith
1947	Imprudence	Rae Johnstone
1948	Queenpot	Gordon Richards
1949	Musidora	Edgar Britt
1950	Camaree	Rae Johnstone
1951	Belle of All	Gordon Richards
1952	Zabara	Ken Gethin
1953	Happy Laughter	Manny Mercer
1954	Festoon	Scobie Breasley
1955	Meld	Harry Carr
1956	Honeylight	Edgar Britt
1957	Rose Royale II	Charlie Smirke
1958	Bella Paola	Serge Boullenger
1959	Petite Etoile	Douglas Smith
1960	Never Too Late	Roger Poincelet
1961	Sweet Solera	Bill Rickaby
1962	Abermaid	Bill Williamson
1963	Hula Dancer	Roger Poincelet
1964	Pourparler	Garnie Bougoure
1965	Night Off	Bill Williamson
1966	Glad Rags	Paul Cook
1967	Fleet	George Moore
1968	Caergwrle	Sandy Barclay
1969	Full Dress II	Ron Hutchinson
1970	Humble Duty	Lester Piggott
1971	Altesse Royale	Yves Saint-Martin
1972	Waterloo	Edward Hide
1973	Mysterious	Geoff Lewis
1974	Highclere	Joe Mercer
1975	Nocturnal Spree	Johnny Roe
1976	Flying Water	Yves Saint-Martin
1977	Mrs McArdy	Edward Hide
1978	Enstone Spark	Ernie Johnson
1979	One In a Million	Joe Mercer
1980	Quick As Lightning	Brian Rouse
1981	Fairy Footsteps	Lester Piggott
1982	On The House	John Reid
1983	Ma Biche	Frederic Head

2000 GUINEAS: A race over 1 mile (1609 m) at Newmarket for three-year-old colts and fillies, first held in 1809. The fastest time is 1 min 35·8 sec by *My Babu*, ridden by Charlie Smirke in 1948. The record number of wins by a jockey is nine by Jem Robinson between 1825 and 1848. The most by a trainer is five by Fred Darling from 1925 to 1947, while the owner's record is also five by the 4th Duke of Grafton, from 1820 to 1827, and also by Lord Jersey, from 1831 to 1837. The largest field was 28 in 1930, and the smallest was two in 1829 and 1830.

1809	Wizard	W. Clift
1810	Hephestion	F. Buckle
1811	Trophonius	S. Barnard
1812	Cwrw	S. Chifney
1813	Smolensko	H. Miller
1814	Olive	W. Arnull
1815	Tigris	W. Arnull
1816	Nectar	W. Arnull
1817	Manfred	W. Wheatley
1818	Interpreter	W. Clift
1819	Antar	E. Edwards
1820	Pindarrie	F. Buckle
1821	Reginald	F. Buckle
1822	Pastilla	F. Buckle
1823	Nicola	W. Wheatley
1824	Schahriar	W. Wheatley
1825	Enamel	J. Robinson
1826	Dervise	J. B. Day
1827	Turcoman	F. Buckle
1828	Cadland	J. Robinson
1829	Patron	F. Boyce
1830	Augustus	P. Conolly
1831	Riddlesworth	J. Robinson
1832	Archibald	A. Pavis
1833	Clearwell	J. Robinson
1834	Glencoe	J. Robinson
1835	Ibrahim	J. Robinson
1836	Bay Middleton	J. Robinson
1837	Achmet	E. Edwards
1838	Grey Momus	J. B. Day
1839	The Corsair	W. Wakefield
1840	Crucifix	J. B. Day
1841	Ralph	J. B. Day
1842	Meteor	W. Scott
1843	Cotherstone	W. Scott

97

The Queen Mother and Princess Margaret taking the traditional ride up the course in a landau at the opening of Royal Ascot. The Royal Family, and particularly the present Queen, are ardent devotees of the sport and own a number of successful horses.

1844	The Ugly Buck	J. Day Jr
1845	Idas	E. Flatman
1846	Sir Tatton Sykes	W. Scott
1847	Conyngham	J. Robinson
1848	Flatcatcher	J. Robinson
1849	Nunnykirk	F. Butler
1850	Pitsford	A. Day

1851	Hernandez	E. Flatman
1852	Stockwell	J. Norman
1853	West Australian	F. Butler
1854	The Hermit	A. Day
1855	Lord of the Isles	T. Aldcroft
1856	Fazzoletto	E. Flatman
1857	Vedette	J. Osborne
1858	Fitz-Roland	J. Wells
1859	The Promised Land	A. Day
1860	The Wizard	T. Ashmall
1861	Diophantus	A. Edwards
1862	The Marquis	T. Ashmall
1863	Macaroni	T. Chaloner
1864	General Peel	T. Aldcroft

1865	Gladiateur	H. Grimshaw
1866	Lord Lyon	R. Thomas
1867	Vauban	G. Fordham
1868	Moslem	T. Chaloner
	dead heat with Formosa	G. Fordham
1869	Pretender	J. Osborne
1870	Macgregor	J. Daley
1871	Bothwell	J. Osborne
1872	Prince Charlie	J. Osborne
1873	Gang Forward	T. Chaloner
1874	Atlantic	F. Archer
1875	Camballo	J. Osborne
1876	Petrarch	H. Luke
1877	Chamant	J. Goater
1878	Pilgrimage	T. Cannon
1879	Charibert	F. Archer
1880	Petronel	G. Fordham
1881	Peregrine	F. Webb
1882	Shotover	T. Cannon
1883	Galliard	F. Archer
1884	Scot Free	W. Platt
1885	Paradox	F. Archer
1886	Ormonde	G. Barrett
1887	Enterprise	T. Cannon
1888	Ayrshire	J. Osborne
1889	Enthusiast	T. Cannon
1890	Surefoot	J. Liddiard
1891	Common	G. Barrett
1892	Bonavista	W. Robinson
1893	Isinglass	T. Loates
1894	Ladas	J. Watts
1895	Kirkconnel	J. Watts
1896	St Frusquin	T. Loates
1897	Galtee More	C. Wood
1898	Disraeli	S. Loates
1899	Flying Fox	M. Cannon
1900	Diamond Jubilee	H. Jones
1901	Handicapper	W. Halsey
1902	Sceptre	H. Randall
1903	Rock Sand	J. Martin
1904	St Amant	K. Cannon
1905	Vedas	H. Jones
1906	Gorgos	H. Jones
1907	Slieve Gallion	W. Higgs
1908	Norman III	O. Madden
1909	Minoru	H. Jones
1910	Neil Gow	D. Maher
1911	Sunstar	G. Stern
1912	Sweeper II	D. Maher
1913	Louvois	J. Reiff
1914	Kennymore	G. Stern
1915	Pommern	S. Donoghue
1916	Clarissimus	J. Clark
1917	Gay Crusader	S. Donoghue
1918	Gainsborough	J. Childs
1919	The Panther	R. Cooper
1920	Tetratema	B. Carslake
1921	Craig an Eran	J. Brennan
1922	St Louis	G. Archibald
1923	Ellangowan	E. Elliott
1924	Diophon	G. Hulme
1925	Manna	S. Donoghue
1926	Colorado	T. Weston
1927	Adam's Apple	J. Leach
1928	Flamingo	E. C. Elliott
1929	Mr Jinks	H. Beasley
1930	Diolite	F. Fox
1931	Cameronian	J. Childs
1932	Orwell	R. A. Jones
1933	Rodosto	R. Brethes
1934	Colombo	W. Johnstone
1935	Bahram	F. Fox
1936	Pay Up	R. Dick
1937	Le Ksar	C. Semblat
1938	Pasch	G. Richards
1939	Blue Peter	E. Smith
1940	Djebel	E. Elliott
1941	Lambert Simnel	E. Elliott
1942	Big Game	G. Richards
1943	Kingsway	S. Wragg
1944	Garden Path	Harry Wragg
1945	Court Martial	Gordon Richards

1946	Happy Knight	Tommy Weston
1947	Tudor Minstrel	Gordon Richards
1948	My Babu	Charlie Smirke
1949	Nimbus	Charlie Elliott
1950	Palestine	Charlie Smirke
1951	Ki Ming	Scobie Breasley
1952	Thunderhead II	Roger Poincelet
1953	Nearula	Edgar Britt
1954	Darius	Manny Mercer
1955	Our Babu	Douglas Smith
1956	Gilles de Retz	Frank Barlow
1957	Crepello	Lester Piggott
1958	Pall Mall	Douglas Smith
1959	Taboun	George Moore
1960	Martial	Ron Hutchinson
1961	Rockavon	Norman Stirk
1962	Privy Councillor	Bill Rickaby
1963	Only For Life	Jimmy Lindley
1964	Baldric II	Bill Pyers
1965	Niksar	Duncan Keith
1966	Kashmir II	Jimmy Lindley
1967	Royal Palace	George Moore
1968	Sir Ivor	Lester Piggott
1969	Right Tack	Geoff Lewis
1970	Nijinsky	Lester Piggott
1971	Brigadier Gerard	Joe Mercer
1972	High Top	Willie Carson
1973	Mon Fils	Frankie Durr
1974	Nonoalco	Yves Saint-Martin
1975	Bolkonski	Gianfranco Dettori
1976	Wollow	Gianfranco Dettori
1977	Nebbiolo	Gabriel Curran
1978	Roland Gardens	Frankie Durr
1979	Tap On Wood	Steve Cauthen
1980	Known Fact	Willie Carson
1981	To-Agori-Mou	Greville Starkey
1982	Zino	Frederic Head
1983	Lomond	Pat Eddery

OAKS: The race is named after the Epsom home of the 12th Earl of Derby. Restricted to three-year-old fillies, the race is over $1\frac{1}{2}$ miles (2414 m) and run at Epsom Downs, Surrey since its institution in 1779, except for wartime races at Newmarket, 1915–18 and 1940–45. The record time is 2 min 34·33 sec by *Bireme*, ridden by Willie Carson in 1980. The most wins by a jockey have been nine by Frank Buckle between 1797 and 1823. The most by a trainer is eight by Alec Taylor from 1910 to 1926, and the record for an owner is six by the 4th Duke of Grafton between 1813 and 1831. The largest field was 26 in 1848.

1779	Bridget	R. Goodison
1780	Teetotum	R. Goodison
1781	Faith	R. Goodison
1782	Ceres	S. Chifney Sr
1783	Maid of the Oakes	S. Chifney Sr
1784	Stella	C. Hindley
1785	Trifle	J. Bird
1786	Perdita filly	J. Edwards
1787	Annette	D. Fitzpatrick
1788	Nightshade	D. Fitzpatrick
1789	Tag	S. Chifney Sr
1790	Hippolyta	S. Chifney Sr
1791	Portia	J. Singleton
1792	Volante	C. Hindley
1793	Caelia	J. Singleton
1794	Hermoine	S. Arnull
1795	Platina	D. Fitzpatrick
1796	Parissot	J. Arnull
1797	Nike	F. Buckle
1798	Bellissima	F. Buckle
1799	Bellina	F. Buckle
1800	Ephemera	D. Fitzpatrick
1801	Eleanor	J. Saunders
1802	Scotia	F. Buckle
1803	Theophania	F. Buckle
1804	Pelisse	W. Clift
1805	Meteora	F. Buckle
1806	Bronze	W. Edwards
1807	Briseis	S. Chifney

1808	Morel	W. Clift	
1809	Maid of Orleans	J. Moss	
1810	Oriana	W. Peirse	
1811	Sorcery	S. Chifney	
1812	Manuella	W. Peirse	
1813	Music	T. Goodison	
1814	Medora	S. Barnard	
1815	Minuet	T. Goodison	
1816	Landscape	S. Chifney	
1817	Neva	F. Buckle	
1818	Corinne	F. Buckle	
1819	Shoveler	S. Chifney	
1820	Caroline	H. Edwards	
1821	Augusta	J. Robinson	
1822	Pastille	H. Edwards	
1823	Zinc	F. Buckle	
1824	Cobweb	J. Robinson	
1825	Wings	S. Chifney	
1826	Lilias	T. Lye	
1827	Gulnare	F. Boyce	
1828	Turquoise	J. B. Day	
1829	Green Mantle	G. Dockeray	
1830	Variation	G. Edwards	
1831	Oxygen	J. B. Day	
1832	Galata	P. Conolly	
1833	Vespa	J. Chapple	
1834	Pussy	J. B. Day	
1835	Queen of Trumps	T. Lye	
1836	Cyprian	W. Scott	
1837	Miss Letty	J. Holmes	
1838	Industry	W. Scott	
1839	Deception	J. B. Day	
1840	Crucifix	J. B. Day	
1841	Ghuznee	W. Scott	
1842	Our Nell	T. Lye	
1843	Poison	F. Butler	
1844	The Princess	F. Butler	
1845	Refraction	H. Bell	
1846	Mendicant	S. Day	
1847	Miami	S. Templeman	
1848	Cymba	S. Templeman	
1849	Lady Evelyn	F. Butler	
1850	Rhedycina	F. Butler	
1851	Iris	F. Butler	
1852	Songstress	F. Butler	
1853	Catherine Hayes	C. Marlow	
1854	Mincemeat	J. Charlton	
1855	Marchioness	S. Templeman	
1856	Mincepie	A. Day	
1857	Pink Bonny	J. Charlton	
1858	Governess	T. Ashmall	
1859	Summerside	G. Fordham	
1860	Butterfly	J. Snowden	
1861	Brown Duchess	L. Snowden	
1862	Feu de Joie	T. Challoner	
1863	Queen Bertha	T. Aldcroft	
1864	Fille de l'Air	A. Edwards	
1865	Regalia	J. Norman	
1866	Tormentor	J. Mann	
1867	Hippia	J. Daley	
1868	Formosa	G. Fordham	
1869	Brigantine	T. Cannon	
1870	Gamos	G. Fordham	
1871	Hannah	C. Maidment	
1872	Reine	G. Fordham	
1873	Marie Stuart	T. Cannon	
1874	Apology	J. Osborne	
1875	Spinaway	F. Archer	
1876	Enguerrande	Hudson	
	Camelia	T. Glover	
1877	Placida	H. Jeffrey	
1878	Jannette	F. Archer	
1879	Wheel of Fortune	F. Archer	
1880	Jenny Howlet	J. Snowden	
1881	Thebais	G. Fordham	
1882	Geheimniss	T. Cannon	
1883	Bonny Jean	J. Watts	
1884	Busybody	T. Cannon	
1885	Lonely	F. Archer	
1886	Miss Jummy	J. Watts	
1887	Reve d'Or	C. Wood	
1888	Seabreeze	W. Robinson	
1889	L'Abbesse de Jouarre	J. Woodburn	
1890	Memoir	J. Watts	
1891	Mimi	F. Rickaby	
1892	La Fleche	G. Barrett	
1893	Mrs Butterwick	J. Watts	
1894	Amiable	W. Bradford	
1895	La Sagessé	S. Loates	
1896	Canterbury Pilgrim	F. Rickaby	
1897	Limasol	W. Bradford	
1898	Airs and Graces	W. Bradford	
1899	Musa	O. Madden	
1900	La Roche	M. Cannon	
1901	Cap and Bells II	M. Henry	
1902	Sceptre	H. Randall	
1903	Our Lassie	M. Cannon	
1904	Pretty Polly	W. Lane	
1905	Cherry Lass	H. Jones	
1906	Keystone II	D. Maher	
1907	Glass Doll	H. Randall	
1908	Signorinetta	W. Bullock	
1909	Perola	F. Wootton	
1910	Rosedrop	C. Trigg	
1911	Cherimoya	F. Winter	
1912	Mirska	J. Childs	
1913	Jest	F. Rickaby Jr	
1914	Princess Dorrie	W. Huxley	
1915	Snow Marten	W. Griggs	
1916	Fifinella	J. Childs	
1917	Sunny Jane	D. Madden	
1918	My Dear	S. Donoghue	
1919	Bayuda	J. Childs	
1920	Charlebelle	A. Whalley	
1921	Love in Idleness	J. Childs	
1922	Pogrom	E. Gardner	
1923	Brownhylda	V. Smyth	
1924	Straitlace	F. O'Neill	
1925	Saucy Sue	F. Bullock	
1926	Short Story	R. A. Jones	
1927	Beam	T. Weston	
1928	Toboggan	T. Weston	
1929	Pennycomequick	H. Jellis	
1930	Rose of England	G. Richards	
1931	Brulette	E. C. Elliott	
1932	Udaipur	M. Beary	
1933	Chatelaine	S. Wragg	
1934	Light Brocade	B. Carslake	
1935	Quashed	H. Jellis	
1936	Lovely Rosa	T. Weston	
1937	Exhibitionist	S. Donoghue	
1938	Rockfel	H. Wragg	
1939	Galatea II	R. A. Jones	
1940	Godiva	D. Marks	
1941	Commotion	Harry Wragg	
1942	Sun Chariot	Gordon Richards	
1943	Why Hurry	Charlie Elliott	
1944	Hycilla	George Bridgland	
1945	Sun Stream	Harry Wragg	
1946	Steady Aim	Harry Wragg	
1947	Imprudence	Rae Johnstone	
1948	Masaka	Willie Nevett	
1949	Musidora	Edgar Britt	
1950	Asmena	Rae Johnstone	
1951	Neasham Belle	Stan Clayton	
1952	Frieze	Edgar Britt	
1953	Ambiguity	Joe Mercer	
1954	Sun Cap	Rae Johnstone	
1955	Meld	Harry Wragg	
1956	Sicarelle	Fred Palmer	
1957	Carrozza	Lester Piggott	
1958	Bella Paola	Max Garcia	
1959	Petite Etoile	Lester Piggott	
1960	Never Too Late	Roger Poincelet	
1961	Sweet Solera	Bill Rickaby	
1962	Monade	Yves Saint-Martin	
1963	Noblesse	Garnie Bougoure	
1964	Homeward Bound	Greville Starkey	
1965	Long Look	Jack Purtell	
1966	Valoris	Lester Piggott	
1967	Pia	Edward Hide	
1968	La Lagune	Gerard Thiboeuf	
1969	Sleeping Partner	John Gorton	
1970	Lupe	Sandy Barclay	

1971	Altesse Royale	Geoff Lewis
1972	Ginevra	Tony Murray
1973	Mysterious	Geoff Lewis
1974	Polygamy	Pat Eddery
1975	Juliette Marny	Lester Piggott
1976	Pawneese	Yves Saint-Martin
1977	Dunfermline	Willie Carson
1978	Fair Salinia	Greville Starkey
1979	Scintillate	Pat Eddery
1980	Bireme	Willie Carson
1981	Blue Wind	Lester Piggott
1982	Time Charter	Billy Newnes
1983	Sun Princess	Willie Carson

ST LEGER: Named after Col Anthony St Leger, who instituted the oldest of the Classics in 1776. It is held over 1 mile 6 furlongs 127 yd (2932 m) at Doncaster, Yorkshire, for three-year-old colts and fillies. The fastest time is 3 min 01·6 sec by *Coronach*, ridden by Joe Childs in 1926, and by *Windsor Lad*, ridden by Charlie Smirke in 1934. The most wins by a jockey is nine by Will Scott between 1821 and 1846, and the most by a trainer is 16 by his brother John Scott from 1827 to 1862. The 9th Duke of Hamilton set an owners record with seven victories between 1786 and 1814. The largest field was 30 in 1825, and the smallest was a wartime substitute race in 1917 with only three runners. In 1789 *Zanga* crossed the line first but was disqualified—the only such occasion in the race's history.

1776	Allabaculia	J. Singleton
1777	Bourbon	J. Cade
1778	Hollandaise	G. Herring
1779	Tommy	G. Lowry Sr
1780	Ruler	J. Mangle
1781	Serina	R. Foster
1782	Imperatrix	G. Searle
1783	Phoenomenon	A. Hall
1784	Omphale	J. Kirton
1785	Cowslip	G. Searle
1786	Paragon	J. Mangle
1787	Spadille	J. Mangle
1788	Young Flora	J. Mangle
1789	Pewett	W. Wilson
1790	Ambidexter	G. Searle
1791	Young Traveller	J. Jackson
1792	Tartar	J. Mangle
1793	Ninety-Three	W. Peirse
1794	Beningbrough	J. Jackson
1795	Hambletonian	R. D. Boyce
1796	Ambrosia	J. Jackson
1797	Lounger	J. Shepherd
1798	Symmetry	J. Jackson
1799	Cockfighter	T. Fields
1800	Champion	F. Buckle
1801	Quiz	J. Shepherd
1802	Orville	J. Singleton Jr
1803	Remembrancer	B. Smith
1804	Sancho	F. Buckle
1805	Staveley	J. Jackson
1806	Fyldener	T. Carr
1807	Paulina	W. Clift
1808	Petronius	B. Smith
1809	Ashton	B. Smith
1810	Octavian	W. Clift
1811	Soothsayer	B. Smith
1812	Otterington	R. Johnson
1813	Altisidora	J. Jackson
1814	William	J. Shepherd
1815	Filho da Puta	J. Jackson
1816	The Duchess	B. Smith
1817	Ebor	R. Johnson
1818	Reveller	R. Johnson
1819	Antonio	T. Nicholson
1820	St Patrick	R. Johnson
1821	Jack Spigot	W. Scott
1822	Theodore	J. Jackson
1823	Barefoot	T. Goodisson
1824	Jerry	B. Smith
1825	Memnon	W. Scott
1826	Tarrare	G. Nelson

1827	Matilda	J. Robinson
1828	The Colonel	W. Scott
1829	Rowton	W. Scott
1830	Birmingham	P. Conolly
1831	Chorister	J. B. Day
1832	Margrave	J. Robinson
1833	Rockingham	S. Darling
1834	Touchstone	G. Calloway
1835	Queen of Trumps	T. Lye
1836	Elis	J. B. Day
1837	Mango	S. Day Jr
1838	Don John	W. Scott
1839	Charles the Twelfth	W. Scott
1840	Launcelot	W. Scott
1841	Satirist	W. Scott
1842	The Blue Bonnet	T. Lye
1843	Nutwith	J. Marson
1844	Foig a Ballagh	H. Bell
1845	The Baron	F. Butler
1846	Sir Tatton Sykes	W. Scott
1847	Van Tromp	J. Marson
1848	Surplice	E. Flatman
1849	The Flying Dutchman	C. Marlow
1850	Voltigeur	J. Marson
1851	Newminster	S. Templeman
1852	Stockwell	J. Norman
1853	West Australian	F. Butler
1854	Knight of St George	R. Basham
1855	Saucebox	J. Wells
1856	Warlock	E. Flatman
1857	Imperieuse	E. Flatman
1858	Sunbeam	L. Snowden
1859	Gamester	T. Aldcroft
1860	St Albans	L. Snowden
1861	Caller Ou	T. Chaloner
1862	The Marquis	T. Chaloner
1863	Lord Clifden	J. Osborne
1864	Blair Athol	J. Snowden
1865	Gladiateur	H. Grimshaw
1866	Lord Lyon	H. Custance
1867	Achievement	T. Chaloner
1868	Formosa	T. Chaloner
1869	Pero Gomez	J. Wells
1870	Hawthornden	J. Grimshaw
1871	Hannah	C. Maidment
1872	Wenlock	C. Maidment
1873	Marie Stuart	T. Osborne
1874	Apology	J. Osborne
1875	Craig Millar	T. Chaloner
1876	Petrarch	J. Goater
1877	Silvio	F. Archer
1878	Jannette	F. Archer
1879	Rayon d'Or	J. Goater
1880	Robert the Devil	T. Cannon
1881	Iroquois	F. Archer
1882	Dutch Oven	F. Archer
1883	Ossian	J. Watts
1884	The Lambkin	J. Watts
1885	Melton	F. Archer
1886	Ormonde	F. Archer
1887	Kilwarlin	W. T. Robinson
1888	Seabreeze	W. T. Robinson
1889	Donovan	F. Barrett
1890	Memoir	J. Watts
1891	Common	G. Barrett
1892	La Fleche	J. Watts
1893	Isinglass	T. Loates
1894	Throstle	M. Cannon
1895	Sir Visto	S. Loates
1896	Persimmon	J. Watts
1897	Galtee More	C. Wood
1898	Wildflower	C. Wood
1899	Flying Fox	M. Cannon
1900	Diamond Jubilee	H. Jones
1901	Doricles	K. Cannon
1902	Sceptre	F. W. Hardy
1903	Rock Sand	D. Maher
1904	Pretty Polly	W. Lane
1905	Challacombe	O. Madden
1906	Troutbeck	G. Stern
1907	Wool Winder	W. Halsey
1908	Your Majesty	Wal Griggs

1909	Bayardo	D. Maher
1910	Swynford	F. Wootton
1911	Prince Palatine	F. O'Neill
1912	Tracery	G. Bellhouse
1913	Night Hawk	E. Wheatley
1914	Black Jester	Wal Griggs
1915	Pommern	S. Donoghue
1916	Hurry On	C. Childs
1917	Gay Crusader	S. Donoghue
1918	Gainsborough	J. Childs
1919	Keysoe	B. Carslake
1920	Caligual	A. Smith
1921	Polemarch	J. Childs
1922	Royal Lancer	R. A. Jones
1923	Tranquil	T. Weston
1924	Salmon-Trout	B. Carslake
1925	Solario	J. Childs
1926	Coronach	J. Childs
1927	Book Law	H. Jelliss
1928	Fairway	T. Weston
1929	Trigo	M. Beary
1930	Singapore	G. Richards
1931	Sandwich	H. Wragg
1932	Firdaussi	F. Fox
1933	Hyperion	T. Weston
1934	Windsor Lad	C. Smirke
1935	Bahram	C. Smirke
1936	Boswell	P. Beasley
1937	Chulmleigh	G. Richards
1938	Scottish Union	B. Carslake
1939	No Race	
1940	Turkhan	Gordon Richards
1941	Sun Castle	George Bridgland
1942	Sun Chariot	Gordon Richards
1943	Herringbone	Harry Wragg
1944	Tehran	Gordon Richards
1945	Chamossaire	Thomas Lowrey
1946	Airborne	Thomas Lowrey
1947	Sayajirao	Edgar Britt
1948	Black Tarquin	Edgar Britt
1949	Ridge Wood	Michael Beary
1950	Scratch II	Rae Johnstone
1951	Talma II	Rae Johnstone
1952	Tulyar	Charlie Smirke
1953	Premonition	Eph Smith
1954	Never Say Die	Charlie Smirke
1955	Meld	Harry Carr
1956	Cambremer	Fred Palmer
1957	Ballymoss	Tom Burns
1958	Alcide	Harry Carr
1959	Cantelo	Edward Hide
1960	St Paddy	Lester Piggott
1961	Aurelius	Lester Piggott
1962	Hethersett	Harry Carr
1963	Ragusa	Garnie Bougoure
1964	Indiana	Jimmy Lindley
1965	Provoke	Joe Mercer
1966	Sodium	Frankie Durr
1967	Ribocco	Lester Piggott
1968	Ribero	Lester Piggott
1969	Intermezzo	Ron Hutchinson
1970	Nijinsky	Lester Piggott
1971	Athens Wood	Lester Piggott
1972	Boucher	Lester Piggott
1973	Peleid	Frankie Durr
1974	Bustino	Joe Mercer
1975	Bruni	Tony Murray
1976	Crow	Yves Saint-Martin

Twice champion National Hunt jockey JonJo O'Neill leaving *Alverton* **in the 1979 Grand National. The non-smoking, teetotal Irishman has had his fair share of falls in his illustrious career, and surprisingly has never finished the Grand National course.**

1977	Dunfermline	Willie Carson
1978	Julio Mariner	Edward Hide
1979	Son Of Love	Alain Lequeux
1980	Light Cavalry	Joe Mercer
1981	Cut Above	Joe Mercer
1982	Touching Wood	Paul Cook

GRAND NATIONAL: The forerunner of the race was run at Maghull in 1837 and 1838 although not regarded by all authorities as official. In 1839 at Aintree the race was named the Grand Liverpool Steeplechase and took its present title in 1847. Always run at Aintree except for 1916–18 when it was held at Gatwick, Surrey. The course is 4½ miles (7242 m) long and consists of 30 jumps. Until 1930 five-year-old horses were eligible but since then only six-year-olds and over have been allowed. The only horse to win on three occasions was *Red Rum* in 1973, 1974 and 1977, which also came second in 1975 and 1976. Between 1895 and 1904 *Manifesto* ran eight times, winning twice, placing second three times and coming fourth once. The fastest time was set by *Red Rum*, carrying 65·7 kg (10 stone 5 lb), ridden by Brian Fletcher, with 9 min 1·9 sec in 1973. This represents an average speed of 47·96 km/h (29·80 mph). The highest jump is the 15th, known as 'The Chair', which is 1·57 m (5 ft 2 in) high and 1·14 m (3 ft 9 in) thick. The only jockey to have ridden five winners is George Stevens between 1856 and 1870. The only trainer to have had four victories is Fred Rimell in 1956, 1961, 1970 and 1976, but the Hon Aubrey Hastings won three at Aintree, 1906, 1915 and 1924, as well as a wartime race in 1917. Owners who have won three times are Capt Henry Machell, Sir Charles Assheton-Smith, and Noel Le Mare. The biggest field was 66 runners in 1929, while the smallest was 10 in 1841 and 1883. The highest weight carried to victory has been 85·8 kg (12 st 7 lb) in 1893, 1899, 1912 and 1919. The oldest horses to win have been the 13-year-olds *Why Not* in 1894 and *Sergeant Murphy* in 1923, while the youngest jockey to ride a winner was 17-year-old Bruce Hobbs on *Battleship* in 1938.

1837	The Duke	Mr Potts
1838	Sir Henry	T. Oliver
1839	Lottery	J. Mason
1840	Jerry	B. Bretherton
1841	Charity	Powell
1842	Gay Lad	T. Oliver
1843	Vanguard	T. Oliver
1844	Discount	Crickmere
1945	Cureall	W. Loft
1846	Pioneer	Taylor
1847	Matthew	D. Wynne
1848	Chandler	Capt Little
1849	Peter Simple	T. Cunningham
1950	Abd-el-Kader	C. Green
1951	Abd-el-Kader	T. Abbott
1952	Miss Mowbray	Mr A. Goodman
1953	Peter Simple	T. Oliver
1954	Bourton	Tasker
1855	Wanderer	J. Hanlon
1856	Free Trader	G. Stevens
1857	Emigrant	C. Boyce
1858	Little Charlie	W. Archer
1859	Half Caste	C. Green
1860	Anatis	Mr Thomas
1861	Jealousy	J. Kendall
1862	Huntsman	H. Lamplugh
1863	Emblem	G. Stevens
1864	Emblematic	G. Stevens
1865	Alcibiade	Capt Coventry
1866	Salamander	Mr A. Goodman
1867	Cortolvin	J. Page
1868	The Lamb	Mr Edwards
1869	The Colonel	G. Stevens
1870	The Colonel	G. Stevens
1871	The Lamb	Mr Thomas
1872	Casse Tete	J. Page
1873	Disturbance	Mr J. Richardson
1874	Reugny	Mr J. Richardson

1875	Pathfinder	Mr Thomas
1876	Regal	J. Cannon
1877	Austerlitz	Mr E. Hobson
1878	Shifnal	J. Jones
1879	Liberator	Mr G. Moore
1880	Empress	Mr T. Beasley
1881	Woodbrook	Mr T. Beasley
1882	Seaman	Lord Manners
1883	Zoedone	Count C. Kinsky
1884	Voluptuary	Mr E. Wilson
1885	Roquefort	Mr E. Wilson
1886	Old Joe	T. Skelton
1887	Gamecock	W. Daniells
1888	Playfair	Mawson
1889	Frigate	Mr T. Beasley
1890	Ilex	A. Nightingall
1891	Come Away	Mr H. Beasley
1892	Father O'Flynn	Capt R. Owen
1893	Cloister	Dollery
1894	Why Not	A. Nightingall
1895	Wild Man From Borneo	Mr J. Widger
1896	The Soarer	Mr D. Campbell
1897	Manifesto	T. Kavanagh
1898	Drogheda	J. Gourley
1899	Manifesto	G. Williamson
1900	Ambush II	A. Anthony
1901	Grudon	A. Nightingall
1902	Shannon Lass	D. Read
1903	Drumcree	P. Woodland
1904	Moifaa	A. Birch
1905	Kirkland	F. Mason
1906	Ascetic's Silver	Hon. A. Hastings
1907	Eremon	A. Newey
1908	Rubio	H. Bletsoe
1909	Lutteur III	G. Parfremont
1910	Jenkinstown	R. Chadwick
1911	Glenside	Mr J. Anthony
1912	Jerry M	E. Piggott
1913	Covercoat	P. Woodland
1914	Sunloch	W. Smith
1915	Ally Sloper	Mr J. Anthony
1916	Vermouth	J. Reardon
1917	Ballymacad	E. Driscoll
1918	Poethlyn	E. Piggott
1919	Poethlyn	E. Piggott
1920	Troytown	Mr J. Anthony
1921	Shaun Spadah	F. Rees
1922	Music Hall	L. Rees
1923	Sergeant Murphy	Capt G. Bennett
1924	Master Robert	R. Trudgill
1925	Double Chance	Maj J. Wilson
1926	Jack Horner	W. Watkinson
1927	Sprig	T. E. Leader
1928	Tipperary Tim	Mr W. P. Dutton
1929	Gregalach	R. Everett
1930	Shaun Goilin	T. Cullinan
1931	Grakle	R. Lyall
1932	Forbra	J. Hamey
1933	Kellsboro' Jack	D. Williams
1934	Golden Miller	G. Wilson
1935	Reynoldstown	Mr F. Furlong
1936	Reynoldstown	Mr F. Walwyn
1937	Royal Mail	E. Williams
1938	Battleship	B. Hobbs
1939	Workman	T. Hyde
1940	Bogskar	M. Jones
1941–45	No race	
1946	Lovely Cottage	Capt Robert Petre
1947	Caughoo	Edward Dempsey
1948	Sheila's Cottage	Arthur Thompson
1949	Russian Hero	Liam McMorrow
1950	Freebooter	Jimmy Power
1951	Nickel Coin	Johnny Bullock
1952	Teal	Arthur Thompson
1953	Early Mist	Bryan Marshall
1954	Royal Tan	Bryan Marshall
1955	Quare Times	Pat Taaffe
1956	E.S.B.	Dave Dick
1957	Sundew	Fred Winter
1958	Mr. What	Arthur Freeman
1959	Oxo	Michael Scudamore
1960	Merryman II	Gerald Scott

1961	Nicolaus Silver	Bobby Beasley
1962	Kilmore	Fred Winter
1963	Ayala	Pat Buckley
1964	Team Spirit	Willie Robinson
1965	Jay Trump	Tommy Smith
1966	Anglo	Tim Norman
1967	Foinavon	John Buckingham
1968	Red Alligator	Brian Fletcher
1969	Highland Wedding	Eddie Harty
1970	Gay Trip	Pat Taaffe
1971	Specify	John Cook
1972	Well To Do	Graham Thorner
1973	Red Rum	Brian Fletcher
1974	Red Rum	Brian Fletcher
1975	L'Escargot	Tommy Carberry
1976	Rag Trade	John Burke
1977	Red Rum	Tommy Stack
1978	Lucius	Bob Davies
1979	Rubstick	Maurice Barnes
1980	Ben Nevis	Charlie Fenwick
1981	Aldaniti	Bob Champion
1982	Grittar	Dick Saunders
1983	Corbiere	Ben De Haan

CHELTENHAM GOLD CUP: A steeplechase first held in 1924 at Cheltenham. The distance, having varied slightly over the years, is now 3 miles 516 yd (5·29 km), and all horses carry 12 stone (76·2 kg). *Golden Miller* won a record five times, consecutively 1932–36, and the most wins by a jockey is four by Pat Taaffe between 1964 and 1968. The highest priced winners, at 33–1, have been *Gay Donald* in 1955, and *L'Escargot* in 1970. The odds on *Arkle* were 1–10 in 1966 when it won for the third consecutive time.

1924	Red Splash	F. Rees
1925	Ballinode	T. Leader
1926	Koko	J. Hamey
1927	Thrown In	H. Grosvenor
1928	Patron Saint	F. Rees
1929	Easter Hero	F. Rees
1930	Easter Hero	T. Cullinan
1931	No Race	
1932	Golden Miller	T. Leader
1933	Golden Miller	W. Stott
1934	Golden Miller	G. Wilson
1935	Golden Miller	G. Wilson
1936	Golden Miller	E. Williams
1937	No Race	
1938	Morse Code	D. Morgan
1939	Brendan's Cottage	G. Owen
1940	Roman Hackle	E. Williams
1941	Poet Prince	R. Burford
1942	Medoc II	H. Nicholson
1943–44	No Race	
1945	Red Rower	D. Jones
1946	Prince Regent	Tim Hyde
1947	Fortina	Richard Black
1948	Cottage Rake	Aubrey Brabazon
1949	Cottage Rake	Aubrey Brabazon
1950	Cottage Rake	Aubrey Brabazon
1951	Silver Frame	Martin Molony
1952	Mont Tremblant	Dave Dick
1953	Knock Hard	Tim Molony
1954	Four Ten	Tommy Cusack
1955	Gay Donald	Tony Grantham
1956	Limber Hill	Jimmy Power
1957	Linwell	Michael Scudamore
1958	Kerstin	Stan Hayhurst
1959	Roddy Owen	Bobby Beasley
1960	Pas Seul	Bill Rees
1961	Saffron Tartan	Fred Winter
1962	Mandarin	Fred Winter
1963	Mill House	Willie Robinson
1964	Arkle	Pat Taaffe
1965	Arkle	Pat Taaffe
1966	Arkle	Pat Taaffe
1967	Woodland Venture	Terry Biddlecombe
1968	Fort Leney	Pat Taaffe
1969	What a Myth	Paul Kelleway

1970	L'Escargot	Tommy Carberry
1971	L'Escargot	Tommy Carberry
1972	Glencaraig Lady	Frank Berry
1973	The Dikler	Ron Barry
1974	Captain Christy	Bobby Beasley
1975	Ten Up	Tommy Carberry
1976	Royal Frolic	John Burke
1977	Davy Lad	Dessie Hughes
1978	Midnight Court	Johnny Francome
1979	Alverton	Jonjo O'Neill
1980	Master Smudge	Richard Hoare
1981	Little Owl	Jim Wilson
1982	Silver Buck	Robert Earnshaw
1983	Bregawn	Graham Bradley

CHAMPION HURDLE: A steeplechase, held at Cheltenham, now standardised at 2 miles 200 yd (3·4 km). Three horses have won on three occasions, *Hatton's Grace* 1949–51, *Sir Ken* 1952–54, and *Persian War* 1968–70. The most wins by a jockey have been four by Tim Molony 1951–54. The highest priced winner was *Kirriemuir* at 50–1 in 1965.

1927	Blaris	G. Duller
1928	Brown Jack	F. Rees
1929	Royal Falcon	F. Rees
1930	Brown Tony	T. Cullinan
1931	No race	
1932	Insurance	T. Leader
1933	Insurance	W. Stott
1934	Chenango	D. Morgan
1935	Lion Courage	G. Wilson
1936	Victor Norman	H. Nicholson
1937	Free Fare	G. Pellerin
1938	Our Hope	Capt R. Harding
1939	African Sister	K. Piggott
1940	Solford	S. Magee
1941	Seneca	R. Smyth
1942	Forestation	R. Symth
1943–44	No Race	
1945	Brains Trust	T. Rimell
1946	Distel	Robert O'Ryan
1947	National Spirit	Danny Morgan
1948	National Spirit	Ron Symth
1949	Hatton's Grace	Aubrey Brabazon
1950	Hatton's Grace	Aubrey Brabazon
1951	Hatton's Grace	Tim Molony
1952	Sir Ken	Tim Molony
1953	Sir Ken	Tim Molony
1954	Sir Ken	Tim Molony
1955	Clair Soleil	Fred Winter
1956	Doorknocker	Harry Sprague
1957	Merry Deal	Granville Underwood
1958	Bandalore	George Slack
1959	Fare Time	Fred Winter
1960	Another Flash	Bobby Beasley
1961	Eborneezer	Fred Winter
1962	Anzio	Willie Robinson
1963	Winning Fair	Alan Lillingston
1964	Magic Court	Pat McCarron
1965	Kirriemuir	Willie Robinson
1966	Salmon Spray	Johnny Haine
1967	Saucy Kit	Roy Edwards
1968	Persian War	Jimmy Uttley
1969	Persian War	Jimmy Uttley
1970	Persian War	Jimmy Uttley
1971	Bula	Paul Kelleway
1972	Bula	Paul Kelleway
1973	Comedy of Errors	Bill Smith
1974	Lanzarote	Richard Pitman
1975	Comedy of Errors	Ken White
1976	Night Nurse	Paddy Broderick
1977	Night Nurse	Paddy Broderick
1978	Monksfield	Tommy Kinane
1979	Monksfield	Dessie Hughes
1980	Sea Pigeon	Jonjo O'Neill
1981	Sea Pigeon	Johnny Francome
1982	For Auction	Colin Magnier
1983	Gaye Brief	Richard Linley

Monksfield on his way to winning the 1978 Champion Hurdle. The following year he won again but with a different jockey.

THE TRIPLE CROWN

There are three different Triple Crowns, depending on the sex of the horse and the country involved. In Britain, that for colts is the combination of the Derby, St Leger and the 2000 Guineas, while for fillies it is the Oaks, St Leger and the 1000 Guineas. In the USA it comprises three races for three-year-olds. They are the Kentucky Derby, instituted 1875, and held over 1¼ miles (2012 m) at Churchill Downs, Louisville, Kentucky; the Belmont Stakes, instituted 1867, and held over 1½ miles (2414 m) at Belmont Park, New York; and the Preakness Stakes, instituted 1873, and held over 1 mile 330 yd (1911 m). There have been 15 winners of the British colt's combination, the most recent being *Nijinsky* in 1970. Six fillies have won their combination, the most recent being *Meld* in 1955. The American Triple Crown has been won by 11 horses, the most recent was *Affirmed* in 1978.

PRIX DE L'ARC DE TRIOMPHE: The most important race in Europe outside Britain, it is run at Longchamp, Paris over a distance of 2400 m (1 mile 864 yd). Open to horses of all ages it was first held in 1920, and the record time of 2 min 28 sec is held by *Detroit*, ridden by Pat Eddery in 1980. The most successful jockeys, both with four wins, have been Jacques Doyasbère, between 1942 and 1951, and Frederic Head, between 1966 and 1979. The trainer's record is four by Charles Semblat from 1942 to 1949, while the owner's best is six by Marcel Boussac between 1936 and 1949. The largest field was 30 in 1967.

Winners from 1970:

1970	Sassafras	Yves Saint-Martin
1971	Mill Reef	Geoff Lewis
1972	San San	Frederic Head
1973	Rheingold	Lester Piggott
1974	Allez France	Yves Saint-Martin
1975	Star Appeal	Greville Starkey
1976	Ivanjica	Frederic Head
1977	Alleged	Lester Piggott
1978	Alleged	Lester Piggott
1979	Three Troikas	Frederic Head
1980	Detroit	Pat Eddery
1981	Gold River	Gary Moore
1982	Akiyda	Yves Saint-Martin

MELBOURNE CUP: Australia's most prestigious race, instituted in 1861, is held on the first Tuesday in November at Flemington Racecourse, Melbourne, Victoria. Two jockeys have won on four occasions: Robert Lewis between 1902 and 1927, and Harry White between 1974 and 1979. Lewis was also second four times and third once. The most successful trainer has been J. Bart Cummings with seven winners, and four second places, between 1965 and 1979. The record for the race, since 1972 held over 3200 m (1 mile 1739 yd) is 3 min 18·4 sec by *Gold and Black* in 1977, but the time of *Rain Lover* in 1968 of 3 min 19·1 sec for 2 miles (3218 m) is intrinsically faster.

Ice Hockey

The young American Eric Strobel surrounded by Soviet players in the 1980 Olympic ice hockey game in which the unheralded United States team caused a major surprise by beating the USSR, the favourites, by four goals to three, and then went on to win the gold medal.

A game akin to hockey on ice called *Kalv* was played in Holland in the early 16th century, but the birth of modern ice hockey took place in Canada, probably at Kingston, Ontario where English soldiers played with hockey sticks and a puck-like object at Christmas 1855. Halifax, Nova Scotia also claims to be its birthplace, but the first rules were formulated by students of McGill University in Montreal and their club, formed in 1880, was the first recognised team. The first game recorded in the USA was in 1893. In 1908 the International Ice Hockey Federation was formed, and World and Olympic championships inaugurated in 1920. The National Hockey League (NHL) in North America was founded in 1917. The World Hockey Association (WHA) was formed in 1971 and disbanded in 1979, when four of its teams joined the NHL.

OLYMPIC GAMES: The title has been won six times by Canada between 1920 and 1952. A record three gold medals were won by four Soviet players who were members of the USSR winning teams in 1964, 1968 and 1972. Great Britain scored a major upset when it won its sole Olympic gold medal in 1936, having won its only other medal, a bronze, in 1924.

WORLD CHAMPIONSHIPS: Initially the same as the Olympic title, a separate tournament was instituted in 1930, held annually, but in conjunction with the Olympic title in Games years until 1972. Canada and the USSR have won 19 championships each. The championships were confined to amateurs until 1976.

1970	USSR	1977	Czechoslovakia
1971	USSR	1978	USSR
1972	Czechoslovakia	1979	USSR
1973	USSR	1980	Not held
1974	USSR	1981	USSR
1975	USSR	1982	USSR
1976	Czechoslovakia	1983	USSR

STANLEY CUP: Presented in 1893 by Lord Stanley of Preston, the then Governor-General of Canada, as a trophy for the amateur championship of Canada. In 1910 the National Hockey Association, the forerunner of the NHL, took it over as the professional trophy. Since 1926 only NHL teams have been eligible. The Cup has been won most times by the Montreal Canadiens with 22 victories between 1916 and 1979. Henri Richard (Montreal Canadiens) played in a record 11 finals up to 1973. *Winners from 1970:*

1970	Boston Bruins
1971	Montreal Canadiens
1972	Boston Bruins
1973	Montreal Canadiens
1974	Philadelphia Flyers
1975	Philadelphia Flyers
1976	Montreal Canadiens
1977	Montreal Canadiens
1978	Montreal Canadiens
1979	Montreal Canadiens
1980	New York Islanders
1981	New York Islanders
1982	New York Islanders
1983	New York Islanders

SPEED
The game is considered to be the fastest in the world and the greatest speed recorded by a player was 47·7 km/h (29·7 mph) by Bobby Hull of the Chicago Black Hawks in the early 1960s. He has also been credited with the highest puck speed, off his left-handed slap shot, of 190·3 km/h (118·3 mph).

HIGH SCORING
The most goals scored in a major ice hockey match was in the 1949 World championships when Canada beat Denmark by 47–0. The record for an NHL match is a total of 21 when Montreal Canadiens defeated Toronto St Patricks 14–7 in 1920. The highest score by one team is also by the Canadiens when they beat Quebec Bulldogs 16–3 two months later that same year. The most goals scored in one game by an individual is seven by Joe Malone for Quebec Bulldogs against Toronto St Patricks on 31 January 1920. Six players, Harvey Jackson (Toronto), Max Bentley, Clint Smith and Grant Mulvey (Chicago), Red Berenson (St Louis) and Bryan Trottier (New York Islanders) have scored four goals in one period (20 minutes).

In a 32-year career in the professional leagues, Gordie Howe (Can) totalled 1071 goals, 1518 assists for 2589 points. He holds the NHL goal record with 801, the points record with 1850 and the assists mark at 1049. Starting his career in 1946 with the Detroit Red Wings, he later played in the WHA on a team that included his two sons, Mark and Marty. He retired aged 52 in 1980 when he was back in the NHL with the Hartford Whalers, having played in 2421 major league games. He won both the Hart Memorial Trophy, for the most valuable player in the NHL, and the Art Ross Trophy, for leading scorer, on six occasions, and once won the WHA Trophy named after him.

In the 1981–82 season Wayne Gretzky shattered all NHL scoring records. The 21-year-old centre from Ontario, Canada scored 92 goals (breaking the previous record of 76 by Phil Esposito), including ten occasions on which he scored hat-tricks, another record. He also made 120 assists to set a league mark of 212 points. This represents an outstanding average of 2·65 points per game. Additionally, in the Stanley Cup playoffs, he scored another five goals and made seven assists for a further 12 points. With his assistance his club, the Edmonton Oilers, scored team records of 417 goals and 1123 points in the same season. In 1982–83 he improved his assists mark to 121, and helped the Oilers to set a new team scoring record of 424 goals.

THE BRITISH LEAGUE CHAMPIONSHIP: It was instituted in 1934 as the English League Championship and has been won a record four times by Wembley Lions, between 1936 and 1957, and by Streatham (now Redskins) between 1950 and 1982. The major British club trophy is the Icy Smith Cup, first held in 1966. It has been won a record nine times by Murrayfield Racers. In 1982 a British club championship was inaugurated, and won by Dundee Rockets.

The highest score in a British league match has been 41–2, when Cleveland Bombers beat Richmond Flyers in February 1983. A record 14 goals were scored by Roy Halpin when Dundee Rockets beat Durham Wasps 24–1 in April 1982. Halpin also holds records of 151 goals and 254 points set in the 1981–82 season. Cleveland's Ted Phillips set a British points record of 20 (13 goals and 7 assists) in their record defeat of Richmond. In March 1955 Kenny Westman scored a hat-trick in 30 seconds playing for Nottingham Panthers against Brighton Tigers.

Ice Skating

The earliest skates were made of animal bones, such as those found in France and thought to be 20 000 years old. The first reference to skating is in early Norse literature c AD 200 but the earliest report of skating as a sport or pastime is in a British chronicle by William Fitzstephen of 1175. The first club was founded in Edinburgh in 1742, and the earliest artificial ice rink was opened in London in December 1842. Speed skating or racing must have taken place from the earliest times, although curved rinks, especially for racing, did not appear until the 1880s. Two Americans developed figure skating into an art. E. W. Bushnell invented steel blades in 1850 and thereby provided the precision skate needed for ever more intricate figures, and the first true innovator and teacher was Jackson Haines. He was a ballet master who transferred the artistry of the dance to the ice when he went to Vienna in 1864. One of his pupils, Louis Rubinstein, was a founder of the Amateur Skating Association of Canada in 1878, the first national governing body in the world. A year later the NSA of Great Britain was organised, and in 1892 the International Skating Union was set up at Schweringen, Netherlands.

WORLD CHAMPIONSHIPS—FIGURE SKATING:

First held in 1896 at St Petersburg (now Leningrad), USSR, the title was won by Gilbert Fuchs (Ger). The 1898 championships were held in London on the site of what is now the Palladium Theatre in Argyll Street. When the meeting was held in London, again in 1902, a real sensation was caused by a British woman, Madge Syers, who applied for entry into what had always been a men's preserve. As there was no rule against women competing her entry was accepted, and she finished second to the defending champion Ulrich Salchow (Swe). A separate women's championship was held from 1906—the first two being won by Mrs Syers. The most titles won is 10 by Salchow between 1901 and 1911, and by Sonja Henie (Nor) from 1927 to 1936. The record for pairs titles (first held in 1908) is also 10 by Irina Rodnina (USSR), four of them with Alexei Ulanov 1969–72, and six with her subsequent husband Aleksandr Zaitsev 1973–78. The most titles won in ice dancing (introduced in 1952) is six by Ludmila Pakhomova and Aleksandr Gorshkov (USSR) between 1970 and 1976. The greatest number of 'sixes' (the maximum possible) awarded in one competition to a solo skater was seven to the 1962 world champion Donald Jackson (Can) at Prague, Czechoslovakia. *Winners from 1947:*

Men	Women
1947 Hans Gerschwiler (Swi)	Barbara Ann Scott (Can)
1948 Richard Button (USA)	Barbara Ann Scott (Can)
1949 Richard Button (USA)	Aja Vrzanova (Cz)
1950 Richard Button (USA)	Aja Vrzanova (Cz)
1951 Richard Button (USA)	Jeanette Altwegg (GB)
1952 Richard Button (USA)	Jeanette Altwegg (GB)
1953 Hayes Jenkins (USA)	Tenley Albright (USA)
1954 Hayes Jenkins (USA)	Gundi Busch (Ger)
1955 Hayes Jenkins (USA)	Tenley Albright (USA)
1956 Hayes Jenkins (USA)	Carol Heiss (USA)
1957 David Jenkins (USA)	Carol Heiss (USA)
1958 David Jenkins (USA)	Carol Heiss (USA)
1959 David Jenkins (USA)	Carol Heiss (USA)
1960 Alain Giletti (Fra)	Carol Heiss (USA)
1961 Not held	
1962 Donald Jackson (Can)	Sjoukje Dijkstra (Hol)
1963 Donald McPherson (Can)	Sjoukje Dijkstra (Hol)
1964 Manfred Schnelldorfer (Ger)	Sjoukje Dijkstra (Hol)
1965 Alain Calmat (Fra)	Petra Burka (Can)
1966 Emmerich Danzer (Aut)	Peggy Fleming (USA)
1967 Emmerich Danzer (Aut)	Peggy Fleming (USA)
1968 Emmerich Danzer (Aut)	Peggy Fleming (USA)
1969 Tim Wood (USA)	Gabriele Seyfert (GDR)
1970 Tim Wood (USA)	Gabriele Seyfert (GDR)
1971 Ondrej Nepela (Cz)	Beatrix Schuba (Aut)
1972 Ondrej Nepela (Cz)	Beatrix Schuba (Aut)
1973 Ondrej Nepela (Cz)	Karen Magnussen (Can)
1974 Jan Hoffmann (GDR)	Christine Errath (GDR)
1975 Sergei Volkov (USSR)	Dianne de Leeuw (Hol)
1976 John Curry (GB)	Dorothy Hamill (USA)
1977 Vladimir Kovalyev (USSR)	Linda Fratiane (USA)
1978 Charles Tickner (USA)	Annett Pötzsch (GDR)
1979 Vladimir Kovalyev (USSR)	Linda Fratiane (USA)
1980 Jan Hoffmann (GDR)	Annett Pötzsch (GDR)
1981 Scott Hamilton (USA)	Denise Beillmann (Swi)
1982 Scott Hamilton (USA)	Elaine Zayak (USA)
1983 Scott Hamilton (USA)	Rosalynn Sumners (USA)

Pairs
1947 Pierre Baugniet & Micheline Lannoy (Bel)
1948 Pierre Baugniet & Micheline Lannoy (Bel)
1949 Ede Király & Andrea Kékessy (Hun)
1950 Peter Kennedy & Karol Kennedy (USA)
1951 Paul Falk & Ria Baran/Falk (Ger)
1952 Paul Falk & Ria Baran/Falk (Ger)
1953 John Nicks & Jennifer Nicks (GB)
1954 Norris Bowden & Frances Dafoe (Can)
1955 Norris Bowden & Frances Dafoe (Can)
1956 Kurt Oppelt & Sissy Schwarz (Aut)
1957 Robert Paul & Barbara Wagner (Can)
1958 Robert Paul & Barbara Wagner (Can)
1959 Robert Paul & Barbara Wagner (Can)
1960 Robert Paul & Barbara Wagner (Can)
1961 Not held
1962 Otto Jelinek & Maria Jelinek (Can)
1963 Hans-Jürgen Bäumler & Marika Kilius (Ger)
1964 Hans-Jürgen Bäumler & Marika Kilius (Ger)
1965 Oleg & Lyudmila Protopopov (USSR)
1966 Oleg & Lyudmila Protopopov (USSR)
1967 Oleg & Lyudmila Protopopov (USSR)
1968 Oleg & Lyudmila Protopopov (USSR)
1969 Alexei Ulanov & Irina Rodnina (USSR)
1970 Alexei Ulanov & Irina Rodnina (USSR)
1971 Alexei Ulanov & Irina Rodnina (USSR)
1972 Alexei Ulanov & Irine Rodnina (USSR)
1973 Aleksandr Zaitsev & Irina Rodnina (USSR)
1974 Aleksandr Zaitsev & Irina Rodnina (USSR)
1975 Aleksandr Zaitsev & Irina Rodnina (USSR)
1976 Aleksandr Zaitsev & Irina Rodnina (USSR)
1977 Aleksandr Zaitsev & Irina Rodnina (USSR)
1978 Aleksandr Zaitsev & Irina Rodnina (USSR)
1979 Randy Gardner & Tai Babilonia (USA)
1980 Sergei Shakrai & Marina Tcherkasova (USSR)
1981 Igor Lisovsky & Irina Vorobyeva (USSR)
1982 Tassilo Thierbach & Sabine Baess (GDR)
1983 Oleg Vasiliyev & Yelena Valova (USSR)

Ice Dancing
1952 Lawrence Demmy & Jean Westwood (GB)
1953 Lawrence Demmy & Jean Westwood (GB)
1954 Lawrence Demmy & Jean Westwood (GB)
1955 Lawrence Demmy & Jean Westwood (GB)
1956 Paul Thomas & Pamela Weight (GB)
1957 Courtney Jones & June Markham (GB)
1958 Courtney Jones & June Markham (GB)
1959 Courtney Jones & Doreen Denny (GB)
1960 Courtney Jones & Doreen Denny (GB)
1961 Not held
1962 Pavel Roman & Eva Romanova (Cz)
1963 Pavel Roman & Eva Romanova (Cz)
1964 Pavel Roman & Eva Romanova (Cz)
1965 Pavel Roman & Eva Romanova (Cz)
1966 Bernard Ford & Diane Towler (GB)
1967 Bernard Ford & Diane Towler (GB)
1968 Bernard Ford & Diane Towler (GB)
1969 Bernard Ford & Diane Towler (GB)
1970 Aleksandr Gorshkov & Ludmila Pakhomova (USSR)
1971 Aleksandr Gorshkov & Ludmila Pakhomova (USSR)
1972 Aleksandr Gorshkov & Ludmila Pakhomova (USSR)
1973 Aleksandr Gorshkov & Ludmila Pakhomova (USSR)
1974 Aleksandr Gorshkov & Ludmila Pakhomova (USSR)
1975 Andrei Minenkov & Irina Moiseyeva (USSR)
1976 Aleksandr Gorshkov & Ludmila Pakhomova (USSR)
1977 Andrei Minenkov & Irina Moiseyeva (USSR)
1978 Gennadi Karponosov & Natalia Linichuk (USSR)
1979 Gennadi Karponosov & Natalia Linichuk (USSR)
1980 Andras Sallay & Krisztine Regoczy (Hun)
1981 Christopher Dean & Jayne Torvill (GB)
1982 Christopher Dean & Jayne Torvill (GB)
1983 Christopher Dean & Jayne Torvill (GB)

Tai Babilonia and Randy Gardner of the United States in a 'death spiral'. In 1979 they became the first American couple to win the world pairs title and they were among the favourites for the 1980 Olympic crown until an injury to Randy in training caused their withdrawal.

OLYMPIC GAMES—FIGURE SKATING:

Winter Games as such were not organised until 1924, but there were ice skating events held in the Summer Games at 1908 and 1920. Among the winners in London in 1908 were Britain's Madge Syers, and Nikolai Panin, the only Russian to win an Olympic gold medal at any sport before 1952. The most gold medals won is three by Gillis Gråafstrom (Swe) in 1920, 1924 and 1928, by Sonja Henie (Nor) in 1928, 1932 and 1936, and by Irina Rodnina (USSR) in the pairs event in 1972, 1976 and 1980. Ice dancing was not included until 1976. Post war winners have been:

Men		*Women*	
1948	Richard Button (USA)	1948	Barbara Ann Scott (Can)
1952	Richard Button (USA)	1952	Jeanette Altwegg (GB)
1956	Hayes Jenkins (USA)	1956	Tenley Albright (USA)
1960	David Jenkins (USA)	1960	Carol Heiss (USA)
1964	Manfred Schnelldorfer (Ger)	1964	Sjoukje Dijkstra (Hol)
1968	Wolfgang Schwarz (Aut)	1968	Peggy Fleming (USA)
1972	Ondrej Nepela (Cz)	1972	Beatrix Schuba (Aut)
1976	John Curry (GB)	1976	Dorothy Hamill (USA)
1980	Robin Cousins (GB)	1980	Annette Pötzsch (GDR)

Ice Dancing
1976 Aleksandr Gorshkov & Ludmila Pakhomova (USSR)
1980 Gennadi Karponosov & Natalia Linichuk (USSR)

Pairs
1948 Pierre Baugniet & Micheline Lannoy (Bel)
1952 Paul & Ria Falk (Ger)
1956 Kurt Oppelt & Sissy Schwarz (Aut)
1960 Robert Paul & Barbara Wagner (Can)
1964 Oleg Protopopov & Ludmila Belousova (USSR)
1968 Oleg Protopopov & Ludmila Belousova (USSR)
1972 Alexei Ulanov & Irina Rodnina (USSR)
1976 Aleksandr Zaitsev & Irina Rodnina (USSR)
1980 Aleksandr Zaitsev & Irina Rodnina (USSR)

RINKS AND RACES

The complex of the Fujikyu Highland Promenade Rink in Japan is the largest artificial rink in the world, with a total area of 26 500 square metres (285 244 square feet). Indoors the largest is in the Moscow Olympic arena which can accommodate a rink of 8 064 square metres (86 800 square feet). The longest known race, regularly held, is the Elfstedentocht, or Tour of the Eleven Towns, in Holland. The record time for the 200 km (124·27 miles) is 7 hr 35 min by Jeen van den Berg (Hol) in 1954, thus averaging 26·38 km/h (16·39 mph). The first report of the event was in 1763.

THE TRIPLE CROWN

As in other sports there are three competitions forming a Grand Slam of the highest honours attainable. In skating they are the World, European and Olympic championships. Both Karl Schäfer (Aut) and Sonja Henie (Nor) achieved double Triple Crowns in 1932 and 1936. The only Briton to win all three titles in the same year is John Curry in 1976.

JUMP TO IT

Many of the most difficult jumps in skating are named after their originators, such as the Axel (after Axel Paulsen of Norway) and the Salchow (after Ulrich Salchow of Sweden). The first woman to attempt a jump in major competition is said to have been Theresa Weld (USA) who was reprimanded for her 'unfeminine behaviour' in the 1920 Olympic events. Cecilia Colledge (GB) was the first woman to achieve two turns in the air a few years later. In the 1962 World championships Donald Jackson (Can) performed the first triple Lutz in a major competition and in the 1978 championships Vern Taylor, another Canadian, achieved the first triple Axel. Among women, the first triple Salchow was done by Sonja Morgenstern (GDR) in 1972, and the first triple Lutz by Denise Beilmann (Swi) in the 1978 European championships. Incidentally, the latter has a spin named after her. The first quadruple twist was performed by Marina Tcherkasova and Sergei Shakrai (USSR) in a pairs competition in Helsinki in 1977. They were able to achieve this because of the unusual difference in size between the tiny 12-year-old girl and her tall male partner. A backward somersault jump was successfully negotiated by Terry Kubicka (USA) in the 1976 world championships but it was immediately banned as being too dangerous.

Ken Lebel (USA) jumped over 17 barrels, a record distance of 8·73 m (28 ft 8 in) at Liberty, New York in February 1965. One more barrel, 18, was cleared by Yvon Jolin (Can) at Quebec in 1980, but they measured 30 cm (1 ft) less in total distance. The best jump by a female skater is 11 barrels, measuring 6·21 m (20 ft 4½ in) by Janet Hainstock (USA) in March 1980.

BRITISH CHAMPIONSHIPS—FIGURE SKATING: The most individual titles won is 11 by Jack Page between 1922 and 1933, while the most by a woman is six by Cecilia Colledge between 1935 and 1946. Miss Colledge was the youngest ever member of a British Olympic team in 1932 when she was only 11 yr 24 days old. Jack Page also won nine pairs titles for a grand total of 20. Winning the British Ice Dance title on 19 November 1981 at Nottingham, Jayne Torvill and Christopher Dean were awarded seven maximums (of six points) out of a possible nine, for artistic impression. In the World championships at Helsinki, Finland on 12 March 1983 they were awarded a unique nine maximums in the same category.

WORLD CHAMPIONSHIPS—SPEED SKATING: Speed skating as a sport developed in Holland in the middle of the 17th century. The first reported race in Britain was on the Fens, East Anglia in 1763. At the instigation of the National Skating Association of Great Britain the first international competition was organised in Hamburg, Germany in 1885. The first world championships were held at Amsterdam in 1889, but were not given full official recognition, thus the series is officially dated from 1893. Although Dutch women were known to have taken part in races as early as 1805, the first world titles for women were not held till 1936. The greatest number of overall titles won is five by Oscar Mathisen (Nor) between 1908 and 1914, and by Clas Thunberg (Fin) from 1923 to 1931. The record for a woman is four by Inga Artomonova-Voronina (USSR) from 1957 to 1964, and by Atje Keulen-Deelstra (Hol) between 1970 and 1974.

Left: **Jayne Torvill and Christopher Dean attained virtual perfection in their 1983 World Championship performance of their routine based on the theatrical show *Barnum*.**

Overall champions from 1970:

	Men	Women
1970	Ard Schenk (Hol)	Atje Keulen-Deelstra (Hol)
1971	Ard Schenk (Hol)	Nina Statkevich (USSR)
1972	Ard Schenk (Hol)	Atje Keulen-Deelstra (Hol)
1973	Goran Claesson (Swe)	Atje Keulen-Deelstra (Hol)
1974	Sten Stensen (Nor)	Atje Keulen-Deelstra (Hol)
1975	Harm Kuipers (Hol)	Karin Kessow (GDR)
1976	Piet Kleine (Hol)	Sylvia Burka (Can)
1977	Eric Heiden (USA)	Vera Bryndzey (USSR)
1978	Eric Heiden (USA)	Tatyana Averina (USSR)
1979	Eric Heiden (USA)	Beth Heiden (USA)
1980	Hilbert van der Duim (Hol)	Natalia Petruseva (USSR)
1981	Amund Sjöbrend (Nor)	Natalia Petruseva (USSR)
1982	Hilbert van der Duim (Hol)	Karin Busche-Enke (GDR)
1983	Rolf Falk-Larsen (Nor)	Andrea Schöne (GDR)

Three times world champion speed skater Eric Heiden hit the jackpot at Lake Placid in 1980 with a record five Olympic gold medals from five events. To make it a true family occasion his sister Beth won a bronze medal.

OLYMPIC GAMES—SPEED SKATING: First held at Chamonix, France in 1924, for men only. Women's events were not included until 1960 although there had been demonstration races in 1932. The most gold medals won is six by Lidia Skoblikova (USSR) in 1960 and 1964. The most by a man is five by Clas Thunberg (Fin) in 1924 and 1928, and by Eric Heiden (USA) who uniquely made a clean sweep of all the titles in 1980. The most successful countries have been, in the men's events,

The speed skating oval at Inzell in Bavaria where many world records have been set. Note that the skater in the outside lane is not penalised, as in all races the competitors have to change lanes at set intervals so that both skaters cover the same total distance.

Norway with 18 wins (including two shared), and in the women's events, the USSR with 12 victories. Combining the results of male and female events the USSR has won a record total of 20 titles (including one shared).

WORLD RECORDS—SPEED SKATING (As at 30 April 1983)—Outdoors

	Men				Women	
Distance	min sec			min sec		
500 m	36·57*	Pavel Pegov (USSR)	1983	39·69	Christa Rothenburger (GDR)	1983
1000 m	1 12·58	Pavel Pegov (USSR)	1983	1 19·31	Natalia Petruseva (USSR)	1983
1500 m	1 54·26	Igor Zhelezovsky (USSR)	1983	2 04·04	Natalia Petruseva (USSR)	1983
3000 m	4 04·06	Dmitri Oglobin (USSR)	1979	4 21·70	Gaby Schönbrunn (GDR)	1981
5000 m	6 51·17	Sergei Pribikov (USSR)	1982	7 40·97	Andrea Schöne (GDR)	1983
10 000 m	14 23·59	Tomas Gustavsson (Swe)	1982	—	—	—

* This represents an average speed of 49·22 km/h (30·58 mph).

WORLD SHORT-TRACK SPEED SKATING (As at 30 April 1983)—Indoors

	Men				Women	
Distance	min sec			min sec		
500 m	45·37	Louis Grenier (Can)	1983	49·49	Sylve Daigle (Can)	1983
800 m	1 15·51	Tatsuyoshi Ishihara (Jap)	1981	1 25·29	Bonnie Blair (USA)	1983
1000 m	1 37·91	Guy Daignault (Can)	1982	1 43·66	Sylve Daigle (Can)	1983
1500 m	2 27·27	Tatsuyoshi Ishihara (Jap)	1981	2 41·75	Sylve Daigle (Can)	1983
3000 m	5 08·15	Tatsuyoshi Ishihara (Jap)	1983	5 32·31	Sylve Daigle (Can)	1983

Judo

Judo was devised in 1882 by a Japanese educationalist Dr Jigoro Kano in the Eishoji Temple, Tokyo. It is based on a combination of various pre-Christian era Japanese and Chinese combat methods, notably Ju-jitsu. Dr Kano came to Britain in 1885, and a school opened in Paris in the early years of the new century, but the sport did not catch on in Europe until the opening of the London Budokwai in 1918. The first known international match was between a German team and the London Budokwai in 1926. The British Judo Association was formed in 1949 and the International Judo Federation in 1951. Inaugural European championships were held in 1951 and the first world titles were in 1956.

WORLD CHAMPIONSHIPS: Six weight divisions were included in the first championships but the weights were altered in 1979 to make eight classes. The championships are now contested biennially, although the 1977 competition was cancelled. Shozo Fujii (Jap) has won a record four titles in the 80 kg class in 1971, 1973 and 1975, and the 78 kg class in 1979. Women's championships were instituted in 1980 and Jane Bridge, in the 48 kg class, won Britain's first world title.
Winners from 1969:

Open		*Over 95 kg (formerly over 93 kg)*
1969	Masatoshi Shinomaki (Jap)	Shuja Suma (Jap)
1971	Masatoshi Shinomaki (Jap)	Wim Ruska (Hol)
1973	Kazuhiro Ninomiya (Jap)	Chonufuhe Tagaki (Jap)
1975	Haruki Uemura (Jap)	Sumio Endo (Jap)
1979	Sumio Endo (Jap)	Yasuhiro Yamashita (Jap)
1981	Yasuhiro Yamashita (Jap)	Yasuhiro Yamashita (Jap)

95 kg (formerly 93 kg)		*86 kg (formerly 80 kg)*
1969	Fumio Sasahara (Jap)	Isamu Sonoda (Jap)
1971	Fumio Sasahara (Jap)	Shozo Fujii (Jap)
1973	Nobuyaki Sato (Jap)	Shozo Fujii (Jap)
1975	Jean-Luc Rouge (Fra)	Shozo Fujii (Jap)
1979	Tengiz Khubuluri (USSR)	Detlef Ultsch (GDR)
1981	Tengiz Khubuluri (USSR)	Bernard Tchoullouyan (Fra)

78 kg		*65 kg*
1979	Shozo Fujii (Jap)	Nikolai Soludkhin (USSR)
1981	Neil Adams (GB)	Katsuhiko Kashiwazaki (Jap)

70 kg (formerly 71 kg)		*60 kg (formerly 63 kg)*
1969	Hiroshi Minatoya (Jap)	Yoshio Sonoda (Jap)
1971	Hizashi Tsuzawa (Jap)	Takao Kawaguchi (Jap)
1973	Kazutoyo Nomura (Jap)	Yoshiharu Minamo (Jap)
1975	Vladimir Nevzorov (USSR)	Yoshiharu Minamo (Jap)
1979	Kyoto Katsuki (Jap)	Thierry Ray (Fra)
1981	Chong Hak Park (SK)	Yasuhiko Moriwaki (Jap)

OLYMPIC GAMES: Included since 1964, with the exception of 1968. Only Wim Ruska (Hol) has won more than one title, with the over 93 kg and the Open classes in 1972. One of the biggest upsets to national pride in any sport occurred in 1964 when the giant 1·98 m (6 ft 6 in) Dutchman, Anton Geesink, won the Open category in Tokyo before some 15 000 partisan Japanese spectators.

Open		*Over 95 kg (formerly over 93 kg)*
1964	Anton Geesink (Hol)	Isao Inokuma (Jap)
1972	Wim Ruska (Hol)	Wim Ruska (Hol)
1976	Haruki Uemura (Jap)	Sergei Novikov (USSR)
1980	Dietmar Lorenz (GDR)	Angelo Parisi (Fra)

Fiery Lancashire redhead Jane Bridge about to dispose of an opponent. At the first ever world championships for women in New York in 1980 Jane won Britain's only title in the 48 kg category.

113

	95 kg (formerly 93 kg)	86 kg (formerly 80 kg)	70 kg (formerly 71 kg)	60 kg (formerly 63 kg)
1964	Not held	Isao Okano (Jap)	Not held	Takehide Nakatani (Jap)
1972	Shota Chochoshvili (USSR)	Shinobu Sekine (Jap)	Kazutoyo Nomura (Jap)	Takao Kawaguchi (Jap)
1976	Kazuhiro Ninomiya (Jap)	Isamu Sonoda (Jap)	Vladimir Nevzorov (USSR)	Hector Rodriguez (Cub)
1980	Robert van de Walle (Bel)	Jürg Röthlisberger (Swi)	Ezio Gamba (Ita)	Thierry Ray (Fra)

	78 kg	65 kg
1980	Shota Khabareli (USSR)	Nikolai Soludkhin (USSR)

BRITISH OPEN: Champions since 1977, when weight categories were altered to match international standards:

	Over 95 kg	95 kg	86 kg
1977	Bryan Dew	Robert Van de Walle (Bel)	Bertil Strom (Swe)
1978	Arthur Mapp	Robert Van de Walle (Bel)	Brian Jacks
1979	Clemens Jehle (Swi)	Paul Radburn	Peter Donnelly
1980	Paul Radburn	Peter Donnelly	Bertil Strom (Swe)
1981	Arthur Schnabel (FRG)	Mark Chittenden	Stewart Williams
1982	Alexander Van der Groeben (GDR)	Gunther Neureuther (Hol)	William Ward
1983	Juha Salonen (Fin)	Robert Van de Walle (Bel)	Ben Spijkers (Hol)

	78 kg	71 kg	65 kg	60 kg
1977	Vacinuff Morrison	Neil Adams	Raymond Neenan	Keith Cannaby
1978	Jean-Pierre Gilbert (Fra)	Chris Bowles	Raymond Neenan	Keith Cannaby
1979	William Ward	Neil Adams	Wolfgang Bierdron (Swe)	Keith Cannaby
1980	Neil Adams	Chris Bowles	Raymond Neenan	Reino Fagerlund (Fin)
1981	Neil Adams	Bernard Tambour (Bel)	Sandro Rosati (Ita)	Felice Mariani (Ita)
1982	Neil Adams	Jürgen Fuchtmeyer (FRG)	Kerrith Brown	Peter Middleton
1983	Neil Adams	Serge Dyot (Fra)	Kerrith Brown	Guy Lebaupin (Fra)

BRITISH CHAMPIONSHIPS: First held in 1966 for men and 1971 for women. The most titles won is nine by Dave Starbrook, at middleweight, light-heavyweight and the Open class between 1969 and 1975. The record for women is held by Christine Child with six titles at heavyweight and the Open class between 1971 and 1975.

By winning his sixth British title in the 1983 championships, Neil Adams gave notice that he intends to improve on his 1980 Olympic silver medal at Los Angeles.

Lacrosse

The early white settlers in North America found the Indians had a game called *baggataway*, often involving hundreds of participants and played across country for many miles. The French clergyman, Pierre de Charlevoix, saw a resemblance to a bishop's crozier in the hooked sticks used and called it *la crosse*. Another legend has the French naming it after an old game of their own—Chouler à la crosse—which dated from 1381. Yet another story is that the game was brought to the Indians by early Norse explorers. The famous Ottawa chieftain, Pontiac, used the game, which was performed as an entertainment for the soldiers, as a ruse to enter the gates and massacre the British garrison at Fort Michillmackinac, Canada on the occasion of the celebration of George III's birthday in June 1763. However, by the 1830s the Europeans were playing it themselves. In 1867 some Indians gave demonstrations in Britain, and the first club was formed in Glasgow. The English Lacrosse Union was formed in 1892. The first international match was between Canada and the United States in 1868. The game is played by two 10-a-side teams.

WORLD CHAMPIONSHIPS: The International Federation of Amateur Lacrosse (AFAL) was formed in 1928, but the game was not standardised sufficiently to hold world championships until 1967 for men and 1969 for women. However, it had been played in the Olympic Games in 1904, when Canada beat the USA, and in 1908, when Canada beat Great Britain, and there had been demonstration games in 1928, 1932 and 1948. The only man to play in all three world championships held so far is Englishman Mike Roberts.

Men		Women	
1967	USA	1969	Great Britain
1974	USA	1974	USA
1978	Canada	1978	Canada
1982	USA	1982	USA

ENGLISH CHAMPIONSHIPS: The Iroquois Cup, awarded to the English Club champions, has been won 15 times by Stockport between 1897 and 1934. The highest score achieved in the competition was 30–5 when Sheffield University beat Hampstead in the 1982 final.

HIGH SCORES

The most goals scored in an international match was 28–4 when the USA beat Canada at Stockport in July 1978. The highest by England was their 19–11 defeat of Canada at Melbourne in 1974.

A hectic moment in a lacrosse game clearly illustrates much of the equipment used in this hard and fast sport which originated among the Indians of North America. Fittingly the cup for the English club championship is named after one of those tribes, the Iroquois.

Modern Pentathlon

In the ancient Olympics the Pentathlon was the most prestigious event of the Games. Traditionally inspired by the city of Sparta, it consisted of the discus and javelin throws, running, jumping and wrestling, and the competitors were eulogised by Aristotle. The concept of the five-event all-round sporting contest was held dear by the founder of the modern Games, Baron de Coubertin, but it was not until 1912 that it was first held. The events are riding (an 800 m course with 15 fences), fencing, shooting, swimming (300 m freestyle), and finally a 4000 m cross-country run, each event held on a different day. There is a story that the competitor is supposed to represent a King's messenger. First he rides like the wind to outdistance his pursuers, then when his horse is brought down he fences his way out of trouble, following up with some good shooting to drive back the enemy's reserves. Then he crosses the final obstacle, a river, and finally runs home to deliver his message. Certainly the qualities required of a Modern Pentathlete are not far removed from those of the messenger in the story. Points are awarded for each activity and the winner is the one with the highest total after the five events. Initially only military personnel competed but since the founding of the Union Internationale de Pentathlon Moderne et Biathlon (UIPMB) in 1948 non-military competitors have been allowed.

A silver medal in the first world modern pentathlon championships for women in 1977 did not satisfy Reading's Kathy Tayler, so she set her sights a little higher and won the World Cup (the unofficial world title) two years later.

Jim Fox, a member of Britain's gold medal winning team at the 1976 Olympics, in the riding segment of the event.

OLYMPIC GAMES: Lars Hall (Swe) is the only man to have won two individual titles in 1952 and 1956. The most gold medals, two team and one individual, and the most total medals, three gold and two silver, have been won by András Balczó (Hun) between 1960 and 1972. The highest individual placing by a Briton is fourth by Jim Fox in 1972. Perhaps the greatest margin of victory was achieved by Willie Grut (Swe) in 1948, when the scoring was based on actual placings in the different events. He started by winning both the riding and fencing, came fifth in the shooting, first again in the swimming and finally eighth in the running, for a total of 16 points—31 ahead of the silver medallist.

Olympic Champions

Individual
1912 Gosta Lilliehöök (Swe)
1920 Gustaf Dyrssen (Swe)
1924 Bo Lindman (Swe)
1928 Sven Thofelt (Swe)
1932 Johan Oxenstierna (Swe)
1936 Gotthardt Handrick (Ger)
1948 Willie Grut (Swe)

	Individual	Team
1952	Lars Hall (Swe)	Hungary
1956	Lars Hall (Swe)	USSR
1960	Ferenc Németh (Hun)	Hungary
1964	Ferenc Török (Hun)	USSR
1968	Björn Ferm (Swe)	Hungary
1972	András Balczó (Hun)	USSR
1976	Janusz Pyciak-Peciak (Pol)	GB
1980	Anatoli Starostin (USSR)	USSR

WORLD CHAMPIONSHIPS: First held in 1949, and annually since, except in Olympic years when the titles are held simultaneously. The most world titles won is six by András Balczó (Hun), including the 1972 Olympic title, between 1963 and 1972. The highest placing by a Briton is third by Jim Fox in 1975. A competition for women was instituted in 1977, followed by unofficial championships, under the title of World Cup, until 1981. *Winners of the men's title from 1970:*

Men

	Individual	Team
1970	Paul Kelemen (Hun)	Hungary
1971	Boris Onischenko (USSR)	USSR
1973	Pavel Lednev (USSR)	USSR
1974	Pavel Lednev (USSR)	USSR
1975	Pavel Lednev (USSR)	Hungary
1977	Janusz Pyciak-Peciak (Pol)	Poland
1978	Pavel Lednev (USSR)	Poland
1979	Robert Nieman (USA)	USA
1981	Janusz Pyciak-Peciak (Pol)	Poland
1982	Daniele Masala (Ita)	USSR

Women

	Individual	Team
1977	Virginia Swift (USA)	—
1978*	Wendy Skipworth (GB)	GB
1979*	Kathy Tayler (GB)	GB
1980*	Wendy Norman (GB)	GB
1981	Anne Ahlgren (Swe)	GB
1982	Wendy Norman (GB)	GB

*World Cup

BRITISH CHAMPIONSHIPS: Jim Fox won a record 10 British titles (instituted 1929) from 1963 to 1974, while in the women's championship (instituted in 1977) Wendy Norman has won three times. *Winners from 1970:*

Men
1970 Jim Fox
1971 Jim Fox
1972 Jim Fox
1973 Jim Fox
1974 Jim Fox
1975 Adrian Parker

	Men		Women
1976	Danny Nightingale		
1977	Danny Nightingale	1977	Sarah Parker
1978	Danny Nightingale	1978	Wendy Norman
1979	Richard Phelps	1979	Wendy Norman
1980	Michael Mumford	1980	Wendy Norman
1981	Richard Phelps	1981	Janet Savage
1982	Richard Phelps	1982	Wendy Norman

Motorcycle Racing

The earliest known race was held in the grounds of Sheen House, Richmond, Surrey in November 1897, over a mile (1609 m) oval course and won by Charles Jarrott (GB) on a Fournier. In the early days many races were for both motorcycles and motor cars, and often took the form of long distance inter-city or inter-country events. These were heavily criticised following the aborted Paris to Madrid race of 1903 which led to a number of deaths of competitors and spectators. In 1904 the International Cup Race was held in France for motorcycles only, and on a closed road circuit. Badly organised and chauvinistic, the British team, in particular, suffered from sabotage and the result was eventually declared void. However, in 1905 the race was held again, and this is recognised as the first international motorcycling event. The venue was Dourdon near Paris, and it was organised by the newly formed Fédération Internationale des Clubs Motocyclistes (FICM), the predecessor of the Fédération Internationale Motocycliste (FIM). The race was a success and was won by an Austrian named Wondrick.

WORLD CHAMPIONSHIPS: Started in 1949 by the FIM, competitors gain points from a series of Grand Prix races. The championships are currently held for the following classes of motorcycles: 50 cc, 125 cc, 250 cc, 350 cc, 500 cc, and sidecars. Giacomo Agostini (Ita) won a record 15 titles in the 350 cc 1968–74 and the 500 cc in 1966–72 and 1975. He also uniquely won two titles in five consecutive years, both the 350 cc and 500 cc in 1968–72. In total, Agostini won a record 122 races in the world titles series between 1965 and 1976, including a single year record of 19 in 1970. This latter mark had first been achieved by Mike Hailwood (GB) in 1966. In sidecar racing Klaus Enders (FRG) won six titles between 1967 and 1974. The youngest rider to win a world championship was Johnny Cecotto (Ven) in 1975 when he won the 350 cc title aged 19 yr 211 days. The oldest was Hermann-Peter Müller (FRG), aged 46 when he won the 250 cc class in 1955.

In the Manufacturers' category Italian MV-Agusta machines won a record 37 world championships between 1952 and 1973, and a record 276 race victories in world championship competition. In 1966 the Japanese Honda bikes won five of the six available world titles and 29 races. In the sidecar class BMW machines won an unprecedented 19 consecutive championships between 1955 and 1973.

Barry Sheene (number 7) and Kenny Roberts (number 2) in one of their many hard-fought races.

WORLD CHAMPIONS

50 cc

1962 Ernst Degner (Ger)	Suzuki
1963 Hugh Anderson (NZ)	Suzuki
1964 Hugh Anderson (NZ)	Suzuki
1965 Ralph Bryans (Ire)	Honda
1966 Hans-Georg Anscheidt (Ger)	Suzuki
1967 Hans-Georg Anscheidt (Ger)	Suzuki
1968 Hans-Georg Anscheidt (Ger)	Suzuki
1969 Angel Nieto (Spa)	Derbi
1970 Angel Nieto (Spa)	Derbi
1971 Jan de Vries (Hol)	Kreidler
1972 Angel Nieto (Spa)	Derbi
1973 Jan de Vries (Hol)	Kreidler
1974 Henk van Kessel (Hol)	Kreidler
1975 Angel Nieto (Spa)	Kreidler
1976 Angel Nieto (Spa)	Bultaco
1977 Angel Nieto (Spa)	Bultaco
1978 Ricardo Tormo (Spa)	Bultaco
1979 Eugenio Lazzarini (Ita)	Kreidler
1980 Eugenio Lazzarini (Ita)	Kreidler
1981 Ricardo Tormo (Spa)	Bultaco
1982 Stefan Dörflinger (Swi)	MBA

125 cc

1949 Nello Pagani (Ita)	Mondial
1950 Bruno Ruffo (Ita)	Mondial
1951 Carlo Ubbiali (Ita)	Mondial
1952 Cecil Sandford (GB)	MV
1953 Werner Haas (Ger)	NSU
1954 Rupert Hollaus (Aut)	NSU
1955 Carlo Ubbiali (Ita)	MV
1956 Carlo Ubbiali (Ita)	MV
1957 Tarquinio Provini (Ita)	Mondial
1958 Carlo Ubbiali (Ita)	MV
1959 Carlo Ubbiali (Ita)	MV
1960 Carlo Ubbiali (Ita)	MV
1961 Tom Phillis (Aus)	Honda
1962 Luigi Taveri (Swi)	Honda
1963 Hugh Anderson (NZ)	Suzuki
1964 Luigi Taveri (Swi)	Honda
1965 Hugh Anderson (NZ)	Suzuki
1966 Luigi Taveri (Swi)	Honda
1967 Bill Ivy (GB)	Yamaha
1968 Phil Read (GB)	Yamaha
1969 Dave Simmonds (GB)	Kawasaki
1970 Dieter Braun (FRG)	Suzuki
1971 Angel Nieto (Spa)	Derbi
1972 Angel Nieto (Spa)	Derbi
1973 Kent Andersson (Swe)	Yamaha
1974 Kent Andersson (Swe)	Yamaha
1975 Paolo Pileri (Ita)	Morbidelli
1976 Pier-Paolo Bianchi (Ita)	Morbidelli
1977 Pier-Paolo Bianchi (Ita)	Morbidelli
1978 Fugenio Lazzarini (Ita)	MBA
1979 Angel Nieto (Spa)	Morbidelli
1980 Pier-Paolo Bianchi (Ita)	MBA
1981 Angel Nieto (Spa)	Minarelli
1982 Angel Nieto (Spa)	Garelli

250 cc

1949 Bruno Ruffo (Ita)	Guzzi
1950 Dario Ambrosini (Ita)	Benelli
1951 Bruno Ruffo (Ita)	Guzzi
1952 Enrico Lorenzetti (Ita)	Guzzi
1953 Werner Haas (Ger)	NSU
1954 Werner Haas (Ger)	NSU
1955 Herman Müller (Ger)	NSU
1956 Carlo Ubbiali (Ita)	MV
1957 Cecil Sandford (GB)	Mondial
1958 Tarquinio Provini (Ita)	MV
1959 Carlo Ubbiali (Ita)	MV
1960 Carlo Ubbiali (Ita)	MV
1961 Mike Hailwood (GB)	Honda
1962 Jim Redman (Rho)	Honda
1963 Jim Redman (Rho)	Honda
1964 Phil Read (GB)	Yamaha
1965 Phil Read (GB)	Yamaha
1966 Mike Hailwood (GB)	Honda
1967 Mike Hailwood (GB)	Honda
1968 Phil Read (GB)	Yamaha
1969 Kel Caruthers (Aus)	Benelli
1970 Rod Gould (GB)	Yamaha
1971 Phil Read (GB)	Yamaha
1972 Jarno Saarinen (Fin)	Yamaha
1973 Dieter Braun (FRG)	Yamaha
1974 Walter Villa (Ita)	Harley-Davidson
1975 Walter Villa (Ita)	Harley-Davidson
1976 Walter Villa (Ita)	Harley-Davidson
1977 Mario Lega (Ita)	Morbidelli
1978 Kork Ballington (Saf)	Kawasaki
1979 Kork Ballington (Saf)	Kawasaki
1980 Anton Mang (FRG)	Kawasaki
1981 Anton Mang (FRG)	Kawasaki
1982 Jean-Louis Tournadre (Fra)	Yamaha

350 cc

1949 Freddie Frith (GB)	Velocette
1950 Bob Foster (GB)	Velocette
1951 Geoff Duke (GB)	Norton
1952 Geoff Duke (GB)	Norton
1953 Fergus Anderson (GB)	Guzzi
1954 Fergus Anderson (GB)	Guzzi
1955 Bill Lomas (GB)	Guzzi
1956 Bill Lomas (GB)	Guzzi
1957 Keith Campbell (Aus)	Guzzi
1958 John Surtees (GB)	MV
1959 John Surtees (GB)	MV
1960 John Surtees (GB)	MV
1961 Gary Hocking (Rho)	MV
1962 Jim Redman (Rho)	Honda
1963 Jim Redman (Rho)	Honda
1964 Jim Redman (Rho)	Honda
1965 Jim Redman (Rho)	Honda
1966 Mike Hailwood (GB)	Honda
1967 Mike Hailwood (GB)	Honda
1968 Giacomo Agostini (Ita)	MV
1969 Giacomo Agostini (Ita)	MV
1970 Giacomo Agostini (Ita)	MV
1971 Giacomo Agostini (Ita)	MV
1972 Giacomo Agostini (Ita)	MV
1973 Giacomo Agostini (Ita)	MV
1974 Giacomo Agostini (Ita)	Yamaha
1975 Johnny Cecotto (Ven)	Yamaha
1976 Walter Villa (Ita)	Harley-Davidson
1977 Takazumi Katayama (Jap)	Yamaha
1978 Kork Ballington (Saf)	Kawasaki
1979 Kork Ballington (Saf)	Kawasaki
1980 Jon Ekerold (Saf)	Yamaha
1981 Anton Mang (FRG)	Kawasaki
1982 Anton Mang (FRG)	Kawasaki

500 cc

1949 Leslie Graham (GB)	AJS
1950 Umberto Masetti (Ita)	Gilera
1951 Geoff Duke (GB)	Norton
1952 Umberto Masetti (Ita)	Gilera
1953 Geoff Duke (GB)	Gilera
1954 Geoff Duke (GB)	Gilera
1955 Geoff Duke (GB)	Gilera
1956 John Surtees (GB)	MV
1957 Libero Liberati (Ita)	Gilera
1958 John Surtees (GB)	MV
1959 John Surtees (GB)	MV
1960 John Surtees (GB)	MV
1961 Gary Hocking (Rho)	MV
1962 Mike Hailwood (GB)	MV
1963 Mike Hailwood (GB)	MV
1964 Mike Hailwood (GB)	MV
1965 Mike Hailwood (GB)	MV
1966 Giacomo Agostini (Ita)	MV
1967 Giacomo Agostini (Ita)	MV
1968 Giacomo Agostini (Ita)	MV
1969 Giacomo Agostini (Ita)	MV
1970 Giacomo Agostini (Ita)	MV
1971 Giacomo Agostini (Ita)	MV
1972 Giacomo Agostini (Ita)	MV

1973	Phil Read (GB)	MV
1974	Phil Read (GB)	MV
1975	Giacomo Agostini (Ita)	Yamaha
1976	Barry Sheene (GB)	Suzuki
1977	Barry Sheene (GB)	Suzuki
1978	Kenny Roberts (USA)	Yamaha
1979	Kenny Roberts (USA)	Yamaha
1980	Kenny Roberts (USA)	Yamaha
1981	Marco Lucchinelli (Ita)	Suzuki
1982	Franco Uncini (Ita)	Suzuki

750 cc

1977	Steve Baker (USA)	Yamaha
1978	Johnny Cecotto (Ven)	Yamaha
1979	Patrick Pons (Fra)	Yamaha
1980	Lost World Championship Status	

Side Cars

1949	Eric Oliver (GB)	Norton
1950	Eric Oliver (GB)	Norton
1951	Eric Oliver (GB)	Norton
1952	Cyril Smith (GB)	Norton
1953	Eric Oliver (GB)	Norton
1954	Wilhelm Noll (Ger)	BMW
1955	Wilhelm Faust (Ger)	BMW
1956	Wilhelm Noll (Ger)	BMW
1957	Fritz Hillebrand (Ger)	BMW
1958	Walter Schneider (Ger)	BMW
1959	Walter Schneider (Ger)	BMW
1960	Helmut Fath (Ger)	BMW
1961	Max Deubel (Ger)	BMW
1962	Max Deubel (Ger)	BMW
1963	Max Deubel (Ger)	BMW
1964	Max Deubel (Ger)	BMW
1965	Fritz Scheidegger (Swi)	BMW
1966	Fritz Scheidegger (Swi)	BMW
1967	Klaus Enders (Ger)	BMW
1968	Helmut Fath (Ger)	URS
1969	Klaus Enders (Ger)	BMW
1970	Klaus Enders (FRG)	BMW
1971	Horst Owesle (FRG)	Munch
1972	Klaus Enders (FRG)	BMW
1973	Klaus Enders (FRG)	BMW
1974	Klaus Enders (FRG)	Busch BMW
1975	Rolf Steinhausen (FRG)	Konig
1976	Rolf Steinhausen (FRG)	Busch Konig
1977	George O'Dell (GB)	Yamaha
1978	Rolf Biland (Swi)	Yamaha
1979	Rolf Biland (Swi)	Yamaha
1980	Jock Taylor (GB)	Yamaha
1981	Rolf Biland (Swi)	Yamaha
1982	Werner Schwärzel (FRG)	Yamaha

The Swiss side car pair of Rolf Biland and Kurt Waltisperg in their Yamaha during the Austrian Grand Prix. In 1981 they won the world championship for their event for the third time.

TOURIST TROPHY (TT) RACES: The TT Races on the Isle of Man are the most important series of road races in the sport. The British team for the 1905 International Cup race was at a distinct disadvantage due to the various restrictions imposed on motorcycles in Britain. However, the Manx authorities were sympathetic to their plight and the team trials were held on a 25·44 km (15·81 miles) course. The following year the Auto Cycle Club, formed in 1903 and the forerunner of the Auto Cycle Union, formulated the idea that led to the inauguration in 1907 of the first Tourist Trophy races. In 1911 the 60·72 km (37·73 miles) Mountain course (with 264 curves and corners) came into use, and apart from some minor changes this is the course currently used.

The greatest number of wins in the TT races is 14 by Mike Hailwood between 1961 and 1979, including a unique three events (out of a possible seven) in one year, which he achieved twice in 1961 and 1967. The only Senior (500 cc) race that has been won on a lower capacity machine was in 1921 when Howard Davies rode a 350 cc AJS to victory. The longest competitive span was by C. W. Johnston from 1922 to 1951, during which time he only won once in the 1926 lightweight race. The fastest times have been by Mick Grant on a 750 cc Kawasaki in the 1978 Open Classic race, in which he set a race average speed of 180·89 km/h (112·4 mph) and by Joey Dunlop, on a Honda, who set a lap record of 185·71 km/h (115·40 mph) in the 1981 Classic. The first rider to lap the circuit at an average of over 100 mph (160·9 km/h) was Bob McIntyre in 1957 on a Gilera with 162·73 km/h (101·12 mph). *Winners of the Senior TT race from 1970:*

1970	Giacomo Agostini (Ita)	MV-Agusta
1971	Giacomo Agostini (Ita)	MV-Agusta
1972	Giacomo Agostini (Ita)	MV-Agusta
1973	Jack Findlay (GB)	Suzuki
1974	Phil Carpenter (GB)	Yamaha
1975	Mick Grant (GB)	Kawasaki
1976	Tom Herron (GB)	Yamaha
1977	Phil Read (GB)	Suzuki
1978	Tom Herron (GB)	Suzuki
1979	Mike Hailwood (GB)	Suzuki
1980	Graham Crosby (GB)	Suzuki
1981	Mick Grant (GB)	Suzuki
1982	Norman Brown (GB)	Suzuki

MOTO-CROSS (Scrambling)
This is a very specialised sport in which the competitors race over rough country including steep climbs and drops, sharp turns, sand, mud and water. The sport originated at Camberley, Surrey, in 1924 when some riders competed in 'a rare old scramble'. Until the second World War it remained mainly a British interest but the Moto-Cross des Nations was inaugurated in 1947, and became an annual event, with the current rules formulated in 1963. In 1961 the Trophée des Nations, for 250 cc machines, was introduced by the FIM. World championships had been instituted in 1957. The most titles won are six by Joel Robert (Bel) between 1964 and 1972, during which period he also won a record fifty 250 cc Grands Prix. The youngest to win a world championship was Joel Robert (Bel) who was 20 yr 8 months when he won the 250 cc title in 1964. *Winners from 1970:*

Moto-Cross des Nations		*Trophée des Nations*	
1970	Sweden	**1970**	Belgium
1971	Sweden	**1971**	Belgium
1972	Belgium	**1972**	Belgium
1973	Belgium	**1973**	Belgium
1974	Sweden	**1974**	Belgium
1975	Czechoslovakia	**1975**	Belgium
1976	Belgium	**1976**	Belgium
1977	Belgium	**1977**	Belgium
1978	USSR	**1978**	Belgium
1979	Belgium	**1979**	USSR
1980	Belgium	**1980**	Belgium
1981	USA	**1981**	USA
1982	USA	**1982**	USA

The world 500 cc Moto-Cross champion André Malherbe almost takes flight on his way to victory in 1980. He is the latest in a long line of superb riders who have helped Belgium dominate this type of motorcycle activity.

TRIALS

Trials riding began in the early days of motorcycle sport and was mainly confined to the British Isles. From its beginnings the Auto-Cycle Union organised regular competitions and the Scottish Six Days Trial first took place in 1909. The first International Six Days Trial took place in 1913 and has become the major event in the sport. The British championships, originally the A-CU Stars has been won 11 times by Sammy Miller from 1959 to 1969. A world title was introduced in 1975, and the winners are:

1975 Martin Lampkin (GB)
1976 Yrjo Vesterinen (Fin)
1977 Yrjo Vesterinen (Fin)
1978 Yrjo Vesterinen (Fin)
1979 Bernie Schreiber (USA)
1980 Ulf Karlsson (Swe)
1981 Gilles Burgat (Fra)
1982 Eddy Lejeune (Bel)

Motor Racing

The first known race between automobiles was over 323 km (201 miles) from Green Bay to Madison, Wisconsin in 1878, and was won by an Oshkosh steamer. However, it is generally accepted that the first 'real' race was the Paris to Bordeaux and back run of 1178 km (732 miles) in June 1895, won by Emile Levassor (Fra). He was driving a Panhard-Levassor two-seater, powered by a 1·2 litre Daimler engine, and achieved an average speed of 24·15 km/h (15·01 mph). The first closed circuit race was in September 1896 at Narragansett Park, Cranston, Rhode Island and was won by A. H. Whiting driving a Riker electric car. The oldest regularly run race still in existence is the RAC Tourist Trophy on the Isle of Man which was first held in 1905. The oldest Grand Prix is that of France, inaugurated in 1906.

WORLD CHAMPIONSHIPS: Inaugurated in 1950, the Drivers' Championship has been won most often by Juan-Manuel Fangio (Arg) with five championships between 1951 and 1957. When he won for the last time in August 1957 he was the oldest ever winner, aged 46 yr 55 days. The youngest has been Emerson Fittipaldi (Bra) who was 25 yr 273 days old in 1972. The Manufacturers' Championship has been won by Ferrari six times since it was introduced in 1958.

	Champion Driver	Champion Car
1950	Giuseppe Farina (Ita)	—
1951	Juan Manuel Fangio (Arg)	—
1952	Alberto Ascari (Ita)	—
1953	Alberto Ascari (Ita)	—
1954	Juan Manuel Fangio (Arg)	—
1955	Juan Manuel Fangio (Arg)	—
1956	Juan Manuel Fangio (Arg)	—
1957	Juan Manuel Fangio (Arg)	—
1958	Mike Hawthorn (GB)	Vanwall
1959	Jack Brabham (Aus)	Cooper-Climax
1960	Jack Brabham (Aus)	Cooper-Climax
1961	Phil Hill (USA)	Ferrari
1962	Graham Hill (GB)	BRM
1963	Jim Clark (GB)	Lotus-Climax
1964	John Surtees (GB)	Ferrari
1965	Jim Clark (GB)	Lotus-Climax
1966	Jack Brabham (Aus)	Repco-Brabham
1967	Denny Hulme (NZ)	Repco-Brabham
1968	Graham Hill (GB)	Lotus-Ford
1969	Jackie Stewart (GB)	Matra-Ford
1970	Jochen Rindt (FRG)	Lotus-Ford
1971	Jackie Stewart (GB)	Tyrell-Ford
1972	Emerson Fittipaldi (Bra)	JPS Lotus
1973	Jackie Stewart (GB)	JPS Lotus
1974	Emerson Fittipaldi (Bra)	McLaren
1975	Niki Lauda (Aut)	Ferrari
1976	James Hunt (GB)	Ferrari
1977	Niki Lauda (Aut)	Ferrari
1978	Mario Andretti (USA)	JPS Lotus
1979	Jody Scheckter (Saf)	Ferrari
1980	Alan Jones (Aus)	Williams-Ford
1981	Nelson Piquet (Bra)	Williams-Ford
1982	Keke Rosberg (Fin)	Ferrari

GRAND PRIX RACING

The greatest number of Grands Prix won is 27 by Jackie Stewart (GB) between 1965 and 1973. The most in one year is seven by Jim Clark (GB) in 1963. Graham Hill (GB) set a record of 176 starts in Grand Prix races, from 1958 to January 1975, out of a possible 184 he could have contested. This included 90 consecutive races from November 1960 to October 1969. The youngest driver to win a Grand Prix was Bruce McLaren (NZ) in 1959 when he won the US race at the age of 22 yr 104 days. However, the youngest driver to take part in a Grand Prix was Mike Thackwell (NZ) who was aged 19 yr 182 days when he competed in the Canadian GP in 1980. The oldest winner was Tazio Nuvolari (Ita) aged 53 yr 240 days when he won the 1946 Albi GP in France. The oldest GP driver was Louis Chiron of Monaco, who finished sixth in the 1955 Monaco GP when aged 55 yr 292 days.

Above: **The 1981 world champion Nelson Piquet Soutomaior of Brazil clinched the title by winning three Grands Prix and placing in four others. In 1980 on the British Grand Prix circuit at Silverstone he set a new lap record in a test run.** *Right:* **One of the many sharp bends on the circuit which makes the Monaco race the toughest in Grand Prix racing. Not surprisingly the race and lap records are the slowest of all events counting towards the world championship.**

The toughest GP course is that at Monaco, first run in 1929, which stretches for 3312 km (2·05 miles) around the streets and harbour of the Principality. With its 11 sharp corners, and severe gradients, it has been estimated that a driver makes about 1600 gear changes during the 76 laps of the race—totalling 251·7 km (156·4 miles). The fastest time for the race has been 1 hr 54 min 11·259 sec, averaging 132·30 km/h (82·21 mph) by Riccardo Patrese (Ita) in a Brabham-Ford in 1982. The race lap record is 1 min 26·354 sec, average speed 138·073 km/h (85·79 mph) by Patrese in 1982. The practice lap best is 1 min 23·28 sec, at an average speed of 143·17 km/h (88·96 mph), by René Arnoux (Fra) in a Renault Elf Turbo in 1982.

BRITISH GRAND PRIX: Originally run at Brooklands, Surrey in 1926 and 1927 as the RAC GP, it was then held as the Donington GP from 1935–38. Restarted at Silverstone in 1948, the race was given its current name the following year. It was won a record five times by Jim Clark between 1962 and 1967.

The venue now alternates between Silverstone and Brands Hatch. The fastest time for the race is 1 hr 26 min 11·17 sec, averaging 223·37 km/h (138·80 mph) by Clay Regazzoni (Swi) in 1979, when driving a Saudia-Williams in which he also set a Silverstone lap, 4·719 km (2·932 miles), race record of 1 min 14·40 sec, averaging 228·31 km/h (141·87 mph). The practice lap mark is 1 min 11·00 sec, averaging 239·24 km/h (148·66 mph) by René Arnoux (Fra) in a Renault Elf Turbo in 1981.

Year	Driver	Car
1926	Robert Sénéchal/Louis Wagner (Fra)	Delage
1927	Robert Benoist (Fra)	Delage
1935	Richard Shuttleworth (GB)	Alfa Romeo
1936	Hans Ruesch (Ger) Richard Seaman (GB)	Alfa Romeo
1937	Bernd Rosemeyer (Fer)	Auto-Union
1938	Tazio Nuvolari (Ita)	Auto-Union
1948	Luigi Villoresi (Ita)	Maserati
1949	Baron Emmanuel de Graffenried (Swi)	Maserati
1950	Giuseppe Farina (Ita)	Alfa Romeo
1951	José Froilan Gonzalez (Arg)	Ferrari
1952	Alberto Ascari (Ita)	Ferrari
1953	Alberto Ascari (Ita)	Ferrari
1954	José Froilan Gonzalez (Arg)	Ferrari
1955	Stirling Moss (GB)	Mercedes-Benz
1956	Juan Manuel Fangio (Arg)	Ferrari
1957	Tony Brooks/Stirling Moss (GB)	Vanwall
1958	Peter Collins (GB)	Ferrari
1959	Jack Brabham (Aus)	Cooper-Climax
1960	Jack Brabham (Aus)	Cooper-Climax
1961	Wolfgang von Trips (Ger)	Ferrari
1962	Jim Clark (GB)	Lotus-Climax
1963	Jim Clark (GB)	Lotus-Climax
1964	Jim Clark (GB)	Lotus-Climax
1965	Jim Clark (GB)	Lotus-Climax
1966	Jack Brabham (Aus)	Repco Brabham
1967	Jim Clark (GB)	Lotus-Ford
1968	Joseph Siffert (Swi)	Lotus-Ford
1969	Jackie Stewart (GB)	Matra-Ford
1970	Jochen Rindt (FRG)	Lotus-Ford
1971	Jackie Stewart (GB)	Tyrell-Ford
1972	Emerson Fittipaldi (Bra)	JPS Ford
1973	Peter Revson (USA)	McLaren-Ford
1974	Jody Scheckter (Saf)	Tyrell-Ford
1975	Emerson Fittipaldi (Bra)	McLaren-Ford
1976	Niki Lauda (Aut)	Ferrari
1977	James Hunt (GB)	McLaren-Ford
1978	Carlos Reutemann (Arg)	Ferrari
1979	Clay Regazzoni (Swi)	Williams-Ford
1980	Alan Jones (Aus)	Williams-Ford
1981	John Watson (GB)	McLaren-Ford
1982	Niki Lauda (Aut)	McLaren-Ford

Undeterred by the terrible burns he received in his 1976 crash, Niki Lauda is still racing, here in a McLaren in the 1983 French Grand Prix.

LE MANS GRAND PRIX d'ENDURANCE: First held in 1923 on the old Sarthe circuit at Le Mans and conceived as a test for touring cars over a period of 24 hours. The greatest distance covered on the old circuit was 5335·313 km (3315·208 miles) by a Porsche driven by Helmut Marko (Aut) and Gijs van Lennep (Hol) in 1971. On the current 13·64 km (8·475 miles) circuit the record is 5044·52 km (3134·52 miles) by an Alpine Renault driven by the Frenchmen Didier Pironi and Jean-Pierre Jassaud, averaging 210·18 km/h (130·60 mph) in 1978. The race lap record is 3 min 34·2 sec, averaging 229·244 km/h (142·44 mph) by Jean-Pierre Jabouille (Fra) driving an Alpine Renault in 1978, but the practice record is 3 min 27·6 sec, averaging 236·53 km/h (146·97 mph) by Jacky Ickx (Bel) in a Porsche, also in 1978. The most successful driver has been Ickx with six victories between 1969 and 1982. The most wins by a manufacturer have been the nine by Ferrari from 1949 to 1965. The race has been won 13 times by British cars since a Bentley first won in 1924. Crowds of 400 000 have been known, giving the race the record for a single sporting event.

Winners from 1970:

1970	Hans Hermann & Richard Attwood	Porsche
1971	Helmut Marko & Gijs van Lennep	Porsche
1972	Graham Hill & Henri Pescarolo	Matra-Simca
1973	Henri Pescarolo & Gerard Larrousse	Matra-Simca
1974	Henri Pescarolo & Gerard Larrousse	Matra-Simca
1975	Jacky Ickx & Derek Bell	Gulf Ford
1976	Jacky Ickx & Gijs van Lennep	Porsche
1977	Jacky Ickx & Jurgen Barth & Hurley Haywood	Porsche
1978	Didier Pironi & Jean-Pierre Jassaud	Renault Alpine
1979	Klaus Ludwig & Bill and Don Whittington	Porsche
1980	Jean-Pierre Jassaud & Jean Rondeau	Rondeau
1981	Jacky Ickx & Derek Bell	Porsche
1982	Jacky Ickx & Derek Bell	Porsche

The start at the Le Mans Grand Prix d'Endurance—the 24-hours race for touring cars. Record breaking crowds of more than 400 000 people watch the race. The last British car to win was a Ford in 1975.

INDIANAPOLIS 500: First held in 1911 on a 4·02 km (2·5 miles), circuit, the race consists of 200 laps totalling 804 km (500 miles). Held annually on the last Saturday in May, it attracts crowds of about 300 000 spectators. The most wins have been four by Anthony Joseph 'A.J.' Foyt (USA) between 1961 and 1977. The fastest time for the full race has been 3 hr 4 min 5·54 sec by Mark Donohue (USA) who averaged 262·261 km/h (162·962 mph) driving a Sunoco McLaren M16B-Offenhauser in 1972. The race lap record is 46·71 sec, averaging 310·085 km/h (192·678 mph), by the Hawaiian driver Danny Ongais in a Parnelli-Cosworth DFX on lap 42 of the 1977 race. The record speed for a qualifying lap is 335·9 km/h (208·7 mph) by Rick Mears (USA) driving a Penske-Cosworth in 1982. The record prize money for the race was in 1982 at $2 067 475, with the top individual prize of $318 819 going to Johnny Rutherford (USA) in 1980. British drivers have won twice: Jim Clark in 1965 and Graham Hill in 1966. An unusual family achievement was capped in 1981 when, after some controversy, Bobby Unser (USA), was awarded his third win to match his brother Al and make it six for the family since 1968. *Winners from 1970 (all American):*

1970	Al Unser
1971	Al Unser
1972	Mark Donohue
1973	Gordon Johncock
1974	Johnny Rutherford
1975	Bobby Unser
1976	Johnny Rutherford
1977	A. J. Foyt
1978	Al Unser
1979	Rick Mears
1980	Johnny Rutherford
1981	Bobby Unser
1982	Gordon Johncock
1983	Tom Sneva

RALLYING

The first rally was probably the Herkomer Trophy event held in Germany in 1904. The first long rally was that organised by the French newspaper *Le Monde* from Peking to Paris in 1907, distance about 12 000 km (7500 miles). The winner was Prince Scipione Borghese (Ita) in a 40 hp Itala, having taken 61 days. Of the other four starters, three finished some weeks later, and the other one broke down just after the start. The longest rally ever held was the *Singapore Airlines* London to Sydney race in 1977, won by Andrew Cowan, Colin Malkin and Michael Broad, driving a Mercedes 280E over 31 107 km (19 329 miles) in 45 days. The longest annual rally, up to 6234 km (3874 miles), is the Safari, first held in 1953.

It has been won a record five times by Shekhar Mehta (Ken) between 1973 and 1982. The Monte Carlo Rally, first held in 1911, is possibly the most famous motor event in the world. It has been won four times by Sandro Munari (Ita) between 1972 and 1977. The RAC Rally in Britain was instituted in 1932 and recognised by the Fédération Internationale de l'Automobile in 1951. The largest field since then was 242 starters in 1952, but there were 384 in 1934. The most successful driver has been Hannu Mikkola (Fin), who has won four times, driving a Ford Escort in 1978–79 and an Audi Quattro in 1981–82.

Hannu Mikkola and Arne Hertz of Finland in the 1980 RAC Rally. They failed to win, losing to a fellow countryman, but Mikkola notched up his fourth victory in 1982.

Winners of the Monte Carlo Rally from 1970:

1970	Bjorn Waldegaard & Lars Helmer	Porsche
1971	Ove Andersson & David Stone	Alpine Renault
1972	Sandro Munari & Mario Manucci	Lancia Fulvia
1973	Jean-Claude Andruet & 'Biche'★	Alpine Renault
1974	Not held	
1975	Sandro Munari & Mario Manucci	Lancia Stratos
1976	Sandro Munari & Silvio Maiga	Lancia Stratos
1977	Sandro Munari & Mario Manucci	Lancia Stratos
1978	Jean-Pierre Nicolas & Vincent Laverne	Porsche Carrera
1979	Bernard Darniche & Alain Mahe	Lancia Stratos
1980	Walter Röhrl & Christian Geistdorfer	Fiat Abarth
1981	Jean Ragnotti & Jean-Marc Andrié	Renault 5 Turbo
1982	Walter Röhrl & Christian Geistdorfer	Opel Ascona
1983	Walter Röhrl & Christian Geistdorfer	Opel Ascona

★*The first female co-driver in a winning car*

Winning drivers of the RAC Rally from 1970:

1970	Harry Kallstrom (Fin)	Lancia Fulvia
1971	Stig Blomquist (Swe)	Saab
1972	Roger Clark (GB)	Ford Escort
1973	Timo Makinen (Fin)	Ford Escort
1974	Timo Makinen (Fin)	Ford Escort
1975	Timo Makinen (Fin)	Ford Escort
1976	Roger Clark (GB)	Ford Escort
1977	Bjorn Waldegaard (Swe)	Ford Escort
1978	Hannu Mikkola (Fin)	Ford Escort
1979	Hannu Mikkola (Fin)	Ford Escort
1980	Henri Toivonen (Fin)	Talbot Sunbeam Lotus
1981	Hannu Mikkola (Fin)	Audi Quattro
1982	Hannu Mikkola (Fin)	Audi Quattro

In drag racing, especially constructed cars achieve amazing speeds in a matter of seconds.

LADY DRIVERS

The first woman known to have taken part in a race was Madame Laumaillé (Fra) who finished fourth in a two-day event from Marseilles to Nice in 1898. Her husband finished in sixth place. Dorothy Levitt (GB) was the earliest woman driver to win a road race, at Brighton, Sussex in 1905, and she also competed in one of the early Herkomer Trophy rallies in Germany in 1907, finishing fourth out of 172 competitors. The first to drive in a Grand Prix was Maria Teresa de Fillipis (Ita) who drove a Maserati in the 1958 Belgian GP, finishing tenth. Another Italian lady, Lella Lombardi, became the first woman to score in the world championship table when she gained $\frac{1}{2}$ a point for her sixth place in the 1975 Spanish GP at Barcelona, which was stopped due to an accident and the points awarded were halved. In America, Janet Guthrie was the first female driver in the Indianapolis 500 in 1977, although her car developed mechanical problems and she did not finish. She rectified that in 1978, placing ninth. Britain's Pat Moss was the first woman to win a major rally when she took the Liège–Rome–Liège event in 1960 partnered by Anne Wisdom in an Austin Healey 3000.

DRAG RACING

The forerunner of this sport was probably the first sprint meeting ever held, at Acheres Park, near Paris, in December 1898, when cars were clocked over 2000 m (1·24 miles) from a standing start to get two different timings including one for a flying kilometre. Drag racing in specially constructed cars is held over a 440 yd (402 m) course, primarily in America, where it developed after the Second World War. It is now organised by the American Hot-Rod Association who held their first championship meeting in 1955. There are two types of measurement noted—elapsed time (ET), which is that taken to cover the course, and terminal velocity, which is the speed at which the finish line is crossed. The lowest ET recorded is 3·72 sec by Kitty O'Neil (USA) at El Mirage Dry Lake, California in July 1977, when she also set the record for terminal velocity with 631·732 km/h (392·54 mph) in her rocket engined car. The best ET by a piston-engined dragster is 5·484 sec by Gary Beck (USA) at the US Nationals at Indianapolis in 1982. The highest terminal velocity recorded is 412·65 km/h (256·41 mph) by Mark Oswald (USA) in 1982.

Netball

Modern netball grew out of the game of basketball although the Romans and the Greeks played games of similar construction. In 1895, Dr Toles taught the students of a physical training college in London that game, and two years later another American visitor brought slightly differing rules, including rings instead of baskets. The Ling Association (named after the Swede, Per Ling, who devised a system of gymnastic exercises) drew up their own English set of rules in 1901 and coined the name netball. In 1926 the All-England Women's Netball Association was formed, but it had been preceded as the first such national body by that of New Zealand two years earlier. The oldest club still in existence is the Polytechnic Netball Club, London, founded in 1907. The All-England inter-county tournament was first held in 1932, and the first Home Countries internationals in 1949. The earliest international match was that between New Zealand and Australia in 1938. The International Federation was formed in 1960.

WORLD CHAMPIONSHIPS: The first championships were held at Eastbourne, Sussex, England in 1963, and 11 countries took part. Australia has won a record four times since then. The highest score in the championships was achieved when England beat Papua New Guinea by 114–16 in 1975. The most individual goals scored in the tournament is 402 by Judith Heath (Eng) in 1971. *The winners have been:*

1963 Australia
1967 New Zealand
1971 Australia
1975 Australia
1979 Australia, New Zealand, Trinidad & Tobago (all shared)

BRITISH CHAMPIONSHIPS: The national title, first held in 1966, has been won most times by the Sudbury Club with five (including one shared) between 1968 and 1973. The county championship has been won a record 18 times (including one shared) by Surrey between 1949 and 1981.

HIGHEST SCORE
The most points ever scored in an international match is 117–9 when New Zealand beat Singapore in October 1974.

Olympic Games

In 1976, at Montreal, the Olympic flame was lit by two young people, Sandra Henderson from Toronto and Stephane Prefontaine from Montreal, representing the two cultural heritages, English and French, of the host country Canada.

Although recorded details of the ancient Games date only from 776 BC, there is evidence that they were celebrated as far back as 1370 BC. The Games were primarily of religious significance, and indeed a truce between warring states would be declared to enable competitors to travel safely to and from Olympia, some 193 km (120 miles) to the west of Athens, in Greece. Those Games of 776 BC consisted of just one race, a stade of about 176 m (186 yd), and the first known Olympic champion was Coroibos of Elis. In 724 BC a double stade race, the *diaulus*, was added, followed by the *dolichus* of about 4·5 km (2·8 miles) in

128

Olympic champion in the decathlon, Daley Thompson is an excellent performer in many of the individual events. In the high jump, for example, he has flopped over seven feet.

the following celebration. Twelve years later, in 708 BC, the *pentathlon* was added, which consisted of running, jumping, throwing the discus and javelin, and wrestling. In subsequent Games other sports such as chariot racing and boxing were included. In those early Games women were barred, under threat of death, from even watching. The prizes were chaplets of wild olive leaves, but often winning athletes were hugely rewarded by their home cities for the honour they had brought to their birthplace. Gradually the Games went into decline and were finally stopped by a decree of the Roman Emperor Theodosius I in AD 393. They were not revived until 1503 years later,

when at the instigation of Baron Pierre de Coubertin of France the first modern celebration was held in Athens in 1896. The lighting of the Olympic flame, based on the ancient Games ritual of a sacred flame at the altar of Zeus, was introduced in 1928. In 1936 the Germans organised a torch relay to bring the flame by hand from Olympia to Berlin. The 1936 Games were also the first to be televised, albeit on a small scale to a number of special halls not far from the stadium. By the next Games held in Germany in 1972, it was estimated that there was a world-wide television audience of 1000 million people.

The gaiety and colour of the Opening Ceremony of the 1972 Olympic Games at Munich, with the teams drawn up in the centre, thousands of children dancing and singing around the track, and not a seat in the stadium unfilled. Ten days later this was all overshadowed by the blackest day in Olympic history, with the deaths of 11 members of the Israeli team at the hands of terrorists.

OLYMPIC SPORTS

There are 21 different sports currently on the Summer Games programme and eight on the Winter Games schedule, as follows (with year of first inclusion):

Summer
Archery (1900)
Athletics (1896)
Basketball (1936)
Boxing (1904)
Canoeing (1936)
Cycling (1896)
Equestrianism (1900)
Fencing (1896)
Football (Association) (1900)
Gymnastics (1896)
Handball (1972)
Hockey (1908)
Judo (1964)
Modern Pentathlon (1912)
Rowing (1900)
Shooting (1896)
Swimming (including Diving & Water Polo) (1896)
Volleyball (1964)
Weightlifting (1896)
Wrestling (1896)
Yachting (1900)

Winter
Alpine Skiing (1936)
Bobsleigh (1924)
Figure Skating (1908)
Ice Hockey (1920)
Nordic Skiing (including Ski-jumping & Biathlon) (1924)
Speed Skating (1924)
Lugeing (Tobogganing) (1964)

There have been another 17 sports included in the Summer Games either as official events, for which medals were awarded, or as demonstration events, as follows:

Australian Rules Football: *1932, 1936 (both demonstrations)*
Baseball: *1912, 1936, 1956, & 1964 (demonstration)*
Baseball, Finnish: *1952 (demonstration)*
Budo: *1964 (demonstration)*
Cricket: *1900*
Croquet: *1900*

SUMMER AND WINTER

The only person to win gold medals in both summer and winter Olympic Games was Eddie Eagan (USA), who won the light heavyweight boxing title in 1920, and then was a member of the winning 4–man bobsleigh team in 1932. The nearest to this unique achievement was Jacob Thams (Nor), winner of the 1924 ski jumping title and then a member of the silver medal crew in the 8 m Class yachting event in 1936. Another excellent all-rounder was Martin Stokken (Nor), who having placed fourth in the 1948 10 000 m run, won a silver medal in the 4 × 10 km Nordic skiing relay event in the 1952 winter Games. The American Willie Davenport, gold medallist in the 1968 110 m hurdles and bronze in the 1976 event, tried to emulate his countryman, Eagan, when he competed in the 4–man bob in 1980 but his team were only 12th. The only British Medallist to compete in both Games has been Derek Allhusen, a silver medallist in the 1968 equestrian team, who had competed in the 1948 winter Games in the Winter Pentathlon (a demonstration event).

Gliding: *1936 (demonstration)*
Golf: *1900, 1904*
Jeu de Paume (Real Tennis): *1908, 1928*
Lacrosse: *1904, 1908, 1928, 1932, 1948 (last three as demonstrations)*
Motorboating: *1908*
Pelota: *1924, 1968 (both demonstrations)*
Polo: *1900, 1908, 1920, 1924, 1936*
Rackets: *1908*
Roque (Croquet): *1904*
Rugby Union: *1900, 1908, 1920, 1924*
Tennis, Lawn: *1896, 1900, 1904, 1906, 1908, 1912, 1920, 1924, 1968 (demonstration)*

THE GOLD HOARDERS

In the early Games, Leonidas of Rhodos won 12 running titles between 164 and 152 BC, for which he was not awarded gold medals but chaplets of wild olive leaves. In modern times the greatest number of gold medals won is 10 by athlete Ray Ewry (USA) in the standing high, long and triple jumps between 1900 and 1908. The most victories in individual events by a woman is seven by gymnast Vera Caslavska (Cz) in 1964 and 1968. The most won by a British competitor is four by Paul Radmilovic in swimming and water polo between 1908 and 1920, and also by swimmer Henry Taylor in 1906 and 1908. The British-born swimmer Murray Rose won four in 1956 and 1960, but he was representing Australia. The most titles won at one Games is seven by Mark Spitz (USA) in the 1972 swimming events, which included three in relays. The speed skater Eric Heiden (USA) won a record five individual events in 1980, which was also an absolute record for the Winter Games. Only one man has won four consecutive individual titles at the same event, and he is Al Oerter (USA) in the discus throw from 1956 to 1968. Aleksandr Tikhonov (USSR) set a Winter Games record by winning gold medals in the Biathlon relay on four consecutive occasions from 1968 to 1980.

MEDAL TABLES

Although tables of medals by countries are frowned upon by the Olympic authorities—the Games are, in their eyes, for individuals—such compilations are nevertheless of considerable interest. The lists below give the top 10 countries, by total medals, in the Summer and Winter Games from 1896 to 1980. It should be noted that the GDR (or East Germany) was only counted separately from 1968.

Summer Games

	Gold	Silver	Bronze	Total
USA	627	468	417	1512
USSR	340	292	253	885
Great Britain	163	201	176	540
Germany	129	174	169	472
France	142	156	155	453
Sweden	129	125	156	410
Hungary	113	106	130	349
Italy	127	111	108	346
GDR	116	94	97	307
Finland	92	72	102	266

Winter Games

	Gold	Silver	Bronze	Total
Norway	51	55	48	154
USSR	62	38	41	141
USA	36	42	31	109
Finland	25	39	26	90
Austria	25	33	29	87
Sweden	28	23	27	78
Germany	22	21	20	63
GDR	21	17	23	61
Switzerland	16	18	19	53
Canada	12	9	14	35
Netherlands	10	15	10	35

CORNERING THE MARKET

The greatest number of Olympic medals ever won is 18 by Larissa Latynina (USSR), comprising nine golds, five silvers

SUMMER GAMES—VENUES, DATES, COMPETITORS

			Countries	Competitors Male	Female
I	Athens, Greece	6–15 Apr 1896	13	311	—
II	Paris, France	20 May–28 Oct 1900	22	1319	11
III	St Louis, USA	1 July–23 Nov 1904	13	617	8
†	Athens, Greece	22 Apr–2 May 1906	20	877	7
IV	London, UK	27 Apr–31 Oct 1908	22	2013	43
V	Stockholm, Sweden	5 May–22 July 1912	28	2491	55
VI	*Berlin, Germany	1916 (not held)			
VII	Antwerp, Belgium	20 Apr–12 Sept 1920	29	2618	74
VIII	Paris, France	4 May–27 July 1924	44	2956	136
IX	Amsterdam, Netherlands	17 May–12 Aug 1928	46	2724	290
X	Los Angeles, USA	30 July–14 Aug 1932	37	1281	127
XI	Berlin, Germany	1–16 Aug 1936	49	3738	328
XII	*Tokyo, Japan, then Helsinki, Finland	1940 (not held)			
XIII	*London, UK	1944 (not held)			
XIV	London, UK	29 July–14 Aug 1948	59	3714	385
XV	Helsinki, Finland	19 July–3 Aug 1952	69	4407	518
XVI	‡Melbourne, Australia	22 Nov–8 Dec 1956	71	2958	384
XVII	Rome, Italy	25 Aug–11 Sept 1960	83	4738	610
XVIII	Tokyo, Japan	10–24 Oct 1964	93	4457	683
XIX	Mexico City, Mexico	12–27 Oct 1968	112	4749	781
XX	Munich, West Germany	26 Aug–10 Sept 1972	122	6086	1070
XXI	Montreal, Canada	17 July–1 Aug 1976	92	4834	1251
XXII	Moscow, USSR	19 July–3 Aug 1980	81	4238	1088
XXIII	Los Angeles, USA	28 July–12 Aug 1984	—	—	—
XXIV	Seoul, S. Korea	20 Sept–5 Oct 1988	—	—	—

† *Intercalated celebration, not numbered, but officially organised by the International Olympic Committee (IOC)*

‡ *Equestrian events held in Stockholm, Sweden, 10–17 June 1956*

* *Cancelled due to World Wars*

WINTER GAMES—VENUES, DATES, COMPETITORS

			Countries	Competitors Male	Female
I*	Chamonix, France	25 Jan–4 Feb 1924	16	281	13
II	St Moritz, Switzerland	11–19 Feb 1928	25	468	27
III	Lake Placid, USA	4–15 Feb 1932	17	274	32
IV	Garmisch-Partenkirchen, Germany	6–16 Feb 1936	28	675	80
V	St Moritz, Switzerland	20 Jan–8 Feb 1948	28	636	77
VI	Oslo, Norway	14–25 Feb 1952	22	623	109
VII	Cortina d'Ampezzo, Italy	26 Jan–5 Feb 1956	32	687	132
VIII	Squaw Valley, USA	18–28 Feb 1960	30	521	144
IX	Innsbruck, Austria	29 Jan–9 Feb 1964	36	893	200
X	Grenoble, France	6–18 Feb 1968	37	1065	228
XI	Sapporo, Japan	3–13 Feb 1972	35	1015	217
XII	Innsbruck, Austria	4–15 Feb 1976	37	900	228
XIII	Lake Placid, USA	13–24 Feb 1980	37	833	234
XIV	Sarajevo, Yugoslavia	8–19 Feb 1984	—	—	—
XV	Calgary, Canada	1988	—	—	—

There were Winter Games events included in the Summer Games of 1908 (London) and 1920 (Antwerp) which attracted six countries, 14 males and seven females for the first, and 10 countries, 73 males and 12 females for the latter.

and four bronzes, in individual and team competitions from 1956 to 1964. Her compatriot Nikolai Andrianov won seven golds, five silvers and three bronzes to set a male record of 15 from 1972 to 1980. In the Games of 1980 another Russian gymnast Aleksandr Ditiatin won eight medals to set a record for the most won in one celebration.

WE WERE THERE
The only country to have been present at all celebrations of both Summer and Winter Games since 1896 has been Great Britain. Three other countries, Australia, Greece, and Switzerland have attended all the Summer Games.

OLDEST AND YOUNGEST
The oldest person to represent his country at the Olympics was Oscar Swahn (Swe) who won a silver medal for shooting in 1920, aged 72 yr 280 days. He would have set an even more extreme record at the 1924 Games, for which he had qualified, but illness prevented him from competing. Swahn had won a gold medal in 1912 at the record age of 65 yr 258 days. Britain's oldest ever Olympic representative was Lorna Johnstone who

was aged 70 yr 5 days when placed 12th in the Dressage event at Munich in 1972.

The youngest person to win an Olympic gold medal was a French boy who coxed the winning Dutch rowing pairs crew in the 1900 Games. His name is not known as he was a last minute substitute but he was no more than 10 years old and may even have been as young as seven. The youngest female champion was springboard diver Marjorie Gestring (USA), only 13 yr 267 days when she won in 1936. The youngest competitor to represent Great Britain was ice skater Cecilia Colledge who was 11 yr 24 days old at the 1932 Games, only a few weeks younger than her team-mate Megan Taylor.

IF AT FIRST YOU DON'T SUCCEED
The Italian rider Raimondo d'Inzeo competed in a record eight Games from 1948 to 1976, winning one gold, two silver and three bronze medals. The equivalent female record is six Games by fencer Janice Lee York-Romary (USA) from 1948 to 1968, and by discus thrower Lia Manoliu (Rom) who competed from 1952 to 1972, winning a gold in 1968, and bronzes in 1960 and

1964. The Danish fencer Ivan Osier competed over a span of 40 years (winning a silver medal in 1912) from 1908 to 1948 (he missed out in 1936), and he was matched by 1912 and 1920 gold medallist yachtsman Magnus Konow (Nor) also from 1908 to 1948 (but he missed out in 1924, 1928 and 1932). The greatest span of years by a woman was 24 by fencer Ellen Muller-Preis (Aut) from 1932 to 1956, during which time she won one gold and three bronze medals. The most appearances by a Briton is six by fencer Bill Hoskyns from 1956 to 1976, although Durward Knowles competed for Britain in yachting in 1948 and in the next six Games for the Bahamas. Clay pigeon shooter Enoch Jenkins set a British record span of 28 years from 1924 to 1952, while high jumper Dorothy Odam-Tyler is the female record holder from 1936 to 1956.

1980 WINTER OLYMPIC GAMES—CHAMPIONS

Alpine Skiing
Men's Downhill   Leonhard Stock (Aut)
Men's Slalom   Ingemar Stenmark (Swe)
Men's Giant Slalom   Ingemar Stenmark (Swe)
Women's Downhill   Annemarie Moser (Aut)
Women's Slalom   Hanni Wenzel (Lie)
Women's Giant Slalom   Hanni Wenzel (Lie)

Bobsleigh
2-Man   Switzerland I
4-Man   GDR I

Figure Skating
Men   Robin Cousins (GB)
Women   Annette Pötsch (GDR)
Pairs   Irina Rodnina & Aleksandr Zaitsev (USSR)
Dance   Natalia Linichuk & Gennadi Karponosov (USSR)

Ice Hockey
Team   USA

Lugeing
Men—Singles   Bernhard Glass (GDR)
Men—Doubles   Hans Rinn & Norbert Hahn (GDR)
Women—Singles   Vera Zozulia (USSR)

Nordic Skiing—Men
15 km   Thomas Wassberg (Swe)
30 km   Nikolai Zimyatov (USSR)
50 km   Nikolai Zimyatov (USSR)
4 × 10 km Relay   USSR
10 km Biathlon   Frank Ulrich (GDR)
20 km Biathlon   Anatoli Alyabiev (USSR)
4 × 7·5 km Biathlon Relay   USSR
Nordic Combination   Ulrich Wehling (GDR)
70 m Jump   Anton Innauer (Aut)
90 m Jump   Jouko Tormanen (Fin)

Nordic Skiing—Women
5 km   Raisa Smetanina (USSR)
10 km   Barbara Petzold (GDR)
4 × 5 km Relay   GDR

Speed Skating—Men
500 m   Eric Heiden (USA)
1000 m   Eric Heiden (USA)
1500 m   Eric Heiden (USA)
5000 m   Eric Heiden (USA)
10 000 m   Eric Heiden (USA)

Speed Skating—Women
500 m   Karin Enke (GDR)
1000 m   Natalia Petruseva (USSR)
1500 m   Annie Borckink (Hol)
3000 m   Björg-Eva Jensen (Nor)

1980 SUMMER OLYMPIC GAMES—CHAMPIONS

Archery
Men   Tomi Poikolainen (Fin)
Women   Keto Losaberidze (USSR)

Association Football
Team   Czechoslovakia

Athletics—Men
100 m   Allan Wells (GB)
200 m   Pietro Mennea (Ita)
400 m   Viktor Markin (USSR)
800 m   Steve Ovett (GB)
1500 m   Sebastian Coe (GB)
5000 m   Miruts Yifter (Eth)
10 000 m   Miruts Yifter (Eth)
3000 m Steeplechase   Bronislaw Malinowski (Pol)
110 m Hurdles   Thomas Munkelt (GDR)
400 m Hurdles   Volker Beck (GDR)
4 × 100 m Relay   USSR
4 × 400 m Relay   USSR
Marathon   Waldemar Cierpinski (GDR)
20 000 m Walk   Maurizio Damilano (Ita)
50 000 m Walk   Hartwig Gauder (GDR)
High Jump   Gerd Wessig (GDR)
Pole Vault   Wladyslaw Kozakiewicz (Pol)
Long Jump   Lutz Dombrowski (GDR)
Triple Jump   Jaak Uudmae (USSR)
Shot   Vladimir Kiselyev (USSR)
Discus   Viktor Rasshchupkin (USSR)
Hammer   Yuri Sedykh (USSR)
Javelin   Dainis Kula (USSR)
Decathlon   Daley Thompson (GB)

Athletics—Women
100 m   Ludmila Kondratyeva (USSR)
200 m   Barbel Wöckel (GDR)
400 m   Marita Koch (GDR)
800 m   Nadyezda Olizarenko (USSR)
1500 m   Tatyana Kazankina (USSR)
100 m Hurdles   Vera Komisova (USSR)
4 × 100 m Relay   GDR
4 × 400 m Relay   USSR
High Jump   Sara Simeoni (Ita)
Long Jump   Tatyana Kolpakova (USSR)
Shot   Ilona Slupianek (GDR)
Discus   Evelin Jahl (GDR)
Javelin   Maria Colon (Cub)
Pentathlon   Nadyezda Tkachenko (USSR)

Basketball
Men   Yugoslavia
Women   USSR

Boxing
48 kg   Shamil Sabirov (USSR)
51 kg   Petar Lessov (Bul)
54 kg   Juan Hernandez (Cub)
57 kg   Rudi Fink (GDR)
60 kg   Angel Herrara (Cub)
63·5 kg   Patrizio Oliva (Ita)
67 kg   Andres Aldama (Cub)
71 kg   Armando Martinez (Cub)
75 kg   Jose Gomez (Cub)
81 kg   Slobodan Kacar (Yug)
Over 81 kg   Teofilio Stevenson (Cub)

Canoeing—Men
500 m—K1   Vladimir Parfenovich (USSR)
500 m—K2   USSR
1000 m—K1   Rudiger Helm (GDR)
1000 m—K2   USSR
1000 m—K4   GDR
500 m—C1   Sergei Postrekhin (USSR)
500 m—C2   Hungary
1000 m—C1   Lubomir Lubenov (Bul)
1000 m—C2   Romania

Canoeing—Women
500 m—K1   Birgit Fischer (GDR)
500 m—K2   GDR

Cycling
1000 m Sprint   Lothar Thoms (GDR)
1000 m Time Trial   Lutz Hesslich (GDR)
4000 m Individual Pursuit   Robert Dill-Bundi (Swi)
4000 m Team Pursuit   USSR
Individual Road Race   Sergei Soukhorouchenkov (USSR)
Team Road Race   USSR

Equestrianism
Jumping Grand Prix, Individual   Jan Kowalczyk (Pol)
Jumping Grand Prix, Team   USSR

Dressage Grand Prix, Individual	Elisabeth Theurer (Aut)
Dressage Grand Prix, Team	USSR
Three-Day Event, Individual	Frederico Roman (Ita)
Three-Day Event, Team	USSR

Fencing—Men

Foil, Individual	Vladimir Smirnov (USSR)
Foil, Team	France
Epee, Individual	Johan Harmenberg (Swe)
Epee, Team	France
Sabre, Individual	Viktor Krovopouskov (USSR)
Sabre, Team	USSR

Fencing—Women

Foil, Individual	Pascale Trinquet (Fra)
Foil, Team	France

Gymnastics—Men

Overall	Aleksandr Ditiatin (USSR)
Floor Exercises	Roland Bruckner (GDR)
Pommel Horse	Zoltan Magyar (Hun)
Rings	Aleksandr Ditiatin (USSR)
Horse Vault	Nikolai Andrianov (USSR)
Parallel Bars	Aleksandr Tkatchev (USSR)
Horizontal Bars	Stoyan Deltchev (Bul)
Team	USSR

Gymnastics—Women

Overall	Elena Davidova (USSR)
Horse Vault	Natalia Shaposhnikova (USSR)
Assymetrical Bars	Maxi Gnauck (GDR)
Balance Beam	Nadia Comaneci (Rom)
Floor Exercises	Nelli Kim (USSR)
	Nadia Comaneci (Rom)
Team	USSR

Handball

Men	GDR
Women	USSR

Hockey

Men	India
Women	Zimbabwe

Judo

60 kg	Thierry Rey (Fra)
65 kg	Nikolai Soloduchine (USSR)
71 kg	Ezio Gamba (Ita)
78 kg	Shota Khabareli (USSR)
86 kg	Jürg Röthlisberger (Swi)
95 kg	Robert van de Walle (Bel)
Over 95 kg	Angelo Parisi (Fra)
Open	Dietmar Lorenz (GDR)

Modern Pentathlon

Individual	Anatoli Starostin (USSR)
Team	USSR

Rowing—Men

Single Sculls	Pertti Karppinen (Fin)
Double Sculls	GDR
Quad Sculls	GDR
Coxless Pairs	GDR
Coxed Pairs	GDR
Coxless Fours	GDR
Coxed Fours	GDR
Eights	GDR

Rowing—Women

Single Sculls	Sanda Toma (Rom)
Double Sculls	USSR
Quad Sculls	GDR
Coxless Pairs	GDR
Coxed Fours	GDR
Eights	GDR

Shooting

Free Pistol	Aleksandr Melentev (USSR)
Rapid Fire Pistol	Corneliu Ion (Rom)
Small Bore Rifle (3 pos)	Karoly Varga (Hun)
Small Bore Rifle (prone)	Viktor Vlasov (USSR)
Trap Shooting	Luciano Giovanetti (Ita)
Skeet	Hans Kjeld Rasmussen (Den)
Running Game Target	Igor Sokolov (USSR)

Swimming—Men

100 m Free	Jorg Woithe (GDR)
200 m Free	Sergei Kopliakov (USSR)
400 m Free	Vladimir Salnikov (USSR)
1500 m Free	Vladimir Salnikov (USSR)
100 m Breast	Duncan Goodhew (GB)
200 m Breast	Robertas Julpa (USSR)
100 m Back	Bengt Baron (Swe)
200 m Back	Sandor Wladar (Hun)
100 m Butterfly	Par Arvidsson (Swe)
200 m Butterfly	Sergei Fesenko (USSR)
400 m Medley	Aleksandr Sidorenko (USSR)
4 × 100 m Medley Relay	Australia
4 × 200 m Free Relay	USSR
Springboard Diving	Aleksandr Portnov (USSR)
Highboard Diving	Falk Hoffmann (GDR)
Water Polo	USSR

Swimming—Women

100 m Free	Barbara Krause (GDR)
200 m Free	Barbara Krause (GDR)
400 m Free	Ines Diers (GDR)
800 m Free	Michelle Ford (Aus)
100 m Breast	Ute Geweniger (GDR)
200 m Breast	Lina Kachushite (USSR)
100 m Back	Rica Reinisch (GDR)
200 m Back	Rica Reinisch (GDR)
100 m Butterfly	Caren Metschuck (GDR)
200 m Butterfly	Ines Geissler (GDR)
400 m Medley	Petra Schneider (GDR)
4 × 100 m Medley Relay	GDR
4 × 100 m Free Relay	GDR
Springboard Diving	Irina Kalinina (USSR)
Highboard Diving	Martina Jaschke (GDR)

Volleyball

Men	USSR
Women	USSR

Weightlifting

52 kg	Kanybek Osmonaliev (USSR)
56 kg	Daniel Nunez (Cub)
60 kg	Viktor Mazin (USSR)
67·5 kg	Yanko Rusev (Bul)
75 kg	Assen Zlatev (Bul)
82·5 kg	Yurik Vardabyan (USSR)
90 kg	Peter Baczako (Hun)
100 kg	Ota Zaremba (Cz)
110 kg	Leonid Taranemko (USSR)
Over 110 kg	Sultan Rakhmanov (USSR)

Wrestling—Freestyle

48 kg	Claudio Pollio (Ita)
52 kg	Anatoli Beloglazov (USSR)
57 kg	Sergei Beloglazov (USSR)
62 kg	Magomedgasan Abuchev (USSR)
68 kg	Salpulla Absaldov (USSR)
74 kg	Valentin Raitchev (Bul)
82 kg	Ismail Abilov (Bul)
90 kg	Sanasar Oganesyan (USSR)
100 kg	Ilya Mate (USSR)
Over 100 kg	Soysan Andiev (USSR)

Wrestling—Greco-Roman

48 kg	Zaksylik Ushkempirov (USSR)
52 kg	Vakhtang Blagidze (USSR)
57 kg	Shamil Serikov (USSR)
62 kg	Stlianos Migiakis (Gre)
68 kg	Stefan Rusu (Rom)
74 kg	Ferenc Kocsis (Hun)
82 kg	Gennadi Korban (USSR)
90 kg	Norbert Nottny (Hun)
100 kg	Gheorghi Raikov (Bul)
Over 100 kg	Aleksandr Kolchinski (USSR)

Yachting

Finn	Esko Rechardt (Fin)
Tornado	Brazil
Soling	Denmark
Star	USSR
470	Brazil
Flying Dutchman	Spain

135

Orienteering

The term 'orienteering' was first used in Oslo, Norway for an event, held in October 1900, based on military exercises. British soldiers took part in chart and compass races early in the 20th century, but the founding of the modern sport is generally credited to Major Ernst Killander (Swe) in 1918. Originally it was more akin to cross country running, but with the invention of a new type of compass in the 1930s the sport became an entity in its own right. In 1961 an International Orienteering Federation was founded. The first English club was formed in Ribblesdale, Yorkshire in 1964, and the British Federation came into existence three years later.

BRITISH CHAMPIONSHIPS: First held in 1967, Carol McNeill of the Interlopers Club has won a record six women's titles in 1967, 1969, 1972–76. The men's title has been won five times by Geoff Peck, also of Interlopers, in 1971, 1973, 1976–77 and 1979. The men's relay title went to Oxford University twice in 1975 and 1979, and the women's relay was won by Derwent Valley Orienteers in 1975, 1979 and 1980.

WORLD CHAMPIONSHIPS

Inaugurated in 1966, and so far dominated by the Scandinavian countries. In particular, Sweden have won a record 15 championships.

Men	Women
1966 Aage Hadler (Nor)	Ulla Lindquist (Swe)
1968 Karl Johansson (Swe)	Ulla Lindquist (Swe)
1970 Stig Berge (Nor)	Ingrid Hadler (Nor)
1972 Aage Hadler (Nor)	Sarolta Monspart (Fin)
1974 Bernt Frilen (Swe)	Mona Norgaard (Den)
1976 Egil Johansen (Nor)	Liisa Veijalainen (Fin)
1978 Egil Johansen (Nor)	Anne Berit Eid (Nor)
1979 Oyvin Thon (Nor)	Outi Bergonstrom (Fin)
1981 Oyvin Thon (Nor)	Annichen Kringstad (Nor)

	Women's team	Men's team			Women's team	Men's team
1966	Sweden	Sweden		1976	Sweden	Sweden
1968	Sweden	Norway		1978	Norway	Finland
1970	Norway	Sweden		1979	Sweden	Finland
1972	Sweden	Finland		1981	Norway	Sweden
1974	Sweden	Sweden				

A female competitor in an orienteering event. The sport, basically a combination of cross-country running and map reading is very popular in Scandinavia and has an enthusiastic band of followers in Britain.

Powerboat Racing

The first recorded race by powered boats was for steamboats at the Northern Yacht Club Regatta at Rothesay, Scotland in 1827. It was won by *Clarence*, a locally built vessel. Paddle steamers on the Mississippi were often pitted against each other in the 1840s for purely commercial reasons, such as getting to the markets first with their cargoes. In 1870 the *Robert E. Lee* had her famous race with the *Natchez* from New Orleans to St Louis, a distance of 1653 km (1027 miles) which the former won in 90 hr 30 min. This time was not beaten by any boat until 1929. The earliest use of a petrol engine was by Jean Lenoir (Fra) on the River Seine in 1865, and the first race of motor launches took place in 1889. By 1908 the sport had progressed enough to be included in the Olympic Games.

HARMSWORTH CUP: Originally presented in 1903 by Sir Alfred Harmsworth (later Lord Northcliffe), of the *Daily Mail*, for international competition. Of the 25 contests up to 1961 the United States won 16, with the greatest number of individual wins being eight by Commodore Garfield Wood (USA) between 1920 and 1933. The only boat to win three times was the Canadian *Miss Supertest III* driven by Bob Hayward (Can) 1959–61. This boat set the record speed of 191·94 km/h (119·27 mph) at Picton, Canada in 1961. From 1961 to 1977 the competition lapsed, but it was then re-constituted as The Harmsworth British & Commonwealth Trophy. Since then the winners have been:

A dramatic shot taken soon after the start of the 1978 Cowes–Torquay–Cowes powerboat race, which was won by a woman for the first time at a then record average speed of 77·42 mph.

Harmsworth Trophy

	Boat	Nationality	Driver
1977	Limit-Up	England	Michael Doxford & Tim Powell
1978	Limit-Up	England	Michael Doxford & Tim Powell
1979	Uno-Mint-Jewellery	England	Derek Pobjoy
1980	Satisfaction	USA	Bill Elswick
1981	Satisfaction	USA	Paul Clauser
1982	Popeye	USA	Al Copeland

GOLD CUP: Instituted in 1903 by the American Power Boat Association, it has been won a record eight times by Bill Muncey between 1956 and 1979. The highest lap speed reached in the competition is 206·539 km/h (128·338 mph) by the hydroplane *Atlas Van Lines*, driven by Muncey in a qualifying round on the Columbia River, Washington in July 1977, and again in July 1978. Three boats have won on four occasions, *Slo-Mo-Shun IV* 1950–53, *Miss Budweiser* in 1969–70, 1973 and 1980, and *Atlas Van Lines* in 1972, 1977–79. The race speed record is 188·922 km/h (117·391 mph) by *Miss Budweiser* driven by Dean Chenoweth in 1980.

COWES–TORQUAY OFFSHORE RACE: Instituted in 1961 by Sir Max Aitken of the *Daily Express*, and originally held from Cowes to Torquay. In 1968 it was extended to include the return journey, a total distance of 396·11 km (246·13 miles). In 1982 the race became the Cowes International Powerboat Classic. The record for the race is 3 hr 4 min 35 sec by *Satisfaction* driven by Bill Elswick (USA) averaging 128·16 km/h (79·64 mph) in August 1980. The most wins has been three by Tommy Sopwith (GB) between 1961 and 1970. The greatest number of entries was in 1969 when there were 75 starters, of whom 41 finished. In 1970 Sir Max Aitken and his son Maxwell competed in one boat, while Lady Aitken and her daughter Laura competed in another. *Winners from 1970:*

	Boat	Driver
1970	Miss Enfield 2	Tommy Sopwith (GB)
1971	Lady Nara	Ronny Bonelli (Ita)
1972	Aeromarine IX	Carlo Bonomi (Ita)
1973	Unowot	Don Shead (GB)
1974	Dry Martini	Carlo Bonomi (Ita)
1975	Uno Embassy	Don Shead (GB)
1976	I Like It Too	Charles Gill (GB)
1977	Yellowdrama III	Ken Cassir (GB)
1978	Kaama	Betty Cook (USA)
1979	Dry Martini 2	Guido Nicolai (Ita)
1980	Satisfaction	Bill Elswick (USA)
1981	Rombo	Alberto Smania (Ita)
1982	Ego Rothman	Renato Della Valle (Ita)

SPEED RECORDS

The official water speed record is 514·39 km/h (319·627 mph) by Ken Warby (Aus) in a jet-propelled hydroplane *Spirit of Australia* on Blowering Dam Lake, New South Wales in October 1978. However, he had unofficially attained a speed of approximately 556 km/h (345 mph) in November 1977. The official record for a woman is 187·132 km/h (116·279 mph) by Fiona Brothers (GB) in a Seebold marathon hull at Holme Pierrepont, Nottingham on 1 September 1981. However, the fastest attained on water by a woman driver is 305 km/h (190 mph) by Mary Rife (USA) in a drag boat. The highest speed reached in a propeller-driven craft is 355·27 km/h (220·76 mph) by Eddie Hill in his drag boat *The Texan* over a ¼-mile course on Lake Braunig, San Antonio, Texas on 29 August 1981, but the official record, as recognised by the National Drag Boat Association (USA) is 335·22 km/h (208·30 mph) by the same combination at Ski Land, Perris, California on 20 September 1981.

JUMPING

As a stunt for the TV documentary 'The Man Who Fell From The Sky' Peter Horak (USA) jumped his boat, a Glastron Carlson CVX 20 Jet Deluxe, over a distance of 36·57 m (120 ft) in April 1980, from a take-off speed of 88 km/h (55 mph). This beat the previous record which had been set in the famous scene from the James Bond film 'Live and Let Die' in 1972. A new mark was reported, but not confirmed, for a jump of 42·06 m (138 ft) by a Johnson-powered Cobra boat in the film 'Gator' made in 1978.

Fiona Brothers, here seen in the 1981 Bristol race, holds the official water speed record for a woman driver. Powerboating is one of the sports in which women are beginning to match, and sometimes beat, their male counterparts.

Rowing

Warships were driven by human power in ancient times. The earliest literary reference to rowing is by the Roman poet, Virgil in the *Aeneid*, published after his death in 19 BC. Rowing regattas were held in Venice *c* AD 300. The world's oldest annual race was inaugurated on 1 August 1716 by Thomas Doggett, an Irish-born actor. He presented 'an Orange Colour Livery with a Badge' for the winner of a competition for London watermen over a 7·2 km (4½ miles) course from London Bridge to Chelsea. The sport had begun at Eton college some 72 years before the famous 'boating song' was composed in 1865. The oldest surviving club is the Thames-based Leander, formed about 1818. The world governing body, FISA, was founded in 1892, and the first major international meeting, the European championships, was held a year later.

WORLD AND OLYMPIC CHAMPIONSHIPS: Olympic Championships were first held in 1900. Separate world championships were first held for men in 1962 and for women in 1974. The GDR coxless pairs team of Bernd and Jorg Landvoigt have won their event four times in world championships and twice in Olympic competition, setting a record for any event. The female sculler Christine Scheiblich-Hann (GDR) nearly matched this with one Olympic and four world titles. There have been five oarsmen who have won three gold medals in the Olympics: John Kelly (USA), Paul Costello (USA), Jack Beresford Jr (GB), Vyacheslav Ivanov (USSR) and Siegfried Brietzke (GDR). However, only Ivanov won all his titles in the single sculls, in 1956, 1960 and 1964. Kelly and Costello were cousins and won two of their respective medals in the double sculls together in 1920 and 1924. *Champions from 1970:*

Men

	Single Sculls	Double Sculls
1970	Alberto Demiddi (Arg)	Denmark
1972*	Yuri Malishev (USSR)	USSR
1974	Wolfgang Honig (GDR)	GDR
1975	Peter-Michael Kolbe (FRG)	Norway
1976*	Pertti Karppinen (Fin)	Norway
1977	Joachim Dreifke (GDR)	GB
1978	Peter-Michael Kolbe (FRG)	Norway
1979	Pertti Karppinen (Fin)	Norway
1980*	Pertti Karppinen (Fin)	GDR
1981	Peter-Michael Kolbe (FRG)	GDR
1982	Rüdiger Reiche (GDR)	Norway

	Coxless Pairs	Coxed Pairs
1970	FRG	Romania
1972*	GDR	GDR
1974	GDR	USSR
1975	GDR	GDR
1976*	GDR	GDR
1977	USSR	Bulgaria
1978	GDR	GDR
1979	GDR	GDR
1980*	GDR	GDR
1981	USSR	Italy
1982	Norway	Italy

	Coxless Fours	Coxed Fours
1970	GDR	FRG
1972*	GDR	FRG
1974	GDR	GDR
1975	GDR	USSR
1976*	GDR	USSR
1977	GDR	GDR
1978	USSR	GDR
1979	GDR	GDR
1980*	GDR	GDR
1981	USSR	GDR
1982	Switzerland	GDR

	Quadruple Sculls	Eights
1970	Not held	GDR
1972*	Not held	New Zealand
1974	GDR	United States
1975	GDR	GDR
1976*	GDR	GDR
1977	GDR	GDR
1978	GDR	GDR
1979	GDR	GDR
1980*	GDR	GDR
1981	GDR	USSR
1982	GDR	New Zealand

Women

	Single Sculls	Double Sculls
1974	Christine Scheiblich (GDR)	USSR
1975	Christine Scheiblich (GDR)	USSR
1976*	Christine Scheiblich (GDR)	Bulgaria
1977	Christine Scheiblich (GDR)	GDR
1978	Christine Hann (GDR)	Bulgaria
1979	Sanda Toma (Rom)	GDR
1980*	Sanda Toma (Rom)	USSR
1981	Sanda Toma (Rom)	USSR
1982	Irina Fetisova (USSR)	USSR

	Coxless Pairs	Quadruple Sculls
1974	Romania	GDR
1975	GDR	GDR
1976*	Bulgaria	GDR
1977	GDR	GDR
1978	GDR	Bulgaria
1979	GDR	GDR
1980*	GDR	GDR
1981	GDR	USSR
1982	GDR	USSR

	Coxed Fours	Eights
1974	GDR	GDR
1975	GDR	GDR
1976*	GDR	GDR
1977	GDR	GDR
1978	GDR	USSR
1979	USSR	USSR
1980*	GDR	GDR
1981	USSR	USSR
1982	USSR	USSR

* Olympic titles

HENLEY ROYAL REGATTA: First held at Henley-on-Thames, Oxfordshire in March 1839. The length of the course is 2 212 m (1 mile 550 yd). The two major races are The Grand Challenge Cup (instituted 1839) for eights, and the Diamond Sculls (instituted 1844) for single scullers. The Grand has been won by Leander Club on a record 27 occasions between 1840 and 1953, with the fastest time for the event being 6 min 13 sec by Harvard University and a combined Leander & Thames Tradesmen crew, both in 1975, when the latter crew won. The Diamond was won six times consecutively by Australian Stuart Mackenzie 1957–62, while the fastest time is 7 min 40 sec by Sean Drea (Ire) in 1975.

John Kelly was thought to be a victim of class distinction when he was refused entry into the Diamond Sculls at Henley in 1920, being unofficially informed that the muscles he had developed as a bricklayer gave him an unfair advantage over 'gentlemen' competitors. Later, as a rich businessman, he saw his son John Kelly Junior win the Diamond Sculls twice, in 1947 and 1949, and his film-star daughter become Princess Grace of Monaco. Benjamin Spock, later author of a best-selling baby care book, was a member of the Yale crew which represented the USA and won the 1924 Olympic eights.

The Great Britain squad just failing to catch the USSR crew for second place in the coxless fours event of the 1980 Olympic Games. The gold medal was won by the GDR, just one of its seven victories in the eight rowing events.

Henley Winners since 1970:

	Diamond Sculls	Grand Challenge Cup
1970	Jochen Meissner (FRG)	ASK Rostock (GDR)
1971	Alberto Demiddi (Arg)	Tideway Scullers (GB)
1972	Aleksandr Timoshin (USSR)	WMF Moscow (USSR)
1973	Sean Drea (Ire)	Trud Kolomna (USSR)
1974	Sean Drea (Ire)	Trud Kolomna (USSR)
1975	Sean Drea (Ire)	Leander/Thames Tradesmen (GB)
1976	Edward Hale (Aus)	Thames Tradesmen (GB)
1977	Tim Crooks (GB)	Univ. of Washington (USA)
1978	Tim Crooks (GB)	Trakia Club (Bul)
1979	Hugh Matheson (GB)	Thames Tradesmen (GB)
1980	Riccardo Ibarra (Arg)	Charles River R. A. (USA)
1981	Chris Ballieu (GB)	Oxford Univ/Thames Tradesman (GB)
1982	Chris Ballieu (GB)	Leander/London (GB)

SPEED

The greatest speed attained on non-tidal water, over the standard men's rowing distance of 2000 m (2187 yd), is 21·67 km/h (13·46 mph) by the GDR eight at the Montreal Olympics in 1976 when they clocked 5 min 32·17 sec. In 1930, on the Meuse, Belgium, an eight from Pennsylvania AC had clocked 5 min 18·8 sec averaging 22·58 km/h (14·03 mph), but with the help of the river current. The fastest by a female eight is also by a GDR crew, who clocked 2 min 57·38 sec for the standard women's distance of 1000 m (1093·6 yd), achieving an average of 20·29 km/h (12·61 mph) on the Rootsee, Lucerne in 1980. The fastest time over 2000 m by a single sculler, 6 min 49·68 sec by Nikolai Dovgan (USSR) in 1978, represents an average speed of 17·57 km/h (10·92 mph). The best by a female sculler over 1000 m, 3 min 34·31 sec by Christine Scheiblich (GDR) in 1977, represents an average of 16·79 km/h (10·43 mph).

THE BOAT RACE: One of the most famous free shows in sport is the annual Oxford v Cambridge boat race on the Thames. The first race, which Oxford won, was in 1829, from Hambledon Lock to Henley Bridge. The current course, used continuously since 1864, is from Putney to Mortlake, 6779 km (4 miles 374 yd), and the record time is 16 min 58·0 sec by Oxford in 1976, representing an average speed of 23·97 km/h (14·89 mph). Up to and including 1983, there have been 129 races of which Cambridge have won 68, Oxford 60, and a dead heat in 1877. The greatest margin of victory was in 1900 when Cambridge beat Oxford by 20 lengths, although there have been occasions when one of the boats sank. The smallest margin has been 'by a canvas' by Oxford in 1952 and 1980. The heaviest crew was Oxford in 1983 when it averaged 92·7 kg (204·3 lb) per man. The Oxford number 5 in 1976, Stephen Plunkett weighed in at a record 104 kg (229 lb). The lightest rower was the Oxford stroke of 1882, Alfred Higgins who was only 60 kg (132 lb). The lightest ever to compete in the Boat Race were the Cambridge cox of 1862, Francis Archer, and his Oxford counterpart in 1939, Hart Massey, who both weighed only 32·6 kg (72 lb). The first woman to compete was Sue Brown in 1981, when she coxed the Oxford crew to an eight-length victory. The only man to row in six winning crews is Boris Rankov for Oxford from 1978–83.

BOAT RACE WINNERS:

1829 Oxford	1888 Cambridge	1937 Oxford	1964 Cambridge
1836 Cambridge	1889 Cambridge	1938 Oxford	1965 Oxford
1839 Cambridge	1890 Oxford	1939 Cambridge	1966 Oxford
1840 Cambridge	1891 Oxford	1946 Oxford	1967 Oxford
1841 Cambridge	1892 Oxford	1947 Cambridge	1968 Cambridge
1842 Oxford	1893 Oxford	1948 Cambridge	1969 Cambridge
1845 Cambridge	1894 Oxford	1949 Cambridge	1970 Cambridge
1846 Cambridge	1895 Oxford	1950 Cambridge	1971 Cambridge
1849 Cambridge	1896 Oxford	1951 Cambridge	1972 Cambridge
1849 Oxford	1897 Oxford	1952 Oxford	1973 Cambridge
1852 Oxford	1898 Oxford	1953 Cambridge	1974 Oxford
1854 Oxford	1899 Cambridge	1954 Oxford	1975 Cambridge
1856 Cambridge	1900 Cambridge	1955 Cambridge	1976 Oxford
1857 Oxford	1901 Oxford	1956 Cambridge	1977 Oxford
1858 Cambridge	1902 Cambridge	1957 Cambridge	1978 Oxford
1859 Oxford	1903 Cambridge	1958 Cambridge	1979 Oxford
1860 Cambridge	1904 Cambridge	1959 Oxford	1980 Oxford
1861 Oxford	1905 Oxford	1960 Oxford	1981 Oxford
1862 Oxford	1906 Cambridge	1961 Cambridge	1982 Oxford
1863 Oxford	1907 Cambridge	1962 Cambridge	1983 Oxford
1864 Oxford	1908 Cambridge	1963 Oxford	
1865 Oxford	1909 Oxford		
1866 Oxford	1910 Oxford		
1867 Oxford	1911 Oxford		
1868 Oxford	1912 Oxford		
1869 Oxford	1913 Oxford		
1870 Cambridge	1914 Cambridge		
1871 Cambridge	1920 Cambridge		
1872 Cambridge	1921 Cambridge		
1873 Cambridge	1922 Cambridge		
1874 Cambridge	1923 Oxford		
1875 Oxford	1924 Cambridge		
1876 Cambridge	1925 Cambridge		
1877 Dead-heat	1926 Cambridge		
1878 Oxford	1927 Cambridge		
1879 Cambridge	1928 Cambridge		
1880 Oxford	1929 Cambridge		
1881 Oxford	1930 Cambridge		
1882 Oxford	1931 Cambridge		
1883 Oxford	1932 Cambridge		
1884 Cambridge	1933 Cambridge		
1885 Oxford	1934 Cambridge		
1886 Cambridge	1935 Cambridge		
1887 Cambridge	1936 Cambridge		

The winning Oxford crew of the first ever Boat Race in 1829, rowed at Henley-on-Thames over a course of about two miles. In this first race, the result of a challenge from Cambridge, the Oxford crew wore dark blue striped jerseys while the Cambridge men had pink sashes.

An all too familiar sight as Oxford lead Cambridge in the 1983 Boat Race. Oxford achieved their eighth consecutive victory but are still eight wins behind in the series.

Rugby League

Rugby League is one of the few modern games about whose origins there is no doubt. On 29 August 1895, 22 clubs in Lancashire and Yorkshire met in the George Hotel, Huddersfield, to form what was then called The Northern Rugby Football Union, as a breakaway movement from the parent Rugby Union. The main reason for this was the refusal of the governing body to allow the northern clubs to make payments to their players who lost working time and thus wages by playing on a Saturday. Under the new body 'broken time' payments were allowed and three years later full professionalism came into being. Gradually alterations were introduced and in 1906 the major change of reducing the number of players in a team from 15 to 13 was made. The title 'Rugby League' was introduced in 1922. The first foreign touring team was from New Zealand in 1908, and in 1910 the first English team visited Australia.

CHALLENGE CUP: The Cup was inaugurated in 1897, and is contested as an annual knock-out competition. Leeds won a record 10 times between 1910 and 1978, Oldham is the only club to have appeared in four consecutive Finals, in 1924–27 (but only winning twice). The record aggregate score in the Final was 47 points when Featherstone Rovers beat Bradford Northern 33–14 in 1973. The biggest winning margin in the Final was in Huddersfield's defeat of St Helens by 37–3 in 1915. The greatest number of individual points in the Cup is 53 by Tich West (Hull Kingston Rovers) when he scored 10 goals and 11 tries v Brookland Rovers in an early round in 1905. Two men, Alex Murphy, playing for St Helens, Leigh and Warrington from 1961 to 1974 and Brian Lockwood, playing for Castleford, Hull K. R. and Widnes between 1969 and 1981, have won four Cup-winners medals. The youngest ever to play in a Final was Reg Lloyd who was 17 yr 249 days when he played for runners-up Keighley in 1937. A world record attendance, 102 569, for the game was at the Cup Final replay between Warrington and Halifax at Odsal Stadium, Bradford on 5 May 1954, The highest receipts ever were the £591 117 paid for the Hull K. R. v Widnes Final at Wembley Stadium on 2 May 1981.

1897 Batley	1937 Widnes
1898 Batley	1938 Salford
1899 Oldham	1939 Halifax
1900 Swinton	1940 Not held
1901 Batley	1941 Leeds
1902 Broughton R.	1942 Leeds
1903 Halifax	1943 Dewsbury
1904 Halifax	1944 Bradford Northern
1905 Warrington	1945 Huddersfield
1906 Bradford	1946 Wakefield Trinity
1907 Warrington	1947 Bradford Northern
1908 Hunslet	1948 Wigan
1909 Wakefield Trinity	1949 Bradford Northern
1910 Leeds	1950 Warrington
1911 Broughton R.	1951 Wigan
1912 Dewsbury	1952 Workington Town
1913 Huddersfield	1953 Huddersfield
1914 Hull	1954 Warrington
1915 Huddersfield	1955 Barrow
1920 Huddersfield	1956 St Helens
1921 Leigh	1957 Leeds
1922 Rochdale R.	1958 Wigan
1923 Leeds	1959 Wigan
1924 Wigan	1960 Wakefield Trinity
1925 Oldham	1961 St Helens
1926 Swinton	1962 Wakefield Trinity
1927 Oldham	1963 Wakefield Trinity
1928 Swinton	1964 Widnes
1929 Wigan	1965 Wigan
1930 Widnes	1966 St Helens
1931 Halifax	1967 Featherstone R.
1932 Leeds	1968 Leeds
1933 Huddersfield	1969 Castleford
1934 Hunslet	1970 Castleford
1935 Castleford	1971 Leigh
1936 Leeds	1972 St Helens

1973 Featherstone Rovers	1979 Widnes
1974 Warrington	1980 Hull Kingston Rovers
1975 Widnes	1981 Widnes
1976 St Helens	1982 Hull
1977 Leeds	1983 Featherstone Rovers
1978 Leeds	

THE LANCE TODD TROPHY: In 1946 a Trophy was presented in memory of the Nander Lance Todd, who had been killed in a car accident four years earlier, for the 'Man of the Match' in the Cup Final. Only one player has won it twice—Gerry Helme of Warrington in 1950 and 1954.

1946	Billy Stott	Wakefield Trinity
1947	Willie Davies	Bradford Northern
1948	Frank Whitcombe	Bradford Northern
1949	Ernest Ward	Bradford Northern
1950	Gerry Helme	Warrington
1951	Ces Mountford	Wigan
1952	Billy Iveson	Workington Town
1953	Peter Ramsden	Huddersfield
1954	Gerry Helme	Warrington
1955	Jack Grundy	Barrow
1956	Alan Prescott	St Helens
1957	Jeff Stevenson	Leeds
1958	Rees Thomas	Wigan
1959	Brian McTigue	Wigan
1960	Tommy Harris	Hull
1961	Dick Huddart	St Helens
1962	Neil Fox	Wakefield Trinity
1963	Harold Poynton	Wakefield Trinity
1964	Frank Collier	Widnes
1965	Ray Ashby	Wigan
	Brian Gabbitas	Hunslet
1966	Len Killeen	St Helens
1967	Carl Dooler	Featherstone Rovers
1968	Don Fox	Wakefield Trinity
1969	Malcolm Reilly	Castleford
1970	Bill Kirkbride	Castleford
1971	Alex Murphy	Leigh
1972	Kel Coslett	St Helens
1973	Steve Nash	Featherstone Rovers
1974	Derek Whitehead	Warrington
1975	Ray Dutton	Widnes
1976	Geoff Pimblett	St Helens
1977	Steve Pitchford	Leeds
1978	George Nicholls	St Helens
1979	David Topliss	Wakefield Trinity
1980	Brian Lockwood	Hull Kingston Rovers
1981	Mick Burke	Widnes
1982	Eddie Cunningham	Widnes
1983	David Hobbs	Featherstone Rovers

LEAGUE CHAMPIONSHIPS: Instituted in 1907 and decided by play-offs until 1962 and from 1965 to 1973. In 1963–64 and since 1974 the League Champions have been the winners of Division I. Wigan have won a record nine times from 1909 to 1960. *Winners from 1974:*

1974 Salford
1975 St Helens
1976 Salford
1977 Featherstone Rovers
1978 Widnes
1979 Hull Kingston Rovers
1980 Bradford Northern
1981 Bradford Northern
1982 Leigh
1983 Hull

The most individual points scored in a League match were 39 (five tries, 12 goals) by Jimmy Lomas for Salford v Liverpool City in 1907.

PREMIERSHIP TROPHY: First held in 1975 and contested by the leading teams in the League, the winners have been:

1975 Leeds
1976 St Helens
1977 St Helens

1978 Bradford Northern
1979 Leeds
1980 Widnes
1981 Hull Kingston Rovers
1982 Hull
1983 Widnes

Leeds in the process of beating St Helens in 1978 to win a record tenth Rugby League Challenge Cup final. Graham Eccles (11) with the ball for Leeds is watched anxiously by his teammate John Sanderson (7). Their opponents are Noonan (3), Gwilliam (7), Pinner (13) and Pimblett (1).

JOHN PLAYER TROPHY: First held in 1972, the winners have been:

1972	Halifax	1978	Warrington
1973	Leeds	1979	Widnes
1974	Warrington	1980	Bradford Northern
1975	Bradford Northern	1981	Warrington
1976	Widnes	1982	Hull
1977	Castleford	1983	Wigan

MOST VALUABLE PLAYERS
Dave Watkins played for Salford in 140 consecutive games from 1970 to 1974. He scored in 92 successive games between 1972 and 1974 totalling 929 points, comprised of 41 tries and 403 goals. In the season 1972–73 he scored a record 221 goals, and, including 14 points from friendly games, totalled a season's record of 507 points. The most consecutive games played for one club is 239 by Keith Elwell for Widnes from 1977 to 1982. The highest transfer fee paid in Rugby League history is £72 500 by Hull Kingston Rovers to Wigan for fullback George Fairbairn in June 1981.

LANCASHIRE CUP: Instituted in 1905 when it was won by Wigan, who went on to gain a record 17 victories. *Winners from 1970:*

1970	Leigh	1979	Widnes
1971	Wigan	1980	Warrington
1972	Salford	1981	Leigh
1973	Wigan	1982	Warrington
1974	Wigan		
1975	Widnes		
1976	Widnes		
1977	Widnes		
1978	Workington Town		

YORKSHIRE CUP: Instituted in 1905 and first won by Hunslet. The most wins have been 17 by Leeds from 1921 to 1980. *Winners from 1970:*

1970	Leeds	1979	Leeds
1971	Hull Kingston Rovers	1980	Leeds
1972	Leeds	1981	Castleford
1973	Leeds	1982	Hull
1974	Leeds		
1975	Hull Kingston Rovers		
1976	Leeds		
1977	Leeds		
1978	Castleford		

Rod Reddy (Australia) grabbing at Peter Smith (Great Britain) in the 3rd Rugby League Test match in November 1982. Australia won to gain its 40th victory in the series between the countries which began in 1909.

HIGH SCORING GAMES
The highest score ever made in a game involving a senior club was in the first round of the Northern Union Cup in February 1914, when Huddersfield beat Swinton Park Rangers by 119 points (19 goals, 27 tries) to 2 (one goal). When England beat South Australia by 101–0 at Adelaide in May 1914 they set a record for a British touring team. The highest score by a touring team in Britain was at Bramley, Yorkshire in November 1921, when the Australian tourists beat the home team by 92–7.

TEST MATCHES
Mick Sullivan (Huddersfield, Wigan, St Helens, and York) played in a record 46 test matches, for England or Great Britain and scored 43 tries. He also holds the distinction of playing in most games against Australia with 13 Tests and three World Cup matches between 1954 and 1964. The most appearances in solely Test matches against Australia is 15 by Jim Sullivan (no relation) of Wigan from 1924 to 1933.

ALL TEST MATCHES (As at April 1983)

	Played	Won	Lost	Drawn
Great Britain v Australia (instituted 1909)	93	49	40	4
Great Britain v New Zealand (instituted 1908)	64	42	20	2
Great Britain v France (instituted 1957)	38	25	11	2

HIGH SCORING PLAYERS
The Australian-born wing-threequarter, Albert Rosenfeld, playing for Huddersfield, scored 80 tries in 42 matches in the 1913–14 season. Another Australian wing-threequarter, Brian Bevan, scored a total of 796 tries between 1946 and 1964, playing mainly for Warrington, with two seasons for Blackpool Borough. The most points scored in a season, not counting friendly games, is 496 (194 goals, 36 tries) in 1956–57, by Lewis Jones of Leeds. Jim Sullivan of Wigan set a career goal-scoring record of 2860 between 1921 and 1946, including a match record of 22 against Flimby & Fothergill in the Challenge Cup in February 1925. The career record for points in England is held by Neil Fox with 6220 from 1956 to 1979, of which 4488 were for Wakefield Trinity.

WORLD CUP—INTERNATIONAL CHAMPIONSHIP:
First held in 1954 as the World Cup, replaced by the World Championship in 1975 and the International Championship in 1977, the series is now in abeyance. The highest total points score in a World Cup match was 72 when Great Britain beat New Zealand by 53–19 at Pau, France in 1972.

1954 England
1957 Australia
1960 England
1968 Australia
1972 Great Britain
1975 Australia
1977 Australia

Rugby Union

The traditional origin of the game was at Rugby School, in England, when in November 1823 one of the players in a football game, William Webb Ellis, picked up the ball, quite contrary to the rules then in force, and ran with it in his arms. Recent research suggests that this story may be apocryphal, but it is as good a representation of the beginnings of the game as is likely to come to light. *Harpastium*, a Roman game from *c* 400 BC had many similarities to the modern game. The first club was founded at Guy's Hospital, London in 1843, and 20 years later Richmond and Blackheath started an inter-club fixture which remains as the oldest regular match still played. The Rugby Union was formed at the Pall Mall Restaurant, Cockspur Street, London on 26 January 1871. The first ever international match was played in Edinburgh, between England and Scotland on 27 March 1871, with 20 men per side, with the home team winning. Teams were reduced to 15 a side in 1875. In 1888 the first British touring side went to Australia and New Zealand, and the latter, composed mainly of Maoris, toured Britain.

INTERNATIONAL MATCHES

(To give some basis of comparison, scores are shown based on the current scoring values adopted in 1971 of 4 points for a try, 3 points for a penalty, dropped goal, or goal from a mark, and 2 points for a conversion. The actual score using the points system then in force is also given in brackets unless it is the same.) The biggest score in a full international match was 92–0 by France against Spain in March 1979. In the International Championship itself, the highest aggregate has been 75 points when Wales beat France at Swansea in 1910 by 59–16 (49–14). The record for a match between two of the Home nations was set in 1881, before point scoring was even introduced, when England, with 7 goals, 1 dropped goal and 6 tries, beat Wales, by a current margin of 69–0 at Blackheath. The greatest defeat inflicted on one of the Home countries by a touring side is 53–0 (44–0) when South Africa beat Scotland at Murrayfield, Edinburgh in November 1951. The highest individual score in a full international match is 26 by Allan Hewson (NZ) against Australia in September 1982. The most points scored in an international career is 301 by Andy Irvine for Scotland and the British Lions, from 1973 to 10 July 1982. The most international appearances made by a player in matches between the eight International Board countries (see table below) is 69 by Mike Gibson for Ireland between 1964 and 1979. He also played

Andy Irvine, Scotland's record scorer with 273 points in 51 appearances for his country. He has also scored an additional 28 points in international matches while representing the British Lions.

for the British Lions on 12 occasions, making a grand total of 81 'caps'. The most appearances specifically for the British Lions is 17 by Willie John McBride (Ire) from 1962 to 1975. The record for the youngest ever player in an international match is a very close contest between two Scottish players, both from Edinburgh Academy, Ninian Jamieson Finlay and Charles Reid, who played for Scotland v England in 1875 and 1881 respectively. They were both aged 17 yr 36 days, and although Reid is usually quoted as the record holder, recent research indicates that Finlay had one less leap year in his lifetime to the day of his first cap, and thus he holds the outright record. Daniel Carroll played for Australia in the 1908 Olympic Games tournament when only 16 yr 149 days, but that was not considered to be a 'full' international.

INTERNATIONAL MATCHES SINCE 1871
(As at 31 March 1983)

	Played	Won	Lost	Drawn
England v Scotland	99	47	36	16
England v Ireland	95	53	34	8
England v Wales	88	35	41	12
England v France	58	32	20	6
England v Australia	10	4	6	0
England v New Zealand	12	2	10	0
England v S. Africa	7	2	4	1
Wales v Scotland	87	49	36	2
Wales v Ireland	85	52	28	5
Wales v France	56	36	17	3
Wales v Australia	10	7	3	0
Wales v New Zealand	11	3	8	0
Wales v S. Africa	7	0	6	1
Scotland v Ireland	93	46	43	4
Scotland v France	53	25	26	2
Scotland v Australia	9	6	3	0
Scotland v New Zealand	11	0	10	1
Scotland v S. Africa	8	3	5	0
Ireland v France	56	25	27	4
Ireland v Australia	9	6	3	0
Ireland v New Zealand	9	0	8	1
Ireland v S. Africa	10	1	8	1
France v Australia	13	8	4	1
France v New Zealand	18	4	14	0
France v S. Africa	19	3	12	4
Australia v New Zealand	74	18	52	4
Australia v S. Africa	28	21	7	0
New Zealand v S. Africa	37	15	20	2

Teams representing the British Isles have toured Australia, New Zealand and South Africa since 1888, although they were not composed of players from all Home countries until 1924, and the four Home Unions only formally created a Tours committee in 1949. The term 'British Lions', referring to their tie motifs, was first used on a 1924 tour to South Africa. Including the early 'unofficial' tours their results have been as follows:

	Played	Won	Lost	Drawn
British Lions v Australia	14	12	2	0
British Lions v New Zealand	28	5	20	3
British Lions v S. Africa	40	14	20	6

OLYMPIC GAMES: Rugby was included in four celebrations of the Games. In 1900 the title was won by France, in 1908 Australia easily beat a Cornwall team representing Great Britain, and the gold medals in 1920 and 1924 were both won by the United States, leaving them with the surprising honour of being the reigning Olympic champions. Daniel Carroll gained gold medals in the Australian team in 1908 and then, having emigrated in the intervening period, in the USA team in 1920. The founder of the modern Games, Baron Pierre de Coubertin, refereed France's first Rugby international match, against New Zealand, in 1906.

Above: **A line-out during the Welsh Centenary match in 1981 between old rivals Wales and England at Cardiff Arms Park. Wales won 21–19 for their forty-first win out of the 86 games played between the two countries up till then.** *Below:* **When the British Lions played New Zealand Juniors at Wellington in June 1977 it was difficult to decide which team was the 'All Blacks'.**

THE INTERNATIONAL CHAMPIONSHIP

THE INTERNATIONAL CHAMPIONSHIP: First held in 1884 between the four Home countries of England, Ireland, Scotland and Wales, with France included from 1910. Wales has won a record 31 times, including 10 shared titles. Both Wales and England have achieved the Grand Slam—winning all four matches—on eight occasions, but Wales has won the Triple Crown, for beating the other three Home countries, a record 16 times between 1893 and 1979. The highest ever paying attendance at a Rugby match was the 104 000 who watched Scotland beat Wales at Murrayfield in March 1975.

Year	Winner	Year	Winner	Year	Winner
1884	England	1920	England / Scotland / Wales	1953	England
1885	incomplete	1921	England	1954	England / France / Wales
1886	England / Scotland	1922	Wales	1955	France / Wales
1887	Scotland	1923	England	1956	Wales
1888	incomplete	1924	England	1957	England
1889	incomplete	1925	Scotland	1958	England
1890	England / Scotland	1926	Ireland / Scotland	1959	France
1891	Scotland	1927	Ireland / Scotland	1960	England / France
1892	England	1928	England	1961	France
1893	Wales	1929	Scotland	1962	France
1894	Ireland	1930	England	1963	England
1895	Scotland	1931	Wales	1964	Scotland / Wales
1896	Ireland	1932	England / Ireland / Wales	1965	Wales
1897	incomplete	1933	Scotland	1966	Wales
1898	incomplete	1934	England	1967	France
1899	Ireland	1935	Ireland	1968	France
1900	Wales	1936	Wales	1969	Wales
1901	Scotland	1937	England	1970	France / Wales
1902	Wales	1938	Scotland	1971	Wales
1903	Scotland	1939	England / Ireland / Wales	1972	incomplete
1904	Scotland	1947	England / Wales	1973	Quintuple tie
1905	Wales	1948	Ireland	1974	Ireland
1906	Ireland / Wales	1949	Ireland	1975	Wales
1907	Scotland	1950	Wales	1976	Wales
1908	Wales	1951	Ireland	1977	France
1909	Wales	1952	Wales	1978	Wales
1910	England			1979	Wales
1911	Wales			1980	England
1912	England / Ireland			1981	France
1913	England			1982	Ireland
1914	England			1983	France / Ireland

ENGLISH COUNTY CHAMPIONSHIP

ENGLISH COUNTY CHAMPIONSHIP: Inaugurated in 1889, when Yorkshire was declared champion, it has since been organised under four different systems. Gloucestershire has won a record 14 times between 1910 and 1983, and in 1921 beat Leicestershire by the record margin for a final of 31–4. Richard Trickey played in a record 104 matches for Lancashire between 1964 and 1978. *Winners from 1970:*

1970	Staffordshire	1981	Northumberland
1971	Surrey	1982	Lancashire
1972	Gloucestershire	1983	Gloucestershire
1973	Lancashire		
1974	Gloucestershire		
1975	Gloucestershire		
1976	Gloucestershire		
1977	Lancashire		
1978	East Midlands		
1979	Middlesex		
1980	Lancashire		

JOHN PLAYER CUP

JOHN PLAYER CUP: Inaugurated in 1971 as a club knockout competition. The highest score has been in the first round of the 1975 series, when Bedford beat Bournemouth 66–6.

1972	Gloucester	1983	Bristol
1973	Coventry		
1974	Coventry		
1975	Bedford		
1976	Gosforth		
1977	Gosforth		
1978	Gloucester		
1979	Leicester		
1980	Leicester		
1981	Leicester		
1982	Gloucester / Moseley		

THE UNIVERSITY MATCH

THE UNIVERSITY MATCH: The match between Oxford and Cambridge universities was inaugurated in 1872, and except for the 1914–18 War have been held annually, although the 1940–45 matches are not counted in the main series. Thus, after the 101st game played in December 1982, Cambridge lead by 45 games to Oxford's 43, with 13 drawn. The only man to play in six matches was Herbert Fuller for Cambridge from 1878 to 1883, but the most appearances on a winning side is four by Carl Aarvold of Cambridge from 1926 to 1929. The most individual points scored in a game is 19 by Alastair Hignell of Cambridge in 1975. The greatest winning margin is by Oxford who won by 35–3 in 1909, while the highest aggregate of points was in 1975 when Cambridge won by 34–12.

HIGH SCORING MATCHES

Scores of 200 points have been reached in schoolboy matches, eg the 200–0 defeat of Hills Court by Radford School in 1886. However, the highest club score was in Denmark when Comet beat Lindo by 194–0 in November 1973. The record for British teams is the 174–0 victory of the 7th Signal Regiment over the 4 Armoured Workshop, REME team in Germany in November 1980. The New Zealand touring team set a record for any tour match in May 1962 when it beat Northern New South Wales, Australia by 103–0 (under current scoring 125–0).

147

HIGH SCORING PLAYERS

In first class matches between 1971 and 30 April 1983, Dusty Hare scored a record 4666 points comprising 1800 for Nottingham, 2252 for Leicester, 164 for England and 450 in other representative games. The most points scored in a match is 80 by Jannie van der Westhuizen for Carnarvon against Williston at North West Cape, South Africa in March 1972. His total comprised 14 tries, nine conversions, one dropped goal and one penalty goal. However, in a junior house match at the aptly named William Ellis School, Edgware, London, a 12-year-old, Thanos Morphitis, scored 13 tries and 19 conversions in February 1967, to give a total of 90 points under the current values.

The highest number of points scored in first-class matches in a single season is 581 by Sam Doble of Moseley in 52 matches in 1971–72. He also scored another 47 playing for England in South Africa out of season. In a career stretching from 1967 to 1979, Andy Hill scored 312 tries for Llanelli, a record for British club Rugby. In 1928–29, Dan Jones of Neath scored a record 73 tries in a season.

SEVEN-A-SIDES

This form of Rugby originated on 28 April 1883 in Melrose, Scotland, when the town butcher, Ned Haig, put forward the idea in order to raise money for the local club. It has become a very popular part of the game and in 1981 a record 20 countries took part in the International Seven-a-Side tournament held annually since 1976 in Hong Kong. The premier tournament in Britain is the Middlesex Sevens with the finals at the end of the season at Twickenham. Inaugurated in 1926, the most wins have been nine by Richmond between 1951 and 1983. *Winners from 1970:*

1970　Loughborough Colleges
1971　London Welsh
1972　London Welsh
1973　London Welsh
1974　Richmond
1975　Richmond
1976　Loughborough Colleges
1977　Richmond
1978　Harlequins
1979　Richmond
1980　Richmond
1981　Rosslyn Park
1982　Stewart's Melville FP
1983　Richmond

The kicking skills of Ollie Campbell have helped Ireland finish at the top of the International Championship table for the last two years. He holds the Irish record for most points scored in an international match—19 versus Australia in 1979.

Shooting

The first recorded club for gun enthusiasts was the Lucerne Shooting Guild in Switzerland which dates from *c* 1466, and the first known shooting match took place in Zurich in 1472. Early contests had to be over very short range as it was not until rifling, to spin the bullet, was introduced to gun barrels in about 1480 that accuracy over greater distances could be achieved. The National Rifle Association in Britain was founded in 1860, with the profound interest of Queen Victoria, who inaugurated the Queen's Prize by firing the first shot at Wimbledon Common. From 1890 the Prize was contested at Bisley in Surrey. Trapshooting was introduced in the United States in 1830, and by 1893 in England the Inanimate Bird Shooting Association was formed. This became the Clay Bird Shooting Association in 1903 and 25 years later it was finally renamed the Clay Pigeon SA. Skeet shooting was invented in the USA in 1915 and was so called from the old Norse word for 'shoot'.

OLYMPIC GAMES: Seven marksmen have won five gold medals each; one of these, Carl Osburn (USA), won a record 11 medals in all with the addition of four silver and two bronze between 1912 and 1924. The only man to win three individual gold medals, as opposed to team medals, was Gudbrand Skatteboe (Nor) all in 1906. The first woman to win a medal at shooting was Margaret Murdock (USA) in the small-bore rifle (3 positions) event in 1976. It was originally announced that she had won by a single point, but an error was discovered and she was tied with her team-mate Lonny Bassham. Then an examination of the targets indicated that one of the latter's shots was 1/25th of an inch closer to the centre than previously determined, and so the gold medal was given to Bassham, who gallantly invited Murdock to share first place position on the award rostrum.

WORLD CHAMPIONSHIPS—CLAY PIGEON: One lady who has outshot her male counterparts is Susan Nattrass (Can) who has won a record five world titles from 1974 to 1979 at Clay Pigeon shooting. The best by a man has been four championships by Michael Carrega (Fra).

BISLEY—THE QUEEN'S (KING'S) PRIZE: One of the most prestigious trophies in shooting, the Prize has been won three times by Sergeant Arthur Fulton over a span of 19 years from 1912 to 1931. Both his father before him, and his son, were winners. Only one woman has won; in 1930 Marjorie Foster scored 280 out of a possible 300 to secure the title. The record highest score is 294 by the Canadian Alain Marion in 1980.

Evgeni Petrov (USSR), the 1968 Olympic gold medallist, is one of a small number of skeet shooters who have scored the maximum possible of 200 birds, but not in competitions designated as qualifying for world record acceptance.

TRICK SHOOTING

There have been many trick shot specialists, but possibly the most well-known was Phoebe Anne Oakley Mozee, made famous as Annie Oakley in the stage and cinema versions of 'Annie Get Your Gun'. Born in 1860 in America she could score 100 out of 100 in trap shooting until she was in her sixties. Her tricks included splitting a playing card at 30 paces, hitting a small coin in mid-air and shooting a cigarette from the lips of an assistant, usually her husband, Frank Butler, who was himself an excellent marksman. One of the best shots of modern times has been Ed McGivern (USA) who, using a revolver, fired five shots in 0·45 sec into a target, at a range of 4·5 m (15 ft), which could be covered by a coin of 3 cm (1·2 in) diameter. On another occasion he fired 10 shots, using two pistols, in 1·2 sec into two playing cards at the same range.

WORLD SHOOTING RECORDS (Ratified by the Union Internationale de Tir)

Event	Range	Number	Possible Maximum	Score	Name	Year
Free Rifle	300 m	120 shots	1200	1160	Lones Wigger (USA)	1978
	300 m	60 shots prone	600	593	Viktor Danilshenko (USSR)	1982
				593	Malcolm Cooper (GB)	1982
Standard Rifle	300 m	60 shots	600	580	Lones Wigger (USA)	1981
Small-Bore Rifle	50 m	120 shots	1200	1180	Kiril Ivanov (USSR)	1982
	50 m	60 shots prone	600	600	Alistair Allan (GB)	1981
				600	Ernest Van de Zande (USA)	1981
Free Pistol	50 m	60 shots	600	581	Aleksandr Melentev (USSR)	1980
Rapid Fire Pistol	25 m	60 shots	600	599	Igor Puzyrev (USSR)	1981
Centre Fire Pistol	25 m	60 shots	600	597	Thomas Smith (USA)	1963
Standard Pistol	25 m	60 shots	600	583	Ragnar Skanaker (Swe)	1978
				583	Vladas Tourla (USSR)	1982
Running Target	50 m	60 shots	600	595	Igor Sokolov (USSR)	1981
Trap	—	200 birds	200	199	Angelo Scalzone (Ita)	1972
				199	Michael Carrega (Fra)	1974
				199	Daniele Cioni (Ita)	1982
Skeet	—	200 birds	200	200	Matthew Dryke (USA)	1981
Air Rifle	10 m	60 shots	600	590	Harald Stenvaag (Nor)	1982
Air Pistol	10 m	60 shots	600	590	Valdas Tourla (USSR)	1982

Skiing

A ski found in a peat bog, and thus well preserved, at Höting, Sweden has been estimated to be about 4500 years old. However, in 1934 a Russian archaeologist discovered a rock carving of a skier at Bessovysledki, USSR which dates from *c* 6000 BC. These early skiers used the bones of animals whereas wooden skis appear to have been introduced to Europe from Asia. The first reference in literature is in a work by Procopius *c* AD 550 who referred to 'Gliding Finns'. Additionally in the Scandinavian sagas there occur gods of skiing. By 1199 the Danish historian Saxo was reporting the military use of troops on skis by Sigurdsson Sverrir, the Norwegian King. The

modern sport did not develop until 1843 when the first known competition for civilians took place at Tromsö, Norway. The first ever ski club, named the Trysil Shooting and Skiing Club, was founded in Norway in 1861. Twenty years later ski bindings were invented by Sondre Nordheim, from Morgedal in the Telemark area, and the people of this region were the pioneers of the sport. The legendary 'Snowshoe' Thompson, whose parents were Norwegian, was the earliest well-known skier in the United States in 1856 although skiing took place there in the 1840s. It was not until Olaf Kjeldsberg went to Switzerland in 1881 that the sport began to take a hold in that

country, and in 1889 one of the earliest of British exponents, Sir Arthur Conan Doyle, began skiing at Davos. The first downhill race—as opposed to the Scandinavian races across country—was held at Kitzbuhel, Austria in 1908. The first modern slalom race was at Murren, Switzerland in January 1922. The world's first national governing body was the Ski Club of Great Britain founded in 1903, and the International Ski Federation (FIS) followed in 1924.

WORLD AND OLYMPIC CHAMPIONSHIPS: The first Alpine championships were held at Murren in 1931, and Alpine

Sweden's world and Olympic champion Ingemar Stenmark is one of the greatest slalom skiers ever. His so-called 'charges' on the second of the two runs which are contested in slalom racing have become legendary.

events were included in the Olympic Games from 1936. The most titles won is 13 by Christel Cranz (Ger) between 1934 and 1939, comprising four slalom, three downhill and six combined championships. The best by a man is seven by Toni Sailer (Aut) from 1956 to 1958, which included a clean sweep of all four available titles in 1956.

Nordic skiing championships were first held in the Olympics in 1924, with separate world titles instituted in 1929. Galina Koulakova (USSR) won a record nine gold medals between 1968 and 1978, while the best for men has been eight by Sixten Jernberg (Swe) between 1956 and 1964. The most individual titles, excluding relays, is six by Johan Grøttumsbraaten (Nor) from 1926 to 1932. The Nordic Combination title, comprising a 15 km (9·3 miles) cross-country race and a ski jumping contest, has been won four times by Ulrich Wehling (GDR) between 1972 and 1980. The most titles won at Ski-jumping is five by Birger Ruud (Nor) between 1931 and 1937.

The most Biathlon titles, instituted in 1958 as a combination of skiing and shooting, now held over 10 km, 20 km and a 4 × 7·5 km relay, have been won by Aleksandr Tikhonov (USSR). He won individual championships in 1969, 1970, 1973 and 1977, and was in the winning relay teams 10 times between 1968 and 1980 to make a grand total of 14 titles.

ALPINE CHAMPIONSHIPS FROM 1970
(*Olympic Games)

Men

	Downhill	Slalom
1970	Bernhard Russi (Swi)	Jean-Noel Augert (Fra)
1972*	Bernhard Russi (Swi)	Francesco Ochoa (Spa)
1974	David Zwilling (Aut)	Gustavo Thoeni (Ita)
1976*	Franz Klammer (Aut)	Piero Gros (Ita)
1978	Joseph Walcher (Aut)	Ingemar Stenmark (Swe)
1980*	Leonhard Stock (Aut)	Ingemar Stenmark (Swe)
1982	Harti Weirather (Aut)	Ingemar Stenmark (Swe)

	Giant Slalom
1970	Karl Schranz (Aut)
1972*	Gustavo Thoeni (Ita)
1974	Gustavo Thoeni (Ita)
1976*	Heini Hemmi (Swi)
1978	Ingemar Stenmark (Swe)
1980*	Ingemar Stenmark (Swe)
1982	Steve Mahre (USA)

Women

	Downhill	Slalom
1970	Anneroesli Zyrd (Swi)	Ingrid Lafforgue (Fra)
1972*	Marie-Thérèse Nadig (Swi)	Barbara Cochran (USA)
1974	Annemarie Proell (Aut)	Hanni Wenzel (Lie)
1976*	Rosi Mittermaier (FRG)	Rosi Mittermaier (FRG)
1978	Annemarie Moser-Proell (Aut)	Lea Sölkner (Aut)
1980*	Annemarie Moser-Proell (Aut)	Hanni Wenzel (Lie)
1982	Gerry Sorensen (Can)	Erika Hess (Swi)

	Giant Slalom
1970	Betsy Clifford (Can)
1972*	Marie-Thérèse Nadig (Swi)
1974	Fabienne Serrat (Fra)
1976*	Kathy Kreiner (Can)
1978	Maria Epple (FRG)
1980*	Hanni Wenzel (Lie)
1982	Erika Hess (Swi)

WORLD CUP—ALPINE: Introduced in 1967 as a points competition covering most of the season's major events, for men and women. The greatest number of wins is six by Annemarie Moser-Proell (Aut), while the best by a male skiier is four by Gustavo Thoeni (Ita). Ingemar Stenmark (Swe) has won a record 71 slaloms between 1974 and 31 March 1983, including a season best of 14 in 1979. Moser-Proell set a women's best of 62 individual race victories between 1970 and 1979, including a record 11 consecutive downhill wins.

Overall winners:

	Men	Women
1967	Jean-Claude Killy (Fra)	Nancy Greene (Can)
1968	Jean-Claude Killy (Fra)	Nancy Greene (Can)
1969	Karl Schranz (Aut)	Gertrud Gabl (Aut)
1970	Karl Schranz (Aut)	Michele Jacot (Fra)
1971	Gustavo Thoeni (Ita)	Annemarie Proell (Aut)
1972	Gustavo Thoeni (Ita)	Annemarie Proell (Aut)
1973	Gustavo Thoeni (Ita)	Annemarie Proell (Aut)
1974	Piero Gros (Ita)	Annemarie Proell (Aut)
1975	Gustavo Thoeni (Ita)	Annemarie Moser-Proell (Aut)
1976	Ingemar Stenmark (Swe)	Rosi Mittermaier (FRG)
1977	Ingemar Stenmark (Swe)	Lise-Marie Morerod (Swi)
1978	Ingemar Stenmark (Swe)	Hanni Wenzel (Lie)
1979	Peter Luescher (Swi)	Annemarie Moser-Proell (Aut)
1980	Andreas Wenzel (Lie)	Hanni Wenzel (Lie)
1981	Phil Mahre (USA)	Marie-Thérèse Nadig (Swi)
1982	Phil Mahre (USA)	Erika Hess (Swi)
1983	Phil Mahre (USA)	Tamara McKinney (USA)

WORLD CUP—NORDIC: The ski jumping cup, inaugurated in 1980, has been won as follows:

1980	Hubert Neuper (Aut)	1981	Armin Kogler (Aut)

The Nordic skiing cup, first held in 1979 although there had been an unofficial competition from 1974, has been won as follows:

	Men	Women
1979	Oddvar Braa (Nor)	Galina Koulakova (USSR)
1980	Juha Mieto (Fin)	Not held
1981	Aleksandr Zavialov (USSR)	Raisa Smetanina (USSR)
1982	Bill Koch (USA)	Berit Aunli (Nor)
1983	Aleksandr Zavialov (USSR)	Marja-Liisa Hämäläinen (Fin)

By winning the downhill section of the 1982–83 World Cup, Austria's 1976 Olympic champion Franz Klammer put himself back in the reckoning for another Olympic title.

SKI JUMPING

Traditionally, the first ski jumping competition is said to have been off the top of a cow shed at Drontheim, Norway in 1797. In the early 1860s the King of Norway awarded a trophy for a jumping contest at Iverslokka, near Oslo, and at the nearby Huseby Hill a jump of 23 m (75 ft 5 in) was made by Troj Hemmestveit from Telemark, in 1879. In 1892 the first jumping competitions were held at the Holmenkollen, on the hills surrounding Oslo, and they have continued there ever since. It was there, for the 1952 Olympics, that the largest crowd ever assembled for an Olympic event was recorded at 150 000 spectators. The first man to jump over 100 m (328 ft) was Joseph Bradl (Aut) at Planica, Yugoslavia in 1936, when he cleared 101 m. Both Planica and Oberstdorf, Germany are special 'ski flying' hills, the latter having a height of 161 m (528 ft). World and Olympic titles are decided from 70 m and 90 m hills. Due to the widely differing construction and general conditions, official records do not exist. The greatest jump recorded to date has been 181 m (593 ft 10 in) by Bogdan Norcic (Yug) on his home hill at Planica in 1977, but he fell on landing. The best jump under 'official' conditions, without falling, is also 181 m by Pavel Ploc (Cz) at Harrachov, Czechoslovakia on 19 March 1983. The greatest distance achieved by a woman is 98 m (321 ft 6 in) by Anita Wold (Nor) at Okura, Japan in January 1975. From a 90 m hill the longest jump has been 128·5 m (421 ft 6 in) by Steve Collins (Can) at Thunder Bay, Canada in December 1980. The Olympic Games best is 117 m (384 ft) by Juoko Tormanen (Fin) at Lake Placid in 1980. The best by a Briton is still the 61 m (200 ft 1 in) jumped by Guy Nixon on the Bolgenschanze, Davos, Switzerland on 24 February 1931.

SPEED

The current fastest time on skis over a measured 1000 m course, is 208·092 km/h (129·303 mph) by Franz Weber (Aut) at Silverton, Colorado in April 1983. The best by a woman is 194·384 km/h (120·785 mph) by Kirsten Culver (USA) also at Silverton on 23 April 1983. The fastest achieved in Olympic competition was 102·82 km/h (63·89 mph) by Franz Klammer (Aut) at Innsbruck, in February 1976.

GREAT RACES

The longest downhill race in the world is The Inferno, held over a 14 km (8·7 miles) course from the top of the Schilthorn to Lauterbrunnen in Switzerland. It was first held in 1928 under the auspices of the British-run Kandahar Club, and won by Harold Mitchell (GB). In 1981, when it was won in the fastest ever time of 15 min 44·57 sec by Heinz Fringer (Swi), there was a record entry of 1401 participants. The greatest Nordic ski race is the Vasaloppet in Sweden. It commemorates the achievement of Gustav Vasa, later King Gustavus Eriksson, who skied from Mora to Salen in 1521, a distance of 85·8 km (53·3 miles). The annual race, in the reverse direction of Vasa's journey, attracted a record 12 000 entrants in 1981. The fastest time has been 3 hr 58 min 8 sec by Konrad Hallenbarter (Swi) in 1983. In 1977 the present King, Carl Gustav, competed in the race. The narrowest winning margin in a long distance race occurred in the 1980 Olympic 15 km (9·3 miles) event at Lake Placid when Thomas Wassberg (Swe) won by one hundredth of a second from Juha Mieto (Fin) with a time of 41 min 57·63 sec.

Right: **One of the most thrilling, or perhaps heart-stopping, events in the sporting world. The dual qualities of ice-cold nerve and skill required in ski jumping are all too evident.**

The game originated at the Ootacamund Club, Madras, India where Colonel Sir Neville Chamberlain, of the Devonshire Regiment, made up a hybrid of the then popular 'Black Pool', 'Pyramids', and billiards in 1875. The term 'snooker' derives from the nickname that was given to first-year cadets at the Royal Military Academy, Woolwich. The game reached England about 10 years later after the reigning world billiards champion, John Roberts, had been introduced to snooker while on a trip to India. The rules were not codified until 1919.

WORLD CHAMPIONSHIPS: Since their inauguration in 1927 the Professional championships have been won a record 15 times by Joe Davis (Eng) in 1927–40 and 1946. The youngest player to win the title was Alex 'Hurricane' Higgins of Northern Ireland who was 22 yr 345 days old when he won the 1972 title at Birmingham. The highest break ever compiled in the championship is 147 by Cliff Thorburn (Can) in April 1983 playing against Terry Griffiths. The Amateur title (instituted in 1963) has been won twice by Gary Owen (Eng) in 1963 and 1966, and by Ray Edmonds (Eng) in 1972 and 1974. The youngest winner has been Jimmy White (Eng) who won the 1980 title at Launceston, Tasmania, aged 18 yr 191 days. The professional winners since the championship reverted to an open tournament in 1969, and the Amateur winners since inception are:

Steve Davis contemplating his next shot on the way to winning yet another snooker tournament. Though still only 26 he is already being compared, justifiably, to his famous namesake, Joe, the snooker player *par excellence*.

Professional

1969 John Spencer (Eng)	1976 Ray Reardon (Wal)
1970 Ray Reardon (Wal)	1977 John Spencer (Eng)
1971 John Spencer (Eng)	1978 Ray Reardon (Wal)
1972 Alex Higgins (NI)	1979 Terry Griffiths (Wal)
1973 Ray Reardon (Wal)	1980 Cliff Thorburn (Can)
1974 Ray Reardon (Wal)	1981 Steve Davis (Eng)
1975 Ray Reardon (Wal)	1982 Alex Higgins (NI)
	1983 Steve Davis (Eng)

Amateur

1963 Gary Owen (Eng)	1974 Ray Edmonds (Eng)
1966 Gary Owen (Eng)	1976 Doug Mountjoy (Wal)
1968 David Taylor (Eng)	1978 Cliff Wilson (Wal)
1970 Johathan Barron (Eng)	1980 Jimmy White (Eng)
1972 Ray Edmonds (Eng)	1982 Terry Parsons (Wal)

UNITED KINGDOM PROFESSIONAL CHAMPION-SHIP: Instituted in 1977. The highest break made in the tournament is 139 by Graham Miles (Eng) in 1978.

1977 Patsy Fagan (Ire)	1980 Steve Davis (Eng)
1978 Doug Mountjoy (Wal)	1981 Steve Davis (Eng)
1979 John Virgo (Eng)	1982 Alex Higgins (NI)

BENSON & HEDGES MASTERS CHAMPIONSHIP: Instituted in 1975, the championship record break is 136 by Terry Griffiths in 1980 and Tony Meo in 1982.

1975 John Spencer (Eng)	1980 Terry Griffiths (Wal)
1976 Ray Reardon (Wal)	1981 Alex Higgins (NI)
1977 Doug Mountjoy (Wal)	1982 Steve Davis (Eng)
1978 Alex Higgins (NI)	1983 Cliff Thorburn (Can)
1979 Perrie Mans (Saf)	

YOUNGEST CHAMPIONS

Jimmy White is both the youngest ever winner of a world snooker title (the 1980 Amateur crown) and the youngest player to win a major professional tournament, the 1981 Langs Supreme Scottish Masters title at the age of 19 yr 146 days. In Australia, Fiona Johncock won the Tasmanian Open Women's title in July 1981 aged only 12 yr 286 days.

POT BLACK CHAMPIONSHIP: Instituted specifically for BBC Television presentation in 1969, it has become a highlight of the snooker year.

1969 Ray Reardon (Wal)	1977 Perrie Mans (Saf)
1970 John Spencer (Eng)	1978 Doug Mountjoy (Wal)
1971 John Spencer (Eng)	1979 Ray Reardon (Wal)
1972 Eddie Charlton (Aus)	1980 Eddie Charlton (Aus)
1973 Eddie Charlton (Aus)	1981 Cliff Thorburn (Can)
1974 Graham Miles (Eng)	1982 Steve Davis (Eng)
1975 Graham Miles (Eng)	1983 Steve Davis (Eng)
1976 John Spencer (Eng)	

Belfast-born Alex 'Hurricane' Higgins nearly became a jockey but increasing weight put him back on the path to snooker fame.

ENGLISH AMATEUR CHAMPIONSHIP: Instituted in 1916, it has been won a record four times by Marcus Owen from 1958 to 1973. The youngest winner was Jimmy White in 1979 the age of 16 yr 340 days. *Winners from 1970:*

1970 Jonathan Barron	1977 Terry Griffiths
1971 Jonathan Barron	1978 Terry Griffiths
1972 Jonathan Barron	1979 Jimmy White
1973 Marcus Owen	1980 Joe O'Boye
1974 Ray Edmonds	1981 Vic Harris
1975 Sid Hood	1982 David Chalmers
1976 Chris Ross	

HIGHEST BREAKS

The maximum break possible under 'normal' conditions is 147, and it was first compiled by E. J. 'Murt' O'Donoghue (NZ) in Griffiths, New South Wales, Australia on 1 September 1934. However, that and other 147s by Horace Lindrum (Aus) in 1941, Leo Levitt (Can) in 1948, and Clark McConachy (NZ) in 1952 were not officially accepted. The official record is held by Joe Davis (Eng) who made his 147 against Willie Smith at the Leicester Square Hall, London on 22 January 1955, and by Rex Williams (Eng), against Manuel Francisco at Cape Town, South Africa on 22 December 1965. More than 150 other maximum scores have been recorded under 'unofficial' conditions. There have been three 147s scored in major competitions. The first was by John Spencer in the Holsten Lager International in 1979. Steve Davis made the first maximum seen on television in the Lada Classic on 11 January 1982. The first ever officially accepted total clearance was a break of 133 by Sidney Smith (Eng) in December 1936. In February 1976 Alex Higgins (NI) became the first player to make a 16-red clearance, including a free ball from a foul by his opponent, when he scored 146 at the YMCA, Leicester. Theoretically, with a combination of the most abnormal and unlikely circumstances, it is possible to score a break of 155. In the 1983 World Championships, Cliff Thorburn (Can) scored 151, with four points from his opponent for a foul shot added to his maximum break.

The official amateur record is 140 by Joe Johnson (Eng) in a televised tournament at the TUC Club, Middlesbrough in 1978.

Speedway

The sport as we now know it originated in Australia at the West Maitland Agricultural Show, New South Wales in November 1923 when local riders took part in a race on a grass circuit temporarily covered with cinders from a nearby slag heap. The first proper dirt-track was constructed at Sydney Show Ground in 1926. The first event on cinders in Britain was at High Beech, Essex on 19 February 1928, although an earlier motorcycle race meeting, on a sandy circuit, was held at Camberley, Surrey the previous year. By early 1929 a league competition had been organised, and in 1930 the first matches between England and Australia took place. In September 1936, under the auspices of the Fédération Internationale Motocycliste (FIM), the first world championships were held at Wembley.

WORLD CHAMPIONSHIPS: Instituted in 1936 as an individual contest, a team competition was inaugurated in 1960. Ivan Mauger (NZ) won a record six individual titles between 1968 and 1979. His countryman, Barry Briggs, made a record 17 appearances in the finals from 1954 to 1970, during which time he won four titles and scored a record total of 201 points. New Zealand riders have won the title on 12 occasions. The world team championship has been won most times by Great Britain with seven between 1968 and 1977. The world pairs cup (first held in 1968) has been won five times by England, with both Malcolm Simmons (Eng) and Anders Michanek (Swe) being members of three winning pairs. *Winners from 1970:*

	Individual	Team
1970	Ivan Mauger (NZ)	Sweden
1971	Ole Olsen (Den)	GB
1972	Ivan Mauger (NZ)	GB
1973	Jerzy Szczakiel (Pol)	GB
1974	Anders Michanek (Swe)	England
1975	Ole Olsen (Den)	England
1976	Peter Collins (Eng)	Australia
1977	Ivan Mauger (NZ)	England
1978	Ole Olsen (Den)	Denmark
1979	Ivan Mauger (NZ)	New Zealand
1980	Mike Lee (Eng)	England
1981	Bruce Penhall (USA)	Denmark
1982	Bruce Penhall (USA)	USA

	Pairs
1970	Ronnie Moore & Ivan Mauger (NZ)
1971	Jerzy Szczakiel & Andrzej Wyglenda (Pol)
1972	Ray Wilson & Terry Betts (Eng)
1973	Anders Michanek & Tommy Jansson (Swe)
1974	Anders Michanek & Soren Sjösten (Swe)
1975	Anders Michanek & Tommy Jansson (Swe)
1976	Malcolm Simmons & John Louis (Eng)
1977	Malcolm Simmons & Peter Collins (Eng)
1978	Malcolm Simmons & Gordon Kennett (Eng)
1979	Ole Olsen & Hans Nielsen (Den)
1980	Dave Jessup & Peter Collins (Eng)
1981	Bruce Penhall & Bobby Schwartz (USA)
1982	Dennis Sigalos & Bobby Schwartz (USA)

BRITISH LEAGUE: Instituted in 1932 as the National League, and replaced in 1965 by the British League which also encompassed the Provincial League (formed in 1960) as the

Right: **The cornering technique of Ivan Mauger which helped him become the only speedway rider to win three consecutive world championships. After only one season of riding in his native New Zealand he arrived in Britain in 1957 and joined the Wimbledon team.**

156

result of an inquiry by the RAC into the organisation of the sport in Britain. The Wembley Lions won the National League eight times between 1932 and 1953, while the British League title has been won a record four times by Belle Vue 1970–72 and 1982. The highest team score was by Bristol when they beat Glasgow by 70–14 points in 1949. The most points scored by an individual in a season is 480 by Pete Lansdale for Plymouth in 1949.

Winners from 1965:

1965 West Ham	1971 Belle Vue	1977 White City
1966 Halifax	1972 Belle Vue	1978 Coventry
1967 Swindon	1973 Reading	1979 Coventry
1968 Coventry	1974 Exeter	1980 Reading
1969 Poole	1975 Ipswich	1981 Cradley Heath
1970 Belle Vue	1976 Ipswich	1982 Belle Vue

Squash

Squash developed out of a game used for the practice of Rackets, which itself had developed from one played by the inmates of the Fleet Prison, London, about the middle of the 18th century. Some hundred years later the boys of Harrow School would knock-up on adjacent walls while waiting for games on the Rackets courts. They used a softer ball, thus the term 'squashy' came about, and gradually the new game spread. Surprisingly, the first national governing body was that of the United States, and the winner of their first championships in 1907, John Miskey, was the first major titlist in the world. The English Squash Rackets Association was not formed until 1928.

Since he won the world title in 1981, Jahangir Khan has dominated the squash scene and reestablished his country, Pakistan, and indeed his family, at the very top of the sport.

WORLD OPEN CHAMPIONSHIPS: First held in 1976 the youngest winner was Jahangir Khan (Pak) aged 17 yr 354 days when he took the 1981 title.

	Men	Women
1976	Geoff Hunt (Aus)	Heather McKay (Aus)
1977	Geoff Hunt (Aus)	not held
1978	not held	not held
1979	Geoff Hunt (Aus)	Heather McKay (Aus)
1980	Geoff Hunt (Aus)	not held
1981	Jahangir Khan (Pak)	Rhonda Thorne (Aus)
1982	Jahangir Khan (Pak)	not held

WORLD AMATEUR CHAMPIONSHIPS: First held in 1967, the youngest winner was Jahangir Khan (Pak) aged 15 yr 309 days in 1979.

	Individual	Team
1967	Geoff Hunt (Aus)	Australia
1969	Geoff Hunt (Aus)	Australia
1971	Geoff Hunt (Aus)	Australia
1973	Cameron Nancarrow (Aus)	Australia
1975	Kevin Shawcross (Aus)	Great Britain
1977	Maqsood Ahmed (Pak)	Pakistan
1979	Jahangir Khan (Pak)	Great Britain
1981	Steve Bowditch (Aus)	Pakistan

BRITISH OPEN CHAMPIONSHIPS—MEN: From their institution in 1930 until the inauguration of the World Amateur in 1967, the winners of these titles were considered to be the unofficial world champions. Until 1947 the holder only played in the final challenge round. Geoff Hunt (Aus) won a record eight titles between 1969 and 1981, while the previous record holder, Hashim Khan (Pak), who won seven times in the 1950s, also won the Vintage title four times 1978–81.

1930	Don Butcher (GB)
1931	Don Butcher (GB)
1932	Abdel Fattah Amr Bey (Egy)
1933	Not held
1934	Abdel Fattah Amr Bey (Egy)
1935	Abdel Fattah Amr Bey (Egy)
1936	Abdel Fattah Amr Bey (Egy)
1937	Abdel Fattah Amr Bey (Egy)
1938	James Dear (GB)
1946	Mahmoud el Karim (Egy)
1947	Mahmoud el Karim (Egy)
1948	Mahmoud el Karim (Egy)
1949	Mahmoud el Karim (Egy)
1950	Hashim Khan (Pak)
1951	Hashim Khan (Pak)
1952	Hashim Khan (Pak)
1953	Hashim Khan (Pak)
1954	Hashim Khan (Pak)
1955	Hashim Khan (Pak)
1956	Roshan Khan (Pak)
1957	Hashim Khan (Pak)
1958	Azam Khan (Pak)
1959	Azam Khan (Pak)
1960	Azam Khan (Pak)
1961	Azam Khan (Pak)
1962	Mohibullah Khan (Pak)
1963	Abou Taleb (Egy)
1964	Abou Taleb (Egy)
1965	Abou Taleb (Egy)
1966	Abou Taleb (Egy)
1967	Jonah Barrington (GB)
1968	Jonah Barrington (GB)
1969	Geoff Hunt (Aus)
1970	Jonah Barrington (GB)
1971	Jonah Barrington (GB)
1972	Jonah Barrington (GB)
1973	Jonah Barrington (GB)
1974	Geoff Hunt (Aus)
1975	Qamar Zaman (Pak)
1976	Geoff Hunt (Aus)
1977	Geoff Hunt (Aus)
1978	Geoff Hunt (Aus)
1979	Geoff Hunt (Aus)
1980	Geoff Hunt (Aus)
1981	Geoff Hunt (Aus)
1982	Jahangir Khan (Pak)
1983	Jahangir Khan (Pak)

BRITISH OPEN CHAMPIONSHIPS—WOMEN: First held in 1922, the title has been won 16 times by Heather McKay (Aus) consecutively from 1962 to 1977. Her domination of the women's game is virtually unequalled at this level in any other sport, for from 1959 to 1980 she lost only two games.

1922	Joyce Cave (GB)
1922	Sylvia Huntsman (GB)
1923	Nancy Cave (GB)
1924	Joyce Cave (GB)
1925	Cecily Fenwick (GB)
1926	Cecily Fenwick (GB)
1928	Joyce Cave (GB)
1929	Nancy Cave (GB)
1930	Nancy Cave (GB)
1931	Cecily Fenwick (GB)
1932	Susan Noel (GB)
1933	Susan Noel (GB)
1934	Susan Noel (GB)
1934	Margot Lumb (GB)
1935	Margot Lumb (GB)
1936	Margot Lumb (GB)
1937	Margot Lumb (GB)
1938	Margot Lumb (GB)
1939	Margot Lumb (GB)
1947	Joan Curry (GB)
1948	Joan Curry (GB)
1949	Joan Curry (GB)
1950	Janet Morgan (GB)
1951	Janet Morgan (GB)
1952	Janet Morgan (GB)
1953	Janet Morgan (GB)
1954	Janet Morgan (GB)
1955	Janet Morgan (GB)
1956	Janet Morgan (GB)
1957	Janet Morgan (GB)
1958	Janet Morgan (GB)
1960	Sheila Macintosh (GB)
1961	Fran Marshall (GB)
1962	Heather McKay (Aus)
1963	Heather McKay (Aus)
1964	Heather McKay (Aus)
1965	Heather McKay (Aus)
1966	Heather McKay (Aus)
1967	Heather McKay (Aus)
1968	Heather McKay (Aus)
1969	Heather McKay (Aus)
1970	Heather McKay (Aus)
1971	Heather McKay (Aus)
1972	Heather McKay (Aus)
1973	Heather McKay (Aus)
1974	Heather McKay (Aus)
1975	Heather McKay (Aus)
1976	Heather McKay (Aus)
1977	Heather McKay (Aus)
1978	Susan Newman-King (Aus)
1979	Barbara Wall (Aus)
1980	Vicki Hoffman (Aus)
1981	Vicki Hoffman (Aus)
1982	Vicki Hoffman-Cardwell (Aus)
1983	Vicki Hoffman-Cardwell (Aus)

BRITISH AMATEUR CHAMPIONSHIPS: Instituted in 1922, and won most times by Abdel Amr Bey—later Egypt's Ambassador to Britain—between 1931 and 1937. The longest known match at championship level anywhere in the world took place in the Amateur of 1976, when Murray Lilley (NZ) beat Barry O'Connor of Kent after playing for 2 hr 35 min. The second game alone, which went 10–8 to Lilley, took 58 min. The tournament as such came to an end in 1979, when the distinction between amateurs and professionals in squash was abolished.

Swimming and Diving

Egyptian hieroglyphics, c 3000 BC, indicate swimming figures, and a bronze of a diver dating from c 510 BC was found near Perugia, Italy. Both Julius Caesar and Charlemagne were known to be good swimmers. Competitions took place in Japan in 36 BC, and that country was the first to take to the sport in a major way with an Imperial edict by the Emperor G-Yozei decreeing its introduction in schools. In Britain, sea bathing was practised as early as 1660 at Scarborough, but competitive swimming was not introduced until 1837, when competitions were held in London's artificial pools organised by the National Swimming Society, founded in that year. Australia was in the forefront of modern developments and an unofficial world 100 yd championship was held in Melbourne in 1858. With the foundation of the Amateur Swimming Association (though not known by this name till later) in 1869 came the distinction between amateurs and professionals.

STROKES AND BEATS

The first recognisable stroke style seems to have been the breaststroke, although the 'dog-paddle' technique may well have preceded it. From this developed the sidestroke, which is the breaststroke performed sideways, a style which was last used by an Olympic champion in 1904, when Emil Rausch (Ger) won the 1 mile event. About the middle of the 19th century, some American Indians had swum in London exhibiting a style resembling the crawl. An Englishman, John Trudgen, noted a variation of this style while on a trip to South America in the 1870s. His forerunner to the modern crawl used the legs in basically a breaststroke way. However, from ancient carvings and wall paintings it would seem that the Trudgen stroke was in use in early times. Another 'throwback' was the front crawl which is credited to a British emigrant to Australia, Frederick Cavill, and his sons, who noticed the unusual style of South Sea Island natives, and modified it to their own use. American swimmers developed this even further by variations of the kicking action of the legs. At the beginning of the 20th century some had shown their prowess by attempting the breaststroke on their backs, and later the crawl action was tried in the same position. Thus the backstroke was born. In the 1930s the idea of recovering the arms over the water in the breaststroke was developed, and led to a drastic revision of the record book, until the new style was recognised as a separate stroke, the butterfly, in 1952. Also in the 1930s came the introduction, mainly in the USA, of medley events in which swimmers use all four major strokes during one event, a real test of all-round ability.

WORLD CHAMPIONSHIPS: Instituted in 1973, and now held quadrenially, the most medals won is 10 by Kornelia Ender (GDR) with eight gold and two silver in 1973 and 1975. The record for a male swimmer is eight, five gold and three silver, by Rowdy Gaines (USA) in 1978 and 1982. In 1978 Tracy Caulkins (USA) collected a record five golds and one silver medal at one celebration. The most successful country in the championships has been the USA with a total of 50 swimming, nine diving and eight synchronised swimming titles. However, in women's swimming events alone the GDR has a record total of 31 victories. Other than relays, the only gold medallist in the same event at three championships is Phil Boggs (USA) in the springboard diving. The only Briton to gain a world title is David Wilkie who won three breaststroke events in 1973 and 1975.

OLYMPIC GAMES: The record number of gold medals is nine by Mark Spitz (USA), who also won a record 11 medals of all colours, with a silver and a bronze in 1968. The most gold medals in individual events is four, by Spitz, Charles Daniels (USA) in 1904–08, Pat McCormick (USA) in diving events 1952–56, and Roland Matthes (GDR) in 1968–72. The record number of medals by a woman is eight by Dawn Fraser (Aus) with four golds and four silvers from 1956 to 1964, Kornelia Ender (GDR) also with four golds and four silvers in 1972 and 1976, and Shirley Babashoff (USA) with two golds, and six silvers in 1972 and 1976. Dawn Fraser is the only swimmer, male or female, to have won the same event on three successive occasions with the 100 m freestyle from 1956 to 1964. However, the diver Klaus Dibiasi, Austrian-born but representing Italy, took the highboard event on three successive occasions, while amassing a diving medal record of five, including two silvers, between 1964 and 1976. The highest placed British diver in Olympic competition was Eileen Armstrong, the silver medallist in the 1920 highboard event, while the best by a British male diver is a bronze medal by Harold Clarke in 1924 and Brian Phelps in 1960. The British record for swimming gold medals is four by Henry Taylor in 1906 and 1908, and Paul Radmilovic with three at Water Polo from 1908 to 1920 and another in the 4 × 200 m relay in 1908. Taylor also collected a silver and three bronzes for a record total of eight medals. No British girl has more than one gold medal but Joyce Cooper won the most medals, four, with a silver and three bronzes in 1928 and 1932.

Viktor Salnikov (USSR) has broken all the records for freestyle swimming over 400 m, 800 m and 1500 m since he won three gold medals in the 1980 Olympic Games.

Olympic Champions
MEN

100 metres freestyle
1896 Alfred Hajos (Hun) 1:22·2
1900 Not held
1904 Zoltan Halmay (Hun) 1:02·8*
1906 Charles Daniels (USA) 1:13·4
1908 Charles Daniels (USA) 1:05·6
1912 Duke Kahanamoku (USA) 1:03·4
1920 Duke Kahanamoku (USA) 1:01·4
1924 Johnny Weissmuller (USA) 59·0
1928 Johnny Weissmuller (USA) 58·6
1932 Yasuji Miyazaki (Jap) 58·2

1936 Ferenc Csik (Hun) 57·6
1948 Walter Ris (USA) 57·3
1952 Clarke Scholes (USA) 57·4
1956 Jon Henricks (Aus) 55·4
1960 John Devitt (Aus) 55·2
1964 Donald Schollander (USA) 53·4
1968 Michael Wenden (Aus) 52·2
1972 Mark Spitz (USA) 51·22
1976 Jim Montgomery (USA) 49·99
1980 Jorg Woithe (GDR) 50·40
* 100 yards

200 metres freestyle
1900 Freddy Lane (Aus) 2:52·2
1904 Charles Daniels (USA) 2:44·2*
1906–64 Not held
1968 Michael Wenden (Aus) 1:55·2
1972 Mark Spitz (USA) 1:52·78
1976 Bruce Furniss (USA) 1:50·29
1980 Sergei Kopliakov (USSR) 1·49·81
* 220 yards

400 metres freestyle
1896 Paul Neumann (Aut) 8:12·6†
1900 Not held
1904 Charles Daniels (USA) 6:16·2*
1906 Otto Scheff (Aut) 6:22·8
1908 Henry Taylor (GB) 5:36·8
1912 George Hodgson (Can) 5:24·4
1920 Norman Ross (USA) 5:26·6
1924 Johnny Weismuller (USA) 5:04·2
1928 Alberto Zorilla (Arg) 5:01·6
1932 Buster Crabbe (USA) 4:48·4
1936 Jack Medica (USA) 4:44·5
1948 William Smith (USA) 4:41·0
1952 Jean Boiteaux (Fra) 4:30·7
1956 Murray Rose (Aus) 4:27·3
1960 Murray Rose (Aus) 4:18·3
1964 Donald Schollander (USA) 4:12·2
1968 Michael Burton (USA) 4:09·0
1972 Bradford Cooper (Aus) 4:00·27
1976 Brian Goodell (USA) 3:51·93
1980 Vladimir Salnikov (USSR) 3:51·31
† 500 metres
* 440 yards

1500 metres freestyle
1896 Alfred Hajos (Hun) 18:22·2†
1900 John Jarvis (GB) 13:40·2‡
1904 Emil Rausch (Ger) 27:18·2*
1906 Henry Taylor (GB) 28:28·0*
1908 Henry Taylor (GB) 22:48·4
1912 George Hodgson (Can) 22:00·0
1920 Norman Ross (USA) 22:23·2
1924 Andrew Charlton (Aus) 20:06·6
1928 Arne Borg (Swe) 19:51·8
1932 Kusuo Kitamura (Jap) 19:12·4
1936 Noboru Terada (Jap) 19:13·7
1948 James McLane (USA) 19:18·5
1952 Ford Konno (USA) 18:30·0
1956 Murray Rose (Aus) 17:58·9
1960 Jon Konrads (Aus) 17:19·6
1964 Robert Windle (Aus) 17:01·7
1968 Michael Burton (USA) 16:38·9
1972 Michael Burton (USA 15:52·58
1976 Brian Goodell (USA) 15:02·40
1980 Vladimir Salnikov (USSR) 14:58·27
† 1200 metres
‡ 1000 metres
* 1 mile

100 metres backstroke
1904 Walter Brack (Ger) 1:16·8*
1906 Not held
1908 Arno Bieberstein (Ger) 1:24·6
1912 Harry Hebner (USA) 1:21·2
1920 Warren Kealoha (USA) 1:15·2
1924 Warren Kealoha (USA) 1:13·2
1928 George Kojac (USA) 1:08·2
1932 Masaji Kiyokawa (Jap) 1:08·6
1936 Adolf Kiefer (USA) 1:05·9
1948 Allen Stack (USA) 1:06·4
1952 Yoshinobu Oyakawa (USA) 1:05·4
1956 David Thiele (Aus) 1:02·2
1960 David Thiele (Aus) 1:02·2

1964 Not held
1968 Roland Matthes (GDR) 58·7
1972 Roland Matthes (GDR) 56·58
1976 John Naber (USA) 55·49
1980 Bengt Baron (Swe) 56·53
* 100 yards

200 metres backstroke
1900 Ernst Hoppenberg (Ger) 2:47·0
1904–60 Not held
1964 Jed Graef (USA) 2:10·3
1968 Roland Matthes (GDR) 2:09·6
1972 Roland Matthes (GDR) 2:02·82
1976 John Naber (USA) 1:59·19
1980 Sandor Wladar (Hun) 2:01·93

100 metres butterfly
1896–1964 Not held
1968 Douglas Russell (USA) 55·9
1972 Mark Spitz (USA) 54·27
1976 Matt Vogel (USA) 54·35
1980 Par Arvidsson (Swe) 54·92

200 metres butterfly
1896–1952 Not held
1956 William Yorzyk (USA) 2:19·3
1960 Michael Troy (USA) 2:12·8
1964 Kevin Berry (Aus) 2:06·6
1968 Carl Robie (USA) 2:08·7
1972 Mark Spitz (USA) 2:00·70
1976 Michael Bruner (USA) 1:59·23
1980 Sergei Fesenko (USSR) 1:59·76

100 metres breaststroke
1896–1964 Not held
1968 Donald McKenzie (USA) 1:07·7
1972 Nobutaka Taguchi (Jap) 1:04·94
1976 John Hencken (USA) 1:03·11
1980 Duncan Goodhew (GB) 1:03·34

200 metres breaststroke
1908 Frederick Holman (GB) 3:09·2
1912 Walther Bathe (Ger) 3:01·8
1920 Hakan Malmroth (Swe) 3:04·4
1924 Robert Skelton (USA) 2:56·6
1928 Yoshiyuki Tsuruta (Jap) 2:48·8
1932 Yoshiyuki Tsuruta (Jap) 2:45·5
1936 Tetsuo Hamuro (Jap) 2:41·5
1948 Joseph Verdeur (USA) 2:39·3
1952 John Davies (Aus) 2:34·4
1956 Masura Furukawa (Jap) 2:34·7
1960 William Mulliken (USA) 2:37·4
1964 Ian O'Brien (Aus) 2:27·8
1968 Felipe Munoz (Mex) 2:28·7
1972 John Hencken (USA) 2:21·55
1976 David Wilkie (GB) 2:15·11
1980 Robertas Zulpa (USSR) 2:15·85

200 metres individual medley
1896–1964 Not held
1968 Charles Hickcox (USA) 2:12·0
1972 Gunnar Larsson (Swe) 2:07·17
1976–80 Not held

400 metres individual medley
1896–1960 Not held
1964 Richard Roth (USA) 4:45·4
1968 Charles Hickcox (USA) 4:48·4
1972 Gunnar Larsson (Swe) 4:31·98
1976 Rod Strachan (USA) 4:23·68
1980 Aleksandr Sidorenko (USSR) 4:22·89

4 × 100 metres freestyle relay
1896–1960 Not held
1964 USA 3:33·2
1968 USA 3:31·7
1972 USA 3:26·42
1976–80 Not held

4 × 200 metres freestyle relay
1906 Hungary 16:52·4*
1908 GB 10:55·6
1912 Australasia 10:11·6
1920 USA 10:04·4
1924 USA 9:53·4
1928 USA 9:36·2

1932 Japan 8:58·4
1936 Japan 8:51·5
1948 USA 8:46·0
1952 USA 8:31·1
1956 Australia 8:23·6
1960 USA 8:10·2
1964 USA 7:52·1
1968 USA 7:52·3
1972 USA 7:35·78
1976 USA 7:23·22
1980 USSR 7:23·50
* 4 × 250 metres

4 × 100 metres medley relay
1896–1956 Not held
1960 USA 4:05·4
1964 USA 3:58·4
1968 USA 3:54·9
1972 USA 3:48·16
1976 USA 3:42·22
1980 Australia 3:45·70

Springboard diving
1908 Albert Zurner (Ger) 85·5
1912 Paul Gunther (Ger) 79·23
1920 Louis Kuehn (USA) 675·4
1924 Albert White (USA) 696·4
1928 Pete Desjardins (USA) 185·04
1932 Micky Galitzen (USA) 161·38
1936 Dickie Degener (USA) 163·57
1948 Bruce Harlan (USA) 163·64
1952 David Browning (USA) 205·29
1956 Robert Clotworthy (USA) 159·56
1960 Gary Tobian (USA) 170·00
1964 Kenneth Sitzberger (USA) 159·90
1968 Bernard Wrightson (USA) 170·15
1972 Vladimir Vasin (USSR) 594·09
1976 Philip Boggs (USA) 619·05
1980 Aleksandr Portnov (USSR) 905·025

Platform diving (highboard)
1904 George Sheldon (USA) 12·66
1906 Gottlob Walz (Ger) 156·00
1908 Hjalmar Johansson (Swe) 83·75
1912 Erik Adlerz (Swe) 73·94
1920 Clarence Pinkson (USA) 100·67
1924 Albert White (USA) 97·46
1928 Pete Desjardins (USA) 98·74
1932 Harold Smith (USA) 124·80
1936 Marshall Wayne (USA) 113·58
1948 Samuel Lee (USA) 130·05
1952 Samuel Lee (USA) 156·28
1956 Joaquin Capilla (Mex) 152·44
1960 Robert Webster (USA) 165·56
1964 Robert Webster (USA) 148·58
1968 Klaus Dibiasi (Ita) 164·18
1972 Klaus Dibiasi (Ita) 504·12
1976 Klaus Dibiasi (Ita) 600·51
1980 Falk Hoffman (GDR) 835·650

WOMEN

100 metres freestyle
1912 Fanny Durack (Aus) 1:22·2
1920 Ethelda Bleibtrey (USA) 1:13·6
1924 Ethel Lackie (USA) 1:12·4
1928 Albina Osipowich (USA) 1:11·0
1932 Helene Madison (USA) 1:06·8
1936 Rie Mastenbroek (Hol) 1:05·9
1948 Greta Andersen (Den) 1:06·3
1952 Katalin Szöke (Hun) 1:06·8
1956 Dawn Fraser (Aus) 1:02·0
1960 Dawn Fraser (Aus) 1:01·2
1964 Dawn Fraser (Aus) 59·5
1968 Jan Henne (USA) 1:00·0
1972 Sandra Neilson (USA) 58·59
1976 Kornelia Ender (GDR) 55·65
1980 Barbara Krause (GDR) 54·79

200 metres freestyle
1912–1964 Not held
1968 Debbie Meyer (USA) 2:10·5
1972 Shane Gould (Aus) 2:03·56
1976 Kornelia Ender (GDR) 1:59·26
1980 Barbara Krause (GDR) 1:58·33

400 metres freestyle
1912 Not held
1920 Ethelda Bleibtrey (USA) 4:34·0*
1924 Martha Norelius (USA) 6:02·2
1928 Martha Norelius (USA) 5:42·8
1932 Helene Madison (USA) 5:28·5
1936 Rie Mastenbroek (Hol) 5:26·4
1948 Ann Curtis (USA) 5:17·8
1952 Valeria Gyenge (Hun) 5:12·1
1956 Lorraine Crapp (Aus) 4:54·6
1960 Christine von Saltza (USA) 4:50·6
1964 Virginia Duenkel (USA) 4:43·3
1968 Debbie Meyer (USA) 4:31·8
1972 Shane Gould (Aus) 4:19·04
1976 Petra Thuemer (GDR) 4:09·89
1980 Ines Diers (GDR) 4:08·76
* 300 metres

800 metres freestyle
1912–64 Not held
1968 Debbie Meyer (USA) 9:24·0
1972 Keena Rothhammer (USA) 8:53·68
1976 Petra Thuemer (GDR) 8:37·14
1980 Michelle Ford (Aus) 8:28·90

100 metres backstroke
1912–20 Not held
1924 Sybil Bauer (USA) 1:23·2
1928 Maria Braun (Hol) 1:22·0
1932 Eleanor Holm (USA) 1:19·4
1936 Dina Senff (Hol) 1:18·9
1948 Karen Harup (Den) 1:14·4
1952 Joan Harrison (Saf) 1:14·3
1956 Judy Grinham (GB) 1:12·9
1960 Lynn Burke (USA) 1:09·3
1964 Cathy Ferguson (USA) 1:07·7
1968 Kaye Hall (USA) 1:06·2
1972 Melissa Belote (USA) 1:05·78
1976 Ulrike Richter (GDR) 1:01·83
1980 Rica Reinisch (GDR) 1:00·86

200 metres backstroke
1912–64 Not held
1968 Lillian Watson (USA) 2:24·8
1972 Melissa Belote (USA) 2:19·19
1976 Ulrike Richter (GDR) 2:13·43
1980 Rica Reinisch (GDR) 2:11·77

100 metres butterfly
1912–52 Not held
1956 Shelley Mann (USA) 1:11·0
1960 Carolyn Schuler (USA) 1:09·5
1964 Sharon Stouder (USA) 1:04·7
1968 Lynette McClements (USA) 1:05·5
1972 Mayumi Aoki (Jap) 1:03·34
1976 Kornelia Ender (GDR) 1:00·13
1980 Caren Metschuck (GDR) 1:00·42

200 metres butterfly
1912–64 Not held
1968 Ada Kok (Hol) 2:24·7
1972 Karen Moe (USA) 2:15·57
1976 Andrea Pollack (GDR) 2:11·41
1980 Ines Geissler (GDR) 2:10·44

100 metres breaststroke
1912–64 Not held
1968 Djurdica Bjedov (Yug) 1:15·8
1972 Catherine Carr (USA) 1:13·58
1976 Hannelore Anke (GDR) 1:11·16
1980 Ute Geweniger (GDR) 1:10·22

200 metres breaststroke
1912–20 Not held

1924 Lucy Morton (GB) 3:33·2
1928 Hilde Schrader (Ger) 3:12·6
1932 Clare Dennis (Aus) 3:06·3
1936 Hideko Maehata (Jap) 3:03·6
1948 Petronella van Vliet (Hol) 2:57·2
1952 Eva Székely (Hun) 2:51·7
1956 Ursula Happe (Ger) 2:53·1
1960 Anita Lonsborough (GB) 2:49·5
1964 Galina Prozumenshchikova (USSR) 2:46·4
1968 Sharon Wichman (USA) 2:44·4
1972 Beverley Whitfield (Aus) 2:41·71
1976 Marina Koshevaia (USSR) 2:33·35
1980 Lina Kachushite (USSR) 2:29·54

200 metres individual medley
1912–64 Not held
1968 Claudia Kolb (USA) 2:24·7
1972 Shane Gould (Aus) 2:23·07
1976–80 Not held

400 metres individual medley
1912–1960 Not held
1964 Donna de Varona (USA) 5:18·7
1968 Claudia Kolb (USA) 5:08·5
1972 Gail Neall (Aus) 5:02·97
1976 Ulrike Tauber (GDR) 4:42·77
1980 Petra Schneider (GDR) 4:36·29

4 × 100 metres freestyle relay
1912 GB 5:52·8
1920 USA 5:11·6
1924 USA 4:58·8
1928 USA 4:47·6
1932 USA 4:38·0
1936 Holland 4:36·0
1948 USA 4:29·2
1952 Hungary 4:24·4
1956 Australia 4:17·1
1960 USA 4:08·9
1964 USA 4:03·8
1968 USA 4:02·5
1972 USA 3:55·19
1976 USA 3:44·82
1980 GDR 3:42·71

4 × 100 metres medley relay
1912–56 Not held
1960 USA 4:41·1
1964 USA 4:33·9
1968 USA 4:28·3
1972 USA 4:20·75
1976 GDR 4:07·95
1980 GDR 4:06·67

Springboard diving
1912 Not held
1920 Aileen Riggin (USA) 539·9
1924 Elizabeth Becker (USA) 474·50
1928 Helen Meany (USA) 78·62
1932 Georgia Coleman (USA) 87·52
1936 Marjorie Gestring (USA) 89·27
1948 Victoria Draves (USA) 108·74
1952 Patricia McCormick (USA) 147·30
1956 Patricia McCormick (USA) 142·36
1960 Ingrid Krämer (Ger) 155·81
1964 Ingrid Engel (née Krämer) (Ger) 145·00
1968 Sue Gossick (USA) 150·77
1972 Micki King (USA) 450·03
1976 Jennifer Chandler (USA) 506·19
1980 Irina Kalinina (USSR) 725·910

Platform diving (highboard)
1912 Greta Johanasson (Swe) 39·9
1920 Stefani Fryland-Clausen (Den) 34·6
1924 Caroline Smith (USA) 33·2
1928 Elizabeth Pinkston (USA) 31·60
1932 Dorothy Poynton (USA) 40·26
1936 Dorothy Poynton (USA) 33·93
1948 Victoria Draves (USA) 68·87
1952 Patricia McCormick (USA) 79·37
1956 Patricia McCormick (USA) 84·85
1960 Ingrid Krämer (Ger) 91·28
1964 Lesley Bush (USA) 99·80
1968 Milena Duchková (Cz) 109·59
1972 Ulrika Knape (Swe) 390·00
1976 Elena Vaytsekhovskaya (USSR) 406·59
1980 Martina Jaschke (GDR) 596·250

EUROPEAN CUP
Competitions for European nations' teams for both men and women were first held in 1969. In December 1980 the events were held in a 25-metre pool, as compared to the usual 50-metre pools used in the summer months.

MEN
1969 GDR
1971 USSR
1973 GDR
1975 USSR
1976 USSR
1979 USSR
1980 USSR
1981 USSR
1982 USSR

WOMEN
1969 GDR
1971 GDR
1973 GDR
1975 GDR
1976 USSR
1979 GDR
1980 GDR
1981 GDR
1982 GDR

LIKE A FISH
Though human speed in the water has increased tremendously in the last few decades, it is still far from equalling that of other inhabitants of the water. A number of fish have been attributed with speeds in excess of 64 km/h (40 mph) and the sailfish is reputed to have exceeded 100 km/h (62 mph). The fastest reached by a human is 7·98 km/h (4·96 mph) by Robin Leamy (USA) when he swam a length of 50 m (54·6 yd) in 22·54 sec at Milwaukee in August 1981.

The closest finish in any major championship race was in the 400 m individual medley event at the Olympic Games in Munich, on 30 August 1972. The Swede, Gunnar Larsson was given the verdict over Tim McKee (USA) with the electric timing showing a difference of two-thousandth of a second, 4 min 31·981 sec to 4 min 31·983 sec. It has been calculated that this margin of about 3 mm represents the length grown by a fingernail over a period of three weeks. However, even this minute margin was not the ultimate in judging a swimmer's fate, as in the 1964 Games at Tokyo, Hans-Joachim Klein (Ger) was awarded the bronze medal because the timing equipment had shown that he was one-thousandth of a second ahead of Gary Ilman (USA) in the 100 m freestyle event. The Munich incident led to a change in the rules so that now times and placings are determined to one-hundredths only, and swimmers with the same times under those conditions are credited with dead-heating.

Mark Spitz, the only man in any sport to win seven gold medals at one Olympic Games, when at Munich in 1972 he also picked up a world record plaque in each of the events. Four years earlier, at Mexico City, he had been disappointed to gain only two golds and a bronze.

RECORD-BREAKER EXTRAORDINARY

One of the most remarkable swimmers in history is Mark Spitz (USA) who won an unprecedented seven gold medals in the 1972 Games in Munich, a feat that will probably never be equalled. His total of nine Olympic firsts has only been bettered by one sportsman or woman in history—athlete Ray Ewry in the early 1900s. His total of world records, 26, has only been beaten by swimmers from the era before the modern standardisation of distances and pool lengths. Oddly enough his first world record in June 1967 was at the 400 m freestyle event, whereas he achieved his fame at shorter distances. His Olympic triumphs were in the individual 100 m and 200 m freestyle and butterfly races, and 4 × 100 m and 4 × 200 m freestyle and 4 × 100 m medley relays.

Kornelia Ender (GDR) holds the modern record for most world records by a woman with 23 between 1973 and 1976. After the Montreal Games she married countryman Roland Matthes, a superlative backstroke swimmer, who himself won seven Olympic medals, including four golds. With his 18 marks they now have a family total of 41 world records.

Along with these current stars one must mention the Danish girl, Ragnhild Hveger, who, under the rules and conditions then in force, set an all-time total of 42 individual world records between 1936 and 1942. Known as 'The Golden Torpedo' she set marks over 18 different events. She was a virtual certainty to win at the 1940 Games, but, of course, war intervened. Retiring in 1945, she made a comeback for the 1952 Games and placed fifth in the 400 m freestyle.

Duncan Goodhew improved on his seventh place in the 100 m breast-stroke four years previously to win Britain's only swimming gold medal in the 1980 Olympic Games. In national championships he won the 100 m/200 m breaststroke double on five occasions from 1976 to 1980.

The biggest swimming pool in the world is at Casablanca, Morocco the 480 m (525 yd) long and 75 m (82 yd) wide sea-water Orthlieb Pool. In 1925 the Fleishhacker Pool in San Francisco was opened as the largest heated-water enclosed swimming pool in the world, measuring 308·8 m (333·3 yd) by 46 m (50 yd), but it is no longer in use. The largest is now at Osaka, Japan where there is room for 13 614 spectators. The largest in Great Britain is the Royal Commonwealth Pool in Edinburgh, opened in 1970. The pool at Earl's Court, London, opened in 1937 but no longer used, is 59·50 m (65 yd) long and 29 m (32 yd) wide, and could accommodate an audience of 12 000.

BRITISH CHAMPIONSHIPS: The championships have been under the auspices of the Amateur Swimming Association (ASA) since 1886, but the first national title was organised by the ASA's predecessor, the Metropolitan Swimming Association, in 1869. This was over 1 mile, and was originally contested in the River Thames. Jack Hatfield won a record 40 individual titles from 1912 to 1931, and that total would undoubtedly have been greater but for the cessation of competition from 1915 to 1919, due to war. The record for a woman is 21 by Sharon Davies between 1976 and 1980.

CHANNEL SWIMMING

One of the greatest challenges in long distance swimming is the English Channel, 'only' 33·8 km (21 miles) wide but, due to tides, temperatures and weather conditions, a tremendous test of strength and ability. The first man to swim it, Capt Matthew Webb (GB), in August 1875 swam a distance of 61 km (38 miles), indicating the problems involved. Though Webb is acknowledged officially as being the first, there is good evidence that Jean-Marie Saletti, a Frenchman held in a British prison hulk off Dover in 1815, slipped over the side and swam to Boulogne and freedom.

The first woman to succeed was Gertrude Ederle (USA) in August 1926. She has another claim to fame as the youngest person in a non-mechanical sport to have set a world record, when she broke the 880 yd freestyle mark in 1919, at the age of 12 yr 298 days. The first British girl to swim the Channel was Mercedes Gleitze, who succeeded at her eighth attempt in October 1927, but was not given the credit for 53 years, as it was always assumed, mistakenly, that she was German. In 1981 Mercedes, then Mrs Carey, received her rightful recognition.

To the end of 1982 there have been 386 successful crossings by some 242 swimmers, although there have been about 2500 attempts recorded. It has been estimated that in a crossing of 13 hr duration the swimmer makes about 51 000 strokes.

The youngest conqueror of the Channel has been Marcus Hooper (GB), aged 12 yr 53 days when he made it in 1974, and the oldest is Ashby Harper of Albuquerque, USA who was 65 yr 332 days old when he swam from Dover to Cap Blanc Nez on 28 Aug 1982. The youngest and oldest women have been respectively Abla Adel Khairi (Egy) at 13 yr 326 days in 1974, and Stella Taylor (GB) who was 45 yr 350 days in 1975. As long distance swimming seems one of the few areas in sport where women are equal—if not actually superior—to men, it is no surprise to find that the record time for the swim across the Channel is held by Penny Dean (USA) with 7 hr 40 min, from England to France, in July 1978. Even more outstanding is the double crossing record of 18 hr 55 min by the pretty Canadian, Cindy Nicholas, in August 1982, which was over 10 hours faster than the previous male best. That mark had been held by Jon Erikson (USA), and he answered the challenge with the first ever triple crossing, in 38 hr 27 min, in August 1981. For a number of years there had been a rivalry between an Australian businessman, Des Renford, and a British nutritionist, Mike

Twenty-year-old University of Florida student Tracy Caulkins has won more US swimming titles than any other swimmer in history. Her total currently stands at 46 indoor and outdoor championships. She won five gold medals in the 1978 world championships.

Read, for the greatest number of successful crossings. Both tied at 19 in August 1980, but Read has now gone well clear with 25 to the end of 1982, and has the title of 'King of the Channel'. Cindy Nicholas holds the woman's best of 15 crossings.

The Channel 'season' lasts for about four months in the summer, and the extremes of success have occurred on 6 June, by Dorothy Perkins (GB) in 1961, and 28 October by Mike Read (GB) in 1979.

One cannot end this section without a mention of perhaps the most courageous of Channel swimmers, Henry Sullivan, from Massachusetts. In August 1923 he became the third person to make the crossing, from England to France, but it took him 26 hr 50 min, and due to the perversity of the tides he swam an estimated 90 km (56 miles) in all.

RECORDS (As at 31 May 1983)

MEN

Event	World			Commonwealth			British		
Freestyle	min sec			min sec			min sec		
100 metres	49·36	Rowdy Gaines (USA)	1981	51·09	Neil Brooks (Aus)	1982	51·69	David Lowe	1982
200 metres	1 48·93	Rowdy Gaines (USA)	1982	1 50·27	Peter Szmidt (Can)	1980	1 51·52	Andrew Astbury	1982
400 metres	3 48·32	Vladimir Salnikov (USSR)	1983	3 50·49	Peter Szmidt (Can)	1980	3 53·29	Andrew Astbury	1982
800 metres	7 52·83	Vladimir Salnikov (USSR)	1982	8 02·91	Steve Holland (Aus)	1976	8 13·83	Simon Gray	1980
1500 metres	14 54·76	Vladimir Salnikov (USSR)	1983	15 04·66	Steve Holland (Aus)	1976	15 31·42	Simon Gray	1978
4 × 100 metres Relay	3 19·26	United States	1982	3 24·17	Australia	1982	3 26·98	England Team	1982
4 × 200 metres Relay	7 20·82	United States	1978	7 28·81	Australia	1982	7 30·00	England Team	1982
Breaststroke									
100 metres	1 02·53	Steve Lundquist (USA)	1982	1 02·82	Victor Davis (Can)	1982	1 02·93	Adrian Moorhouse	1982
200 metres	2 14·77	Victor Davis (Can)	1982	2 14·77	Victor Davis (Can)	1982	2 15·11	David Wilkie	1976
Backstroke									
100 metres	55·49	John Naber (USA)	1976	56·50	Mark Kerry (Aus)	1979	57·72	Gary Abraham	1980
200 metres	1 59·19	John Naber (USA)	1976	2 02·61	Mark Kerry (Aus)	1979	2 04·23	Douglas Campbell	1980
Butterfly									
100 metres	53·81	William Paulus (USA)	1981	54·71	Don Thompson (Can)	1982	55·42	Gary Abraham	1980
200 metres	1 58·01	Craig Beardsley (USA)	1981	2 00·21	Phil Hubble (Eng)	1981	2 00·21	Phil Hubble	1981
Medley									
200 metres	2 02·25	Alex Baumann (Can)	1982	2 02·25	Alex Baumann (Can)	1982	2 05·83	Robin Brew	1982
400 metres	4 19·78	Ricardo Prado (Bra)	1982	4 22·39	Alex Baumann (Can)	1981	4 27·09	Stephen Poulter	1982
4 × 100 metres Relay	3 40·84	United States	1982	3 45·70	Australia	1980	3 47·71	National Team	1980

WOMEN

Event	World			Commonwealth			British		
Freestyle									
100 metres	54·79	Barbara Krause (GDR)	1980	56·60	Carol Klimpel (Can)	1981	56·60	June Croft	1982
200 metres	1 58·23	Cynthia Woodhead (USA)	1979	1 59·74	June Croft (Eng)	1982	1 59·74	June Croft	1982
400 metres	4 06·28	Tracey Wickham (Aus)	1978	4 06·28	Tracey Wickham (Aus)	1978	4 11·67	Jackie Willmott	1982
800 metres	8 24·62	Tracey Wickham (Aus)	1978	8 24·62	Tracey Wickham (Aus)	1978	8 32·61	Jackie Willmott	1982
1500 metres	16 04·49	Kim Linehan (USA)	1979	16 06·63	Tracey Wickham (Aus)	1979	16 46·48	Jackie Willmott	1980
4 × 100 metres Relay	3 42·71	GDR	1980	3 47·86	Canada	1980	3 51·06	National Team	1981
Breaststroke									
100 metres	1 08·60	Ute Geweniger (GDR)	1981	1 10·99	Anne Ottenbrite (Can)	1982	1 11·05	Susan Brownsdon	1981
200 metres	2 28·36	Lina Kachushite (USSR)	1979	2 32·07	Anne Ottenbrite (Can)	1982	2 34·43	Susan Brownsdon	1981
Backstroke									
100 metres	1 00·86	Rica Reinisch (GDR)	1980	1 03·28	Nancy Garapick (Can)	1976	1 04·44	Beverley Rose	1982
200 metres	2 09·91	Cornelia Sirch (GDR)	1982	2 13·46	Lisa Forrest (Aus)	1982	2 17·66	Jane Admans	1981
Butterfly									
100 metres	57·93	Mary Meagher (USA)	1981	1 01·22	Lisa Curry (Aus)	1982	1 01·93	Ann Osgerby	1980
200 metres	2 05·96	Mary Meagher (USA)	1981	2 11·29	Michelle Ford (Aus)	1978	2 13·91	Ann Osgerby	1982
Medley									
200 metres	2 11·73	Ute Geweniger (GDR)	1981	2 16·94	Lisa Curry (Aus)	1982	2 17·31	Sharron Davies	1980
400 metres	4 36·10	Petra Schneider (GDR)	1982	4 46·83	Sharron Davies (Eng)	1980	4 46·83	Sharron Davies	1980
4 × 100 metres Relay	4 05·88	GDR	1982	4 12·24	England	1980	4 12·24	National Team	1980

WORLD SHORT-COURSE RECORDS (in 25 m pools)
(As at 31 May 1983)

MEN

Event	min sec	Name/Nationality	Year
50 m freestyle	22·09	Jorg Woithe (GDR)	1981
100 m freestyle	48·52	David McCagg (USA)	1980
200 m freestyle	1 44·50	Michael Gross (FRG)	1982
400 m freestyle	3 42·96	Vladimir Salnikov (USSR)	1982
800 m freestyle	7 38·90	Vladimir Salnikov (USSR)	1983
1500 m freestyle	14 37·60	Vladimir Salnikov (USSR)	1982
100 m breaststroke	1 01·00	Gerald Moerken (FRG)	1978
200 m breaststroke	2 11·54	Victor Davis (Can)	1982
100 m backstroke	54·55	Bengt Baron (Swe)	1981
200 m backstroke	1 58·24	Frank Baltrusch (GDR)	1981
100 m butterfly	53·17	Per Arvidsson (Swe)	1981
200 m butterfly	1 56·18	Michael Gross (FRG)	1982
200 m medley	1 59·84	Aleksandr Sidorenko (USSR)	1981
400 m medley	4 12·67	Alex Baumann (Can)	1981

WOMEN

Event	min sec	Name/Nationality	Year
50 m freestyle	25·28	Caren Metschuck (GDR)	1982
100 m freestyle	53·99	Birgit Meineke (GDR)	1983
200 m freestyle	1 56·35	Birgit Meineke (GDR)	1983
400 m freestyle	4 02·59	Cynthia Woodhead (USA)	1978
800 m freestyle	8 17·32	Petra Schneider (GDR)	1982
1500 m freestyle	15 43·31	Petra Schneider (GDR)	1982

100 m breaststroke	1 07·47	Tracy Caulkins (USA)	1981	100 m butterfly	Not as good as 50 m pool record		
200 m breaststroke	2 26·17	Ute Geweniger (GDR)	1982	200 m butterfly	2 05·65	Mary Meagher (USA)	1981
100 m backstrokè	59·97	Kristin Otto (GDR)	1983	200 m medley	2 10·60	Petra Schneider (GDR)	1982
200 m backstroke	2 07·74	Cornelia Sirch (GDR)	1983	400 m medley	4 33·44	Tracy Caulkins (USA)	1981

YOU OUGHT TO BE IN PICTURES

The ability to move well in water has been the key to a movie career for a number of champion swimmers. The first 'star' was Australian Annette Kellerman who made a number of silent films, and was the first woman to wear a one-piece costume. However, it was the 1924 and 1928 Olympic gold medallist, Johnny Weissmuller (USA), who became the first major box-office attraction from the swimming world, playing the role of Tarzan in a dozen films. His 1928 Olympic team-mate, Clarence Crabbe, who later won the 1932 400 m freestyle title, also went to Hollywood, where as 'Buster' Crabbe he was the hero in the long-running Buck Rogers and Flash Gordon serials.

Another 1932 Olympic champion, the glamorous Eleanor Holm (USA) made several movies, although she did not go to Hollywood until she was dropped from the 1936 team for disciplinary reasons. Perhaps the best known of these swimming stars was Esther Williams, American 100 m champion in 1939 and favourite for the soon-to-be-cancelled Olympics of 1940. Turning professional she created a new vogue in the cinema, the swimming musical, in which she was supreme throughout the 1940s. One of her co-stars was Fernando Lamas, who had been a national swimming champion in his native Argentina, and who she later married.

The Soviet diving star, Irina Kalinina won the Olympic gold medal in the 1980 springboard event to the three titles she had won in the 1975 and 1978 world championships. Surprisingly, despite competing in three championships, she has never won a European title.

167

Table Tennis

In 1879 some Cambridge University students indulged in a diversion in which they hit champagne corks to each other over a table, using cigar boxes as crude bats. From this humble beginning came a new sport. Rubber balls soon followed, but it was not until James Gibb, a former English world record-breaking runner, introduced a celluloid ball to the game that *gossima*, as it had previously been called, took the name of *ping pong*, after the noise the ball made when hit back and forth. The game thrived for a period, and in 1902 the Ping Pong Association was formed in Britain. But the monotony of play due to plain wooden bats soon led to a decline in interest until the 1920s when E. C. Goode fixed a studded rubber mat, from a chemist's shop, to his bat and proceeded to sweep all before him with the spin thus imparted to the ball. In April 1927 the English Table Tennis Association was founded and rules were standardised. In view of their current dominance it is noteworthy that organised table tennis in China dates from 1923.

WORLD CHAMPIONSHIPS: First held in December 1926 in London, originally as European championships, but later, retrospectively, upgraded. A men's team championship was instituted for a cup donated by Lady Swaythling, and a similar competition for women was included in 1934 for the Marcel Corbillon cup. Both are now held biennially. During the period to 1957, when they were held annually, Maria Mednyanszky (Hun) won a record 18 titles from 1927 to 1935, and Viktor Barna (Hun) set a male mark of 15, between 1929 and 1939, including a unique five singles championships. Romania's Angelica Rozeanu won six consecutive women's singles 1950–55. The most successful partnerships have been Viktor Barna and Miklos Szabados (Hun) with six wins in the men's doubles between 1929 and 1935, Maria Mednyanszky and Anna Sipos (Hun) also with six, consecutively, in the women's doubles 1930–35, and Szabados and Mednyanszky in the mixed doubles in which they won a record three titles together between 1930 and 1934. The 1939 meeting in Cairo, Egypt, was the first world championship for any sport to be held on the continent of Africa. A unique distinction was achieved by the 1929 singles champion, Fred Perry (GB), in that he later became the first person to achieve the Grand Slam of the major titles at Lawn Tennis.

	Men	Women
1927	Roland Jacobi (Hun)	Maria Mednyanszky (Hun)
1928	Zoltan Mechlovits (Hun)	Maria Mednyanszky (Hun)
1929	Fred Perry (GB)	Maria Mednyanszky (Hun)
1930	Viktor Barna (Hun)	Maria Mednyanszky (Hun)
1931	Miklos Szabados (Hun)	Maria Mednyanszky (Hun)
1932	Viktor Barna (Hun)	Anna Sipos (Hun)
1933	Viktor Barna (Hun)	Anna Sipos (Hun)
1934	Viktor Barna (Hun)	Marie Kettnerova (Cz)
1935	Viktor Barna (Hun)	Marie Kettnerova (Cz)
1936	Standa Kolar (Cz)	Ruth Aarons (USA)
1937	Richard Bergmann (Aut)	Vacant
1938	Bohumil Vana (Cz)	Trude Pritzi (Aut)
1939	Richard Bergmann (Aut)	Vlasha Depetrisova (Cz)
1947	Bohumil Vana (Cz)	Gizi Farkas (Hun)
1948	Richard Bergmann (Eng)	Gizi Farkas (Hun)
1949	Johnny Leach (Eng)	Gizi Farkas (Hun)
1950	Richard Bergmann (Eng)	Angelica Rozeanu (Rom)
1951	Johnny Leach (Eng)	Angelica Rozeanu (Rom)
1952	Hiroji Satoh (Jap)	Angelica Rozeanu (Rom)
1953	Ferenc Sido (Hun)	Angelica Rozeanu (Rom)
1954	Ichiro Ogimura (Jap)	Angelica Rozeanu (Rom)
1955	Toshiaki Tanaka (Jap)	Angelica Rozeanu (Rom)
1956	Ichiro Ogimura (Jap)	Timo Okawa (Jap)
1957	Toshiaki Tanaka (Jap)	Fujie Eguchi (Jap)
1959	Jung Kuo-tuan (Chn)	Kimiyo Matsuzaki (Jap)
1961	Chuang Tse-tung (Chn)	Chiu Chung-hui (Chn)
1963	Chuang Tse-tung (Chn)	Kimiyo Matsuzaki (Jap)
1965	Chuang Tse-tung (Chn)	Naoko Fukazu (Jap)
1967	Nobuhiko Hasegawa (Jap)	Sachiko Morisawa (Jap)
1969	Shigeo Ito (Jap)	Toshiko Kowada (Jap)
1971	Stellan Bengtsson (Swe)	Lin Hui-Ching (Chn)
1973	Hsi En-Ting (Chn)	Hu Yu-Lan (Chn)
1975	Istvan Jonyer (Hun)	Pak Yung-Sun (NK)
1977	Mitsuru Kohno (Jap)	Pak Yung-Sun (NK)
1979	Seiji Ono (Jap)	Ke Hsin-Ai (Chn)
1981	Guo Yue-Hua (Chn)	Ting Ling (Chn)
1983	Guo Yue-Hua (Chn)	Cao Yan-Hua (Chn)

	Venue	Men	Women
1927	London, UK	Hungary	—
1928	Stockholm, Sweden	Hungary	—
1929	Budapest, Hungary	Hungary	—
1930	Berlin, Germany	Hungary	—
1931	Budapest, Hungary	Hungary	—
1932	Prague, Czechoslovakia	Czechoslovakia	—
1933	Baden, Germany	Hungary	—
1934	Paris, France	Hungary	Germany
1935	London, UK	Hungary	Czechoslovakia
1936	Prague, Czechoslovakia	Austria	Czechoslovakia
1937	Baden, Germany	USA	USA
1938	London, UK	Hungary	Czechoslovakia
1939	Cairo, Egypt	Czechoslovakia	Germany
1947	Paris, France	Czechoslovakia	England
1948	London, UK	Czechoslovakia	England
1949	Stockholm, Sweden	Hungary	USA
1950	Budapest, Hungary	Czechoslovakia	Romania
1951	Vienna, Austria	Czechoslovakia	Romania
1952	Bombay, India	Hungary	Japan
1953	Budapest, Hungary	England	Romania
1954	London, UK	Japan	Japan
1955	Utrecht, Holland	Japan	Romania
1956	Tokyo, Japan	Japan	Romania
1957	Stockholm, Sweden	Japan	Japan
1959	Dortmund, Germany	Japan	Japan
1961	Peking, China	China	Japan
1963	Prague, Czechoslovakia	China	Japan
1965	Llubljana, Yugoslavia	China	China
1967	Stockholm, Sweden	Japan	Japan
1969	Munich, Germany	Japan	USSR
1971	Nagoya, Japan	China	Japan
1973	Sarajevo, Yugoslavia	Sweden	South Korea
1975	Calcutta, India	China	China
1977	Birmingham, UK	China	China
1979	Pyongyang, N. Korea	Hungary	China
1981	Novi Sad, Yugoslavia	China	China
1983	Tokyo, Japan	China	China

Mixed Doubles
1965	Koji Kimura & Masako Seki (Jap)
1967	Nobuhiko Hasegawa & Noriko Yamanaka (Jap)
1969	Nobuhiko Hasegawa & Yasuka Konno (Jap)
1971	Chang Shih-Lin & Lin Hui-Ching (Chn)
1973	Liang Ko-Liang & Li Li (Chn)
1975	Stanislav Gomozko & Anna Ferdman (USSR)
1977	Jacques Secretin & Claude Bergeret (Fra)
1979	Liang Ko-Liang & Ke Hsin-Ai (Chn)
1981	Xie Saike & Huang Junquin (Chn)
1983	Guo Yue-Hua & Ni Xialin (Chn)

Men's Doubles
1965	Chung Tse-tung & Hsu Yin-sheng (Chn)
1967	Hans Alser & Kjell Johansson (Swe)
1969	Hans Alser & Kjell Johansson (Swe)
1971	Istvan Jonyer & Tibor Klampar (Hun)
1973	Stellan Bengtsson & Kjell Johansson (Swe)
1975	Gabor Gergely & Istvan Jonyer (Hun)
1977	Chen-Shih Li & Liang Ko-Liang (Chn)
1979	Dragutin Surbek & Anton Stipancic (Yug)
1981	Cai Zhen-Hua & Li Zhen-Shi (Chn)
1983	Dragutin Surbek & Zoran Kalinic (Yug)

Women's Doubles
1965	Cheng Min-chih & Lin Hui-ching (Chn)
1967	Saeko Hirota & Sachiko Morisawa (Jap)
1969	Svetlana Grinberg & Zoya Rudnova (USSR)
1971	Cheng Min-Chih & Lin Hui-Ching (Chn)
1973	Maria Alexandru (Rom) & Miho Hamada (Jap)
1975	Maria Alexandru (Rom) & Shoko Takashima (Jap)
1977	Yong Ok Pak (NK) & Ying Yang (Chn)
1979	Zhang Li & Zhang Deijing (Chn)
1981	Cao Yan-Hua & Zhang Deijing (Chn)
1983	Shen Jianping & Dai Lili (Chn)

The 1981 world table tennis champion from China, Guo Yue-Hua, about to serve. He won the title after twice being runner-up to Japanese players in the previous championships in 1977 and 1979. To emphasise its strength, China became the first country to win all seven available titles in 1981.

SWAYTHLING AND CORBILLON CUPS: The world team championship for men has been won 12 times by Hungary, including five from 1927 to 1931. The championship for women's teams, the Corbillon cup, has been won on a record eight occasions by Japan, with China winning five consecutively, 1975–83. England has won the Swaythling cup once, in 1953, and the Corbillon cup twice in 1947 and 1948. The longest match ever recorded in major competition lasted 11 hours and took place between Austria and Romania in the Swaythling Cup final in 1936. In the preliminary rounds of the same competition a record was set in the game between Alex Ehrlich (Pol) and Farcas Paneth (Rom) when their opening rally lasted for 1 hr 58 min.

ENGLISH CHAMPIONSHIPS: Since the Open championships were first held in 1921 the most titles won has been 20 by the Hungarian-born Viktor Barna, comprising five singles, eight mixed and seven men's doubles between 1931 and 1953. Richard Bergman, who was born in Austria but like Barna later represented Great Britain, won a record six singles from 1939 to 1954. The women's record for most titles is held by Diane Rowe with 17, made up of 12 women's doubles, four mixed doubles and one singles championship. Seven of the doubles were with her twin sister Rosalind. The most women's singles victories is six by Maria Alexandru (Rom) from 1963 to 1974. In the English Closed championships, Jill Hammersley-Parker has won seven singles titles from 1973 to 1981.

In specially staged efforts players have achieved some exceptional exploits, such as the two young Americans who rallied for 8 hr 33 min in July 1978. Another American, Gary Fisher, standing to the side of the table totalled 5000 successive volleys with himself in 1979 using a bat in either hand, and taking nearly three-quarters of an hour. Even top class players get the bug, as when English international representatives Desmond Douglas and Nicky Jarvis set up a record of 162 consecutive hits in 60 sec at the aptly named Eccentric Club, London in December 1976. Douglas and Paul Day equalled that mark in March 1977. The record for women is 148 by Linda Howard and Melodi Ludi, at Blackpool in October 1977.

Jill Hammersley-Parker, who has been Britain's top woman singles player for many years, has regularly placed high on the European rankings.

Tennis

The game of Lawn Tennis evolved from the indoor game of Real (or Royal) Tennis, which itself originated as *Jeu de Paume* in French monasteries about the middle of the 11th century. There is a mention of 'Field tennis' in a magazine dated September 1793. In 1858 Major Harry Gem laid out a 'court' on the lawn of his friend, Augurio Perera in Edgbaston, Birmingham, and in 1872 founded the first club in Leamington Spa. Two years later Major Walter Wingfield patented and popularised a form of the game that he called *sphairistike*, or 'sticky' as it was soon nicknamed. Soon after his patent lapsed, in April 1877, the All England Croquet Club added the words Lawn Tennis to its name and held their first championships. The United States National Lawn Tennis Association (now the USLTA) was founded in 1881, and the English Lawn Tennis Association (LTA) followed in 1888. The International Lawn Tennis Federation was formed in Paris in March 1913.

WIMBLEDON CHAMPIONSHIPS: The All England championships, held at Wimbledon, London since 1877, is generally considered to be the most important tournament in the world. Until 1922 it was held on a Challenge Round basis with the winner playing the defending champion for the title. The greatest number of titles collected is 20 by Billie Jean King (USA) between 1961 and 1979, comprising six singles, ten women's doubles and four mixed doubles. The most by a male player is 13 by Lawrence Doherty (GB) with five singles, and a record eight men's doubles with his brother Reggie, from 1897 to 1905. The most doubles titles is 19 by Elizabeth Ryan (USA), who won 12 women's and seven mixed between 1912 and 1934. The most singles victories have been eight by Helen Wills-Moody (USA) from 1927 to 1938, and the most by a man, since the Challenge Round was abolished, is five by Bjorn Borg (Swe) 1976–80. In the early days of the tournament Charles Renshaw (GB) was champion seven times between 1881 and 1889, including six consecutively. The oldest person to win a title was Margaret Osborne-duPont (USA) aged 44 yr 4 months in the 1962 mixed doubles, while the oldest man was Gardner Mulloy (USA) aged 43 yr 7 months when part of the winning men's doubles in 1957. The oldest men's singles champion was Wentworth Gore (GB) in 1909 aged 41 yr 6 months, and the oldest women's singles champion was Charlotte Cooper-Sterry (GB) aged 37 yr 7 months in 1908. The oldest competitor has been Jean Borotra (Fra), who last played in 1964 aged 65 yr 10 months, just missing the record 36 appearances by Wentworth Gore (GB) between 1888 and 1927. Borotra subsequently played in the Veterans event until 1976. The oldest female player has been Agnes Tuckey (GB) who played in the mixed doubles with her son, Raymond, in 1932 at the age of 54 yr 11 months.

The first of tennis's female superstars Suzanne Lenglen was unbeaten at singles between 1916 and 1926, except for a forced retirement in the 1921 US championships. The French woman's other achievements include two Olympic gold medals.

The youngest champion was Lottie Dod (GB) aged only 15 yr 285 days when she won the singles in 1887. The youngest male has been Dennis Ralston (USA) aged 17 yr 340 days in the winning men's doubles in 1960, while the youngest male singles champion has been Wilfred Baddeley (GB) aged 19 yr 175 days in 1891. The youngest ever competitor is thought to be Mita Klima (Aut) who was reputed to be only 13 yr in 1907. The youngest of modern times has been Kathy Rinaldi (USA) aged 14 yr 91 days at the start of the 1981 championships, while the youngest seeded player was Andrea Jaeger (USA) at 15 yr 19 days for the 1980 tournament. The biggest single day crowd was 38 291 on 27 June 1979 and in 1981 there was a record for the whole championships of 358 250 spectators.

Suzanne Lenglen (Fra) was the first player to take all three titles available when she took the singles, women's doubles and mixed doubles in 1920. During her eight-year domination of Wimbledon from 1919 to 1926 she won six singles, six women's doubles and three mixed doubles. She was undefeated in singles, and in all lost only three of her 94 matches.

WIMBLEDON CHAMPIONS

	Men	Women			
1877	Spencer W. Gore (GB)	—	1894	Joshua Pim (GB)	Blanche Hillyard (GB)
1878	Frank Hadow (GB)	—	1895	Wilfred Baddeley (GB)	Charlotte Cooper (GB)
1879	Rev. John Hartley (GB)	—	1896	Harold Mahony (GB)	Charlotte Cooper (GB)
1880	Rev. John Hartley (GB)	—	1897	Reginald Doherty (GB)	Blanche Hillyard (GB)
1881	William Renshaw (GB)	—	1898	Reginald Doherty (GB)	Charlotte Cooper (GB)
1882	William Renshaw (GB)	—	1899	Reginald Doherty (GB)	Blanche Hillyard (GB)
1883	William Renshaw (GB)	—	1900	Reginald Doherty (GB)	Blanche Hillyard (GB)
1884	William Renshaw (GB)	Maud Watson (GB)	1901	Arthur W. Gore (GB)	Charlotte Sterry (née Cooper) (GB)
1885	William Renshaw (GB)	Maud Watson (GB)	1902	Laurence Doherty (GB)	Muriel Robb (GB)
1886	William Renshaw (GB)	Blanche Bingley (GB)	1903	Laurence Doherty (GB)	Dorothea Douglass (GB)
1887	Herbert Lawford (GB)	Lottie Dod (GB)	1904	Laurence Doherty (GB)	Dorothea Douglass (GB)
1888	Ernest Renshaw (GB)	Lottie Dod (GB)	1905	Laurence Doherty (GB)	May Sutton (USA)
1889	William Renshaw (GB)	Blanche Hillyard (née Bingley) (GB)	1906	Laurence Doherty (GB)	Dorothea Douglass (GB)
1890	Willoughby Hamilton (GB)	Helene Rice (GB-Ire)	1907	Norman Brookes (Aus)	May Sutton (USA)
1891	Wilfred Baddeley (GB)	Lottie Dod (GB)	1908	Arthur W. Gore (GB)	Charlotte Sterry (GB)
1892	Wilfred Baddeley (GB)	Lottie Dod (GB)	1909	Arthur W. Gore (GB)	Dora Boothby (GB)
1893	Joshua Pim (GB)	Lottie Dod (GB)	1910	Tony Wilding (NZ)	Dorothea Lambert Chambers (née Douglass) (GB)

Men	Women
1911 Tony Wilding (NZ)	Dorothea Lambert Chambers (GB)
1912 Tony Wilding (NZ)	Ethel Larcombe (GB)
1913 Tony Wilding (NZ)	Dorothea Lambert Chambers (GB)
1914 Norman Brookes (Aus)	Dorothea Lambert Chambers (GB)
1919 Gerald Patterson (Aus)	Suzanne Lenglen (Fra)
1920 Bill Tilden (USA)	Suzanne Lenglen (Fra)
1921 Bill Tilden (USA)	Suzanne Lenglen (Fra)
1922 Gerald Patterson (Aus)	Suzanne Lenglen (Fra)
1923 William Johnston (USA)	Suzanne Lenglen (Fra)
1924 Jean Borotra (Fra)	Kathleen McKane (GB)
1925 René Lacoste (Fra)	Suzanne Lenglen (Fra)
1926 Jean Borotra (Fra)	Kathleen Godfree (née McKane) (GB)
1927 Henri Cochet (Fra)	Helen Wills (USA)
1928 René Lacoste (Fra)	Helen Wills (USA)
1929 Henri Cochet (Fra)	Helen Wills (USA)
1930 Bill Tilden (USA)	Helen Wills Moody (USA)
1931 Sidney Wood (USA)	Cilly Aussem (Ger)
1932 Ellsworth Vines (USA)	Helen Wills Moody (USA)
1933 Jack Crawford (Aus)	Helen Wills Moody (USA)
1934 Fred Perry (GB)	Dorothy Round (GB)
1935 Fred Perry (GB)	Helen Wills Moody (USA)
1936 Fred Perry (GB)	Helen Jacobs (USA)
1937 Donald Budge (USA)	Dorothy Round (GB)
1938 Donald Budge (USA)	Helen Wills Moody (USA)
1939 Bobby Riggs (USA)	Alice Marble (USA)
1946 Yvon Petra (Fra)	Pauline Betz (USA)
1947 Jack Kramer (USA)	Margaret Osborne (USA)
1948 Bob Falkenburg (USA)	Louise Brough (USA)
1949 Ted Schroeder (USA)	Louise Brough (USA)
1950 Budge Patty (USA)	Louise Brough (USA)
1951 Dick Savitt (USA)	Doris Hart (USA)
1952 Frank Sedgman (Aus)	Maureen Connolly (USA)
1953 Vic Seixas (USA)	Maureen Connolly (USA)
1954 Jaroslav Drobny (Cz)	Maureen Connolly (USA)
1955 Tony Trabert (USA)	Louise Brough (USA)
1956 Lew Hoad (Aus)	Shirley Fry (USA)
1957 Lew Hoad (Aus)	Althea Gibson (USA)
1958 Ashley Cooper (Aus)	Althea Gibson (USA)
1959 Alex Olmedo (USA)	Maria Bueno (Bra)
1960 Neale Fraser (Aus)	Maria Bueno (Bra)
1961 Rod Laver (Aus)	Angela Mortimer (GB)
1962 Rod Laver (Aus)	Karen Susman (USA)
1963 Chuck McKinley (USA)	Margaret Smith (Aus)
1964 Roy Emerson (Aus)	Maria Bueno (Bra)
1965 Roy Emerson (Aus)	Margaret Smith (Aus)
1966 Manuel Santana (Spa)	Billie Jean King (USA)
1967 John Newcombe (Aus)	Billie Jean King (USA)
1968 Rod Laver (Aus)	Billie Jean King (USA)
1969 Rod Laver (Aus)	Ann Jones (GB)
1970 John Newcombe (Aus)	Margaret Smith-Court (Aus)
1971 John Newcombe (Aus)	Evonne Goolagong (Aus)
1972 Stan Smith (USA)	Billie Jean King (USA)
1973 Jan Kodes (Cz)	Billie Jean King (USA)
1974 Jimmy Connors (USA)	Chris Evert (USA)
1975 Arthur Ashe (USA)	Billie Jean King (USA)
1976 Bjorn Borg (Swe)	Chris Evert (USA)
1977 Bjorn Borg (Swe)	Virginia Wade (GB)
1978 Bjorn Borg (Swe)	Martina Navratilova (Cz)
1979 Bjorn Borg (Swe)	Martina Navratilova (Cz)
1980 Bjorn Borg (Swe)	Evonne Goolagong-Cawley (Aus)
1981 John McEnroe (USA)	Chris Evert-Lloyd (USA)
1982 Jimmy Connors (USA)	Martina Navratilova (Cz)

Men's Doubles
1879 L. R. Erskine & H. F. Lawford (GB)
1880 William & Ernest Renshaw (GB)
1881 William & Ernest Renshaw (GB)
1882 J. T. Hartley & R. T. Richardson (GB)
1883 C. W. Grinstead & C. E. Welldon (GB)
1884 William & Ernest Renshaw (GB)
1885 William & Ernest Renshaw (GB)
1886 William & Ernest Renshaw (GB)
1887 Herbert Wilberforce & Patrick Bowes-Lyon (GB)
1888 William & Ernest Renshaw (GB)
1889 William & Ernest Renshaw (GB)
1890 Joshua Pim & Frank Stoker (GB)
1891 Wilfred & Herbert Baddeley (GB)
1892 Ernest Lewis & Harry Barlow (GB)
1893 Joshua Pim & Frank Stoker (GB)

1894 Wilfred & Herbert Baddeley (GB)
1895 Wilfred & Herbert Baddeley (GB)
1896 Wilfred & Herbert Baddeley (GB)
1897 Reginald & Lawrence Doherty (GB)
1898 Reginald & Lawrence Doherty (GB)
1899 Reginald & Lawrence Doherty (GB)
1900 Reginald & Lawrence Doherty (GB)
1901 Reginald & Lawrence Doherty (GB)
1902 Sidney Smith & Frank Riseley (GB)
1903 Reginald & Lawrence Doherty (GB)
1904 Reginald & Lawrence Doherty (GB)
1905 Reginald & Lawrence Doherty (GB)
1906 Sidney Smith & Frank Riseley (GB)
1907 Norman Brookes (Aus) & Anthony Wilding (NZ)
1908 Anthony Wilding (NZ) & Josiah Ritchie (GB)
1909 Arthur Gore & Roper Barrrett (GB)
1910 Anthony Wilding (NZ) & Josiah Ritchie (GB)
1911 Andre Gobert & Max Decugis (Fra)
1912 Charles Dixon & Roper Barrett (GB)
1913 Charles Dixon & Roper Barrett (GB)
1914 Norman Brookes (Aus) & Anthony Wilding (NZ)
1915–18 Not held
1919 Ronald Thomas & Pat O'Hara Wood (Aus)
1920 Richard Williams & Charles Garland (USA)
1921 Randolph Lycett & Max Woosnam (GB)
1922 James Anderson (Aus) & Randolph Lycett (GB)
1923 Leslie Godfree & Randolph Lycett (GB)
1924 Frank Hunter & Vincent Richards (USA)
1925 Jean Borotra & Rene Lacoste (Fra)
1926 Jacques Brugnon & Henri Cochet (Fra)
1927 Frank Hunter & William Tilden (USA)
1928 Jacques Brugnon & Henri Cochet (Fra)
1929 William Allison & John Van Ryn (USA)
1930 William Allison & John Van Ryn (USA)
1931 George Lott & John Van Ryn (USA)
1932 Jean Borotra & Jacques Brugnon (Fra)
1933 Jean Borotra & Jacques Brugnon (Fra)
1934 George Lott & Lester Stoefen (USA)
1935 Jack Crawford (USA) & Adrian Quist (Aus)
1936 Pat Hughes & Raymond Tuckey (GB)
1937 Don Budge & Gene Mako (USA)
1938 Don Budge & Gene Mako (USA)
1939 Ellwood Cooke & Bobby Riggs (USA)
1940–45 Not held
1946 Tom Brown & Jack Kramer (USA)
1947 Bob Falkenburg & Jack Kramer (USA)
1948 John Bromwich & Frank Sedgman (Aus)
1949 Ricardo Gonzales & Frank Parker (USA)
1950 John Bromwich & Adrian Quist (Aus)
1951 Ken McGregor & Frank Sedgman (Aus)
1952 Ken McGregor & Frank Sedgman (Aus)
1953 Lew Hoad & Ken Rosewall (Aus)
1954 Rex Hartwig & Mervyn Rose (Aus)
1955 Rex Hartwig & Lew Hoad (Aus)
1956 Lew Hoad & Ken Rosewall (Aus)
1957 Budge Patty & Gardnar Mulloy (USA)
1958 Sven Davidson & Ulf Schmidt (Swe)
1959 Roy Emerson & Neale Fraser (Aus)
1960 Rafael Osuna (Mex) & Dennis Ralston (USA)
1961 Roy Emerson & Neale Fraser (Aus)
1962 Bob Hewitt & Fred Stolle (Aus)
1963 Rafael Osuna & Antonio Palafox (Mex)
1964 Bob Hewitt & Fred Stolle (Aus)
1965 John Newcombe & Tony Roche (Aus)
1966 Ken Fletcher & John Newcombe (Aus)
1967 Bob Hewitt & Frew McMillan (Saf)
1968 John Newcombe & Tony Roche (Aus)
1969 John Newcombe & Tony Roche (Aus)
1970 John Newcombe & Tony Roche (Aus)
1971 Roy Emerson & Rod Laver (Aus)
1972 Bob Hewitt & Frew McMillan (Saf)
1973 Jimmy Connors (USA) & Ilie Nastase (Rom)
1974 John Newcombe & Tony Roche (Aus)
1975 Vitas Gerulaitis & Sandy Mayer (USA)
1976 Brian Gottfried (USA) & Raul Ramirez (Mex)
1977 Ross Case & Geoff Masters (Aus)
1978 Bob Hewitt & Frew McMillan (Saf)
1979 John McEnroe & Peter Fleming (USA)
1980 Peter McNamara & Paul McNamee (Aus)
1981 John McEnroe & Peter Fleming (USA)
1982 Peter McNamara & Paul McNamee (Aus)

Women's Doubles

1913 Winifred McNair & Dora Boothby (GB)
1914 Agnes Morton (GB) & Elizabeth Ryan (USA)
1915–18 Not held
1919 Suzanne Lenglen (Fra) & Elizabeth Ryan (USA)
1920 Suzanne Lenglen (Fra) & Elizabeth Ryan (USA)
1921 Suzanne Lenglen (Fra) & Elizabeth Ryan (USA)
1922 Suzanne Lenglen (Fra) & Elizabeth Ryan (USA)
1923 Suzanne Lenglen (Fra) & Elizabeth Ryan (USA)
1924 Hazel Wightman & Helen Wills (USA)
1925 Suzanne Lenglen (Fra) & Elizabeth Ryan (USA)
1926 Mary Browne & Elizabeth Ryan (USA)
1927 Helen Wills & Elizabeth Ryan (USA)
1928 Peggy Saunders & Phyllis Watson (GB)
1929 Peggy Saunders-Michell & Phyllis Watson (GB)
1930 Helen Wills-Moody & Elizabeth Ryan (USA)
1931 Phyllis Mudford & Dorothy Barron (GB)
1932 Doris Metaxa (Fra) & Josane Sigart (Bel)
1933 Simone Mathieu (Fra) & Elizabeth Ryan
1934 Simone Mathieu (Fra) & Elizabeth Ryan
1935 Freda James & Kay Stammers
1936 Freda James & Kay Stammers
1937 Simone Mathieu (Fra) & Billie Yorke (GB)
1938 Sarah Fabyan & Alice Marble (USA)
1939 Sarah Fabyan & Alice Marble (USA)
1940–45 **Not held**
1946 Louise Brough & Margaret Osborne (USA)
1947 Pat Todd & Doris Hart (USA)
1948 Louise Brough & Margaret Osborne-duPont (USA)
1949 Louise Brough & Margaret Osborne-duPont (USA)
1950 Louise Brough & Margaret Osborne-duPont (USA)
1951 Doris Hart & Shirley Fry (USA)
1952 Doris Hart & Shirley Fry (USA)
1953 Doris Hart & Shirley Fry (USA)
1954 Louise Brough & Margaret Osborne-duPont (USA)
1955 Angela Mortimer & Anne Shilcock (GB)
1956 Angela Buxton (GB) & Althea Gibson (USA)
1957 Althea Gibson & Darlene Hard (USA)
1958 Maria Bueno (Bra) & Althea Gibson (USA)
1959 Jean Arth & Darlene Hard (USA)
1960 Maria Bueno (Bra) & Darlene Hard (USA)
1961 Karen Hantze & Billie Jean Moffitt (USA)
1962 Karen Hantze-Susman & Billie Jean Moffitt (USA)
1963 Maria Bueno (Bra) & Darlene Hard (USA)
1964 Margaret Smith & Lesley Turner (Aus)
1965 Maria Bueno (Bra) & Billie Jean Moffitt (USA)
1966 Maria Bueno (Bra) & Nancy Richey (USA)
1967 Rosemary Casals & Billie Jean Moffitt-King (USA)
1968 Billie Jean King & Rosemary Casals (USA)
1969 Margaret Smith-Court & Judy Tegart (Aus)
1970 Billie Jean King & Rosemary Casals (USA)
1971 Billie Jean King & Rosemary Casals (USA)
1972 Billie Jean King (USA) & Betty Stove (Hol)
1973 Billie Jean King & Rosemary Casals (USA)
1974 Evonne Goolagong (Aus) & Peggy Michel (USA)
1975 Ann Kiyomura (USA) & Kazuko Sawamatsu (Jap)
1976 Chris Evert (USA) & Martina Navratilova (Cz)
1977 Helen Cawley (Aus) & Joanne Russell (USA)
1978 Kerry Reid & Wendy Turnbull (Aus)
1979 Billie Jean King (USA) & Martina Navratilova (Cz)
1980 Kathy Jordan & Anne Smith (USA)
1981 Martina Navratilova (Cz) & Pam Shriver (USA)
1982 Martina Navratilova & Pam Shriver (USA)

Mixed Doubles

1913 Agnes Tuckey & Hope Crisp (GB)
1914 Ethel Larcombe & James Parke (GB)
1915–18 Not held
1919 Elizabeth Ryan (USA) & Randolph Lycett (GB)
1920 Suzanne Lenglen (Fra) & Gerald Patterson (Aus)
1921 Elizabeth Ryan (USA) & Randolph Lycett (GB)
1922 Suzanne Lenglen (Fra) & Pat O'Hara Wood (USA)
1923 Elizabeth Ryan (USA) & Randolph Lycett (GB)
1924 Kitty McKane & Brian Gilbert (GB)
1925 Suzanne Lenglen & Jean Borotra (Fra)
1926 Kitty McKane-Godfree & Leslie Godfree (GB)
1927 Elizabeth Ryan & Frank Hunter (USA)
1928 Elizabeth Ryon (USA) & Pat Spence (Saf)
1929 Helen Wills & Frank Hunter (USA)
1930 Elizabeth Ryan (USA) & Jack Crawford (Aus)

1931 Anna Harper & George Lott (USA)
1932 Elizabeth Ryan (USA) & Enrique Maier (Spa)
1933 Hilda Krahwinkel & Gottfried von Cramm (Ger)
1934 Dorothy Round (GB) & Ryuki Miki (Jap)
1935 Dorothy Round & Fred Perry (GB)
1936 Dorothy Round & Fred Perry (GB)
1937 Alice Marble & Don Budge (USA)
1938 Alice Marble & Don Budge (USA)
1939 Alice Marble & Bobby Riggs (USA)
1940–45 Not held
1946 Louise Brough & Tom Brown (USA)
1947 Louise Brough (USA) & John Bromwich (Aus)
1948 Louise Brough (USA) & John Bromwich (Aus)
1949 Sheila Summers & Eric Sturgess (Saf)
1950 Louise Brough (USA) & Eric Sturgess (Saf)
1951 Doris Hart (USA) & Frank Sedgman (Aus)
1952 Doris Hart (USA) & Frank Sedgman (Aus)
1953 Doris Hart & Vic Seixas (USA)
1954 Doris Hart & Vic Seixas (USA)
1955 Doris Hart & Vic Seixas (USA)
1956 Shirley Fry & Vic Seixas (USA)
1957 Darlene Hard (USA) & Mervyn Rose (Aus)
1958 Loraine Coghlan & Bob Howe (Aus)
1959 Darlene Hard (USA) & Rod Laver (Aus)
1960 Darlene Hard (USA) & Rod Laver (Aus)
1961 Lesley Turner & Fred Stolle (Aus)
1962 Margaret Osborne-duPont (USA) & Neale Fraser (Aus)
1963 Margaret Smith & Ken Fletcher (Aus)
1964 Lesley Turner & Fred Stolle (Aus)
1965 Margaret Smith & Ken Fletcher (Aus)
1966 Margaret Smith & Ken Fletcher (Aus)
1967 Billie Jean Moffitt-King (USA) & Owen Davidson (Aus)
1968 Margaret Smith-Court & Ken Fletcher (Aus)
1969 Ann Jones (GB) & Fred Stolle (Aus)
1970 Rosemary Casals (USA) & Ilie Nastase (Rom)
1971 Billie Jean King (USA) & Owen Davidson (Aus)
1972 Rosemary Casals (USA) & Ilie Nastase (Rom)
1973 Billie Jean King (USA) & Owen Davidson (Aus)
1974 Billie Jean King (USA) & Owen Davidson (Aus)
1975 Margaret Smith-Court (Aus) & Marty Reissen (USA)

The most dominant female player in tennis today, Martina Navratil-ova. The Czech-born American, here winning her third Wimbledon title in 1982, is the richest sportswoman in the world.

1976 Françoise Durr (Fra) & Tony Roche (Aus)
1977 Greer Stevens & Bob Hewitt (Saf)
1978 Betty Stove (Hol) & Frew McMillan (Saf)
1979 Greer Stevens & Bob Hewitt (Saf)
1980 Tracy Austin & John Austin (USA)
1981 Betty Stove (Hol) & Frew McMillan (Saf)
1982 Anne Smith (USA) & Kevin Curren (Saf)

FASTEST SERVE

There is much controversy about who has had the fastest serve in tennis. In 1931, with the measuring equipment then available, 'Big Bill' Tilden, who had won the Wimbledon title the previous year, was timed at 263 km/h (163·6 mph). The fastest server to be timed with modern electronic equipment is Scott Carnahan (USA) who was clocked at 220 km/h (137 mph) at the third annual Cannonball Classic organised by *Tennis* magazine at Los Angeles in 1976. However, some players and experts consider that the 1948 Wimbledon champion, Bob Falkenburg (USA) was the fastest ever.

John and Tracy Austin became the first ever brother and sister pairing to win the mixed doubles at Wimbledon. In the previous year they had been eliminated in the first round. Tracy was only 14½ when she first competed at Wimbledon in 1977.

Jimmy Connors, twice Wimbledon singles champion and runner-up on three other occasions. His first title at Wimbledon was in the men's doubles in 1973.

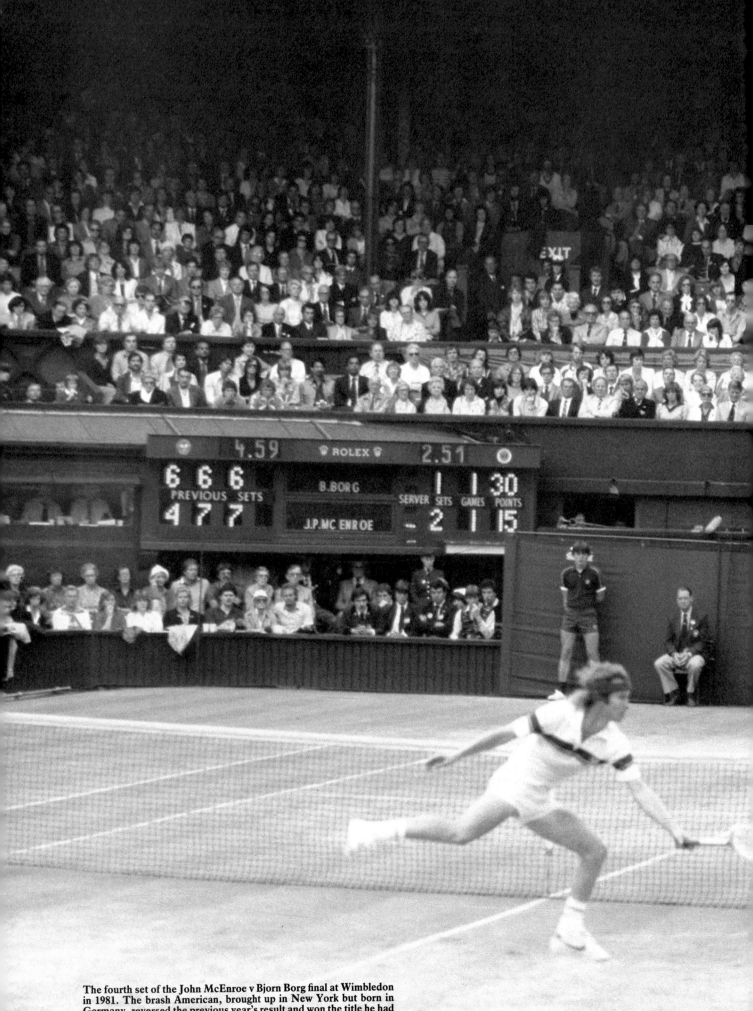

The fourth set of the John McEnroe v Bjorn Borg final at Wimbledon in 1981. The brash American, brought up in New York but born in Germany, reversed the previous year's result and won the title he had first contested in 1977. For Borg it was a halt to a series of Wimbledon triumphs which began with the junior title in 1972.

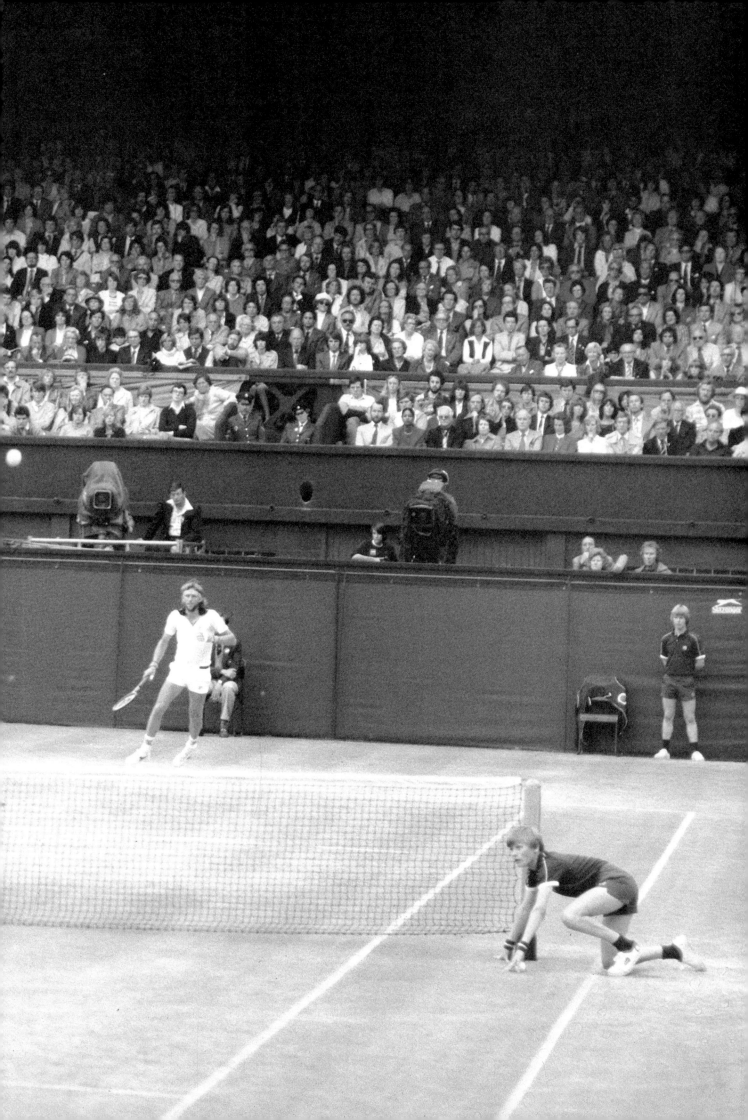

US CHAMPIONSHIPS: First held at Newport, Rhode Island in 1881, for men only. The women's championships started in 1887, and, like the men's tournament, continued until 1969, when they were replaced by the US Open championships which had first taken place in 1968. Currently all titles are contested at Flushing Meadows, New York. Margaret Osborne-duPont won a record 25 titles between 1941 and 1960, including a record 13 women's doubles, a record nine mixed doubles and three singles. The best by a man is 16 by Bill Tilden with seven singles, five men's doubles and four mixed doubles from 1913 to 1927. The most singles titles won is eight by Norwegian-born Molla Bjurstedt-Mallory from 1915 to 1926, including two war-time tournaments, although Helen Wills-Moody won seven between 1923 and 1931. The male record is seven, from 1881 to 1887 by Richard Sears, who also won the most men's doubles with six during the same period. The most successful pair has been Margaret Osborne-duPont and Louise Brough who won the women's doubles 12 times between 1942 and 1957, including nine in a row. The best male pairing was Richard Sears and James Dwight who won on five occasions in the 1880s. The youngest person to win a US title is Tracy Austin, the women's singles champion in 1979 at the age of 16 yr 270 days.

	Men	Women
1881	Richard Sears (USA)	—
1882	Richard Sears (USA)	—
1883	Richard Sears (USA)	—
1884	Richard Sears (USA)	—
1885	Richard Sears (USA)	—
1886	Richard Sears (USA)	—
1887	Richard Sears (USA)	Ellen Hansell (USA)

Christine Marie Evert-Lloyd, here playing on a hard court, her favourite surface. Since first competing in the women's singles at Wimbledon in 1972 she has won three times, been runner-up five times, and a semi-finalist on the other three occasions.

1888	Henry Slocum (USA)	Bertha Townsend (USA)
1889	Henry Slocum (USA)	Bertha Townsend (USA)
1890	Oliver Campbell (USA)	Ellen Roosevelt (USA)
1891	Oliver Campbell (USA)	Mabel Cahill (USA)
1892	Oliver Campbell (USA)	Mabel Cahill (USA)
1893	Robert Wrenn (USA)	Aline Terry (USA)
1894	Robert Wrenn (USA)	Helen Helwig (USA)
1895	F. Hovey (USA)	Juliette Atkinson (USA)
1896	Robert Wrenn (USA)	Elisabeth Moore (USA)
1897	Robert Wrenn (USA)	Juliette Atkinson (USA)
1898	Malcolm Whitman (USA)	Juliette Atkinson (USA)
1899	Malcolm Whitman (USA)	Marion Jones (USA)
1900	Malcolm Whitman (USA)	Myrtle McAteer (USA)
1901	William Larned (USA)	Elisabeth Moore (USA)
1902	William Larned (USA)	Marion Jones (USA)
1903	Lawrence Doherty (GB)	Elisabeth Moore (USA)
1904	Halcombe Ward (USA)	May Sutton (USA)
1905	Beals Wright (USA)	Elisabeth Moore (USA)
1906	William Clothier (USA)	Helen Homans (USA)
1907	William Larned (USA)	Evelyn Sears (USA)
1908	William Larned (USA)	Maud Barger-Wallach (USA)
1909	William Larned (USA)	Hazel Hotchkiss (USA)
1910	William Larned (USA)	Hazel Hotchkiss (USA)
1911	William Larned (USA)	Hazel Hotchkiss (USA)
1912	Maurice McLoughlin (USA)	Mary Browne (USA)
1913	Maurice McLoughlin (USA)	Mary Browne (USA)
1914	Richard Williams (USA)	Molla Bjurstedt (USA)
1915	William Johnston (USA)	Molla Bjurstedt (USA)
1916	Richard Williams (USA)	Molla Bjurstedt (USA)
1917	Lindley Murray (USA)	Molla Bjurstedt (USA)
1918	Lindley Murray (USA)	Molla Bjurstedt (USA)
1919	William Johnston (USA)	Hazel Hotchkiss-Wightman (USA)
1920	William Tilden (USA)	Molla Bjurstedt-Mallory (USA)
1921	William Tilden (USA)	Molla Bjurstedt-Mallory (USA)
1922	William Tilden (USA)	Molla Bjurstedt-Mallory (USA)
1923	William Tilden (USA)	Helen Wills (USA)
1924	William Tilden (USA)	Helen Wills (USA)
1925	William Tilden (USA)	Helen Wills (USA)
1926	Rene Lacoste (Fra)	Molla Bjurstedt-Mallory (USA)
1927	Rene Lacoste (Fra)	Helen Wills (USA)
1928	Henri Cochet (Fra)	Helen Wills (USA)
1929	William Tilden (USA)	Helen Wills (USA)
1930	John Doeg (USA)	Betty Nuthall (GB)
1931	Ellsworth Vines (USA)	Helen Wills Moody (USA)
1932	Ellsworth Vines (USA)	Helen Jacobs (USA)
1933	Fred Perry (GB)	Helen Jacobs (USA)
1934	Fred Perry (GB)	Helen Jacobs (USA)
1935	Wilmer Allison (USA)	Helen Jacobs (USA)
1936	Fred Perry (GB)	Alice Marble (USA)
1937	Don Budge (USA)	Anita Lizana (Chi)
1938	Don Budge (USA)	Alice Marble (USA)
1939	Bobby Riggs (USA)	Alice Marble (USA)
1940	Donald McNeill (USA)	Alice Marble (USA)
1941	Bobby Riggs (USA)	Sarah Cooke (USA)
1942	Fred Schroeder (USA)	Pauline Betz (USA)
1943	Joseph Hunt (USA)	Pauline Betz (USA)
1944	Frank Parker (USA)	Pauline Betz (USA)
1945	Frank Parker (USA)	Sarah Cooke (USA)
1946	Jack Kramer (USA)	Pauline Betz (USA)
1947	Jack Kramer (USA)	Louise Brough (USA)
1948	Ricardo Gonzales (USA)	Margaret Osborne-duPont (USA)
1949	Ricardo Gonzales (USA)	Margaret Osborne-duPont (USA)
1950	Arthur Larsen (USA)	Margaret Osborne-duPont (USA)
1951	Frank Sedgman (USA)	Maureen Connolly (USA)
1952	Frank Sedgman (USA)	Maureen Connolly (USA)
1953	Tony Trabert (USA)	Maureen Connolly (USA)
1954	Vic Seixas (USA)	Doris Hart (USA)
1955	Tony Trabert (USA)	Doris Hart (USA)
1956	Ken Rosewall (Aus)	Shirley Fry (USA)
1957	Malcolm Anderson (Aus)	Althea Gibson (USA)
1958	Ashley Cooper (Aus)	Althea Gibson (USA)
1959	Neale Fraser (Aus)	Maria Bueno (Bra)
1960	Neale Fraser Aus)	Darlene Hard (USA)
1961	Roy Emerson (Aus)	Darlene Hard (USA)
1962	Rod Laver (Aus)	Margaret Smith (Aus)
1963	Rafael Osuna (Mex)	Maria Bueno (Bra)
1964	Roy Emerson (Aus)	Maria Bueno (Bra)
1965	Manuel Santana (Spa)	Margaret Smith (Aus)
1966	Fred Stolle (Aus)	Maria Bueno (Bra)
1967	John Newcombe (Aus)	Billie Jean Moffitt-King (USA)
1968*	Arthur Ashe (USA)	Margaret Smith-Court (Aus)
1968	Arthur Ashe (USA)	Virginia Wade (GB)

Year	Men's Champion	Women's Champion
1969*	Stan Smith (USA)	Margaret Smith-Court (Aus)
1969	Rod Laver (Aus)	Margaret Smith-Court (Aus)
1970	Ken Rosewall (Aus)	Margaret Smith-Court (Aus)
1971	Stan Smith (USA)	Billie Jean King (USA)
1972	Ilie Nastase (Rom)	Billie Jean King (USA)
1973	John Newcombe (Aus)	Margaret Smith-Court (Aus)
1974	Jimmy Connors (USA)	Billie Jean King (USA)
1975	Manuel Orantes (Spa)	Chris Evert (USA)
1976	Jimmy Connors (USA)	Chris Evert (USA)
1977	Guillermo Vilas (Arg)	Chris Evert (USA)
1978	Jimmy Connors (USA)	Chris Evert (USA)
1979	John McEnroe (USA)	Tracy Austin (USA)
1980	John McEnroe (USA)	Chris Evert-Lloyd (USA)
1981	John McEnroe (USA)	Tracy Austin (USA)
1982	Jimmy Connors (USA)	Chris Evert-Lloyd (USA)

* *In 1968 & 1969 'National' titles were also held.*

AUSTRALIAN CHAMPIONSHIPS: Organised in 1905 by the LTA of Australasia (combining Australia and New Zealand) which had been formed the previous year. Margaret Smith-Court won 22 titles between 1960 and 1973, including a record 11 singles. The most titles by a man have been 13 by Adrian Quist, comprising three singles and a record 10 men's doubles from 1936 to 1950. Eight of the doubles (all consecutive) were with John Bromwich, between 1938 and 1950, which included a five-year break due to cancellation of the championships during the war. Thelma Long set a record total of 16 doubles titles, including 12 women's doubles, between 1936 and 1958, thus also achieving a unique span of 22 years between her first and last titles. The longest span for a male player is 19 years by Ken Rosewall who was the youngest to win the singles, in 1953 aged 18 yr 2 months, and the oldest to win the title, in 1972 aged 37 yr 2 months. The most wins in the men's singles has been six by Roy Emerson from 1961 to 1967.

Year	Men's Champion	Women's Champion
1905	Rodney Heath (Aus)	—
1906	Anthony Wilding (NZ)	—
1907	H. Rice (Aus)	—
1908	Fred Alexander (USA)	—
1909	Anthony Wilding (NZ)	—
1910	Rodney Heath (Aus)	—
1911	Norman Brookes (Aus)	—
1912	James Parke (GB)	—
1913	E. Parker (Aus)	—
1914	Pat O'Hara Wood (Aus)	—
1915	F. Lowe (GB)	—
1916–18	Not held	—
1919	Algernon Kingscote (GB)	—
1920	Pat O'Hara Wood (Aus)	—
1921	R. Gemmell (Aus)	—
1922	James Anderson (Aus)	M. Molesworth (Aus)
1923	Pat O'Hara Wood (Aus)	M. Molesworth (Aus)
1924	James Anderson (Aus)	Sylvia Lance (Aus)
1925	James Anderson (Aus)	Daphne Akhurst (Aus)
1926	John Hawkes (Aus)	Daphne Akhurst (Aus)
1927	Gerald Patterson (Aus)	E. Boyd (Aus)
1928	Jean Borotra (Fra)	Daphne Akhurst (Aus)
1929	Colin Gregory (GB)	Daphne Akhurst (Aus)
1930	E. Moon (Aus)	Daphne Akhurst (Aus)
1931	Jack Crawford (Aus)	C. Buttsworth (Aus)
1932	Jack Crawford (Aus)	C. Buttsworth (Aus)
1933	Jack Crawford (Aus)	Joan Hartigan (Aus)
1934	Fred Perry (GB)	Joan Hartigan (Aus)
1935	Jack Crawford (Aus)	Dorothy Round (GB)
1936	Adrian Quist (Aus)	Joan Hartigan (Aus)
1937	Viv McGrath (Aus)	Nancye Wynne (Aus)
1938	Don Budge (USA)	May Bundy (USA)
1939	John Bromwich (Aus)	V. Westacott (Aus)
1940	Adrian Quist (Aus)	Nancye Wynne (Aus)
1941–45	Not held	Not held
1946	John Bromwich (Aus)	Nancye Wynne-Bolton (Aus)
1947	Dinny Pails (Aus)	Nancye Wynne-Bolton (Aus)
1948	Adrian Quist (Aus)	Nancye Wynne-Bolton (Aus)
1949	Frank Sedgman (Aus)	Doris Hart (USA)
1950	Frank Sedgman (Aus)	Louise Brough (USA)
1951	Dick Savitt (USA)	Nancye Wynne-Bolton (Aus)
1952	Hen McGregor (Aus)	Thelma Long (Aus)
1953	Ken Rosewall (Aus)	Maureen Connolly (USA)
1954	Mervyn Rose (Aus)	Thelma Long (Aus)
1955	Ken Rosewall (Aus)	Beryl Penrose (Aus)

MOST TITLES
Margaret Smith-Court (Aus) won a record 63 major titles, singles and doubles, from her first Australian singles victory in 1960 to the 1975 US women's doubles title. They comprised 10 Wimbledon wins, 18 in the US championships, 22 Australian and 13 French titles. In the less important Italian, German and South African championships she won an additional 26, plus four US 'National' titles.

Year	Men's Champion	Women's Champion
1956	Lew Hoad (Aus)	Mary Carter (Aus)
1957	Ashley Cooper (Aus)	Shirley Fry (USA)
1958	Ashley Cooper (Aus)	Angela Mortimer (GB)
1959	Alex Olmedo (USA)	Mary Carter-Reitano (Aus)
1960	Rod Laver (Aus)	Margaret Smith (Aus)
1961	Roy Emerson (Aus)	Margaret Smith (Aus)
1962	Rod Laver (Aus)	Margaret Smith (Aus)
1963	Roy Emerson (Aus)	Margaret Smith (Aus)
1964	Roy Emerson (Aus)	Margaret Smith (Aus)
1965	Roy Emerson (Aus)	Margaret Smith (Aus)
1966	Roy Emerson (Aus)	Margaret Smith (Aus)
1967	Roy Emerson (Aus)	Nancy Richey (USA)
1968	Bill Bowrey (Aus)	Billie Jean Moffitt-King (USA)
1969	Rod Laver (Aus)	Margaret Smith-Court (Aus)
1970	Arthur Ashe (USA)	Margaret Smith-Court (Aus)
1971	Ken Rosewall (Aus)	Margaret Smith-Court (Aus)
1972	Ken Rosewall (Aus)	Virginia Wade (GB)
1973	John Newcombe (Aus)	Margaret Smith-Court (Aus)
1974	Jimmy Connors (USA)	Evonne Goolagong-Cawley (Aus)
1975	John Newcombe (Aus)	Evonne Goolagong-Cawley (Aus)
1976	Mark Edmondson (Aus)	Evonne Goolagong-Cawley (Aus)
1977	Roscoe Tanner (USA)	Kerry Reid (Aus)
1978	Vitas Gerulaitis (USA)	Evonne Goolagong-Cawley (Aus)
1979	Guillermo Vilas (Arg)	Christine O'Neill (Aus)
1980	Guillermo Vilas (Arg)	Barbara Jordan (USA)
1981	Brian Teacher (USA)	Hana Mandlikova (Cz)
1982	Johan Kriek (Saf)	Martina Navratilova (USA)
1983*	Johan Kriek (Saf)	Chris Evert-Lloyd (USA)

* *Held in December of previous year*

BATTLE OF THE SEXES
Bobby Riggs (USA), the 1939 Wimbledon champion, challenged the top female players in 1973 when he was 55 years old. He beat Margaret Smith-Court (Aus), probably then past her best, at Ramona, California, but he more than met his match against Billie Jean King (USA) at the Houston Astrodome, Texas on 20 September. The tremendous publicity, based on the male *v* female angle, drew the greatest crowd ever to watch a game of tennis, 30 472, plus an estimated television audience of 50 million, who saw Riggs beaten by 6–4, 6–3, 6–3.

WORLD CHAMPIONSHIP TENNIS (WCT): When the distinction between amateur and professional began to be eliminated in 1968, eight of the world's top players signed up for WCT which had been founded by some American entrepreneurs. In 1970 a $1 million circuit was announced embracing 20 events and 32 players. The first WCT Masters championships were held in 1971 in Dallas, Texas, and winners have been:

1971	Ken Rosewall (Aus)	1978	Vitas Gerulaitis (USA)
1972	Ken Rosewall (Aus)	1979	John McEnroe (USA)
1973	Stan Smith (USA)	1980	Jimmy Connors (USA)
1974	John Newcombe (Aus)	1981	John McEnroe (USA)
1975	Arthur Ashe (USA)	1982	Ivan Lendl (Cz)
1976	Bjorn Borg (Swe)	1983	John McEnroe (USA)
1977	Jimmy Connors (USA)		

A WCT doubles tournament was introduced in 1973, and winners have been:

1973 Bob Lutz & Stan Smith (USA)
1974 Bob Hewitt & Frew McMillan (Saf)
1975 Brian Gottfried (USA) & Raul Ramirez (Mex)
1976 Wojtek Fibak (Pol) & Karl Meiler (FRG)
1977 Vijay Amritraj (Ind) & Dick Stockton (USA)
1978 Wojtek Fibak (Pol) & Tom Okker (Hol)
1979 Peter Fleming & John McEnroe (USA)
1980 Brian Gottfried (USA) & Raul Ramirez (Mex)
1981 Peter McNamara & Paul McNamee (Aus)
1982 Heinz Gunthardt (Swi) & Balasz Taroczy (Hun)
1983 Heinz Gunthardt (Swi) & Balasz Taroczy (Hun)

DAVIS CUP: The cup was donated by an American, Dwight Davis, who was himself a top flight player and played in the first two matches. Although open to international competition, only Britain took up the challenge originally. In 1972, when the Challenge Round was abolished, the number of countries entered was a record 55. Inclusive of 1982, the cup has been won 28 times by the USA, 24 by Australia/Australasia, nine by Great Britain/British Isles, six by France, and one each by South Africa, Sweden, Italy and Czechoslovakia. The USA set a record of seven consecutive victories in 1920–26. Nicola Pietrangeli (Ita) played in a record 66 ties and 164 rubbers between 1954 and 1972, winning 120 of them, including 78 of his 110 singles and 42 of 54 doubles matches. Australia's Roy Emerson competed in a record nine successive Challenge Rounds from 1959 to 1967, and was only once on the losing side. The longest rubber ever held in the competition was one of 122 games in the 1973 American zone final, when Stan Smith and Erik Van Dillen (USA) beat Jaime Fillol and Pat Cornejo (Chi) 7–9, 37–39, 8–6, 6–1, 6–3. The most one-sided tie was in 1904 when the British Isles beat Belgium and only lost 17 games in all. The greatest ever crowd for a normal competition tennis match was 25 578 people at Sydney, Australia to watch the home team play the USA on the first day of the Challenge Round on 27 December 1954.

GRAND SLAM
The first man to achieve the Grand Slam (holding the Wimbledon, US, Australian and French titles at the same time) was Don Budge (USA) in 1938. The only other player to achieve it was Australian left-hander, Rod Laver, in 1962, and again in 1969. At men's doubles the only pair to do so has been Frank Sedgeman and Ken McGregor (Aus) in 1951. The women's singles Grand Slam was first achieved by Maureen 'Little Mo' Connolly (USA) in 1953. Ten years later Margaret Court-Smith (Aus) did it in mixed doubles with countryman Ken Fletcher, and then in 1970 became only the second woman ever to achieve it in women's singles.

DAVIS CUP
Winners from 1972:

1972	USA	1977	Australia
1973	Australia	1978	USA
1974	South Africa	1979	USA
1975	Sweden	1980	Czechoslovakia
1976	Italy	1981	USA
		1982	USA

WIGHTMAN CUP: Originally donated by Hazel Wightman (USA) in 1920 for competition among various nations, but only the USA and Great Britain showed any interest. The first competition was held in 1923 and won by the USA 7–0. Since then the USA have won another 43 times, with Britain victorious on 10 occasions. Virginia Wade (GB) played in a record 18 ties between 1965 and 1982.

FEDERATION CUP: The female equivalent of the Davis cup, it is an international team competition for a trophy donated by the ILTF and first held in 1963. The USA has won a record 11 times, with Australia gaining seven, and South Africa and Czechoslovakia one each. The most victories by an individual is 34 by Margaret Smith-Court (Aus) between 1963 and 1971.

OLYMPIC GAMES: Lawn Tennis was part of the Olympic programme up until 1924 and it was also a demonstration sport at Mexico City in 1968. The most gold and total medals won was by 1911 Wimbledon doubles champion Max Decugis (Fra) with four gold, one silver and one bronze in 1900, 1906 and 1920. Kitty McKane-Godfree (GB) set a women's record with one gold, two silver and two bronze in 1920 and 1924. In the latter year she won the first of her two Wimbledon singles championships. The 1908 Olympic titles were played at the All-England Club, Wimbledon.

Trampolining

Springboards were known in the Middle Ages in Europe when a Frenchman named Du Trampoline was one of the leading circus acrobats. In the period just before the First World War a show business group, 'The Walloons', were using equipment similar to current trampolines, but the prototype 'T' model was perfected by George Nissen (USA) in a garage in Cedar Rapids, Iowa in 1936 and patented in 1939.

WORLD CHAMPIONSHIPS: Instituted in 1964 and since 1968 held biennially.

	Men	*Women*
1964	Danny Millman (USA)	Judy Wills (USA)
1965	George Irwin (USA)	Judy Wills (USA)
1966	Wayne Miller (USA)	Judy Wills (USA)
1967	Dave Jacobs (USA)	Judy Wills (USA)
1968	Dave Jacobs (USA)	Judy Wills (USA)
1970	Wayne Miller (USA)	Renee Ransom (USA)
1972	Paul Luxon (GB)	Alexandra Nicholson (USA)
1974	Richard Tisson (Fra)	Alexandra Nicholson (USA)
1976	Richard Tisson (Fra) / Evgeni Janes (USSR)	Svetlana Levina (USSR)
1978	Evgeni Janes (USSR)	Tatyana Anisimova (USSR)
1980	Stewart Matthews (GB)	Ruth Keller (Swi)
1982	Carl Furrer (GB)	Ruth Keller (Swi)

BRITISH CHAMPIONSHIPS: First held in 1959 at RAF, Stanmore, Middlesex. Between 1969 and 1977 Wendy Wright won a record seven British titles, while the most won by a man is five by Stewart Matthews 1976–80.

Volleyball

Called *Minnonette* in its early days, volleyball was invented by an American YMCA instructor, William Morgan, at Holyoke, Massachusetts, in 1895, as a game for those who found basketball too strenuous. The name volleyball was suggested a year later by Dr Holsted of Springfield College. The game quickly spread world-wide and reached Britain in 1914, but it never caught on here as it did in most other countries. The first international tournament was the inaugural European championships in 1948, the year after the founding of the International Volleyball Federation. In the men's game the height of the net is 2·43 m (7 ft 11¾ in) and in the women's 2·24 m (7 ft 4¼ in). An Italian game, *Pallone*, played in the 16th century was very similar to modern volleyball.

OLYMPIC GAMES: First put forward by the United States for inclusion in the 1924 Games, volleyball was not accepted until 1964. Since then the only player to win four medals has been the Russian woman Inna Ryskal with gold in 1968 and 1972, and silver in 1964 and 1976. The best by a male player is gold medals in 1964 and 1968, and a bronze in 1972 by Yuri Poyarkov (USSR).

WORLD CHAMPIONSHIPS: Instituted in 1949 for men and 1952 for women, the greatest number of wins have been by teams from the USSR with six men's and four women's titles. In 1952 when the championships were held in Moscow, there was a record crowd of 60 000 people.

	Men		Women
1949	USSR	1952	USSR
1952	USSR	1956	USSR
1956	Czechoslovakia	1960	USSR
1960	USSR	1962	Japan
1962	USSR	1964★	Japan
1964★	USSR	1966	Japan
1966	Czechoslovakia	1968★	USSR
1968★	USSR	1970	USSR
1970	GDR	1972★	USSR
1972★	Japan	1974	Japan
1974	Poland	1976★	Japan
1976★	Poland	1978	Cuba
1978	USSR	1980★	USSR
1980★	USSR	1982	China
1982	USSR	*★Olympic Games*	

EUROPEAN CHAMPIONSHIPS: Instituted in 1948 for men and in 1949 for women, these championships have been dominated by the USSR with eight men's and ten women's titles.

	Men		Women
1948	Czechoslovakia	1949	USSR
1950	USSR	1950	USSR
1951	USSR	1951	USSR
1955	Czechoslovakia	1955	Czechoslovakia
1958	Czechoslovakia	1958	USSR
1963	Romania	1963	USSR
1967	USSR	1967	USSR
1971	USSR	1971	USSR
1975	USSR	1975	USSR
1977	USSR	1977	USSR
1979	USSR	1979	USSR
1981	USSR	1981	Bulgaria

The 1980 Olympic women's volleyball final in which the USSR, in red, beat the GDR team 3–1 to win the title for the third time. One of the fastest-growing and popular sports in Europe and the Far East, it has not met with much success in Britain so far.

Water Skiing

The sport originated with people walking on water with planks attached to their feet, possibly as early as the 14th century. Aquaplaning on large boards was first seen on the Pacific coast of America in the early 1900s. In July 1914 a plank-gliding competition was held at Scarborough, Yorkshire, but water-skiing as we now know it was pioneered by Ralph Samuelson (USA) on Lake Pepin, Minnesota in the summer of 1922. The 18-year-old Samuelson first tried using snow skies and then made his own pine board skis with which he gave exhibitions for the next few years, culminating in the first jump, off a greased ramp, in 1925. During the same year he was towed by a Curtiss flying-boat at about 130 km/h (80 mph). Claims have also been made, but unsubstantiated, for a parallel development on Lake Annecy, France at about the same time. One of the earliest British aquaplaners was the Duke of York, later King George VI, who was introduced to the fad at Cowes, Isle of Wight, in 1921 by Lord Louis Mountbatten, himself one of the early band of true water skiers. Other early *aficionados* of the new sport in the 1930s were film stars David Niven and Errol Flynn. The first national governing body was the American Water Ski Association founded in 1939, and they organised the first national championships in that year. A world body, the Union Internationale de Ski Nautique was set up in July 1946, and the British Water Ski Federation was formed in 1954.

Mike Hazelwood in the middle of one of his superlative jumps. Though this is his strongest event, he is also competent enough at slalom and tricks to have won the overall championship title at national, European and world levels.

MIKE HAZELWOOD

Britain's greatest ever water ski exponent is Mike Hazelwood, the son of a Lincolnshire farmer, who began in the sport when only eight years old. Despite a serious back injury in 1974, which meant having part of his spine fused, he broke his first major record, the European jumping mark, in 1976. Since then he has won the world overall title in 1977, and the world jump crown in 1979 and 1981, and is the former world record holder in that event. His other victories include four in the prestigious US Masters championships and a unique five wins in the Moomba Masters in Australia.

JUMPING

When Samuelson first jumped about 50 ft (15·24 m) in 1925 he set a standard that was not exceeded officially until 1947, but then improvements came quickly. The 100 ft mark was beaten by both Dick Binette (USA) and Butch Rosenberg (USA) in the 1954 American National championships with 102 ft (31·09 m), and the first woman to do it was Barbara Cooper Clack (USA) in 1964. The longest jump recorded is 61·60 m (202 ft) by Glen Thurlow (Aus) at Moomba, Australia on 14 March 1983. The women's record is 44·90 m (174 ft 4 in) by Kathy Hulme (GB) at Kirton's Farm, Reading on 1 August 1982. The British men's record is 60·00 m (196 ft 10 in) by Mike Hazelwood in 1981.

WORLD CHAMPIONSHIPS: Following the first European championships in 1947, the inaugural world titles were held in 1949 at Juan Les Pins, France. The most overall championships won have been three by Willa Worthington-McGuire (USA) in 1949, 1950, 1955, and by Liz Allan-Shetter (USA) in 1965, 1969 and 1975. The most won by a male skier have been two, by Alfredo Mendoza (USA), Mike Suyderhoud (USA) and George Athans (Can). Liz Allan-Shetter also won a record eight individual events, and the United States have won the team title on all 13 occasions that it has been held since 1957. The first British titlist, and only woman so far, was Jeannette Stewart-Wood, who won the overall and jump championships in 1967. Since then, Mike Hazelwood and Andy Mapple have also won world titles. *World champions from 1969:*

BRITISH CHAMPIONSHIPS: The most British overall titles (inaugurated in 1954) won have been nine by Karen Morse, in the women's competition, between 1971 and 1981. The men's record is six by Mike Hazelwood from 1974 to 1981. In the three individual events of the championships, tricks, slalom and jumping, Karen Morse won 19 between 1971 and 1982, and Mike Hazelwood holds the record for men with 13 between 1973 and 1981.

SPEED

Samuelson's unofficial speed of 130 km/h (80 mph) was not bettered officially until the late 1950s, when Butch Peterson (USA), towed by a powerboat, was the first to go faster than 161 km/h (100 mph). The fastest ever recorded, but not yet ratified, is 219·44 km/h (136·35 mph) by Grant Torrens (Aus) on the Hawkesbury River, NSW, Australia on 7 March 1982. The fastest by a female water skier is 178·81 km/h (111·11 mph) by Donna Brice (USA) at Long Beach, California in August 1977. The respective British bests are 131·217 km/h (81·53 mph) by Billy Rixon in 1973, and 122·187 km/h (75·92 mph) by Elizabeth Hobbs in 1982, both achieved on Lake Windermere, Cumbria.

TRICKS

The tricks, or freestyle figures event, involves various manoeuvres for which points are given, according to the degree of difficulty and the speed at which they are performed. The current records are 9580 points by Cory Pickos (USA), which he achieved in October 1982, and for women, 7650 points (not yet ratified) by Natalia Rumiantseva (USSR) in 1982. The British marks are 7830 points by John Battleday at Walton Hall, Yorkshire on 18 September 1982, and 5520 points by Nicola Rasey at Martiges, France in October 1982.

SLALOM

In the slalom event the skier has to negotiate a course of six buoys, set at predetermined distances, using one special slalom ski. The tow boat's speed is increased after each successful pass up to a maximun of 58 km/h (36 mph) for men and 55 km/h (34 mph) for women. When those speeds have been reached, the tow line is progressively shortened. The world's best is by Bob LaPoint (USA) who negotiated three buoys on a 10·75 m (35 ft 3 in) line at the maximum speed in Florida in September 1980. This was equalled by his brother Kris in 1982. The record for a woman is one and a half buoys on a 11·25 m (37 ft) line by the late Sue Fieldhouse (Aus) at Thorpe, Surrey in the 1981 world championships.

	Overall	*Tricks*	*Slalom*	*Jumps*
1969 (Copenhagen, Denmark)				
Men	Mike Suyderhoud (USA)	Bruce Cockburn (Aus)	Victor Palomo (Spa)	Wayne Grimditch (USA)
Women	Liz Allan (USA)	Liz Allan (USA)	Liz Allan (USA)	Liz Allan (USA)
1971 (Banolas, Spain)				
Men	George Athans (Can)	Ricky McCormick (USA)	Mike Suyderhoud (USA)	Mike Suyderhoud (USA)
Women	Christy Weir (USA)	Willi Stahle (Hol)	Christy Freeman (USA)	Christy Weir (USA)
1973 (Bogota, Colombia)				
Men	George Athans (Can)	Wayne Grimditch (USA)	George Athans (Can)	Ricky McCormick (USA)
Women	Lisa St. John (USA)	Maria Victoria Carrasco (Ven)	Sylvie Maurial (Fra)	Liz Allan-Shetter (USA)
1975 (Thorpe, England)				
Men	Carlos Suarez (Ven)	Wayne Grimditch (USA)	Roby Zucchi (Ita)	Ricky McCormick (USA)
Women	Liz Allan-Shetter (USA)	Maria Victoria Carrasco (Ven)	Liz Allan-Shetter (USA)	Liz Allan-Shetter (USA)
1977 (Milan, Italy)				
Men	Mike Hazelwood (GB)	Carlos Suarez (Ven)	Bob LaPoint (USA)	Mike Suyderhoud (USA)
Women	Cindy Todd (USA)	Maria Victoria Carrasco (Ven)	Cindy Todd (USA)	Linda Giddens (USA)
1979 (Toronto, Canada)				
Men	Joel McClintock (Can)	Patrice Martin (Fra)	Bob LaPoint (USA)	Mike Hazelwood (GB)
Women	Cindy Todd (USA)	Natalia Rumiantseva (USSR)	Pat Messner (Can)	Cindy Todd (USA)
1981 (Thorpe, England)				
Men	Sammy Duvall (USA)	Cory Pickos (USA)	Andy Mapple (GB)	Mike Hazelwood (GB)
Women	Karin Roberge (USA)	Ana Maria Carrasco (Ven)	Cindy Todd (USA)	Deena Brush (USA)

BRITISH CHAMPIONSHIPS

		Overall	Tricks	Slalom	Jumps
1975	Men	Paul Seaton	Paul Seaton	Paul Seaton	Paul Seaton
	Women	Karen Morse	Ann Pitt	Ann Pitt	Jackie Dobson
1976	Men	Mike Hazelwood	Mike Hazelwood	Mike Hazelwood	James Carne
	Women	Karen Morse	Ann Pitt	Philippa Roberts	Karen Morse / Jackie Dobson
1977	Men	Mike Hazelwood	John Battleday	Mike Hazelwood	Mike Hazelwood
	Women	Philippa Roberts	Philippa Roberts	Philippa Roberts	Karen Morse
1978	Men	Mike Hazelwood	Mike Hazelwood	Mike Hazelwood	Mike Hazelwood
	Women	Karen Morse	Philippa Roberts	Karen Morse	Karen Morse
1979	Men	Mike Hazelwood	Mike Hazelwood	Mike Hazelwood	John Battleday
	Women	Kathy Hulme	Philippa Roberts	Kathy Hulme	Karen Morse
1980	Men	Andy Mapple	John Battleday	John Battleday	Steve Lawrence
	Women	Karen Morse	Philippa Roberts	Karen Morse	Karen Morse
1981	Men	Mike Hazelwood	John Battleday	Mike Hazelwood	Mike Hazelwood
	Women	Karen Morse	Jane Bubear	Karen Morse	Karen Morse
1982	Men	John Battleday	John Battleday	Andy Mapple	David Frost
	Women	Philippa Roberts	Nicola Rasey	Karen Morse	Kathy Hulme

BAREFOOT SKIING

The first person to ski barefooted was Dick Pope Jr (USA) in 1947, thereby introducing a new element to the sport. By 1978 his countryman, Billy Nichols, had set a duration record of 2 hr 42 min 39 sec, and an Australian, Paul McManus, had set a backwards record of 39 min. The official speed mark is 177·06 km/h (110·02 mph) by Lee Kirk (USA) at Firebird Lake, Arizona in June 1977, with the best of his two statutory runs being clocked at nearly 6 km/h (3·7 mph) faster. The

Reigning world slalom champion Andy Mapple from Preston scored an upset victory to take the title in 1981, the first time that it had been won by a British competitor. Strangely, his only national title to that date had been the 1980 overall category.

women's record is 109·72 km/h (68·18 mph) by Lorraine Nelson (USA) in 1980. The fastest by a British barefoot skier is 114·86 km/h (71·37 mph) by Richard Mainwaring at Holme Pierrepoint, Nottingham in December 1978.

Weightlifting

The earliest country to have shown an official interest in weight-lifting as an exercise appears to have been China from c 3500 BC. Certainly during the Chou Dynasty, which ended in 249 BC, it had become a necessary military test. In Greece, c 600 BC, 'the Age of Strength' gave rise to many deeds of great strength. In Europe, strong-men were to be seen primarily at fairgrounds, and by the 17th and 18th centuries there were many well-documented stories of prodigious lifts. The amateur sport is of comparatively modern vintage, with the first reports of competitions dating from 1854 and 1870, the latter in New York. The first International championships of importance were held at the Café Monico, London on 28 March 1891.

WORLD AND OLYMPIC CHAMPIONSHIPS: The 1891 competition is often referred to as a 'world' title meeting, although the winner, Lawrence Levy (GB) never called it such. It was not until the founding of the International Weightlifting Federation in 1920 that proper world championships came into being, the first in 1922. The Olympic Games of 1896 had included a weightlifting contest, in which Launceston Elliot (GB) became the only Briton to win an Olympic title. The most World titles won have been eight by John Davis (USA) between 1938 and 1952, Tommy Kono (USA) from 1952 to 1959, and Vasili Alexeyev (USSR) consecutively 1970–77. From 1922 to 1982 there have been 274 gold medals awarded in the overall (or total) category of the different classes, of which the USSR has taken 124. Only one British lifter, the Jamaican-born Louis Martin, has won at the world championships, with four titles between 1959 and 1965. The record for all Olympic medals is four, by Norbert Schemansky (USA) with a gold, a silver and two bronzes between 1948 and 1964. Overall class champions between 1928 and 1972 were those with the best totals from the recognised three lifts—snatch, jerk, clean and press. The latter lift was then dropped from the programme, and the overall champions from 1973 are: (* Olympic)

52 kg
		kg
1973	Mohammed Nassiri (Irn)	240·0
1974	Mohammed Nassiri (Irn)	232·5
1975	Zigmunt Smalczerz (Pol)	237·5
1976*	Aleksandr Voronin (USSR)	242·5
1977	Aleksandr Voronin (USSR)	247·5
1978	Kanybek Osmonaliev (USSR)	240·0
1979	Kanybek Osmonaliev (USSR)	242·5
1980*	Kanybek Osmonaliev (USSR)	245·0
1981	Kanybek Osmonaliev (USSR)	247·5
1982	Stefan Leletko (Pol)	250·0

56 kg
1973	Atanas Kirov (USSR)	257·5
1974	Atanas Kirov (USSR)	255·0
1975	Atanas Kirov (USSR)	255·0
1976*	Norair Nurikyan (Bul)	262·5
1977	Jiro Hosotani (Jap)	252·5
1978	Daniel Nunez (Cub)	260·0
1979	Anton Kodiabashev (Bul)	267·5
1980*	Daniel Nunez (Cub)	275·0
1981	Anton Kodiabashev (Bul)	272·5
1982	Anton Kodiabashev (Bul)	280·0

60 kg
1973	Dito Shanidze (USSR)	272·5
1974	Georgi Todorov (Bul)	280·0
1975	Georgi Todorov (Bul)	285·0
1976*	Nikolai Kolesnikov (USSR)	185·0
1977	Nikolai Kolesnikov (USSR)	280·0
1978	Nikolai Kolesnikov (USSR)	270·0
1979	Marek Seweryn (USSR)	290·0
1980*	Viktor Mazin (USSR)	290·0
1981	Beloslav Manolov (Bul)	302·5
1982	Yurik Sarkisian (USSR)	302·5

67·5 kg
1973	Mukharbi Kirzhinov (USSR)	305·0
1974	Pyotr Korol (USSR)	305·0
1975	Pyotr Korol (USSR)	312·5
1976*	Pyotr Korol (USSR)	305·0
1977	Roberto Urrutia (Cub)	315·0
1978	Yanko Russev (Bul)	310·0
1979	Yanko Russev (Bul)	332·5
1980*	Yanko Russev (Bul)	342·5
1981	Joachim Kunz (GDR)	340·0
1982	Piotr Mandra (Pol)	325·0

75 kg
1973	Nedelcho Kolev (Bul)	337·5
1974	Nedelcho Kolev (Bul)	335·0
1975	Peter Wenzel (GDR)	335·0
1976*	Jordan Mitkov (Bul)	335·0
1977	Yuri Vardanyan (USSR)	345·0
1978	Roberto Urrutia (Cub)	347·5
1979	Roberto Urrutia (Cub)	345·0
1980*	Assen Zlatev (Bul)	360·0
1981	Yanko Russev (Bul)	360·0
1982	Yanko Russev (Bul)	365·0

82·5 kg
1973	Vladimir Rizhenkov (USSR)	350·0
1974	Trendafil Stoychev (Bul)	350·0
1975	Valeri Shary (USSR)	357·5
1976*	Valeri Shary (USSR)	365·0
1977	Gennadiy Bessonov (USSR)	352·5
1978	Yuri Vardanyan (USSR)	377·5
1979	Yuri Vardanyan (USSR)	370·0
1980*	Yuri Vardanyan (USSR)	400·0
1981	Yuri Vardanyan (USSR)	392·5
1982	Asen Zlatev (Bul)	400·0

90 kg
1973	David Rigert (USSR)	365·0
1974	David Rigert (USSR)	387·5
1975	David Rigert (USSR)	377·5
1976*	David Rigert (USSR)	382·5
1977	Sergei Poltoratski (USSR)	375·0
1978	Rolf Milser (Ger)	377·5
1979	Gennadiy Bessonov (USSR)	380·0
1980*	Peter Baczako (Hun)	377·5
1981	Blagoi Blagoyev (Bul)	405·0
1982	Blagoi Blagoyev (Bul)	415·0

100 kg
1973–76	Not held	
1977	Anatoli Kozlov (USSR)	367·5
1978	David Rigert (USSR)	390·0
1979	Pavel Sirchin (USSR)	385·0
1980*	Ota Zaremba (Cz)	395·0
1981	Viktor Sots (USSR)	407·5
1982	Viktor Sots (USSR)	422·5

110 kg
1973	Pavel Pervushin (USSR)	385·0
1974	Vladimir Ustyuzhin (USSR)	380·0
1975	Valentin Khristov (Bul)	417·5
1976*	Yuri Saitsev (USSR)	385·0
1977	Valentin Khristov (Bul)	405·0
1978	Yuri Saitsev (USSR)	402·5
1979	Sergei Arakelov (USSR)	410·0
1980*	Leonid Taranenko (USSR)	422·5
1981	Valeri Kravchuk (USSR)	415·0
1982	Sergei Arakelov (USSR)	427·5

+110 kg
1973	Vasili Alexeyev (USSR)	402·5
1974	Vasili Alexeyev (USSR)	425·0
1975	Vasili Alexeyev (USSR)	427·5
1976*	Vasili Alexeyev (USSR)	440·0
1977	Vasili Alexeyev (USSR)	430·0
1978	Jurgen Heuser (GDR)	417·5
1979	Sultan Rakhmanov (USSR)	430·0
1980*	Sultan Rakhmanov (USSR)	440·0
1981	Anatoli Pisarenko (USSR)	425·0
1982	Anatoli Pisarenko (USSR)	445·0

Double Olympic weightlifting champion Vasili Alexeyev, the most prolific world record breaker at any sport.

WORLD RECORDS

The greatest number of world records broken by one man in any sport is the 80 official weightlifting marks set by Vasili Alexeyev (USSR) from 20 January 1970 to 1 November 1977. The current records (as at 31 May 1983) are as follows: (S = Snatch, J = Jerk, T = Total)

Weight Class		kg	lb	Name	Venue	Year
52 kg	S	115	253½	Jacek Gutowski (Pol)	Ljubljana, Yugoslavia	1982
	J	143·5	316¼	Stefan Leletko (Pol)	Ljubljana, Yugoslavia	1982
	T	252·5	556½	Lubomir Khadjiev (Bul)	Tatabanya, Hungary	1982
56 kg	S	126·5	278¾	Wu Shu-Teh (Chn)	Nagoya, Japan	1981
	J	160·5	353¾	Andreas Letz (GDR)	Varna, Bulgaria	1983
	T	282·5	622¾	Oksen Mirzoyan (USSR)	Odessa, USSR	1983
60 kg	S	137·5	303	Daniel Nunez (Cub)	Copenhagen, Denmark	1982
	J	171	376¾	Stefan Topurov (Bul)	Haskovo, Bulgaria	1982
	T	302·5	666¾	Beloslav Manolov (Bul)	Lille, France	1981
67·5 kg	S	154	339½	Vladimir Gratchev (USSR)	Odessa, USSR	1983
	J	196	432	Joachim Kunz (GDR)	Karl Marx Stadt, GDR	1981
	T	345	760½	Joachim Kunz (GDR)	Karl Marx Stadt, GDR	1981
75 kg	S	163·5	360¼	Vladimir Kuznetsov (USSR)	Odessa, USSR	1983
	J	209	460¾	Yanko Russev (Bul)	Ljubljana, Yugoslavia	1982
	T	367·5	810	Aleksandr Varbanov (Bul)	Lille, France	1983
82·5 kg	S	180	396¾	Asen Zlatev (Bul)	Ljubljana, Yugoslavia	1982
	J	223·5	492½	Alexsandr Pervi (USSR)	Frunze, USSR	1982
	T	400	881¾	Yurik Vardanyan (USSR)	Moscow, USSR	1980
90 kg	S	195·5	431	Blagoi Blagoyev (Bul)	Varna, Bulgaria	1983
	J	228·5	503¾	Adam Saidoulayev (USSR)		1982
	T	420	920¼	Blagoi Blagoyev (Bul)	Varna, Bulgaria	1983
100 kg	S	200	440¾	Yuri Zakharevich (USSR)	Odessa, USSR	1983
	J	240	529	Yuri Zakharevich (USSR)	Odessa, USSR	1983
	T	440	970	Yuri Zakharevich (USSR)	Odessa, USSR	1983
110 kg	S	196·5	433	Leonid Taranenko (USSR)	Odessa, USSR	1983
	J	242	533½	Leonid Taranenko (USSR)	Odessa, USSR	1983
	T	435	959	Leonid Taranenko (USSR)	Moscow, USSR	1982
Over 110 kg	S	203	447½	Anatoli Pisarenko (USSR)	Odessa, USSR	1983
	J	260	573	Vladimir Marchuk (USSR)	Moscow, USSR	1982
	T	457·5	1008½	Anatoli Pisarenko (USSR)	Dnepropetrovsk, USSR	1982

POWERLIFTING

The international Powerlifting Federation was founded in 1972. The three basic powerlifts are squat (or deep knee bend), bench press, and dead lift. It is probably true to say that these lifts require less technical skill than the Olympic-type lifts, but involve possibly more sheer basic strength. The greatest total achieved of all three lifts was by Paul Anderson (USA), when as a professional he squatted with 544 kg (1200 lb) and aggregated 1200 kg (2647 lb). The first man to lift a total of 11 times his bodyweight was Precious McKenzie (GB and New Zealand) who, weighing 55 kg (121 lb), achieved 607·5 kg (1339 lb) at Honolulu, Hawaii in May 1979. Later that year Lamar Gant (USA) became the first to deadlift five times his bodyweight (56 kg, 123¼ lb) with a lift of 280 kg (617 lb) at Dayton, Ohio. The only man to hold simultaneously the total records in four different classes is Mike Bridges (USA) who did so on 8 November 1980 with the marks in the 67·5 kg, 75 kg, 82·5 kg and 90 kg categories. A rather unusual category of record is the deadlift for two men, ie both men holding the bar at the same time. Brothers Clay and Doug Patterson (USA) lifted a record 656·8 kg (1448 lb) in December 1979. The greatest power lift by a woman is 247 kg (545½ lb) by Jan Todd (USA) at Columbus, Ohio in January 1981. The official three-lift total for women is 574·5 kg (1267 lb) by Australian Bev Francis at Honolulu on 12 May 1981.

EXCEPTIONAL LIFTS

The greatest known weight ever raised by a human being is 2844 kg (2·8 tons) in a back lift, in which the weight is raised off trestles, by Paul Anderson (USA) at Toccoa, Georgia on 12 June 1957, nearly seven months after he had won the Olympic title. The greatest weight lifted by a woman was 1616 kg (1½ tons) by Josephine Blatt (USA), in a hip and harness lift at the Bijou Theatre, Hoboken, New Jersey in April 1895. In April 1960 it was reported that an hysterical woman, Mrs Maxwell Rogers, had lifted one end of a station wagon, which weighed 1632 kg (1·6 tons) to free her son, on whom it had fallen off a jack. She only weighed 56 kg (8 st 11 lb) herself, and was later taken to hospital with cracked vertebrae.

WORLD POWERLIFTING RECORDS (As at 1 January 1983)
(S = squat, B = bench press, D = dead lift, T = total).

Weight Class		kg	lb	Name	Venue (where known)	Year
52 kg	S	242·5	534½	J Cunha (USA)		1981
	B	146·5	323	J Cunha (USA)		1982
	D	232·5	512½	Haruji Watanabe (Jap)	Tokyo, Japan	1980
	T	567·5	1251	Hideaki Inaba (Jap)	Arlington, Texas	1980
56 kg	S	237·5	523½	Hideaki Inaba (Jap)		1982
	B	147·5	325	H Isagawa (Jap)		1981
	D	289·5	638	Lamar Gant (USA)		1982
	T	625	1378	Lamar Gant (USA)		1982
60 kg	S	295	650½	Joe Bradley (USA)	Arlington, Texas	1980
	B	180	397	Joe Bradley (USA)	Phoenix, Arizona	1980
	D	285	628½	Lamar Gant (USA)	Arlington, Texas	1980
	T	707·5	1560	Joe Bradley (USA)		1982
67·5 kg	S	296·5	653½	R Wahl (USA)		1982
	B	194	427½	K Hulecki (Swe)		1982
	D	312·5	689	R Välineva (Fin)		1981
	T	732·5	1615	Joe Bradley (USA)		1981
75 kg	S	327·5	722	Mike Bridges (USA)	Auburn, Alabama	1980
	B	217·5	479½	James Rouse (USA)	Arlington, Texas	1980
	D	325	716½	R. Välineva (Fin)		1982
	T	850	1874	Rick Gaugler (USA)		1982
82·5 kg	S	379·5	836½	Mike Bridges (USA)	Arlington, Texas	1982
	B	240	529	Mike Bridges (USA)		1981
	D	357·5	788	Veli Kumpuniemi (Fin)	Zurich, Switzerland	1980
	T	952·5	2100	Mike Bridges (USA)		1982
90 kg	S	375	826½	Fred Hatfield (USA)	Arlington, Texas	1980
	B	255	562	Mike McDonald (USA)		1980
	D	372·5	821	W Thomas (USA)		1982
	T	937·5	2066½	Mike Bridges (USA)	Huber Heights, Ohio	1980
100 kg	S	400	882	Fred Hatfield (USA)		1982
	B	261·5	576½	Mike McDonald (USA)	Santa Monica, California	1977
	D	377·5	832	J Cash (USA)		1982
	T	952·5	2100	J Cash (USA)		1982
110 kg	S	393·5	867½	D Wohleber (USA)		1981
	B	270	595	J Magruder (USA)		1982
	D	395	870½	John Kuc (USA)	Arlington, Texas	1980
	T	1000	2204½	John Kuc (USA)	Arlington, Texas	1980
125 kg	S	412·5	909½	Dave Waddington (USA)		1982
	B	278·5	614	Tom Hardman (USA)		1982
	D	385	849	Terry McCormick (USA)		1982
	T	1005	2215½	Ernie Hackett (USA)		1981
Over 125 kg	S	445	981	D Fely (USA)		1982
	B	300	661½	Bill Kazmaier (USA)	Columbus, Georgia	1981
	D	402	886½	Bill Kazmaier (USA)		1981
	T	1100	2425	Bill Kazmaier (USA)	Columbus, Georgia	1981

Wrestling

Olympic wrestling, Greco-Roman style, between Andrzej Supron of Poland and Lars-Erik Skiold of Sweden.

Wrestling is one of the oldest sports in the world. Depictions of holds and falls have been found on wall plaques dating from *c* 2750 BC. It was especially popular in ancient Greece and was contested in the Olympic Games from 708 BC. Wrestling developed in varying forms in different countries, with the classical Greco-Roman style popular in Europe, and free style more to the liking of countries in the East and the Americas. The International Amateur Wrestling Federation (FILA) was founded in 1912, but the sport had been included in the first modern Olympics in 1896, and European championships had been held in Vienna in 1898. Around the turn of the century the best wrestlers were undoubtedly professionals, and one of the greatest, the Estonian-born Georges Hackenschmidt, based in Britain, dominated the first decade of the 20th century. The two main styles accepted internationally are free style, and Greco-Roman, but FILA also recognises Sambo wrestling, a form akin to judo popular particularly in the USSR.

WORLD AND OLYMPIC CHAMPIONSHIPS: The most titles by a freestyle wrestler is 10 by Aleksandr Medved (USSR) between 1962 and 1972, in light heavyweight, heavyweight and super heavyweight classes. The only man to gain the same title on six successive occasions was Abdollah Movahed (Irn), with the lightweight crown from 1965 to 1970. The most Greco-Roman titles is seven achieved by Nikolai Balboshin (USSR) at heavyweight and super heavyweight between 1971 and 1979, while the most successive titles is five by featherweight Roman Rurua (USSR) from 1966 to 1970. In the Olympic Games three men have won three titles each: Carl Westergren (Swe) in 1920, 1924 and 1932; Ivar Johansson (Swe) in 1932 (two) and 1936; Aleksandr Medved (USSR) in 1964, 1968 and 1972. Imre Polyak (Hun) holds the record of four medals, with one gold (1964) and three silvers (1952, 1956, 1960) all in the Greco-Roman featherweight class. The heaviest wrestler in the

Olympics has been Chris Taylor, the American bronze medallist in the freestyle super-heavyweight class at Munich in 1972, who was 1·96 m (6ft 5in) tall and weighed over 190 kg (420 lb). The longest recorded bout, under the rules then in force, was between Martin Klein (USSR) and Alfred Asikainen (Fin) in the Greco-Roman middleweight event at Stockholm in 1912. Klein won after 11 hr 40 min.

One of the greatest wrestling champions of all time must have been the famous Greek athlete Milon of Croton, who around 600 BC won six Olympic titles, six at the Pythean Games, nine at the Nemean Games and 10 at the Isthmian Games. It is recorded that he trained by carrying a calf around on his shoulders—thus, as the animal increased in weight every day, becoming the first exponent of weight training. Among modern wrestlers, the 1964 Olympic freestyle featherweight champion, Osamu Watanabe (Jap) was unbeaten in 187 consecutive contests, and Wade Schalles (USA) won 803 bouts between 1964 and 1982. The greatest number of British titles won is 10 by heavyweight Ken Richmond from 1949 to 1960, but an even more remarkable span of years was the 24 from the first title (1909) won by George Mackenzie to his last in 1933. He also represented Britain at five successive Olympic Games from 1908 to 1928.

SUMO WRESTLING

In this form of wrestling, which originated in Japan, about 23 BC, weight and bulk are vital and it is amassed by deliberate over-eating and training. The heaviest ever exponent, *sumotori*, is Kazuhisa Shiki, known first as Genkaiho and then as Rinho. In 1981 he attained a weight of 203 kg (447 lb), at a height of 1·77 m (5 ft 9½ in). Hawaiian-born Jesse Kuhaulua, known as Takamiyama, in 1972 became the first non-Japanese to win an official tournament, and to the end of 1981 he had recorded 1232 consecutive top division bouts. The tallest ever *sumotori* was Ozora, who competed in the early 19th century, and stood 2·20 m (7 ft 3 in) tall. The youngest man to attain the rank of *Yokozuna*, which means Grand Champion, was Kitanoumi in July 1974 when he was 21 yr 2 months old. Four years later he set a record by winning 82 of the 90 bouts that were fought that year. Over a 21-year-period (1789–1810) Raiden lost only 10 of his 254 fights. One of the most famous wrestlers of recent years has been Taiho, meaning Great Bird, who won the Emperor's Cup on 32 occasions.

1980 OLYMPIC WRESTLING CHAMPIONS

	48 kg	52 kg	57 kg
Freestyle	Claudio Pollio (Ita)	Anatoli Beloglasov (USSR)	Sergei Beloglasov (USSR)
Greco-Roman	Zaksylik Ushkempirov (USSR)	Vakhtang Blagidze (USSR)	Shamil Serikov (USSR)

	62 kg	68 kg	74 kg
Freestyle	Magomedgasan Abushev (USSR)	Saipulla Absaidov (USSR)	Valentin Raitchev (Bul)
Greco-Roman	Stilianos Migiakis (Gre)	Stefan Rusu (Rom)	Ferenc Kocsis (Hun)

	82 kg	90 kg	100 kg
Freestyle	Ismail Abilov (USSR)	Sanasar Oganesyan (USSR)	Ilya Mate (USSR)
Greco-Roman	Gennadiy Korban (USSR)	Norbert Nottny (Hun)	Gheorghi Raikov (Bul)

	+ 100 kg
Freestyle	Soslan Andiyev (USSR)
Greco-Roman	Aleksandr Kolchinsky (USSR)

1982 WORLD WRESTLING CHAMPIONS

	48 kg	52 kg	57 kg
Freestyle	Sergei Kornilayev (USSR)	Hartmut Reich (GDR)	Anatoli Beloglasov (USSR)
Greco-Roman	Temiz Kazarashvili (USSR)	Benur Pashayan (USSR)	Piotr Michalik (Pol)

	62 kg	68 kg	74 kg
Freestyle	Sergei Beloglasov (USSR)	Mikhail Karachura (USSR)	Leroy Kemp (USA)
Greco-Roman	Ryszard Swierad (Pol)	Gennadiy Yermilov (USSR)	Stefan Rusu (Rom)

	82 kg	90 kg	100 kg
Freestyle	Taimuraz Dzgoyev (USSR)	Uwe Neupert (GDR)	Ilya Mate (USSR)
Greco-Roman	Nikolai Abhasava (USSR)	Frank Andersson (Swe)	Roman Wroclawski (Pol)

	+ 100 kg
Freestyle	Salman Khasimikov (USSR)
Greco-Roman	Nikolai Dinev (Bul)

The traditional form of wrestling in Japan is Sumo which is conducted with much ceremony and mysticism. The contestants in the picture are Kitanoumi and Takamiyama, two of the greatest ever exponents of the art.

Yachting

The first yachting race took place between King Charles II and his brother, James, Duke of York, for a wager of £100 on the Thames on 1 October 1661 from Greenwich to Gravesend and back. The King won. The first club was the Cork Harbour Water Club (later the Royal Cork Yacht Club) which was estab-

lished in Ireland, and held the first recorded regatta in 1720. The oldest club still active in Britain is the Starcross YC at Powderham Point, on the Exe Estuary, Devon which held its first regatta in 1772. The word 'regatta'—meaning a gathering of boats—is Italian and was applied to the proceedings at Ranelagh

on the Thames in June 1775, The sport did not really prosper until the seas became safer with the end of the Napoleonic Wars in 1815. That year The Yacht Club (later to become The Royal Yacht Squadron) was formed and organised races at Cowes, Isle of Wight, which was the beginning of modern yacht racing. In 1844 the New York YC was founded and held its first regatta the following year. The International Yacht Racing Union (IYRU) was established in 1907.

America's *Bay Bea* leading from Britain's *Marionette* during the 1977 Admiral's Cup series, which was finally won by Great Britain for the seventh time.

THE AMERICA'S CUP: In 1851 the New York YC sent the 170-ton schooner *America* to compete in Britain. Skippered by John Cox Stevens it was invited by the Royal Yacht Squadron to compete against 17 British boats, in a race around the Isle of Wight for the Hundred Guinea Cup. It beat the 47-ton *Aurora* by 18 min on 22 August. Six years later the New York YC put up the trophy as a perpetual challenge cup. The first challenge came in 1870 when James Ashbury in *Cambria* unsuccessfully took on the 14 yachts of the American club at one go. Since then there have been 16 challenges by Britain, six by Australia and two by Canada, but the Americans have never lost a series, and have only been defeated in eight of the 85 races held to 1982. The closest race ever was the fourth race in 1962 when *Weatherly* (skipper, Emil Mosbacher Jr) beat the Australian challenger *Gretel* (Jock Sturrock) by only 3½ lengths, or about 26 sec. The greatest margin of victory was by *Mischief* over the Canadian challenger *Atalanta* which lost the second race of the 1881 series by 38 min 54 sec.

The longest course was 60·3 km (37·5 miles) in 1871. Since 1964 it has been standardised at 39·1 km (24·3 miles), and the fastest time recorded for this triangular course is 2 hr 46 min 58 sec by *Gretel* winning the second race in 1962.

Year	Winner	Challenger
1870	Magic	Cambria (Eng)
1871	Columbia	Livonia (Eng)
1871	Sappho	Livonia (Eng)
1876	Madeleine	Countess of Dufferin (Can)
1881	Mischief	Atalanta (Can)
1885	Puritan	Genesta (Eng)
1886	Mayflower	Galatea (Eng)
1887	Volunteer	Thistle (Sco)
1893	Vigilant	Valkyrie II (Eng)
1895	Defender	Valkyrie III (Eng)
1899	Columbia	Shamrock (Eng)
1901	Columbia	Shamrock II (Eng)
1903	Reliance	Shamrock III (Eng)
1920	Resolute	Shamrock IV (Eng)
1930	Enterprise	Shamrock V (Eng)
1934	Rainbow	Endeavour (Eng)
1937	Ranger	Endeavour II (Eng)
1958	Columbia	Sceptre (Eng)
1962	Weatherly	Gretel (Aus)
1964	Constellation	Sovereign (Eng)
1967	Intrepid	Dame Pattie (Aus)
1970	Intrepid	Gretel II (Aus)
1974	Courageous	Southern Cross (Aus)
1977	Courageous	Australia (Aus)
1980	Freedom	Australia (Aus)

ADMIRAL'S CUP: A series of four races organised by the Royal Ocean Racing Club for the first time in 1957. It consists of a 322 km (200 miles) Channel race, two inshore races in the Solent, and the 974 km (605 miles) race from Cowes to the Fastnet Rock, Ireland and back to Plymouth. The series attracted a record 19 nations in 1975, 1977 and 1979, with each one allowed a maximum of three boats.

1957	Great Britain	1971	Great Britain
1959	Great Britain	1973	Germany
1961	USA	1975	Great Britain
1963	Great Britain	1977	Great Britain
1965	Great Britain	1979	Australia
1967	Australia	1981	Great Britain
1969	USA		

OLYMPIC GAMES: Yachting events were included in the 1900 Games for the first time with 10 boats from four countries taking part. In the 1972 games there were 152 yachts from 42 nations. Paul Elvström (Den) won a record four titles and became the first in any sport to win gold medals in four successive Games, with the Firefly class in 1948, and the Finn class in

1952, 1956, and 1960. The greatest margin of victory in any class was by Rodney Pattisson and Iain Macdonald-Smith (GB) when they won the 1968 Flying Dutchman class in *Superdocious* by over 40 points after winning five, coming second, and being disqualified once, out of seven starts. The yacht is now in the National Maritime Museum, at Greenwich. Pattisson is the only British yachtsman to win at two Olympic regattas, for he repeated his 1968 victory at Kiel, in 1972, with Christopher Davies in *Superdoso*. In this boat he also gained a silver in 1976 with Julian Houghton.

> The greatest number of boats to start in a single race was 1261 in the Round Zealand race over 375 km (233 miles) in Denmark in June 1976. The most in Britain was 1055 keeled yachts and multihulls for the annual Round-the-Island race from Cowes on 27 June 1981 around the Isle of Wight. The world's largest marina for yachts is that at Marina Del Rey, Los Angeles which has 7500 berths, while the largest in Britain and indeed in Europe, is the Brighton Marina with 2313 berths.

THE WHITBREAD ROUND THE WORLD RACE: instituted in 1973, is the longest regular race for yachts. It is held every four years over a distance of 48 515 km (26 180 nautical miles or 30 146 statute miles) from Portsmouth via Cape Town, Auckland and Mar del Plata.

1973–74 Raymond Carlin (Mex) in *Sayula II*
1977–78 Cornelius van Rietschoten (Hol) in *Flyer*
1981–82 Cornelius van Rietschoten (Hol) in *Flyer*

HIGHEST SPEEDS

The official speed record for a sailing boat is 36·04 knots or 66·78 km/h (41·50 mph), by the proa *Crossbow II* on 17 November 1980, over a special 500 m (547 yd) course set out annually in Portland Harbour, Dorset. The skipper was Tim Colman who in October 1978 momentarily reached a speed of 45 knots, or 83 km/h (51 mph). The greatest distance covered in 24 hours by a single-manned yacht is 630 km (340 nautical miles or 391 statute miles) by Nick Keig (GB) in his trimaran *Three Legs of Mann I* during the Falmouth to Azores race in June 1975, averaging 14·16 knots, or 26·23 km/h (16·30 mph).

SINGLE-HANDED TRANSATLANTIC RACE

The first man to navigate the Atlantic Ocean single-handed was Alfred Johnson (USA) who celebrated the centenary of the American Revolution in 1876 by crossing from Gloucester, Massachusetts to Abercastle, Wales in *Centennial*, taking 46 days. In 1891 the first known single-handed race occurred when Josiah Lawlor (USA) in *Sea Serpent* beat William Andrews (USA) in *Mermaid*, taking 45 days from Boston to Coverack, Cornwall. The concept of a regular race was suggested by Col 'Blondie' Hasler and finally came to fruition in 1960. Held every four years, the race is now sponsored by *The Observer* newspaper and raced from Plymouth to Newport, Rhode Island, a distance of about 4828 km (3000 miles).

Year	Name	Yacht	days	hrs	min
1960	Francis Chichester (GB)	*Gipsy Moth III*	40	12	30
1964	Eric Tabarly (Fra)	*Pen Duick II*	27	3	56
1968	Geoffrey Williams (GB)	*Sir Thomas Lipton*	25	20	33
1972	Alain Colas (Fra)	*Pen Duick IV*	20	13	15
1976	Eric Tabarly (Fra)	*Pen Duick VI*	23	20	12
1980	Phil Weld (USA)	*Moxie*	17	23	12

Britain's most successful Olympic yachtsman, Rodney Pattisson, at the helm of *Supercalifragilisticexpialidocious*, a name that was thankfully shortened for official results purposes.